Volume II

A HISTORY
OF THE
HUMAN
COMMUNITY

Volume II

THIRD EDITION

A HISTORY OF THE HUMAN COMMUNITY

1500 *to the Present*

WILLIAM H. McNEILL

Professor Emeritus
The University of Chicago

 PRENTICE HALL, Englewood Cliffs, New Jersey 07632

Library of Congress Cataloging-in-Publication Data

McNeill, William Hardy
  A history of the human community / William H. McNeill.—3rd ed.
    p.   cm.
  Contents: v. 1. Prehistory to 1500—v. 2. 1500 to the present.
  ISBN 0–13–391244–2 (v. 1).—ISBN 0–13–391277–9 (v. 2)
    1. World history.   I. Title.
D20.M485 1990
909—dc20   89–23078
                                              CIP

Editorial/production supervision: Rob DeGeorge
Cover design: William E. Frost Associates Ltd.
Interior design: Maureen Eide
Manufacturing buyer: Ed O'Dougherty
Photo editor: Lori Morris-Nantz
Photo research: Joelle Burrows
Cover photo: *Sales Room in a Foreign Business
Establishment in Yokohama* by Hashimoto Sadahide/The
Metropolitan Museum of Art, Gift of Lincoln Kirstein,
1959. Photograph by Otto E. Nelson.

© 1990, 1987 by William H. McNeill

Printed in the United States of America

10 9 8 7 6 5 4 3 2 1

ISBN 0-13-391277-9

Prentice-Hall International (UK) Limited, *London*
Prentice-Hall of Australia Pty. Limited, *Sydney*
Prentice-Hall Canada Inc., *Toronto*
Prentice-Hall Hispanoamericana, S.A., *Mexico*
Prentice-Hall of India Private Limited, *New Delhi*
Prentice-Hall of Japan, Inc., *Tokyo*
Simon & Schuster Asia Pte. Ltd., *Singapore*
Editora Prentice-Hall do Brasil, Ltda., *Rio de Janeiro*

Contents

Map List

Preface

This book is built around a simple idea: People change their ways mainly because some kind of stranger has brought a new thing to their attention. The new thing may be frightening, it may be delightful; but whatever it is, it has the power to convince key persons in the community of the need to do things differently.

If this is true, then contacts between different cultures become the main drive wheel of history, because such contacts start or keep important changes going. The central theme of human history, after all, is change—how people did new things in new ways, meeting new situations as best they could.

It follows that world history can and should be written to show how in succeeding ages different human groups achieved unusual creativity and then impelled or compelled those around them (and, in time, across long distances) to alter their accustomed style of life to take account of the new things that had come to their attention by what anthropologists call "cultural diffusion" from the center of creativity. There remains a central mystery: How does important creativity occur? Accident, genius, and breakdown of old habit patterns all play a part in provoking inventions. Even more important (because commoner) is the need to readjust other elements in daily life after a major new borrowing resulting from some foreign contact has occurred. So here,

too, I am inclined to emphasize the importance of contacts between strangers as a basic force in increasing the variety and multiplying the openings for all kinds of creative inventions.

This angle of vision upon human affairs came to me from anthropology. In the 1930s, anthropologists studied simple, isolated societies; only a few of them tried to think about relations between such "primitive" peoples and the more complicated civilized societies that occupied so much more of the face of the earth. One of the people who did wonder about the relationships between simple and complex societies was Robert Redfield; my most fundamental ideas took form while sitting in his classroom at the University of Chicago in the summer of 1936.

But even very simple general ideas have to be applied to the data of history with some care before one can really be sure whether they are much use. This took me about twenty-five years: not till I had written *The Rise of the West: A History of the Human Community* (published in 1963) could I know how the history of humankind, insofar as modern scholars have been able to find out about it, would fit into this sort of anthropological framework.

The task was a large one. I had to acquaint myself with recent, more or less standard scholarly writing in all the different fields of historical study and then look for relationships in time and space. This often meant going beyond the bounds of existing scholarly knowledge. Experts have to learn difficult languages and usually do not know very much about what happened outside the time and place where their own special skills allow them to make new contributions to knowledge. And different fields of learning developed different outlooks. Ancient India, for example, has been studied mainly by scholars interested in comparative religion and linguistics; they did not ask political, economic, or technological questions of the Sanskrit texts they used; and until quite lately, they did little archaeological digging. Chinese studies, on the contrary, were directed very much at political institutions and patterns of rule.

An outsider, like myself, asking similar questions of each time and place therefore had to be careful. Guessing too much would be a mistake; not to guess at all, even when available evidence and the state of scholarly knowledge left gaps, would prevent recognition of how the history of one part of the world fit into the pattern of the whole. Yet in spite of such problems, in the end I felt that my effort had been worthwhile. The vision of human history that emerged from my work seemed simple in conception, yet complex in application. The simple pattern of interaction among peoples of different cultures could make room for all the multiplicity and surprisingness of human historical experience.

A lot of other people, ordinary citizens and even professional historians, agreed that my book was good, useful, persuasive. Thinking that such a vision might make the study of history in schools easier and more satisfying to the mind, I then set out to write *The Ecumene: Story of Humanity*, using simple language for the most part, and pruning out details, thinning proper names, defining special terms so that students could understand the ideas of the text more easily.

It is for you, students and readers, to judge how successful this effort has been.

I wish to thank the following for their valuable assistance in reviewing the manuscript for this volume: Guy Beckwith, Auburn University; Douglas Hughes, Washington State University; Ed McGee, Belmont Abbey College; Lysle E. Meyer, Morehead State University; Herbert Ziegler, University of Hawaii.

WILLIAM H. MCNEILL
Chicago, Illinois

Photo Credits

Chapter 15: *350* Art Resource. *355* Zdenek J. Pivecka. *359* Rare Book Division, The New York Public Library, Astor, Lenox and Tilden Foundations (top)/University of Chicago, Department of Art (bottom). *365* McGraw/Three Lions. *367* The Bettmann Archive.

Chapter 16: *376* Alinari/Art Resource (top)/Public Domain (bottom). *378* © Nationalmuseum, Stockholm (left)/Art Resource. *392* Art Resource. *394* Public Domain (top)/From "Rembrandt," courtesy of United Artists Corporation (bottom). *396* The Metropolitan Museum of Art. Gift of Henry G. Marquand, 1889.

Chapter 17: *405* Courtesy of the Metropolitan Museum of Art, bequest of Benjamin Altman, 1913 (14.40.721) (left)/Art Resource (right). *407* William H. McNeill, slide collection (left/right). *411* Marion H. Levy (left)/Sekai Bunka Photo (right). *417* New York Public Library Picture Collection. *423* Library of Congress.

The Use of Plants and Animals in Agriculture: *429* Tim Asch/Anthro-Photo. *431* New York Public Library (top)/Ronald Sheridan's Photo-Library (bottom). *432* William H. McNeill, slide collection (top/bottom). *433* Musee Conde Chantilly/Photographic Giraudan. *435* Metropolitan Museum of Art, Rogers Fund, 1919 (top)/Courtesy Sperry–New Holland (bottom).

Chapter 18: *441* The Bettmann Archives. *444* The Convention and Visitors Bureau of Chamber of Commerce of Greater Philadelphia. *445* Leslie Deeb. *447* Prints Division, The New York Public Library; Astor, Lenox and Tilden Foundations

(left)/Giraudon/Art Resource (right). *454* Cliché des Musées Nationaux (left)/Giraudon/Art Resource (right). *462* Public Domain (left)/Museum of Fine Arts, Boston (right).

Chapter 19· *473* William H. McNeill, slide collection (left/right). *476* William H. McNeill, slide collection. *477* New York Public Library Picture Collection. *481* William H. McNeill, slide collection (left/right). *485* William H. McNeill, slide collection (left)/Courtesy, Museum of Fine Arts, Boston. The Spaulding Collection.

Chapter 20: *500* Fogg Art Museum, Harvard University; Grenville L. Winthrop Bequest (top)/Giraudon/Art Resource (bottom). *502* Giraudon/Art Resource (left)/Museo del Prado, Madrid (right). *512* Louvre Museum, Paris. *516* The Bettmann Archive (left)/Buckingham/Putnam County Historical Society (right). *517* The Metropolitan Museum of Art, Bequest of Mrs. H. O. Havemeyer, 1929. The H. O. Havemeyer Collection (left)/Southern Pacific Photo (right).

Diseases and Their Effects on Human Societies: *521* The Bettmann Archive. *522* American Museum of Natural History. *523* The Bettmann Archive (left column)/Library of Congress (right column).

Chapter 21: *537* The Bettmann Archive. *540* The Bettmann Archive. *541* New York Public Library Picture Collection. *543* Courtesy of the Peabody Museum of Salem. Photo by Mark W. Sexton. *546* Harrison Forman. *547* Courtesy, Museum of Fine Arts, Boston (top)/Library of Congress (bottom). *549* National Archives.

Chapter 22: *561* The Bettmann Archive/BBC Hulton (top/bottom). *562* Courtesy of The Art Institute of Chicago. *566* New York Public Library (left)/AIP Niels Bohr Library (right). *567* Library of Congress (left)/UPI Bettman Newsphotos (right). *571* National Gallery of Art, Washington. Rosenwald Collection (left)/Collection, The Museum of Modern Art, New York. Acquired through the Lillie P. Bliss Bequest.

Chapter 23: *579* Museum of the City of New York. *582* International Harvester (top/bottom). *589* William H. McNeill, slide collection (top)/Painting by John Clymer. Defense Department Photo (Marine Corps) (bottom). *592* Courtesy of the Toshiba Corporation, Tokyo, Japan (top)/William H. McNeill, slide collection (bottom). *597* New York Public Library Picture Collection (top)/The Bettmann Archive/BBC Hulton (bottom). *600* The British Museum, London (Courtesy of the Trustees) (top)/William H. McNeill, slide collection (bottom).

Transportation and Communication: *604* Library of Congress. *605* Illustrated London News, March 21, 1857. *606* Library of Congress (top)/Santa Fe Railway (bottom). *607* Western Union Corporation.

Chapter 24: *610* UPI/Bettmann Newsphotos. *612* National Archives (left/right). *616* The Bettmann Archives (top)/Copyright by Committee on Public Information (bottom). *618* The Bettmann Archives (left)/UPI/Bettmann Newsphotos (right). *623* Public Domain. *625* UPI/Bettmann Newsphotos. *633* Library of Congress. *634* UPI/Bettmann Newsphotos (bottom)/U.S. Department of Defense photo (top).

Chapter 25: *641* Japanese Air Lines (top)/Michal Heron (bottom). *644* Magnum for World Bank (top)/Bruno Barbey/Magnum (bottom). *650* The Bettmann Archive (top)/UPI/Bettmann Newsphotos (bottom). *652* United Nations (top)/Paolo Koch/Photo Researchers (bottom). *659* Marc Riboud/Magnum.

Chapter 26: *666* NASA (left/right). *667* Photograph A. C. Barrington Brown. From J. D. Watson, *The Double Helix*, Atheneum, New York, p. 215 © 1968 by J. D. Watson. *670* Courtesy IBM. *671* AP/Wide World Photos. *674* Philadelphia Museum of Art: Louise and Walter Arensberg Collection (left)/Hirshhorn Museum and Sculpture Garden, Smithsonian Institution (right). *676* Art Resource (top)/UPI/Bettmann Newsphotos (bottom). *677* Courtesy Australian Overseas International Service (top)/Mexican National Tourist Council (bottom).

Breakthroughs in the Use of Energy and Fuel: *682* Bruce Roberts. *683* Library of Congress. *684* News Bureau, General Electric Co. *685* New York Power Authority (top)/AP/Wide World Photos (bottom).

Chapter 15

THE GREAT EUROPEAN DISCOVERIES
1480 to 1550

In our modern age when radio and telephone enable us to maintain instantaneous contact all round the world, it takes an act of imagination to think what it was like to live in a world bounded on every side by the gray shadow of regions utterly unknown, and at a time when news of great happenings in the more distant parts of the known world might take months to reach even the best-informed persons. Yet this was the sort of world in which everyone lived 500 years ago. Of course some people knew more than others about other lands. The immense majority were peasants, who seldom knew or cared anything about regions more than twenty or perhaps fifty miles from where they labored in the fields. Merchants knew more. Some of them traveled thousands of miles to and fro along caravan routes or by sea during all of their active lives. Many such adventurers wandered off the beaten track once in a while; but unless they found something new they could use in trade, they would seldom go back a second time, and whatever they reported about their explorations soon faded from the memories of other merchants and travelers. Merchants' lore about routes and markets, wars and famines spread by word of mouth and was seldom written down. Even such a remarkable adventure as that of Marco Polo, who traveled from Venice to China and back again in the thirteenth century, was recorded by merest chance. In later life, Marco Polo found himself in prison with a fellow prisoner who could write and who chose to write down the strange tale Marco Polo had to tell. Except for these unusual circumstances, we would know absolutely nothing of his adventures at the court of Kublai Khan.

Side by side with the flow of gossip exchanged by long-distance travelers was another and usually quite separate tradition of knowledge about the geography of the earth based on books. From the time of the ancient Greeks, learned Europeans all knew that the earth was spherical. They even had a map of the world based on one drawn up about A.D. 150 by the astronomer and geographer Ptolemy of Alexandria. Moslems shared this Greek inheritance and added to it a substantial body of travelers' reports about remote regions of the Eurasian world. The learned classes of other civilizations were less influenced by the mathematical calculations made by Ptolemy and his predecessors. The Chinese, for instance, took the view that their own land was the center of everything and measured all others by their distance from the "Middle Kingdom." Hindu tradition located a great mountain (the Himalayas?) at the center of the earth. Other people had still different traditional maps of the world's geography. But even the most learned, just like merchants and like simple peasants, always faced a limit beyond which the layout of the earth's surface was a blank.

In the half century between 1492 when Columbus discovered America and 1542 or 1543 when a Portuguese ship first visited Japan, European seafarers filled in many of the blanks that had existed for so long in western Europeans' knowledge of the geography of the earth. Discoveries were pushed inland by missionaries who set out to convert Asians and Amerindians to Christianity, and by military men who overwhelmed the Aztec and Inca empires in the Americas and probed other less-developed regions of the Americas, Africa, and the Spice Islands (the Moluccas) of Indonesia.

It took a while for other civilized people to hear of these great European discoveries; but within Europe itself the news of the American and Asian worlds spread speedily, even among very humble people. Europeans broke down the old separations between learned tradition and the experience of travelers. News of fresh discoveries got into print. Books of exploration found ready sale as stay-at-homes eagerly read about the wonders of far places. Map makers, too, set out to chart the new discoveries and arranged all the newly discovered lands in their proper places according to mathematical methods for projecting a curved surface onto the flat surface of a map.

New knowledge of the world's geography was not the only lasting consequence of the European discoveries. For when the habitable seacoasts of all the earth had been linked together more closely than ever before by European shipping, trade began to follow new routes. Exchanges of goods also attained greater volume than before in many parts of the globe. New crops and new diseases spread widely. Enlarged food supplies and heavier death rates from hitherto unknown diseases resulted.

Reactions in the different parts of the world differed sharply. Western Europe profited most directly. New products, new techniques, new ideas, and a new perspective on the world as a whole all swarmed in upon the nations that had initiated the new patterns of contact among the peoples of the earth. They were free to pick and choose among all the new things that competed for their attention, with no sense of being threatened or endangered by novelty, since it was they and they alone who had started it all in the first place. This openness to change put a special energy behind Europe's self-transformation throughout early modern times.

Eventually, Europe's willingness to experiment with new techniques and ideas put European or western civilization ahead of all the other civilizations of the world in some very important ways. But for a long time, Europe's superiority was not very obvious. Both the Moslems and Far Easterners preferred their own well-worn habits and customs to anything that Europeans had to offer. The strength and skill these people had at their command, together with the distances that separated them from the European center, allowed them to follow their own paths for centuries.

Nevertheless, a new era of world history dawned when the Americas entered for the first time into the interacting circle of civilized humanity and when Europe's restless probing and self-revolution launched a force upon the world with which the rest of humanity, sooner or later, had to cope. The Eurasian Far West, previously at one extreme edge of the civilized world, there-fore became central to the subsequent history of all humankind. When that happened, modern history began.

PROBLEMS OF SEAFARING

The seas and oceans of the world are by no means uniform. Winds, tides, and currents all make an enormous difference, especially to ships that do not have powerful motors to drive them through the water. Only when seafarers learned how to make their ships sail upwind as well as downwind could they hope to travel safely in the stormy, tidal waters of the North Atlantic that touch Europe's western shores. On the other hand, abundant fish life provided a constant lure, for anyone who could sail those stormy seas in safety could make a living by catching fish.

Other seas are not as dangerous as the North Atlantic. In the Mediterranean Sea, for example, for about half the year the trade winds blow steadily from the northeast, and storms do not occur. This was the season when Greek and Roman mariners sailed. A voyage late in the year was considered very risky, for then storms might blow the ship ashore on a rocky coast. Oars could help guide the ship into harbor or out again; but on the open sea sails were essential, even for war galleys with hundreds of rowers. The Romans never mastered the northern seas where storms might occur at any season. Even crossing the channel from France to Britain was a risky enterprise. Longer voyages were rarely attempted.

In the Indian Ocean, however, the monsoons made seafaring comparatively simple. Half the year the winds blew from one direction at almost an even pace; half the year they reversed themselves, so that return voyages were particularly easy. The broad trade-wind zones of the Pacific and Atlantic oceans were like the Mediterranean during the summer months. Throughout these zones a steady northeast wind in the Northern Hemisphere, or a southeast wind in the Southern Hemisphere, could propel sailing ships through bright, cool, clear air every day in the year. Near the American and Asian continents, to be sure, tropical storms could interrupt the regularity of the trade winds. But they occur only during a well-defined season (August to October) and affect the weather for only a few days of the year.

In the tropical zone between the two trade-wind belts the air is often dead calm. Winds are local and usually die away after a few hours. In this region the air is thinned as the sun warms it and then gets pushed aloft by the inrushing denser and cooler air from more northerly and more southerly latitudes. It is this that creates the trade winds, which push toward the tropics to take the place of the thinned and heated air of that region.

Navigation of the tropic zone offered a problem to sailing ships, since light and variable winds might leave a vessel becalmed for weeks on end. Still, there was no great danger in lying becalmed, and ocean currents might allow a skilled captain to travel even without wind in the direction he desired. Conversely, if he had planned his course without due regard for winds and currents, he might find himself traveling backward, willy-nilly. Experiences of this sort quickly taught European navigators where favorable and unfavorable winds and currents could be expected; and as that knowledge spread, voyaging across the vast distances of the oceans became quite easy. Anywhere in the trade-wind zones—and they occupied a large part of the entire ocean area of the earth—a sailing ship could move at least a hundred miles a day. These regions, therefore, became the throughways of the age of the sail.

As soon as European sailors learned how to navigate successfully in the stormy North Atlantic, the trade-wind and tropic zones of the oceans offered no serious dangers. On the contrary, sailing in such gentle waters was easy by comparison with the problems sailors had to solve in the coastal waters of northern Europe.

European Shipbuilding and Navigation

Throughout the Middle Ages, European shipbuilders and sailors made progress in mastering the dangers of the North Atlantic. But not until shortly before 1500 were all the technical and financial problems worked out successfully. The reason was that European mariners decided, from early in the Middle Ages, to try something radically new, building a ship big enough and strong enough to cut through the waves instead of riding upon them, as smaller and lighter vessels did.

Long before the developments of the Middle Ages, a different solution to the problems of navigating on the stormy seas of the North Atlantic had been tried, quite successfully, by early navigators. Small, saucer-shaped craft, made of wickerwork and covered with watertight animal skins, could only carry a few persons—usually no more than three or four. But such *coracles* (to give them their proper name) could sail before the wind across very rough seas, rising and falling with the waves like a cork. Vessels such as these carried Irish missionaries as far as Iceland in the early Middle Ages; and similar craft carried the ancient megalithic folk to and fro along the Atlantic shores of Europe and Africa, beginning about 2000 B.C. Coracles were light enough to be picked up and taken safely ashore by two or three persons, and they were small enough to be rowed or paddled for short distances against the wind. They were, in short, quite seaworthy so long as they stayed close to shore where refuge against headwinds could be found. Coracles actually remained in use for fishing off the shores of Ireland until about 1900.

By A.D. 900 the Vikings put an end to long-distance travel by coracles. The Viking ships were far bigger and carried crews of forty to a hundred men. Coracles were easy prey for such ships; and when travel in unprotected vessels ceased to be safe, sailors soon lost the skills needed for long-distance coracle navigation.

Viking ships were superior to coracles in having a keel, and a steering oar attached at the back of the ship. When the wind blew at an angle to the ship's desired course, the rudder and keel checked the ship's sidewise slip through the water. But, like coracles, Viking ships could not sail against the wind but had to wait on shore until the wind blew from a suitable direction. Since the seas in which the Vikings sailed were in the zone of prevailing westerlies, where cyclonic storms succeeded one another week after week throughout the year, they never had to wait long before the wind changed direction.

The Development of Rigid Hulls and Multiple Masts   Medieval shipbuilders made two major advances over the level attained by the Vikings. First, they made the hulls of their ships stronger and more rigid. This was done by enlarging everything about the Viking hull structure: heavier keel, stouter ribs, double planking attached inside and outside the ribs, and a deck to add strength and keep out water splashed over the gunwales. Medieval shipbuilders eventually learned how to make a hull strong enough to stand the strain of being picked up by two great waves at the bow and stern, leaving little or no water to sustain the weight of the middle portion of the ship. These, then, were the large, stout ships that could safely cut through the waves instead of bouncing about on top of them as light, small vessels had to do.

European sailors also learned that a much safer and more maneuverable ship could be created by substituting rudders for steering oars. Rudders, being larger and attached directly to the rear end of the ship, could exert more force to steer the ship in any desired direction. A second major improvement was to make it easy to adjust sails according to the force and direction of the wind. This was done by placing several masts on the same vessel and dividing the sails on each mast into several different pieces of canvas. If the wind blew very hard, most of the sails could be taken down. By displaying only small storm sails of heavy canvas to the gale, a captain could keep his ship moving through the water fast enough to give the rudder steerage way and thus maintain his course even in stormy weather. With light winds, extra canvas could be spread to make the most of the slightest breath of air.

Sturdy and maneuverable ships built along these lines had another advantage that came by accident. For when European gunsmiths began to make large cannons, the ships which European shipbuilders had learned how to design proved able to withstand the recoil of a heavy gun as easily as they could withstand the buffetings of wind and wave. Lighter and less rigidly constructed ships could and did sail safely in Mediterranean waters and in the Indian Ocean or South China Sea. But such vessels could not carry heavy artillery: the recoil would simply shake them apart. Hence, vessels built for rough seas of the North Atlantic enjoyed an additional and critically important advantage in being able to carry heavier guns than ships of any other design could bear up under.

Multiple masts, rigid hulls, and heavy guns came together in the century between 1400 and 1500. The Portuguese took the lead in developing ship and sail designs. From 1418 on, Prince Henry the Navigator set out systematically to improve the sailing quality of ships with which he wished to explore the Atlantic coast of Africa. Until Prince Henry's death in 1460, Portuguese ships sailed southward almost every year. On his return each captain reported what lands he had found and how his ship had performed. These reports were studied and compared; and when it came time to rig out a new expedition, the practical lessons of preceding years were acted upon. In this way, reliable knowledge of winds, currents, reefs, and harbors accumulated rapidly. The same spirit when applied to ship design led to rapid improvements in the seaworthiness and maneuverability of Portuguese "caravels," as these new oceangoing ships were called.

Development of Cannon   Big guns had a different history. When the Mongols invaded central Europe in 1240–1241, they brought Chinese explosives with them, and European artisans probably learned more about Chinese gunpowder and guns during the century that followed. The first important use of guns in European wars took place at the Battle of Crécy in 1346, where the noise of the explosion scared the horses but did little real damage. The development of guns was closely tied to the mining and metal industries in which Europeans already excelled as early as 1300. Comparatively abundant supplies of metal, in turn, allowed Europeans to outdistance others in the manufacture of artillery by about 1450. For example, the Turkish sultan Mohammed II, when he besieged Constantinople in 1453, employed European artisans to cast enormous guns outside the city's walls, and then batter them down on behalf of the Turks.

The Progress of Navigation   The combination of stout hulls, maneuverability, and heavy guns made European ships clearly superior to all oth-

How to Navigate Accurately This woodcut from a French book illustrates how an explorer, by going ashore and setting up a sighting device on dry land, could measure the highest point in the sun's course with considerable accuracy. The exact angle of the sun's noontide elevation could then be compared with tables, prepared in advance by learned astronomers and mathematicians, that listed the latitude north or south of the equator corresponding to the angle just measured for the particular day of the year on which the measurement was made. The text that accompanied this woodcut explains what must be done to find latitude; but the artist who made the woodcut obviously did not bother to understand what he was supposed to illustrate, for he shows the man sighting away from the sun.

ers. Yet before the exploration of the oceans could proceed, sailors had also to learn how to find their way across the trackless sea and get back home again. This called for skill in navigation. Here, too, Prince Henry of Portugal played a critical role. European sailors had long been accustomed to sighting the North Star and measuring its angle above the horizon in order to tell how far north or south they were. But as soon as a ship crossed the equator this method failed. There was no prominent star near the southern pole that could be used as the North Star was used in the Northern Hemisphere. To meet this problem, therefore, Prince Henry employed expert astronomers and mathematicians to make tables that would show how high the sun stood above the horizon at noon of each day in the year at different latitudes. Then a sea captain could estimate how far north or south of the equator he was by sighting the sun at its highest point in the sky and measuring the angle between the sun and the horizon.

Prince Henry's captains, as soon as they discovered some new cape or estuary along the African coast, put ashore and took careful measurement of the sun's altitude, thus establishing the latitude fairly accurately. This in turn meant that a ship could head for a particular place by sailing far out to sea, safe from the dangers of shoals and rocks, until it reached the right latitude, and then head east until the African coast appeared. Landfalls within thirty to forty miles of the intended goal could regularly be achieved by this method.

Measuring longitude was a different matter. No solution to this problem was discovered until 1761, when John Harrison designed a marine clock that could keep accurate time, even on a pitching ship and for long periods at a stretch. The clock kept Greenwich time; and by noting exactly when the sun reached its noon time height, it became possible to know how far the observer was east or west of the Greenwich meridian. Hours and minutes and seconds, east or west of the Greenwich meridian, could then easily be translated into actual distances (which varied with latitude) by use of tables.

At the time of the great European discoveries, however, ships' captains had no way of tell-

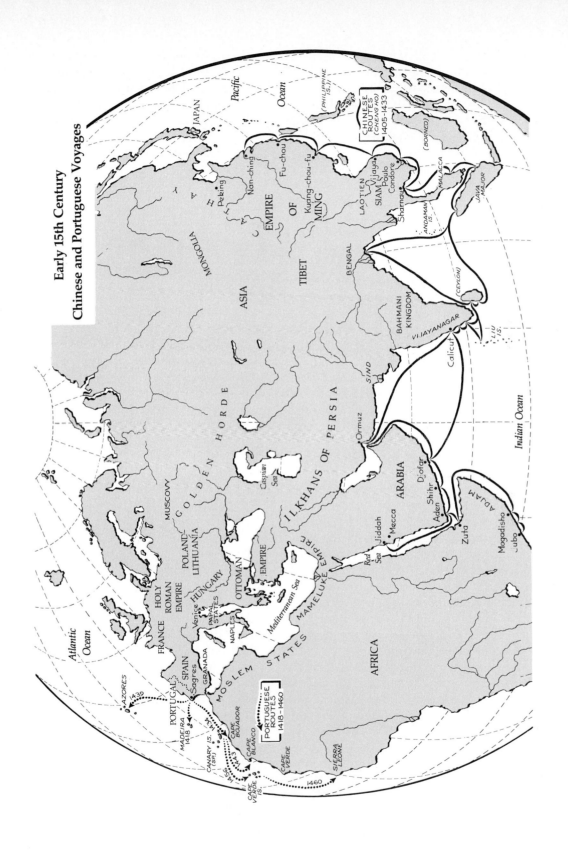

Early 15th Century
Chinese and Portuguese Voyages

ing exactly how far east or west they might be and, as a result, sometimes blundered far off course. Brazil, in fact, was discovered in this way in 1500, when a Portuguese expedition heading for India put farther out to sea than was necessary to clear the coast of west Africa and ran into South America.

But for most purposes, informed guesswork quite adequately took the place of accurate measurement of longitude. This required knowing the ship's speed through the water and then correcting for the speed and direction of ocean currents. The ship's speed through the water was measured by an interesting method. A slender rope with knots tied in it at regular intervals was attached to a "sea anchor" made of canvas and designed to offer so much resistance to being dragged through the water that it would remain almost still while the rope was paid out over the side of the ship. By counting the number of knots that went overboard in a given period of time, the captain would have a fairly accurate measure of how fast his ship was sailing through the water.

Detection of ocean currents was impossible by direct measurement. Instead, captains kept logs in which they entered the estimated distance traveled each day. Then when some large error showed up (for example, when the ship reached land either sooner or later than would be expected by adding up each day's mileage), the difference could be attributed to some current in the ocean. And by comparing records made by many different ships traveling along different courses, the direction and speed of the ocean currents could be defined with reasonable accuracy. The Portuguese became expert in this kind of rule-of-thumb calculation, before other Europeans knew much about oceanic navigation.

The idea that the earth was flat and that if a ship sailed too far it might fall off the edge of the world and never come back may have frightened some sailors. But European navigators and scholars knew better. Measurements of latitude along the coast of Africa had given the Portuguese an accurate idea of how big the earth was. Therefore, when Columbus came to the Portuguese court with his plan for sailing westward to China and the Indies, the experts in Lisbon knew that the Indies were much further away than Columbus believed. They had their own plan for reaching the Indies by sailing around Africa and, quite correctly, decided that Columbus' route was far longer than the one they proposed to take. From the Portuguese point of view, there was absolutely no point in bringing in an ignorant stranger who wanted full rights for himself in anything he might discover. And so they turned Columbus down!

The Value of Navigation Secrets   The Portuguese court treated information about the African coast and ocean navigation as secrets of state. The idea was to keep the trade along the coast for Portuguese ships exclusively. Exactly how much the Portuguese captains and navigators knew about the Atlantic Ocean, before Columbus and the other great explorers opened up knowledge of the New World to all of Europe, is still debated. Perhaps the Portuguese already knew of the existence of Brazil and of the Americas. Or perhaps the store of myths and sailors' yarns about a beautiful land in the west, where the souls of the dead went— an idea as old as Egypt and the megalithic sailors—was all that lay behind the scattered hints about lands beyond the Atlantic that survive in medieval records for modern scholars to read and wonder about.

The Vikings had certainly reached North America from Greenland, where a colony existed until the 1340s. Reports of Leif Ericson's "Vinland" (first visited *c*. 1000) were known in northern Europe; but Viking settlements in the New World did not take root and flourish, though the site of one of them was recently identified and excavated in northern Newfoundland.

A generation or more before Columbus' time, humble fishermen had also begun to sail far out into the Atlantic, and there is some reason to think that Basque and Breton fishermen from the Bay of Biscay may have sailed after cod all the way across the North Atlantic. But fishermen, like members of the Portuguese court, kept their secrets to themselves and certainly did not write books about where the best fishing grounds were to be found.

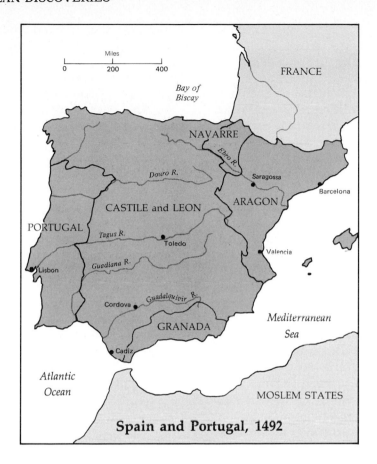

Spain and Portugal, 1492

Problems of Organizing Exploration

Whatever the exact facts were, it is clear that by 1480 European seafarers and shipbuilders had solved the problem of navigating the stormy ocean waters of the North Atlantic so well that no other seas were difficult for them to sail across. The remaining problem was one of money and organization. Who would pay for long voyages to unknown destinations, and how would newfound lands be treated? Spain and Portugal, the two nations that pioneered Europe's ocean contacts with the rest of the world, found two quite different answers to these questions. Under the leadership of Prince Henry the Navigator, Portugal started ocean voyaging and exploration in 1418. At first Prince Henry had to operate on a very modest scale. Funds came from the income of a crusading Order, of which Prince Henry was head. The Order was supposed to devote its resources to fighting the Moslems, and Prince Henry conceived his explorations as part of a grand plan for outflanking the entire Moslem world. Rumor had reached Europe of a great Christian ruler named Prester (that is, Presbyter or Priest) John, whose kingdom was located somewhere in Asia or, perhaps, in East Africa. Prince Henry hoped to be able to find a way to Prester John's kingdom by sailing around Africa. Then, he thought, a combined assault on the Moslem world might lead to final victory over Christendom's traditional enemy.

The existence of Christians in Ethiopia, of Christians in India (said to have been converted by St. Thomas), and of small communities of Nestorian Christians in central Asia provided the basis in fact for the stories of Prester John. But when a Portuguese diplomat named Pedro de Covilhão actually reached Ethiopia in 1487, what he found was disappointing. The Ethiopian Christians were not ready or indeed able to help against the Moslems who surrounded their kingdom.

Dependence on Prester John therefore proved a flimsy hope, and the resources of Prince Henry's Order soon became inadequate to pay for fitting out ships year after year. Borrowing was the next step. Bankers were quite accustomed to lending money to kings for wars and other royal undertakings. They were ready enough to finance the rulers of Portugal, if proper security for the loans could be found. At first this was difficult, for Portugal was not a rich country. But when Prince Henry's ships passed the barren Saharan coast and reached as far south as the Senegal River (1444), a lively trade with the local peoples began to develop. Slaves, gold, and ivory were the main products the Africans offered the Portuguese. Tools, weapons, and knickknacks, offered in exchange, made a trade that seemed advantageous to both sides. This sort of business the bankers of Italy and southern Germany understood. They were ready enough to finance such ventures, making loans and advances against a share in the profits to be expected from each voyage.

PORTUGUESE TRADE AND EMPIRE EXPLORATION

Trade with the African coast sustained the costs of continued exploration, and new exploration added to the extent of trade. The process, in short, became self-sustaining, and the pace of Portuguese discovery picked up accordingly. New and better ships, together with a growing body of experienced crews and captains, could be supplied year by year, since the voyages paid off and the new financing was comparatively easy to find.

A few examples will show how rapidly progress was made once these operational problems were solved. When Prince Henry died in 1460, Portuguese ships had worked their way as far south as the Gambia River and the Cape Verde Islands. Twelve years later (1472) Fernando Po reached the island that still bears his name, lo-

cated near the big bend where the African coast turns south again. Ten years later Diogo Cão discovered the mouth of the Congo River (1482). Five years thereafter Bartholomeu Dias rounded the Cape of Good Hope (1487).

The pace of exploration was interrupted briefly by quarrels with Spain arising from Columbus' discovery in 1492. But progress around Africa was resumed when Vasco da Gama (1497) sailed south through the mid-Atlantic to the latitude of the Cape of Good Hope, then turned eastward until the coast of Africa appeared, after ninety-seven days at sea without sight of land. After coasting along the east shore of Africa, da Gama arrived in Mombasa, where he picked up a pilot who guided him across the Indian Ocean to Calicut in southern India. There the Portuguese were able to load their ships with valuable cargo, and returned in triumph to Portugal (1499). Africa had been rounded at last. The way to the Indies had been discovered in sober fact.

The Spice Trade   The Portuguese set out energetically to develop the possibilities of trade in the Indian Ocean. "Spices" were especially in demand in Europe. Spices meant almost anything that came from the Indian Ocean coastlands and adjacent islands that could be used to flavor food or as a medicine or dye. But the familiar spices of the modern kitchen were always the most important: pepper, cinnamon, cloves. From medieval times, rich Europeans had become accustomed to consuming surprisingly large quantities of these spices. The reason for this was that without refrigeration the meat they ate was nearly always spoiled. Used in large enough quantities, pepper and other spices disguised the taste and smell of decaying meat and were valued accordingly. Spices were also believed to have medicinal effects; and because they were expensive, they also had show-off value.

Different spices came from different parts of the Indian Ocean area. Before da Gama appeared, spices had been gathered by Moslem merchants and shipped from southern India or southern Arabia through the Red Sea to Egypt. From Egypt the spices were forwarded to Venice and other Italian cities and then distributed over western Europe. This trade route involved many exchanges and a fancy price markup with each exchange. Taxes and tolls at each end of the Red Sea also added to the cost of the spices as delivered in Europe. Vasco da Gama interfered with this route by collecting spices in southern India and carrying them in a single, unbroken voyage to Lisbon. This made Lisbon, instead of Venice, the main port for delivery of spices to Europe.

The Portuguese quickly followed up da Gama's successful voyage by sending out a fleet in 1500 (the same fleet that, incidentally, discovered Brazil on its way to India). Other fleets followed. This new route around Africa obviously threatened the Moslem merchants who had been accustomed to making a living by sending spices via the Red Sea route; but the Moslems were not able to stop the Portuguese from doing anything they wanted to do on the high seas. Portuguese ships had guns that could sink enemy vessels at a distance of 100 yards or more. The lightly constructed ships used on the Indian Ocean could

not arm themselves to match the Portuguese, since the recoil of heavy guns was almost as damaging as cannonballs. Hence, when the Moslems assembled a great fleet in 1509, the handful of Portuguese ships that sailed against them had no difficulty in winning a decisive battle off the port of Diu in northwestern India.

This battle marked a drastic revolution in naval tactics as far as the Moslem sea powers of the Indian Ocean were concerned. For at least 2000 years, ramming and boarding had been the methods of fighting at sea in both Mediterranean and Indian Ocean waters. But these close-in tactics became suicidal when cannon fire could sink an approaching vessel before it came close enough even to touch its enemy. In face of such catastrophic change in old patterns of naval warfare, the seafaring peoples of the Indian Ocean did not even try to borrow Portuguese techniques. They submitted instead to paying tolls or risking capture at Portuguese hands.

Portuguese Ship in Japan This large folding screen records the visit of a European ship to Japan. It was made soon after 1542 when such contacts began. Clearly the artist was interested in details of the ship's structure: masts, crow's nests, sails, rigging, guns—all quite accurately portrayed. The white cloud in the foreground represents smoke from a ceremonial salute fired by guns in the bow of the vessel. Fittingly perhaps, it envelops a welcoming party of Japanese on shore, while the visiting Europeans in the foreground remain clearly visible, complete with a horse, perhaps newly landed from the ship. Acute interest in foreign technology—especially guns—evidenced here was characteristic of the earliest Japanese reaction to contact with Europeans. From a European point of view, Japan was the most distant new land they discovered where profitable trade could be conducted. Accordingly, Portuguese ships continued to find a welcome at Japanese ports for nearly a century.

Portuguese Land Bases Overseas   Having demonstrated their command of the seas in such a convincing fashion in 1509, the next problem for the Portuguese was to seize strategic points on land for the control of trade. The port of Goa on the western coast of India (captured 1510) became their headquarters. Ports and naval stations at the mouth of the Persian Gulf (captured 1515) and at Malacca, in the straits between Sumatra and the mainland (captured 1511), made naval control of the whole Indian Ocean possible. Links with home were secured by means of a series of African coastal stations. Still farther east lay the Spice Islands themselves—that is, the Moluccas—and China. A Portuguese explorer reached the south coast of China as early as 1513, and by 1557 the Portuguese had founded a permanent colony at Macao, near Canton. Japan was visited first in 1542.

All these naval operations cost large sums of money. At first, the Portuguese king had no trouble raising the sums needed to build and equip the fleets that sailed to the Indies. Individual voyages came home with cargoes that paid the total costs two or three times over when the spices had been sold in Europe. But windfalls of this sort soon disappeared. The Moslems reorganized themselves to compete once more with the Portuguese. After all, the route around Africa was at least three times as long as the route through the Red Sea, and the costs of building and maintaining the stout oceangoing ships used by the Portuguese were greater than those that had to be met by the flimsier ships of the Indian Ocean. Thus by lowering tolls and taxes and reducing the markup at each change of hands along the route, it was possible for the old pattern of the spice trade to catch up with Portuguese competition within about twenty years.

This in turn meant that the financing of the Portuguese enterprises in the Indian Ocean became more difficult. Local garrisons had to find ways of paying for themselves. Supplies from home came more rarely and in smaller quantity. The first great burst of energy died away, and the Portuguese began to fit into the Indian Ocean scene simply as one group of traders operating in competition with others, with special advantages in the strength of their vessels but with handicaps too—above all, the difficulty of supplying themselves adequately from a distant and by no means wealthy homeland.

In some places, nevertheless, the Portuguese continued to prosper. They carried on trade between Japan and China for nearly a century, for example, and reaped the usual middleman's profits from this trade. Macao thrived on such a role, without any particular support from home. Local merchants could afford to buy the supplies they needed and to equip their ships from their profits. This was a special case, however, made possible by the fact that the Chinese government treated all Japanese merchants as pirates and prohibited direct dealings with them but allowed the Portuguese (who were not, to begin with, much less piratical) to act as go-betweens.

In the Spice Islands, too, the Portuguese were able to extract cloves and other trade goods by demanding them from local rulers as the price for being left in charge of a particular town or island. Since Portuguese ships and crews were equipped with weapons far superior to those that the local people had access to, it was relatively easy for the Portuguese to punish disobedience with sudden catastrophic violence. After a few such terrorist acts, local chiefs and princes found it wise to do what was demanded of them and required their people to work for the Portuguese by gathering cloves or whatever other products the island could produce.

Variations in Local Trade Patterns   Various local trade patterns arose elsewhere. The export of Asian goods to the African coast and exchanges between different regions of the Indian Ocean area offered some trade possibilities. But in general, local traders were in a better position than the Portuguese to develop these commercial relations, since they knew languages, market conditions, and local political relationships better than European intruders. The Portuguese could demand protection money from the ships engaged in such trade, by virtue of their superior armament—and did so with considerable success.

The enduring handicap that the Portuguese faced in the Indian Ocean area and in the Far East was that there were almost no European products that anyone in Asia seemed to want.

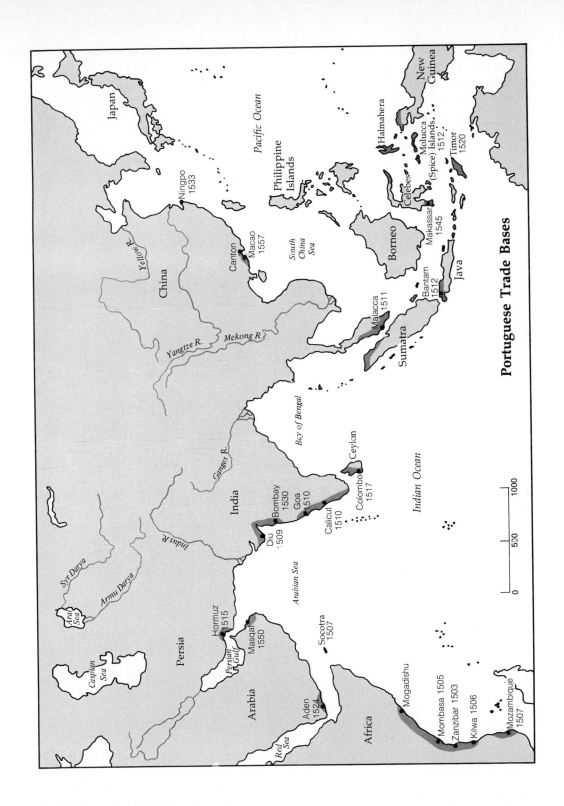

Portuguese Trade Bases

Japan

Pacific Ocean

China

Yellow R.

Ningpo
1533

Canton

Macao
1557

South
China
Sea

Yangtze R.

Mekong R.

Philippine
Islands

Halmahera

Molucca
(Spice) Islands
1512

Celebes

New
Guinea

Timor
1520

Makassar
1545

Borneo

Java

Bantam
1512

Malacca
1511

Sumatra

Bay of Bengal

Ganges R.

India

Ceylon

Colombo
1517

Bombay
1530

Goa
1510

Calicut
1510

Indus R.

Diu
1509

Indian Ocean

Syr Darya

Amu Darya

Aral
Sea

Caspian
Sea

Persia

Hormuz
1515

Masqat
1550

Persian
Gulf

Socotra
1507

Arabian Sea

Arabia

Aden
1524

Red
Sea

Africa

Mogadishu

Mombasa 1505

Zanzibar 1503

Kilwa 1506

Mozambique
1507

0   500   1000

357

European manufactured goods were generally coarse and unattractive to Indian, Chinese, or Japanese consumers. Even in Africa, Asian goods were cheaper and better adapted to African use. Metal and guns interested the Japanese from the start. Elsewhere even these had little market. In any case, it was obviously unwise to sell too many guns to people who might use them to drive the Portuguese away.

A second problem, almost as difficult, was that the king in Portugal had no effective way of controlling his agents in Africa, India, and distant China. The king financed the major expeditions and claimed to rule the forts that had been set up along the trade routes. As early as 1505 a governor went out to India to represent the king. Governors continued to be sent to Goa until 1961, when Portugal finally lost control of that city. But the governors could not easily control the activities of agents scattered over thousands of miles. It was a standing temptation for official representatives of the king of Portugal to trade on their own account. Under these circumstances, profitable undertakings tended to pass into private hands, and dealings that lost money or returned little profit tended to stay on the king's accounts. The result, therefore, was that the king of Portugal seldom had anything to show for his imperial venture in the Indian Ocean. Soon he could not get loans to keep up his forts and ships abroad. Local enterprises, particularly in Macao, did not suffer; but after about 1520 support from home began to slacken, and new ventures into still more distant seas came to a halt. Individuals still might profit handsomely; but the king and the great bankers who had financed the king, in the beginning stages of Portuguese exploration, were not receiving a return on their investment. Accordingly, they stopped advancing money for further ventures.

GROWTH OF SPAIN'S OVERSEAS EMPIRE

The Spaniards came into the business of overseas empire by the back door. Indeed, in 1492 there was no such thing as a kingdom of Spain, for even after the marriage of Ferdinand of Aragon to Isabella of Castile (1469), the two kingdoms retained separate governments. Since it was Isabella who financed Columbus' voyage, her kingdom of Castile fell heir to the Americas. But Castile was an inland kingdom, concerned, over the centuries, with crusading wars against the Moslems. Castile's crusade against Islam reached a climax in 1492, when the last remaining Moslem state in the Spanish peninsula, the kingdom of Granada, was finally conquered. Ferdinand and Isabella followed up this victory by expelling from their kingdoms all Jews (1492) and Moslems (1502) who refused to become converts to Christianity. In this way the crusade was carried through to its local conclusion at the very moment when a vast new field of missionary endeavor opened up in the Americas before the astonished eyes of the Spanish rulers.

The Voyages of Columbus

The fact that Isabella took Columbus seriously was itself an indication of how little experience the Spaniards had in overseas operations. As we just saw, the Portuguese knew better and turned him down cold. But Isabella was impressed by his piety and energy; and when Granada fell, she decided that she could afford the cost of outfitting the three little ships Columbus used on his famous voyage to the "Indies." Moreover, Isabella agreed to make Columbus "Admiral of the Ocean Sea," with wide rights to any new lands that he might discover. The pattern she had in mind, presumably, was the familiar one of lord and vassal. Anything Columbus might find could be treated as another fief of the kingdom of Castile.

Columbus sailed from Spain in August, 1492, and headed south to the Canary Islands, which had belonged to Castile since 1344. Then he headed west and sighted one of the Bahama Islands after only thirty-six days out of sight of land. Since the Canaries lie in the trade-wind zone, Columbus simply let the northeast trades blow his ships across the ocean. For the return, he headed north until he reached the zone of prevailing westerlies and then turned east toward Spain. Columbus was a skilled navigator and knew before he started how to take advantage of

European Encounters with Cannibalism and Idolatry These two woodcuts show how shocking Europeans found the habits of some of the peoples whom they discovered in the century after 1500. Above is a scene from Brazil, showing both nudity and an all-too-human barbeque. The artist took some pains to suggest that the cannibals enjoyed their feast—making their behavior even more shocking. Below are crudely drawn images of three Indian gods, illustrating a popular book that attacked the idolatrous errors of the Hindu religion. Printing allowed information of this kind, as well as much else about newly discovered lands, to circulate widely in Europe in the sixteenth century. On first encountering scenes like these, Europeans reacted with mingled fascination and revulsion. Sharpened awareness of the variety of human habits and customs made older moral certainties harder (and, often, more important) to maintain.

these favoring oceanic wind patterns. From a technical point of view, in fact, his famous voyage was not in the least difficult. Its significance lay in the fact that he opened regular contact between Europe and the Americas for the first time.

Ironically enough, Columbus refused until his dying day to admit that he had discovered a new continent. He believed instead that he had found islands lying somewhere off the coast of Asia. Before his death in 1506 he made three more voyages, discovering Santo Domingo, Cuba, and other islands of the Caribbean Sea, and touching also upon the coast of South America in the region near the Orinoco River. He found small amounts of gold in Santo Domingo. Rumors of untold riches, just over the horizon, ran swiftly through the Spanish court. Footloose nobles and penniless adventurers eagerly took ship to seek their fortunes. The queen continued to make grants of lands yet to be discovered, usually to captains who undertook to organize an expedition at their own expense.

Establishment of Direct Royal Rule   The result in the Americas was wild disorder and bitter quarrels. Columbus soon proved unable to deal with the situation. A royal judge, dispatched from Castile to look into the situation, sent Columbus back to Spain as a prisoner in 1499. The grant of governmental powers to Columbus was canceled; and in principle, though not yet in fact, direct royal administration was extended to the new-found lands on the far side of the Atlantic.

The decision was simply an extension across the ocean of a struggle going on in Castile itself between the royal government and the great feudal nobles, who resisted any increase of royal authority over their lands. The royal government in Castile was making rapid advances, particularly since Ferdinand of Aragon—a much more commanding personality than his wife, Isabella—could give advice and direct policy from behind the scenes. As soon as troubles broke out in Columbus' possessions, therefore, officials took the opportunity to establish direct royal administration over the newly discovered lands.

Such a policy was all very well on paper. But at first the government lacked sufficient income from the New World to pay for the fleets, soldiers, judges, governors, and other officials needed to make royal administration a reality. Hence, the policy of making generous land grants to anyone who would equip an expedition continued to be followed. Such grants sometimes overlapped, since no one knew exactly what was being granted in the first place. Small-scale civil wars and threats of violence therefore continued to break out among the Spaniards in the New World. Royal court decisions and the law applied only spottily, if at all, since there was no way to enforce theoretical rights except by force of arms.

In other words, the turbulent struggle be-

tween king and nobles, which had been decisively won by the agents of the king in Castile just before Columbus sailed, shifted overseas.

Adjustment of Claims Between Spain and Portugal   For a while, news of Columbus' discovery aroused great excitement all over Europe. In 1493 the pope divided the world equally between Spain and Portugal, along arbitrarily chosen meridians of longitude. During the following year, the two governments agreed to modify the pope's line of demarcation by moving it a hundred leagues to the west. The new line brought Brazil within the Portuguese half of the world, but because of the difficulties of measuring longitude, no one was really sure where the line fell in the Far East.

Other European kings did not like to admit the rights of Spain and Portugal, but only the English tried to do anything about it. Henry VII sent John Cabot across the Atlantic to explore more to the north (1497). Cabot discovered no passage to China or the Indies. On the contrary, he found only empty and forbidding forests that offered no obvious attraction to Europeans. After this single venture, therefore, for more than a century the English gave up western exploration as a bad business. No other country even tried.

Discoveries of Vespucci, Balboa, and Magellan

As for the Spaniards, it looked for a while as though the whole venture would soon fall through. Expedition after expedition went out to look for the fabled wealth of the Indies, and each discovered new stretches of the American coast. By 1507 most experts were ready to agree that what had been discovered was not Asia but a new continent. In that year a German scholar, Martin Waldseemüller, published a map on which he entered everything he could find out from the reports of the explorers. For his information about the more southerly parts of the coast of South America, he relied on the report of an Italian captain, Amerigo Vespucci, who had sailed almost as far south as the estuary of La Plata in 1502. In recognition of Amerigo Vespucci's discoveries, Waldseemüller, proposed to call the new land

America. The name stuck, although at first it applied only to South America, and it was not until after 1600 that Europeans agreed that the term should apply to both North and South America.

Any remaining doubt as to what Columbus had discovered was removed when Vasco Nuñez de Balboa, a Spaniard, crossed the Isthmus of Panama in 1513 and sighted the ocean we call the Pacific. Soon thereafter Ferdinand Magellan, a Portuguese sea captain sailing for Spain, discovered the straits that bear his name, at the tip of South America. He then sailed up the western coast of what is now Chile until he reached the trade-wind zone. With the southeast trade winds at his back, Magellan boldly set out across the vast Pacific. The voyage was long and perilous, for Magellan was heading for the Spice Islands, which he knew to be north of the equator. This required him to steer in a northerly direction, so that somewhere in the mid-Pacific he left the trade-wind zone behind and entered the region of tropic calms, where his ships made slow and halting headway. But Magellan was a skilled navigator and eventually made his way to the Philippine Islands, where he was killed in a skirmish with the natives. His companions continued on their way around the world; and one of the five ships with which he had started finally made it back to Spain, arriving in 1522 after three years at sea.

Such feats of seamanship were exciting and impressive but left unanswered the question of how Spain's overseas ventures were ever going to pay for themselves. The gold Columbus gathered from the natives of Santo Domingo did not amount to much. Other American products, however interesting, did not command an immediate market in Europe. The Amerindians whom the Spaniards first met were poor and did not even make good slaves because they died so rapidly from European diseases.

The Conquests of Mexico, Peru, and Chile

Castile's overseas enterprise was saved by the reckless venture of Hernando Cortes against the Aztec Empire of Mexico. Cortes started off from Cuba in 1518 with 600 men and seventeen horses under his command. After sailing for a while along the Mexican coast, he put ashore at Veracruz and set out to march inland toward the Aztec capital, Tenochtitlán. The Spaniards were helped by Indian tribes who resented the Aztec lordship. Montezuma, the Aztec ruler, was nonplused, believing the Spaniards to be supernatural beings. He allowed himself to be taken prisoner and died in captivity. When the Aztecs revolted against the Spaniards in 1520, Cortes was forced to retreat from Tenochtitlán; but the next year, with help from Indian allies, he once more besieged and captured the city. This time he destroyed it and founded Mexico City nearby, as the capital of the new Spanish domain.

What made Cortes' feat so important to the authorities back home was that he discovered enormous quantities of gold and silver in the Aztec capital. Here at last was something really valuable that could pay the costs of exploration and development. The news made credit easy to find and recruits eager to go on overseas adventures.

Cortes' brilliant and brutal success was quickly followed by Francisco Pizarro's conquest of Peru (1531–1536). Only 180 men and twenty-seven horses started out with Pizarro in 1531. Yet the Inca Empire he conquered was larger and much better organized than the Aztec Empire had been. Gold and silver were even more abundant than in Tenochtitlán.

Such amazing adventures led other Spaniards to start off in every direction, looking for still more cities of gold. A grant from the Spanish government and a few promises to eager followers were enough to get the necessary credit for equipping an expedition. In such a fashion, Hernando de Soto explored what is now the southern United States and discovered the Mississippi River (1539–1542). Francisco Vásquez de Coronado explored what is now New Mexico, Texas, Oklahoma, and part of Kansas in 1540–1543. Yucatan, the home of the Mayas, was explored a little earlier (1527–1535) without yielding returns comparable to the wealth of Mexico and Peru. Similar energies were spent in conquering Chile (complete by 1561), Colombia (1536–1538), sailing down the Amazon from Peru (1541), and exploring Lower California and other nearby regions.

MONTEZUMA

In the year 1502 a handsome young Aztec chieftain succeeded his uncle as ruler of Mexico. The Aztecs were a warrior people, chosen, they believed, by the Sun god to feed him human hearts every day so that he would be strong enough to rise again each morning and dispel the darkness. In the year 1325 the Aztecs took possession of a swampy island in Lake Texcoco and made it their stronghold. By Montezuma's time, the island had become the site of a great city, Tenochtitlán. It was connected with the mainland by narrow causeways. Drawbridges allowed the Aztecs to halt an approaching enemy with ease. Even if a foe should camp where the causeways reached the mainland, boats could bring in supplies from distant shores of the lake. The city of Tenochtitlán was therefore a secure base. From it the Aztec warriors raided far and wide, seeking always to take prisoners alive so as to be able to sacrifice them to the Sun god. Peoples and tribes round about soon agreed to pay tribute to keep the great city supplied with food and all its other needs, rather than run the risk of being captured and sacrificed. So Aztec raiding parties traveled farther and farther to find captives for their god and, doing so, rapidly created a large empire.

This was what Montezuma inherited. He was a capable and pious ruler. Each day priests sacrificed human beings to the Sun god by cutting their still beating hearts from their bodies; each day the Sun rose victoriously in the east, refreshed by human sacrifice. But the Aztecs knew of another god, Quetzalcoatl, who had disappeared long ago after promising to return. Quetzalcoatl

The Organization of Mining   By 1545 it had become clear that no more great empires remained to be conquered and no more Indian hoards of gold and silver awaited Spanish discovery. The great days of the conquistadors had lasted no more than twenty-five years. It was time for officials and administrators, missionaries and bureaucrats, to take over and make Spain's vast overseas empire of the Americas into a more orderly affair.

The first step was to organize mining to keep a flow of precious metals moving toward Spain. Precious metals would pay for everything and keep the authorities at home happy. Gold was found in small quantities at widely scattered locations, mostly as nuggets in stream beds. But the really important new mines produced silver in quantities that Europeans had not seen before. The richest mine was located at Potosi, in the high Andes. The mine was put into regular operation in 1545. Similar mines in central Mexico came into production soon afterward, but Peru remained the largest single source of precious metal. The Spaniards brought the best European techniques to the mines of the New World. The returns were spectacular. Vast quantities of precious metal kept coming year after year after year.

Safe delivery of the silver was a problem, since pirates from other European nations had no scruples about attacking a treasure-laden Spanish ship on its way home. A convoy system was therefore set up. Silver from Peru was brought by ship to Panama, carried across the isthmus on muleback, shipped again in armed was white and bearded, a rival to the Aztec Sun god. What he would do when he returned, no one knew.

When Montezuma had ruled for fifteen years, disturbing news came from the eastern coast. Ships as big as houses had been seen; they carried white strangers, wearing beards. Was this a sign that Quetzalcoatl was coming back? Did this foretell the overthrow of the Sun god and of his blood-stained servants, the Aztecs?

Many inhabitants of Mexico thought so. Then, in 1519, a few hundred men and some horses actually came ashore and started to march inland. Hernando Cortes was on his way!

What should Montezuma do? Ought he to welcome Cortes as a god? Should he fight him? No one in Tenochtitlán knew. Montezuma tried at first to persuade the strangers to go back where they had come from. When they refused, he tried to cut off their food supply. But that failed, too, because peoples along the way decided that the Spaniards were gods—or at least so powerful that it was best to treat them as gods.

In the end Montezuma did the same. When Cortes came close to his capital, he went out to welcome him, escorted him into the center of his city, and gave the Spaniards everything they asked for. Montezuma soon found out that Cortes was not Quetzalcoatl, but that did not make him harmless. Quarrels began, and Cortes took Montezuma prisoner. When a riot broke out against the Spaniards, Montezuma tried to tell his people to stop. Instead, they stoned him; soon after, he died, a helpless prisoner. Within a year the empire he ruled and the Sun god he served vanished utterly because the Aztecs' former subjects all rebelled, led and organized by Cortes and his men.

convoy through the Caribbean islands, and then headed for home through the Straits of Florida following the path that Columbus had first sailed in 1492.

Administration according to standard bureaucratic methods became possible as soon as the flow of precious metals had been organized, since the mines paid, and more than paid, for all official salaries. The grants made to the conquistadors in the first days of exploration were canceled. Instead the Spanish lands of the New World were divided between a viceroyalty of Peru, with its capital at Lima, and a viceroyalty of New Spain, with its capital at Mexico City. The viceroy (that is, substitute king) was appointed from Spain and represented the royal authority in the New World. He was assisted by a council of high officials, but all important business had to be approved by a special Council for the Indies that sat in Spain. Various provinces were carved out of each viceroyalty. In these a subordinate council, like that which advised the viceroys, exercised official authority. Each town had a council too, presided over by an appointed officer of the crown.

The wild excesses of the conquistadors' generation were thus effectively tamed. Lawsuits replaced naked force as the way to get and hold property. What had been the wildest and most unruly part of the Castilian kingdom became the most carefully and exactly governed portion. This surprising transformation was not only the work of mining engineers and lawyers; it was also the work of the Catholic Church.

**Spanish and Portuguese Conquest
and Discovery in the New World,
1492-1550**

Spanish colonial territory, c. 1550

Portuguese colonial territory, c. 1550

Aztec Empire, 1519

Maya Empire, 1520

Inca Empire, 1533

Tiahuanaco Aztec, Maya, and
Inca settlements

Cortes' conquest of Mexico: 1519–1531
Pizarro's conquest of Peru: 1531
Coronado's explorations: 1540–1543
DeSoto's explorations: 1539–1542
Dates indicate year of conquest by Spain

The Missionary Thrust

The Spanish kings were accustomed to working closely with the Church. At each stage of the long reconquest of Spain from the Moslems, newly won territory had been made part of the kingdom of Castile through the efforts of royal and Church officials. Indeed, royal officials and Church officials were nearly the same thing. In 1478 Ferdinand and Isabella organized a special Church court system known as the Spanish Inquisition. Its purpose was to search out heretics, particularly former Jews and Moslems who pretended to be Christians but secretly remained loyal to their old faiths. Four years later, in 1482, the pope agreed to give the monarchs of Castile and Aragon almost complete control over appointments to all high Church offices in their respective kingdoms.

These new powers became of the utmost importance to the royal administration. In particular, the Inquisition was almost the only institution that functioned freely and uniformly in both Castile and Aragon. Inquisitors had the power to arrest anyone on suspicion and could hold a prisoner secretly for months, or even for years, while they inquired into the "correctness" of his religious views. Such methods did indeed reveal a good many Jews and Moslems who pretended to be Catholic. But the same methods could be and were used against any opponent of the royal administration. Even if no heresy could be found, the king's critics might simply disap-

The Oldest American Cathedral This is the west doorway of the Cathedral of Santo Domingo in the Dominican Republic. Inside is a tomb of Christopher Columbus, though exactly where his bones are located is a matter of dispute. The building was dedicated in 1540, when this city was still the principal Spanish headquarters in the New World. Its architecture is wholly European since Indian workmen who constructed it had no tradition of building with stone. The size and grandeur of this cathedral demonstrates the importance of the church in Spanish colonial administration. Its location on the central square, next to the vice regal residence, occupied initially by Christopher Columbus, aptly symbolizes the way churchmen were half rivals, half subordinates to secular administrators in managing the Spanish king's new subjects overseas.

pear for an indefinite period. Efforts to inquire what had happened were likely to lead to the disappearance of the person who did the asking. Such arrests, therefore, quickly broke the back of opposition to Ferdinand and Isabella and prepared the way for greater and greater coordination between the two kingdoms.

The Church in the New World   One of the first things the Spanish monarchs did after the news of Columbus' discoveries reached them was to make sure that the Church in the Indies would be under their full control. The pope agreed to this in 1493 and gave the Spanish royal authorities the right to appoint bishops and other Church officials in all their overseas possessions. The Inquisition was not established in the New World until 1569, however, perhaps because it was not needed.

Individual priests and friars accompanied nearly every expedition undertaken by the conquistadors. Believing that millions of souls awaited salvation, the Spanish Church undertook an enormous effort, sending missionaries to every part of the territory that came under Spanish rule. Because the missionaries were interested in the religious welfare of the Indians, they became the special spokesmen for the interests of the Indians. The most famous defender of Indian rights was Bartolemé de Las Casas (1474–1566), a priest, later bishop, who went to Santo Domingo in 1502 and spent the rest of his life trying to plead and argue against enslavement of the Indians. He was successful. When law codes for the Americas were published (1542), Indians were classified as legal dependents, or wards, of the Spanish crown. Their enslavement and mistreatment were prohibited, although Spanish landholders were able to find other ways of controlling Indian labor when it suited them.

Las Casas also made one of the earliest experiments of trying to convert the Indians by setting up a mission. He wished to convert them by persuasion, without use of force. But the Indians usually preferred their own ways, and if left really free would disappear into the forests. Later missions, therefore, combined an element of force with the element of persuasion. Friars and soldiers together rounded up groups of Indians and

invited them to accept Christianity. The Indians seldom refused.

Sometimes a group of Indians tried to sneak away from the mission. Then the soldiers went after them and brought them back. But in general the Indians readily submitted to the friars and priests. The priests and medicine men of their old religions had demanded obedience. So did the Christian priests. It was not difficult for simple farmers to transfer loyalty and obedience from one to the other, particularly when the native religion and political leadership could offer no effective resistance to the Spaniards.

When the great conquistador expeditions ceased about 1540, missions became the means by which the Spaniards continued to extend their hold over the native peoples. The lack of hoarded gold was no obstacle to the expansion of missions. Each mission was expected to pay for itself. This meant putting the Indians to work. Accordingly the Spanish missionaries set out not only to convert the Indians to Catholic Christianity but also to teach them new skills.

Farming methods changed little, since the Indians knew a great deal already about how to raise American food crops. But new metal tools— hoes, axes, spades—often made an enormous difference. Cattle, sheep, and horses, unknown to the Americas before Columbus, also changed the pattern of land use in some parts of Mexico and South America. The missionaries built great churches with Indian labor and taught the Indians how to make all the things needed for church services and for the daily life of the whole community.

In this way, missions could become self-sufficient very quickly. Indeed, missionaries in Paraguay and in some other parts of the New World were later to make missions financially profitable. Indian labor could, after all, be used to produce goods for export. Such commodities when sold in Europe brought in funds that could then be used anywhere in the world; but this was a later development. Most missions were merely self-supporting. This was enough to permit rapid and continuous expansion of their scope within limits set by the number of available Spanish missionaries and companies of soldiers needed to back them.

The mission system was important all along

Spanish Mission of the Alamo This woodcut from the eighteenth century illustrates the social structure of Spanish frontier missions. It shows the clergy, who were in charge, emerging in solemn procession from the church building. In the foreground, four uniformed soldiers bow reverently, while a group of Indians in the background show rather more mixed reaction—some piously on their knees while others stand and stare. In addition to these three groups, a seated figure by the corner of the building, who seems entirely inattentive to the ceremony, is wearing European clothes and may therefore represent a local landowner. Such persons often found themselves competing with clergymen for the control of Indian labor. The figure's apparent indifference to the religious ceremony in progress may therefore have been intended by the artist to give visual form to a pervasive social tension of Spanish colonial society.

the fringes of the Spanish domains in the New World. In the central areas, however, and wherever there were silver mines of any importance, the mission pattern broke down. Indian labor was needed for the mines. It was also needed by the ordinary Spanish immigrant who had come to make his fortune and was not ready to work with his own hands. A common pattern was to lend goods or money to the Indians, who had no idea of what a loan meant and normally could not repay it. Then, as defaulting debtors, they could legally be required to work for their creditors. Low wages and easy credit at the store could then keep the Indians forever in debt and forever bound to work for their creditor. This relationship was called *peonage*, and it differed only in legal form from slavery.

In this way, Spaniards were able to compel Indians to work for them as servants, household artisans, and miners, and in other ways. Where this occurred, Indians and Spaniards both came under the spiritual control of parish priests and bishops, as was customary in Europe. In theory, the Church continued to make efforts to protect the Indians, and government officials backed the priests. In practice, though, loopholes in the law

allowed the immigrant Spaniards to get what they wanted: Indians to do the menial and necessary tasks of the new colonial society in which the Spaniards constituted the upper class. Since the Indians ranked at the bottom, half-breeds—with a Spanish father and an Indian mother—came in between. In regions where Negro slavery became important, other in-between groups arose from intermarriages between Negroes and Indians, and Negroes and Spaniards.

In time these in-between groups became more numerous. This meant that the original simplicity of the Spanish-Indian relationship blurred. But the Church retained its importance always, and so did the official bureaucracy. The two supported each other and together kept the society of the New World in order. Every effort was made to be sure that only Catholics in good standing came from Spain to the New World—and religious doubt or opposition to the Church was energetically suppressed in the Americas. The result was an ordered, stately society sustained by both the silver from the mines and the splendor of church services—and carefully controlled by officials appointed from Spain by the royal council.

Portuguese Missions

Portuguese missionary enterprise had a different history. To outflank Islam had been Prince Henry the Navigator's great goal; and when at last Vasco da Gama rounded Africa, the missionary idea was not forgotten. Friars and priests accompanied the Portuguese explorers; and when regular shore stations were set up, missionary churches were established also. The trouble was that the local inhabitants were not willing to accept the teaching of the missionaries. In India and China, Christianity was not entirely unheard of, and Hindus and Confucians had no use for it. They regarded Christianity as the faith of an unimportant group of outsiders, who might indeed have good ships and guns but who certainly did not know the truth about the nature of God and the universe.

Wherever the Portuguese met Islam—and that was almost everywhere on the shores of the Indian Ocean—the followers of Mohammed were in direct competition with Christian missions. The Moslems usually proved more persuasive, perhaps because they asked local peoples to give up fewer customs and habits than the Christians did. Sufi Islam, after all, had become a very elastic doctrine. Preachers of Islam recognized different ways to God. Christians required observance of all the sacraments. In particular, Christianity prohibited a man from marrying more than one wife, whereas in Africa and in parts of Southeast Asia, rich and important men took several wives and indeed measured their importance, in part, by the number of wives they had. This situation made the Christian gospel unwelcome.

Even when Portuguese missionaries won initial success, long-term results were slight. In the kingdom of Kongo, for example, a usurping ruler became Christian in 1506 and took the name Afonso. King Afonso tried hard to spread Christianity throughout his kingdom, but he also wanted to increase his power by monopolizing the export of slaves. This alienated his subjects; and in fact his kingdom soon broke up, leaving little trace of King Afonso's conversion behind.

Africans mostly preferred to keep their old ways and religion. Nothing had happened to African society to discredit traditional rites and beliefs. The additional fact that Portuguese and other Europeans soon became deeply engaged in the slave trade with the Americas may also have helped to discredit Christianity.

In one land, however, Christian missions had a different reception, for when St. Francis Xavier reached Japan in 1549 he met with considerable success. The Japanese took a remarkable liking to European novelties and, for a while, even imitated European clothing and other outward aspects of their life. Christianity benefited from this interest in foreign things. A community of Japanese Christians soon came into existence and flourished for about a century.

Nowhere else did Portuguese efforts to spread Christianity meet with much response. The Portuguese Empire remained, therefore, a naval and trading empire almost entirely limited to the ports and the high seas. Nothing remotely resembling the vast inland empire that the Spaniards created in the New World resulted from Portuguese exploration. The mark they made on the world was correspondingly temporary, whereas the Spanish conquest of the Indians of the New World gave shape and definition to the society of most of South and Central America.

Brazil was an exception, for here the Portuguese met with Indians similar to those the Spaniards confronted elsewhere. The Portuguese government did not set up a centralized official administration like that which made the Spanish Empire so orderly. Instead, Brazil was divided into a large number of separate local governments. Without silver to pay for everything, officialdom could not keep local energies under control. Efforts to use Indian labor on plantations (especially sugar plantations) proved disastrous, since the Indians died from the unfamiliar diseases brought in by the Portuguese and by slaves from Africa. Soon African slaves began to bear the main burden of producing sugar.

Missionary enterprise in the backwoods never really got started. Portuguese settlers in Brazil wanted laborers, and they raided inland, far and wide, in search of manpower for their sugar fields. The Spanish pattern of protected missions could not arise under such circumstances. On the other hand, plantation owners usually recognized it as part of their duty to provide Christian services for their slaves. By enslavement, therefore, Brazilian Indians and blacks from Africa were at least superficially Christianized.

INDIRECT CONSEQUENCES OF EUROPEAN EXPLORATIONS

The great European discoveries changed everyone's outlook on the world and altered prevailing concepts of the relationships among the major branches of humankind in far-reaching ways. But in addition to conscious changes, there were three worldwide and fundamentally important consequences that resulted from the new patterns of communication, of which contemporaries were largely or completely unaware. These were the so-called price revolution, the spread of diseases to new regions and among new populations, and the spread of American food crops to Europe, Africa, and Asia. Each of these deserves brief explanation.

The Price Revolution

The supply of American silver was so large that the supply of goods that might be bought with coins of silver could not keep up. The result was a rapid rise in prices. More and more silver was needed to buy the same amount of useful goods. Naturally enough, the price revolution was felt first and most strongly in Spain. There prices rose by about 400 percent in a century. In other parts of Europe increases may have been a little less, and they came more slowly. But no part of the European world escaped the effect, since a sharp rise in prices in one market attracted goods from other markets, where prices promptly rose, until some sort of rough balance could be established once more. The effect was not limited to Europe, but spread to the Ottoman Empire and to both India and China.

But as the price revolution spread through the civilized world, it became less important. In Europe more of the people engaged in the purchase and sale of goods than was the case in Asia, where the peasant majority bought and sold very little because they supplied their social superiors with food in the form of rents and taxes in kind. Changes in the price system in China, therefore, did not do much to change relations between peasants and landlords. The same was true in India and in most parts of the Moslem world. In Europe, however, the price revolution disrupted traditional relationships between buyers and sellers, landlords and tenants, government and taxpayers, borrowers and lenders. Some classes benefited, others suffered. Everyone felt uncertain. Nearly everyone believed that greedy, wicked individuals must somehow be responsible for the rise of prices. But in an age when no one understood the relationship between silver supply and price levels measured in silver, it was difficult to find out who was responsible or to pin the blame on anyone in particular.

This did not make the general disturbance of traditional day-by-day relationships any less important or easier to accept. When many suffered and everyone faced new uncertainties in economic matters, the European public was eager to find a scapegoat. The fierce religious quarreling provoked by the Lutheran movement in Germany owes much to the economic dislocation caused by price revolution. It ran through Europe's history for the next hundred years and changed men's lives in detail in innumerable ways. Nothing could be quite the same when prices changed so sharply and, of course, unevenly.

The Spread of Disease

A second, no less important, change was the result of the circulation of disease by ship. Where populations had previously had little contact with the outside world, new diseases brought by sailors from Europe had truly devastating consequences. In particular, the Indians of the Americas suffered enormous loss of life. They lacked any sort of established immunity to the standard childhood diseases of Europe; and thousands died in epidemics of measles, influenza, and whooping cough as well as from the disease more serious to Europeans, smallpox. On top of this exposure, the Amerindians soon had to face diseases brought from West Africa in slave ships—yellow fever, malaria, and the like.

Exposed to such a series of killing diseases, many Indian tribes died out completely. In Mexico and Peru, where millions of farming peasants lived when Cortes and Pizarro first appeared on the scene, the loss of life was even greater. It has been estimated, for example, that in the central part of Mexico the population was between 11 and 20 million when Cortes arrived. By 1650, when smallpox, measles, malaria, and other diseases had done their work, only about 1.5 million people remained, including half-breeds and, of course, all the immigrants from Spain. In other words, more than 85 percent of the population had been wiped out in 130 years. Similar sharp decreases took place in Peru and other parts of South America. The same thing happened wherever a dense population that had not had earlier exposure to civilized diseases came into contact with Europeans.

Civilized populations reacted differently. New plagues and epidemics reached European and Asian port cities by ships. But soon the number of ships and the frequency with which they came and went meant that every active port was infected with a more or less standard assortment of germs, varying only with the climate and living habits of the people.

When diseases became endemic in this manner, heavy loss of life from disease ceased to be an important control on population. Children either died in infancy or early childhood, or else survived with a fair level of immunity to all the standard local diseases. It was not possible any longer for a new disease, or a disease that had not been around for fifty years or more, to arrive in a town and kill half of the inhabitants because the townspeople either never had met the infection before or had lost their biological immunity to it.

In Europe during the later Middle Ages, after the opening of overland trade routes with China under the Mongols, this sort of occasional pestilence had been very common. The Black Death was among the earliest and most severe, but by no means the only example of sudden outbreaks of disease, killing off a large proportion of a town's population in a single summer. But after about 1750 communication had become so much more regular, and levels of infection had become so uniform throughout the civilized world, that such disasters almost ceased to afflict Europe; and they became much less important in India, China, and the Middle East as well.

The result was a remarkable increase in population. From about 1750 civilized populations seem everywhere to have started to grow at a rate unknown before. The new immunity to epidemic diseases was one of the main reasons.

The Spread of New Crops and Livestock

A third result of opening the world's oceans to shipping was the rapid spread of some important food plants and animals into new regions. The Americas gave tobacco, maize, potatoes, sweet potatoes, peanuts, and tomatoes to the rest of the world. In return came the domesticated animals of Europe: horses, cattle, sheep, and goats. The horse revolutionized Indian life on the Great Plains of North America, for mounted on horseback the Indians were able to hunt buffalo with much greater success than before. They developed a warlike hunting way of life, similar in some interesting ways to the life of the nomads of the Eurasion steppelands. (This, incidentally, is the kind of Indian who entered modern legends of the Wild West. But their way of life was still very new when the cowboys from the east arrived to dispute possession of the plains with them.)

Maize and potatoes came to have great importance in Europe and Africa. Sweet potatoes became a major food crop in southern China as well as in West Africa, where peanuts also flourished. Tobacco changed European and Turkish habits and made the fortune of the first English colony in North America. Tomatoes provided Indian and Mediterranean peoples with a valuable source of vitamins.

Taken together, the spread of the food plants from the Americas to the rest of the world greatly increased human food supplies. For example, until maize came from America, Africa had never before had a really high-yielding cereal plant that would do well in the climate of that continent.

As maize spread, the food supply expanded and African populations started to grow. This, in turn, allowed black Africa to withstand the losses due to the slave trade. In southern China, likewise, peasants could plant sweet potatoes on land unsuited for rice paddies and thereby add considerably to the local food resources. Potatoes and maize had similar importance for Europe, although not until after 1650.

The increase in the food supply and the decrease in epidemic diseases, therefore, worked together to allow Old World populations to grow. The depopulation that new diseases brought to other parts of the world made the expansion of civilized disease-experienced populations easier than it might otherwise have been, since local populations often withered away when put into contact with settlers who brought dangerous new diseases with them. Taking the whole globe into account, the European discoveries therefore tipped the balance between civilization and simpler, more isolated communities by favoring the more complex, more varied, more diseased, but also more resistant, populations we call civilized.

CONCLUSION

After about 1550 the first drive and energy of the Portuguese and Spanish expansion slackened. The Portuguese came to depend on tolls and trade profits to support their string of coastal stations in Africa and Asia. The Spaniards had put their new empire on a self-sustaining basis, thanks to the new silver mines. But the period of great, sudden windfalls, of surprising new discoveries, and of derring-do and adventure faded rapidly into the past.

Yet, in the short period of not more than two generations after Columbus returned with the news of his voyage, European discoveries had changed the relationships among the civilizations of the world in a fundamental fashion. The seacoasts of the world had become the most important places where different civilizations met.

To be sure, the frontier between the steppe nomads and civilized peoples, which had played such a large role in history since the time of the Scythians and Assyrians, did not disappear. As a matter of fact, India and China were conquered from the north by peoples coming directly or indirectly from the steppe in the centuries after the European discoveries had opened up the world's oceans to shipping.

But coastal ports where European ships put in began to rival the old steppe frontier as a zone of critical importance. Here Europeans had a chance to learn about the strange ways of other peoples, and other peoples had a chance to study European skills and ideas, if they cared to do so. Goods and ideas, settlers, diseases, and art styles could move more speedily by sea than overland, and did so.

At first the new pattern of movement by sea did not seem to make a great deal of difference in the Far East and India. Merchant ships had traversed the calm waters of the Indian Ocean and the South China Sea for many centuries before Portuguese ships rounded the Cape of Good Hope. The newcomers took over part of the trade and seized some strategic ports, but the goods they had to offer were of little interest, and their ideas were quite unconvincing to most of the people who bothered to listen to them at all.

Even their techniques of seamanship and naval artillery, which were clearly superior to what had been known before in these southern seas, did not make the local peoples change their ways. The costs were too high, and too many changes in old skills would have been required. For ordinary trading, the traditional kind of ship construction, already familiar in those waters, was superior because it was so much cheaper. The Portuguese with their floating castles found it easier to settle back and collect tolls from native ships.

In the Americas, by contrast, the arrival of Europeans changed everything. The Amerindian civilizations were ruthlessly decapitated by the conquistadors. Old priests and chiefs were utterly discredited. The Indian rank and file transferred obedience to the Spaniards. Native traditions sank to the village level and most of the lore of Aztec and Inca priests disappeared forever, since the Spaniards paid little attention to pagan superstition, and Indian priests had not committed their doctrines to writing.

Africa found itself more closely tied in with the rest of the world than before. Sea trade opened new possibilities, particularly in western Africa and in the whole southern half of the continent. Previously, connections with the civilized world had run northward across the Sahara or by caravan eastward along the open savanna country. In both cases, the civilization with which African communities came in touch was Islam. With the Portuguese explorations, however, Christian contacts opened up, and Africans often found themselves in a position to choose between Moslem and Christian styles of civilization. Usually they preferred Islam, even though the Moslems were just as eager slave traders as were the Christians.

Islam continued to expand, not only in Africa but in southeast Asia and in southeastern Europe. European discoveries did upset the Moslems' spice trade for a while, but, as we saw, it recovered after a few years. Trade overland between China and the Moslem lands was also affected somewhat by the opening of sea contact between Europe and China. But as long as the Ottoman Turks continued to win victories in the field against Christian armies, it certainly did not seem as though the great explorations had made any vital difference for Islam.

Yet Islam had been outflanked, just as Prince Henry the Navigator had hoped. The whole of the Americas had been brought, at least potentially, within the circle of European civilizations. The southern seas had been taken over by European shipping, and Moslem merchants faced new and dangerous rivals—even if the Portuguese failed to drive them from the seas.

With the benefit of hindsight, we can now see that the long-range effects of the great European discoveries had yet to show themselves in 1550. It was, in fact, the uses to which Europeans put their discovery of the New World that eventually allowed the Far Western style of civilization to outstrip its rivals in Asia.

The stimulus to Europe's own development was therefore the most important single consequence of opening the world's oceans to European shipping. New wealth, new ideas, new perspectives, new adventures all poured in upon Europe. The various internal deadlocks that had seemed about to freeze European civilization into a "medieval" mold were soon left behind. Europe plunged recklessly and relentlessly into a self-transformation that made the era 1500–1650 the divide between what historians have traditionally called medieval and modern times. We shall examine some of the aspects of that transformation in the next chapter.

Chapter 16

EUROPE'S SELF-TRANSFORMATION

1500 to 1650

Between 1500 and 1650 Europeans began a new age. The Church and religion were transformed by the Reformation, beginning in 1517, and by the Catholic reform that gathered headway a generation afterward. Politics altered as peoples fought and struggled over religious doctrines, dynastic interests, and economic resources. Economic relations were transformed by the price revolution resulting from the influx of American silver, and by new forms of business organization that dominated large-scale enterprises and long-distance trade. Finally, European intellectual horizons enlarged dramatically as voyages of exploration and missionary reports brought in a flood of information about the vast and varied world that lay beyond the seas.

The shock of so many innovations coming so fast was severe. Many people were dismayed and alarmed, and popular movements of the age were all aimed at getting back to a purer, simpler past. But a handful of venturesome persons reacted differently and found new ways to act and think, taking advantage of fresh possibilities that opened before them year after year. Grumbling and protesting, the mass of the European population was dragged along and had to accept more and more novelties because specialists and experts organized, directed, and controlled human and material resources in such ways as to make new techniques and ideas work better than older, customary methods.

Asians did not respond to novelties nearly so actively between 1500 and 1650. This was, therefore, the time when western Europeans began to pull ahead of other civilizations in several important respects, preparing the way for the dominance western civilization was later to acquire over the rest of the globe.

POLITICS AND RELIGION

Ever since the Roman emperor Constantine had allied himself with the Christian Church in A.D. 312, politics and religion had been closely intertwined in Europe's history. The medieval Church had been in the thick of politics. The popes headed an international government that shared authority with secular rulers differently in different places and at different times. Until about 1300 the power of the papacy tended to increase. Thereafter, royal governments in France, Spain, and England took a larger share in church affairs and left less and less real power to the popes. In Germany, however, no strong national government existed. The Holy Roman Empire of the German nation had been wrecked by the quarrel with the popes. When the empire was restored in 1273, the first man elected to the imperial dignity was Rudolph of Hapsburg, a relatively obscure, petty noble who could not possibly challenge the power of the great dukes and princes who ruled the larger states into which the empire had divided. Rudolph did have the rights of his office, however, including the right to reassign any fiefs that happened to fall vacant due to a lack of heirs. During his lifetime a large fief in Austria fell vacant. Rudolph took it for himself, thus planting the Hapsburg family on lands it continued to rule until 1918.

The emperor's powers were limited. In 1356 a constitutional document called the Golden Bull defined how the emperor should be chosen. Seven great princes were named electors, with the right to choose the emperor. In addition, there was a Diet (general assembly or council like the English Parliament) to which all the princes and free cities sent representatives. Both the electors and the Diet were interested in keeping the imperial government weak, so as to leave as many rights to themselves as they could. Hence the empire remained a confusing collection of states, almost but not quite independent of one another, presided over by an emperor who, most of the time, could not get his subjects to obey him, pay him taxes, or cooperate in common policies.

The Hapsburg Empire of Charles V

This situation was changed when the house of Hapsburg acquired new and important territories through a series of fortunate marriages. First, Emperor Maximilian (reigned 1493–1519) married the heiress to the Burgundian lands. This marriage brought the Low Countries (present-day Belgium, Netherlands, and Luxembourg) and nearby territories under Hapsburg rule. He then married his son Philip to the heiress of Spain. Their son, Charles V, therefore, succeeded to the crown of Spain in 1516 when Ferdinand died. Charles succeeded, also, in securing election as Holy Roman Emperor when his grandfather Maximilian I died in 1519.

As emperor, Charles V used his authority to bring together a tremendous though scattered territory. Spain was the greatest power in Europe. Beginning in 1502, Spanish soldiers had conquered part of Italy, and the empire overseas began to pay off after Cortes (1521) and Pizarro (1535) started the flow of precious metals from the Americas to the Spanish royal treasury. In addition, the Low Countries were one of the richest parts of the continent. Austria and nearby lands constituted still a third power cluster, plus whatever Charles V could make out of his imperial title to all the German lands. No European ruler since Charlemagne had presided over such an empire. If the German princes could be brought to heel, as Ferdinand and Isabella had brought the Spanish nobles to heel, Emperor Charles V could hope to become supreme, or very nearly supreme, in all western Europe.

However, Charles V's enemies were as nu-merous as his subjects and his lands lacked any real cohesion. Spaniards, Dutch, Austrians, and Germans had little in common except the same ruler; and Charles was never able to govern them all from a single center or by the same set of laws. From 1522 he gave his brother, Ferdinand I, responsibility for German and Austrian affairs, taking Spain and the Low Countries as his own personal responsibility.

The big issue in Charles' eyes was who was going to control Italy. The French had invaded that country in 1494, upsetting the balance of power between the dozen or so little states into which Italy was divided. Spaniards came in by sea from the south and captured the kingdom of Naples by 1504. The pope and other Italian rulers twisted and turned, caught between the French in the north and Spanish in the south, but they were quite unable to escape foreign control. Time and again, Francis I of France (reigned 1515–1547) marched his armies into Italy. Each time he did so, Charles V went out to meet him, and both sides gathered whatever allies they could find in Italy and elsewhere. Each time Charles won. Bit by bit, Spanish influence seeped northward through the peninsula, snuffing out Italian political independence (except in Venice) and choking off the more pagan aspects of Italian Renaissance culture with the fierce crusading spirit of Spanish Catholicism.

A second problem was almost as critical as the fate of Italy in Charles V's eyes: defense against the Turks. With Constantinople as its capital (since 1453), the Ottoman Empire continued to be a formidable and aggressive military state. After 1499, however, wars waged against the shah of Iran turned Ottoman attention eastward. That did not stop expansion of Turkish power, however, for Sultan Selim the Grim was able to conquer Syria, Palestine, and Egypt between 1512 and 1520. In the next generation, Sultan Suleiman the Lawgiver (ruled 1520–1566) brought the Ottoman Empire to its peak. In 1526 he invaded Hungary, killed the king, and took control of most of that land. A claim to the Hungarian crown, however, passed to Ferdinand of Hapsburg, who had married the sister of the Hungarian king. The Hapsburgs therefore took over the part of Hun-

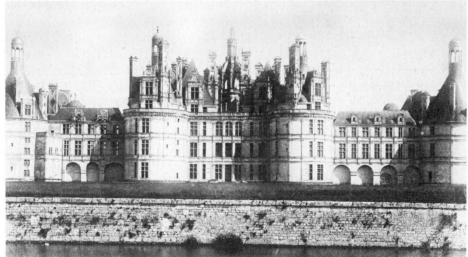

Magnificence in Church and State Architects of the Renaissance era rejected the Gothic principles of construction that their predecessors in western Europe had used so successfully and sought inspiration instead in surviving structures from Roman antiquity. In practice this meant round arches and domes in place of pointed Gothic arches and vaults. Above is the Cathedral of St. Peters, Rome, the seat of papacy, as constructed between 1506 and 1615. Below is the Palace of Chambord, on the Loire river, erected as a royal hunting lodge and rural retreat for King Francis I of France after 1519. St. Peters is one of the largest churches in Christendom and Chambord, with no fewer than 444 separate rooms, was large enough to accommodate a swarm of courtiers as well as the King himself. Both buildings, deliberately echoing Roman imperial style, were designed to express the greatness and magnificence of the popes and kings whose wealth and will had called them into being.

gary that escaped Turkish control. This meant that later Turkish campaigns against Christendom pitted the sultan's forces against Hapsburg imperial armies. In 1529, for example, Suleiman besieged Vienna but failed to capture it. Border warfare became normal, and every once in a while the sultan set forth with his field army to settle accounts with the Christians. Suleiman died on such an expedition in 1566.

Defense against the Turks by land was the special concern of Ferdinand rather than of Charles V. This was also the case with the third of Charles's great problems: how to cope with the disturbance in Germany created by Lutheranism and the religious excitement stirred up by Luther's quarrel with the papacy. From Charles' point of view his wars with the Turks and against the French in Italy were defensive. They were necessary to prevent his enemies from driving his friends and supporters from their rightful positions. However, any systematic effort to suppress heresy in Germany required Charles to exercise powers that had not been in the German emperor's hands for centuries. Moreover, his Spanish and Netherlandish subjects were not eager to see their money or soldiers used to strengthen the emperor's position in Germany. It is therefore not really surprising that Charles could spend only a small part of his time and energy in trying to do something about the Lutheran movement. He had too many other matters to attend to.

Yet in European history, the Protestant Reformation that Luther started in 1517 turned out to be far more significant than the long wars over Italy, for the Reformation divided Europe into opposing religious camps and changed the lives of nearly everyone to some degree. To understand what the great dispute was about, we must know something of Luther's life and his personal pursuit of salvation, for it was these experiences that made him so certain and so persuasive, and gave him courage to defy the highest authorities of Church and state when they commanded him to change his views.

Luther's Reformation

Martin Luther was born in 1483, a miner's son. He started to study law but gave it up to become first a monk, then a priest, and in 1508 a professor of theology at the University of Wittenberg in Saxony. Such a career was unusual only because the young Luther advanced so rapidly. But he took religion far more seriously than most people did. He became a monk because he felt the need of assuring his soul's salvation. In the following years he worked hard to win that salvation. But his best efforts seemed fruitless. He remained—in his own judgment—a sinful man who deserved damnation. How could he, or anyone else, escape the just punishment for sin? How indeed?

The question was an agonizing one for Luther, until one day in 1515 he was reading St. Paul's Epistle to the Romans and came upon the verse that says: "The just shall live by faith." This simple phrase struck Luther with the force of revelation. Here was his answer: God asked only faith—total, unquestioning faith. God did the rest. Faith freed men and women of sin. All efforts to wipe out the penalties of sin by penance and good works were futile, and indeed misleading, since sinners might think that their accounts with God were square when in fact they had failed in the great essential: to have faith and commit all else to God.

The radical consequences of his position became clear to Luther only by degrees. He did not set out to split the Christian Church in two. On the contrary, he always clung to the idea that somehow God would again unite all Christians. When he found his quarrel with the papacy could not be compromised, he appealed to a council of all the bishops, with the idea that this body might reform the Church—always, of course, according to the truth as Luther understood it.

Luther's Attack on Indulgences What triggered the Lutheran Reformation was a campaign to raise money in Germany for the building of St. Peter's cathedral in Rome. One of the ways the popes collected money was by selling indulgences. These were pieces of paper that canceled the penalties of sin. The idea was that the pope could arrange the transfer of merits, accumulated by Christ and the saints, to a soul in need of help. By buying such indulgences, pious persons believed they could relieve themselves or others from having to suffer for their sins in purgatory. The sale of such indulgences had become an important source of income for the popes.

Luther and Pope Leo X These paintings suggest the contrasting character of the protagonists of the earliest phase of the Reformation. On the left, Martin Luther's craggy face and introverted gaze reveals the inward turmoil and firm conviction that impelled him to defy the busy man of affairs, portrayed on the right, who became Pope Leo X. Leo X governed the Church for eight turbulent years, 1513 to 1521, starting when he was just 37 years of age. As befitted a son of Lorenzo the Magnificent, who had ruled renaissance Florence at its peak, the new pope made Rome a center of the arts as never before. Building St. Peters was only one of his many projects and selling indulgences to pay for St. Peters was only one of the ways he set out to raise money for them. Italian politics was an even more urgent concern for Pope Leo X, for he had to steer between rival French and Spanish invaders, who both demanded that local Italian rulers, including the Pope, should support them. By comparison with these urgent and practical concerns, news from Germany of Luther's protest against sale of indulgences counted for little. In 1520 Pope Leo condemned Luther for heresy and left it at that. The next year he died. His successors on the papal throne continued to be so entangled in the Italian wars (1494–1559) that they had little time to bother with Lutheranism or the religious challenge coming from Germany until the 1540s.

Luther was appalled by such an approach to sin, salvation, and finance. In 1517, therefore, when a seller of indulgences came to a nearby town, Luther publicly challenged the usefulness of indulgences. He did this in the customary way, by posting a series of theses on the church door in Wittenberg. These theses were short statements about controversial questions that Luther was prepared to defend in public debate with anyone who chose to argue against him.

Learned theologians were soon able to prove that Luther's views led to heresy. If Christians needed only faith for salvation, what happened to the power of priests to channel God's saving grace to sinners through the rites of the Church? Luther eventually admitted in public that on this and other points he agreed with John Huss, the Czech heretic, who had been burned at the stake for his opinions in 1415.

Even when he had been forced to recognize the radical implications of his position, Luther did not change his convictions. He felt, instead, that the pope must be wrong, because he knew that he was right about faith and salvation—the important thing—and had the words of the Bible to prove it. He put the whole issue before the German public in 1520 by writing three pamphlets in rapid succession: *Address to the Christian Nobility of the German Nation*; *The Babylonian Captivity of the Church*; and *The Liberty of a Christian Man*.

In emphatic language Luther argued his cause, accused the popes of having twisted true doctrine, and invited the German nobility to reform the Church along the lines laid down in the Bible. Appeal to the Bible as the only reliable source of religious truth was, in fact, Luther's strongest and most convincing argument. It soon became obvious that many of the practices of the Church did not have any definite biblical basis. For example, confession, which had been defined as a sacrament only in 1215, in the time of Pope Innocent III, was not clearly authorized by any scriptural passage.

The public response in Germany to Luther's words was tremendous. His arguments seemed convincing to most Germans. Nearly everyone agreed that the Church needed reform—and furthermore, no one in Germany really liked to see good German money being shipped off to Rome to build the new cathedral of St. Peter's. Many Germans were eager to agree with Luther when he accused priests of having taken to themselves rights that were in fact enjoyed by every faithful Christian. The salvation of souls was, after all, a matter of highest importance; and if, in fact, Luther was right, and the popes had been misleading the Christian community for centuries, something had to be done about it, right away.

The newly elected emperor Charles V therefore made the Lutheran question one of the important items of business to be taken up at his first Imperial Diet, which met at the city of Worms in 1521. Luther came in person, on the strength of the emperor's promise that he would not be harmed. Luther reaffirmed his views, despite their condemnation by expert theologians. This was enough to satisfy the emperor, who persuaded the Diet to put Luther under the imperial ban. This meant that anyone who killed Luther would not be tried in an imperial court. Such an act, in effect, invited his assassination.

But the Elector of Saxony, Luther's immediate sovereign, continued to protect his controversial subject. For safety he sent Luther to the Wartburg castle, where he lived incognito for nearly a year. Luther used this time to translate the New Testament into German. A little later, with help from others who knew Hebrew, he also translated the Old Testament. Luther's Bible was widely read. Many ordinary Germans tried to puzzle out religious truth from its pages for themselves. The result was sharp disagreement, since different parts of the Bible lend themselves to very different interpretations.

Some Anabaptists decided that infant baptism was an error because the baptisms recorded in the Bible involved only adults. Other doctrines often combined with this idea. Poor and unhappy people pored over the biblical passages announcing the end of the world and began to expect the opening of the skies at any minute. If the end of the world was really near, people ought to give up most ordinary pursuits, cease from sinning, and prayerfully await the end.

Luther Denounces the Peasant Revolt Religious views of this kind easily spilled over into social and economic protest. In 1524–1525, peasants in southwestern Germany tried to throw off their obligation to pay customary rents and services to their lords. Radical religious views were part of the movement too. This frightened and angered Luther. He felt that the peasants were distorting the meaning of Christian liberty as he had explained it in his famous pamphlet. Faithful Christians, according to Luther, were free because they served their neighbors spontaneously and of their own free will, not because they had no duties or obligations to others. Luther also feared that the peasants and other radicals might discredit his

LUTHER'S KIDNAPPING

When Martin Luther accepted the emperor's summons to the Imperial Diet at Worms in April, 1521, he and his friends recalled how John Huss had gone to the Council of Constance a little more than a century before and, in spite of the emperor's pledge for safe conduct, had been condemned as a heretic and then burned at the stake. Parallels with Christ's visit to Jerusalem and the arrest, trial, and crucifixion that followed also flickered in the minds of Luther's followers. But the young emperor Charles V allowed the troublesome professor to leave Worms unhindered, even though he was about to declare Luther an outlaw.

When Luther was nearing his home in Wittenberg, armed horsemen suddenly appeared along a lonely stretch of road, seized the famous reformer, and with oaths and threats carried him off before the eyes of his horrified companions, who thought he was about to be murdered. Indeed, shortly thereafter a body was discovered and identified as the mortal remains of Dr. Martin Luther. His followers were dismayed but not surprised. Such an event fulfilled the parallels they already had in mind.

Yet his close friends soon began to receive letters from the "dead" Luther; and in December he even visited Wittenberg secretly, disguised as a knight. But it was not until March, 1522, eleven months after he had disappeared so dramatically, that Luther returned openly to Wittenberg and publicly took charge of the tumultuous reform movement he had so suddenly called forth.

reform in the eyes of the German nobles and princes. The result was another pamphlet in which Luther denounced the peasant rebels in extremely harsh language and exhorted their lords to kill them mercilessly.

The peasant revolt was indeed suppressed in blood. Thereafter, the Lutheran movement lost much of the white-hot enthusiasm that Luther's words had stimulated during the first eight years of the Reformation. Instead, Luther and his followers set out to order the Church as it should be ordered—that is, according to the Bible—wherever the secular ruler would agree to undertake the task of reform. Many, but not all, German princes went along with Luther in this task. They had much to gain, for the Lutherans decided that Church property was unnecessary, that monasteries should be suppressed, and that

Church appointments should be treated as another (though supremely important) branch of the governmental bureaucracy.

When Luther died in 1546, reform along these lines had been firmly established in most of northern Germany and in Scandinavia. Emperor Charles V had been far too busy in Italy and elsewhere to check Lutheranism effectively. When he did find time to turn to internal German affairs, it was too late. Confiscated lands and abandoned monasteries could not be restored; in such matters the German princes would not submit to the emperor's will without a fight. Charles V tried to use force, but that failed. In 1555 he therefore reluctantly agreed to the Peace of Augsburg, which gave every German ruler the right to impose either Lutheranism or Roman Catholicism upon his subjects.

The inside story then came out. Frederick the Wise, Elector of Saxony, was Luther's immediate sovereign. He did not want to see Luther killed as an outlaw. Yet he also felt that the famous Wittenberg professor of theology was a hothead and troublemaker. While still at Worms, the Elector decided to take Luther into custody secretly, thus making sure that no harm could come to him and that he could do no further harm himself. So that he might be able truthfully to deny that he knew where Luther was, the Elector ordered his servants to capture the reformer without letting the Elector himself know anything about the details.

When one of the Elector's officers explained the plan to him, Luther agreed, for he was in fear of his life and could not afford to defy the pope, the emperor, and his own prince all at once. The kidnapping was therefore arranged as a device for throwing Luther's enemies off the track. Accordingly, as soon as Luther's abductors were safely hidden in the woods, they paused to allow their "captive" to cast off his monk's cowl and put on a knight's clothing. Then the little party rode, by a roundabout way, to one of Frederick the Wise's more remote castles, the Wartburg. There Luther went into strict seclusion until his hair and beard had grown, disguising the monkish tonsure he had worn up to that time.

Luther used his spare time at the Wartburg to translate the Bible into German. He also carried on a busy correspondence with his friends and never lost touch with the Lutheran movement that continued to convulse Germany. As may be imagined, Luther's reported death and subsequent resurrection did nothing to weaken his hold on the popular imagination of Germany.

John Calvin and the Reformed Churches

Luther's challenge to the papacy did not pass unnoticed outside of Germany. Especially among townspeople in France, Switzerland, England, and the Low Countries, long-standing discontents with the papacy and with the Church burst into flame as news of what had happened in Germany spread through Europe. In many places the reform party was unable to gain control of the government.

Without such power they could only form a church, according to their taste, by withdrawing into some sort of separate body of their own. But in Switzerland, where local cantons (or districts) and cities ruled themselves, religious reformers had only to convince a majority of the city council in order to begin reform.

In this fashion, a fiery preacher, Huldreich Zwingli (1484–1531) started reformation in Zurich in 1518. His ideas paralleled those of Luther on many points, although the two reformers differed on the meaning of the sacrament of the Eucharist. Church reform spread to other Swiss towns, but high in the mountains more conservative communities clung to the old faith. Civil war broke out, and Zwingli was killed in battle. Soon afterward a peace was concluded that left each canton free to choose its own form of religion.

Zwingli's death, however, left the Swiss reformers without a leader. This gap was filled by John Calvin (1509–1564), a Frenchman, who first came to Geneva in 1536 but took up permanent residence there in 1541. Calvin was a far more cool-headed man than Luther. He thought out his opinions carefully and stuck to them with a will of iron. Through his learning and conviction he impressed his views upon all around him.

Like Luther, Calvin took the Bible as the only reliable source of religious truth. In the main, he drew the same lessons from the Bible that Luther had drawn. In his famous book, *Institutes of the Christian Religion*, Calvin gathered together the biblical passages that supported his views on all issues under debate. Calvin arranged his discussion of doctrine systematically so that anyone eager to find out what the Bible had to say about salvation, predestination, faith, and innumerable other questions could discover answers in his book. The *Institutes*, therefore, became a standard reference work for all of the reformed churches.

Calvin's Divergence from Luther   In some matters, however, Calvin disagreed with Luther. Like Zwingli, Calvin interpreted the Eucharist as merely commemorative of the last supper that Jesus Christ had taken with the Apostles. Calvin also emphasized predestination in a way that Luther did not. Luther accepted the idea of predestination, but he never felt it to be particularly important. What mattered was faith in God. Calvin, on the other hand, drew the logical conclusion: Some persons have faith and are saved, but some lack that faith and are therefore damned to all eternity. God makes the choice, not the individuals concerned. God does so for reasons of his own that mere human beings cannot understand.

Such a doctrine emphasized the role of God as judge and ruler. It did not, however, persuade Calvin and his followers to sit back and wait for God to do whatever he had decided to do. Instead, Calvinists developed a tremendous moral drive. No one could ever be absolutely sure that God had chosen him or her to be saved. But a person could try to live as though he or she were among the elect, destined for Heaven. Under Calvin's leadership, Geneva became a school of righteousness. Dissent was suppressed. Morality was enforced by preaching and instruction, and when

that failed, by the force at the disposal of the city government.

Calvin's ideas about the proper relation between Church and state were quite different from Luther's. After 1525 Luther had fallen back upon the support of the German princes and had given them all but complete control over church administration. Calvin combed the Bible for evidence of how the early Church was managed, and came to the conclusion that ministers and elders ought to be in charge of each separate congregation. General questions should be decided by representative assemblies in which both ministers and laymen took part.

Calvin attracted many earnest young men to Geneva to see and study the godly community he had helped to construct there. Such men spread Calvin's ideas far and wide through Europe. In Scotland, John Knox (1505–1572) was able to convert a whole kingdom by fiery preaching and a skillful appeal to nobles who were restless under royal authority. Elsewhere, however, Calvinism spread by attracting the assent of individuals most of whom lived in towns. Calvinists, therefore, remained a minority in France and the Rhinelands. In the Dutch provinces, Calvinists became the majority during a long war against Spain (1568–1648). In both Poland and Hungary, also, Calvinism had a considerable success, mainly among the nobility. Catholic missionaries later reconverted nearly all Polish Calvinists to Roman Catholicism; and in Hungary the majority also returned to Catholicism, although in the eastern parts of Hungary important Calvinist communities still survive.

England's Reformation

The Reformation in England began when Henry VIII (ruled 1509–1547) came to the conclusion that the reason he did not have a male heir was that he had married his dead brother's widow, Catherine of Aragon (the aunt of Charles V and mother of Henry's sickly daughter Mary). King Henry wanted a male heir to assure the continuance of the Tudor family on the English throne. Also, his eye had been caught by the pretty face of a young lady of the court named Anne Boleyn, whom he wished to marry.

The difficulty was that the pope refused to annul Henry's marriage to Catherine of Aragon. The Spanish influence in Rome opposed any such act. Moreover, Henry had married his brother's widow in the first place only on the strength of a special dispensation from the pope; it was awkward for the pope to contradict what before had been officially approved. After waiting in vain for a favorable decision, King Henry asked Parliament in 1534 to declare him to be head of the Church of England. This done, the archbishop of Canterbury declared the king's marriage annulled, freeing him to marry Anne Boleyn. But the king was again denied a male heir, for Anne gave birth to a girl, Elizabeth. King Henry soon tired of Anne and had her head cut off on the charge of unfaithfulness. He later married four other wives in succession, one of whom gave birth to a son, Edward VI (reigned 1547–1553).

Although he quarreled with the pope, Henry VIII had no intention of tampering with doctrine or even with rituals. But Lutheran and, presently, Calvinist ideas could not be prevented from seeping into England. Henry opened one important breach in the old order by seizing lands belonging to monasteries as a way of increasing his income. Under his son, distinctly Protestant phrases were introduced into the officially approved church rituals. Queen Mary (reigned 1553–1558), daughter of Catherine of Aragon and wife of Philip II of Spain, tried to bring England back into the Roman Catholic fold. Her successor, Elizabeth I (reigned 1558–1603), returned to Protestantism, and in 1563 Parliament approved Thirty-nine Articles summing up Christian doctrine. They became the official theological position of the Church of England by Act of Parliament.

These articles had been drawn up with care so as to allow antipapal Christians of many different shades of opinion to accept them. They have remained in force in England ever since. Because Protestantism and English patriotism came to be firmly identified with each other under Queen Elizabeth, most of the English people were well satisfied with the theological compromises of the Thirty-nine Articles. But some enthusiasts felt that the English church needed still further reformation. These "Puritans," as they came to be called, were under strong Calvinist influence. Some felt it possible to work within the established church. Others withdrew to form their own congregations, to preach and practice true and purified Christianity as they understood it.

Roman Catholic Reform

For nearly twenty years the popes in Rome paid little attention to the Protestant movement. They were caught, like all the other rulers of Italy, in the complicated struggle between France and Spain for control of the Italian peninsula. When Charles V's soldiers took and sacked Rome in 1527, how could the pope cooperate effectively with that same emperor to put down the Lutherans in Germany? Moreover, the Renaissance popes were rulers, diplomats, and art patrons— far too much concerned with these affairs to take Luther seriously.

For a long time, too, there was a real ambiguity about the cry for reform. Luther and Calvin never intended to set up separate churches, and they always remained true to the ideal of one universal Church to which all Christians ought to belong. When asked what to do about the corruptions of the papacy, their answer was to appeal to a general council. This sounded like a return to medieval ideas for reforming the Church by means of a council, and the popes could not be expected to welcome revival of this issue. They suspected anyone who urged the need for reform of trying to undermine the authority of the papal office.

Pope Paul III and the Council of Trent Nevertheless, Protestant arguments and the advance of Protestant opinions in so much of Europe could not be overlooked forever. Pope Paul III (reigned 1534–1549) began major reform by appointing scholars and pious individuals to positions of power within the Church. He also approved the establishment of the Society of Jesus (1549), revived the Inquisition (1542), and eventually yielded to widespread demands for a council by calling the Council of Trent (1545–1563, with many recesses).

Europe in the Reformation

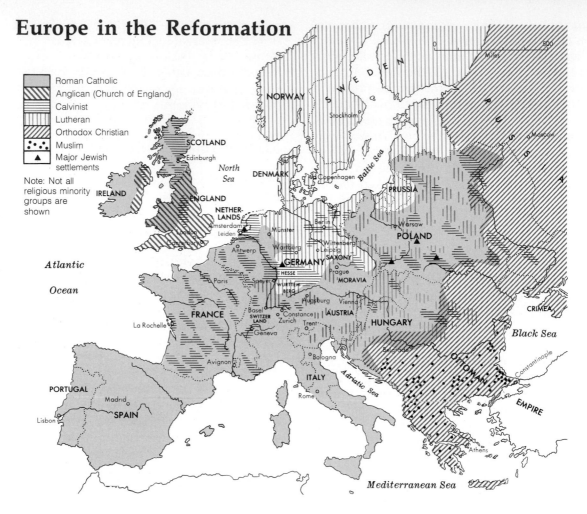

The Council of Trent took care of the main Protestant challenge by declaring that the Bible was not the only source of religious truth. The tradition of the Church, descending without a break from the Apostles, was of equal validity. In other matters of detail, the Council also explained doctrine in an anti-Protestant sense. The gap between the two camps was thus defined clearly, as had not at first been the case. The Council of Trent also reaffirmed the sovereign power of the papacy over the Church and entrusted to the pope the task of carrying out practical reform.

The Jesuit Order   The Society of Jesus played an active part in the deliberations of the Council of Trent. This was a new religious order, founded by St. Ignatius of Loyola (1491–1556). Loyola was a Spanish nobleman, who started out to be a sol-

dier. While recovering from a battle wound, he decided to become a soldier for Christ. His first idea was to concentrate on converting the heathen, and for this he needed theological training. Loyola, therefore, took up study at the University of Paris, where he soon formed a small circle of similarly minded young men. They organized themselves into a religious order in Rome and, in 1540, were given papal blessing as the Society of Jesus.

The Society of Jesus differed from other religious orders in several respects. Its members offered themselves for any sort of service and, like soldiers, swore absolute obedience to their superiors. At the head of the order was a general— to begin with, Loyola himself—and the general took orders only from the pope. The Society of Jesus was thus like the royal standing armies that were coming into existence all over Europe: a body of trained and disciplined men at the disposal of the papacy. They quickly distinguished themselves as teachers, missionaries, and diplomats and became a power in Europe and the world comparable to that of an established state.

To train his shock troops, Loyola developed what he called Spiritual Exercises. Every member of the Jesuit order—as the Society of Jesus is often called—had to undergo special Spiritual Exercises once a year, and in case of need, more frequently. They lasted about a month, during which time the candidate was kept apart from others and commanded to reflect upon his sins, pray for forgiveness, and concentrate his entire attention upon key doctrines of the Church. The Exercises were so emotionally intense as to alter the personalities of those who experienced them. The aim was to strengthen individual character, producing men who would be fully conscious of their religious duty—resolute, self-disciplined, obedient, at all times. St. Ignatius of Loyola was remarkably successful. Thanks largely to the Spiritual Exercises, thousands upon thousands of men who entered the Society of Jesus, from Loyola's day to the present, became new men to a degree seldom equaled by other religious orders or communities.

The Jesuits soon succeeded in checking the advance of the Protestant movement in Germany, and in eastern Europe they were the main agents in reconverting Poland and most of Hungary to Catholicism. Long efforts to bring England back to papal obedience eventually failed. Overseas, however, Jesuits were among the most active and successful Catholic missionaries, both in the Americas and in Asia.

Other important steps were taken to strengthen the Roman Catholic Church. Simple catechisms were introduced to teach the doctrines of the Church to everyone. The papal Inquisition sought out heretics in Italy and punished with death those who refused to recant. The Council of Trent created an Index of prohibited books. The popes kept the Index current by adding titles of new books that were judged damaging to the faith. In countries where the rulers cooperated, such books could not be printed or sold legally. School systems were much enlarged. The Jesuits distinguished themselves by making their schools the best in Europe, combining a thorough training in Latin and mathematics with religious instruction.

The upshot of the Protestant Reformation and the Roman Catholic response was to make Europeans far more conscious of religious duties and doctrines. Both the new Protestant churches of Germany and England and the revived Catholic churches in France, Italy, and Germany were more devout, learned, and serious organizations than had been true before Luther disturbed the religious balance of his time.

Yet religious division was the exact opposite of what everyone sought. There could be only one true Church and only one correct doctrine. All agreed on that. And the salvation of souls depended, everyone believed, on the correctness of beliefs and action in accordance with those beliefs. With these assumptions, no one could rest quietly when confronted by religious error. Their own immortal souls, and those of all persons around them, depended on suppressing mistaken and misguided opinions. It is not strange, therefore, that wars became religious, as Catholics and Protestants tried to impose their different versions of religious truth on each other.

RELIGIOUS AND DYNASTIC WARS

Charles V abdicated in 1556 (effective 1558). He retired to a monastery and died soon after. The bulk of his possessions he left to his son Philip II of Spain. His brother Ferdinand I, however, inherited the Austrian lands and the title of Holy Roman Emperor. The two branches of the Hapsburg family continued to cooperate with each other in most matters, just as had been the case in Charles V's lifetime. Between them, Philip and Ferdinand inherited all the concerns that had distracted Charles V: the Turkish danger from the east, the rivalry with France, the Protestant movement in Germany and elsewhere. But Philip II tended to put a different priority upon the problems he faced. The suppression of Protestantism ranked higher for him than it had for Charles V, and the rivalry with France ranked correspondingly lower.

There was good reason for this, since France passed through a period of internal weakness from 1559 to 1598. In the first of these years, the French signed the Treaty of Cateau-Cambrésis with Philip II, giving up the long struggle over Italy and also surrendering French claims to the Low Countries. For the next few years, weak French kings succeeded one another on the throne, and it became more and more obvious that the Valois royal family was about to die out. This raised the question of succession to the throne.

During the same years, Calvinist preaching was particularly active in France, and a party of Huguenots, as the French Calvinists were called, came into existence. They fought a series of low-grade civil wars against a rival Catholic faction, headed by the family of Guise. After the death of the last of the Valois kings in 1589, Henry of Navarre, a Protestant and first of the Bourbon line, laid claim to the throne. In 1594 he gave up his Protestantism for the Catholic faith, saying, "Paris is worth a Mass," and was crowned king. But Henry IV did not become really secure on the throne until he had come to terms with his former Huguenot allies. This he did through the Edict of Nantes (1598), which allowed great nobles and some towns to maintain Calvinist forms of worship and guaranteed them the same political rights as Catholics. Philip II of Spain died in the same year, and so he never had to face the strength of a reunited France.

As for the Turks, Philip II continued to wage war against them in the Mediterranean on and off until 1580, when he made a peace that recognized Turkish rights over the north coast of Africa as far as Algiers. This agreement represented a considerable gain for the Turks, though in fact they were never able to control North Africa from Constantinople. Algerian pirates preyed upon any and all ships that came their way, with scant regard for their supposed obedience to the Ottoman sultan.

Philip concentrated on the struggle against heresy, and met with much success. As we have seen, the energy and religious conviction of the Roman Catholic church increased greatly, beginning with the pontificate of Pope Paul III (1534–1549). Spanish piety and Spanish ideals played a large part in this revival. Cooperation between the reformed papacy and the two branches of the Hapsburg house remained very close. All of central and eastern Europe felt the impact. Hapsburg officials, Jesuit confessors, and Catholic schools worked together to overwhelm Protestant heresy throughout a broad band of territory that reached from Italy northward across the Alps into Austrian, south German, Hungarian, and Polish lands. Only northern Germany and Scandanavia, together with the parts of Hungary under Turkish rule and areas of the Rhineland under Protestant German princes, escaped the force of this Catholic counteroffensive.

The Limits of Hapsburg Power

In the western parts of Europe, however, Philip II of Spain met with serious setbacks. His wife, the English queen Mary, failed to bring her country back permanently into the Catholic fold. Worse still, the Netherlands revolted in 1567. Seasoned Spanish troops reconquered the southern part of the Netherlands (roughly, modern Belgium), but in the north the Dutch provinces could not be subdued because the Dutch held command of the sea and were able to move supplies and troops to any threatened place more easily than the Spaniards could move overland against them.

The rebels received some help from Queen Elizabeth of England. English pirates, such as John Hawkins and Francis Drake, had also begun to prey upon Spanish ships on the high seas and to plunder Spanish towns in the New World. This eventually persuaded King Philip to try to settle accounts with the English, instead of concentrating everything against the Dutch. He therefore sent a great fleet northward in 1588, intending that it should pick up Spanish troops from the southern Netherlands and then attack England.

But Philip's plan failed. When his fleet, the Spanish Armada, sailed through the English Channel, it suffered repeated attacks from Queen Elizabeth's ships, whose cannon fire damaged the Spanish galleons so badly that the plan of invading England had to be given up. Instead of trying to fight his way back through the Channel, the Armada's commander decided to return to Spain by sailing north around Scotland and Ireland. But his ships were caught in violent storms. Almost none of them got back safely to Spain.

King Philip's death in 1598 marked a turning point in Spanish fortunes. For nearly a century, Spain had been the greatest power in Europe, as well as mistress of the New World. After Philip's death, a reunited France, led by the new Bourbon Dynasty, challenged Spain's political dominance in western Europe. Fifty years later, by 1650, the French monarchy had clearly become more powerful than the Hapsburgs of Spain. During the same years, the naval strength of England and of the Dutch Republic increased on all the oceans of the world at the expense of Spain and Portugal. Within Spain itself, it became more and more difficult for the government to keep up the armies required to defend the imperial position that the country had won between 1492 and 1598.

The Thirty Years' War　On the other hand, between 1618 and 1635, the Austrian branch of the Hapsburg house came close to winning control over all Germany. The progress of the Catholic Reformation in German lands strengthened the position of the Hapsburgs. In 1618, Protestant Bohemian nobles, fearing the consolidation of Catholic power, attempted to throw off Hapsburg control. This action started thirty years of bitter war that soon spread through most of Germany. On the one side stood Ferdinand II, Holy Roman Emperor and champion of Catholicism (reigned 1619–1637). On the other side gathered an unstable collection of Protestant princes. Early in the Thirty Years' War, Ferdinand overcame the Bohemian rebels (1620) and made that extensive kingdom thoroughly subject to his government for the first time. This resulted in a great expansion of his effective power, for Bohemia was richer as well as bigger than the Austrian lands.

Ferdinand also discovered that he could create a vast army by allowing the soldiers to live off the land. Albert of Wallenstein was the imperial general who first showed how effective a force maintained in such a way could be. Each time Wallenstein's army entered a new district, his soldiers plundered it thoroughly. As imperial armies occupied more and more territory, the resulting devastation was enormous.

The intervention of Denmark on the Protestant side (1625) did not check the progress of the emperor's armies; but when Gustavus Adol-phus, king of Sweden, entered the field against them (1630), the balance was temporarily reversed. The Swedes won several famous victories but could not destroy their opponents. In 1632 Gustavus Adolphus died in battle. Two years later Wallenstein, Emperor Ferdinand's most successful general, was assassinated. He had quarreled with his imperial master and may have planned to make himself and his army supreme in Germany.

By now almost everybody was sick and tired of the war, which had become more destructive than any in memory. The aging Emperor Ferdinand died in 1637. He was succeeded by Ferdinand III (reigned 1637–1657), who wanted to make peace. The hope of uniting all Germany again no longer seemed worth the cost. The danger to the Hapsburgs of an overmighty general, such as Wallenstein, and of an army of plunderers had become quite obvious. Nevertheless, the war went on until 1648. The main reason was that the French intervened in 1635, hoping to keep the Austrian Hapsburgs busy in Germany so that they could not come to the aid of their Spanish relatives, who began a war with France in 1622. The war between France and Spain lasted until 1659, when the reluctant Spaniards were compelled to cede a few towns in the Netherlands and territories along the Pyrenees frontier to France.

The Treaty of Westphalia finally ended the Thirty Years' War in 1648, leaving Germany devastated and divided into literally hundreds of separate little states. The Dutch Republic and Switzerland were both formally recognized as separate and independent countries, no longer part of the Holy Roman Empire. France and Sweden emerged as great powers, the one in western Europe, the other in the northeast. The weakened Hapsburgs were no longer a match for the combination of their French, Swedish, and Protestant German enemies. A new era of French predominance in European politics began.

Internal Political Development

In 1500 nearly every ruler in Europe had to bargain with his subjects over paying taxes. Usually a meeting of "Estates" (Diet or Parliament) authorized the ruling king or prince to collect certain taxes for particular purposes and for a lim-

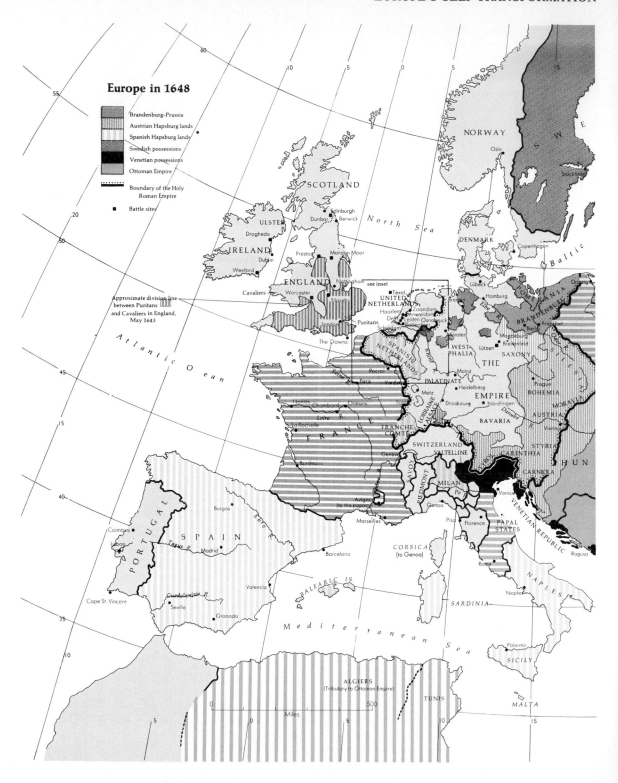

Europe in 1648

- Brandenburg-Prussia
- Austrian Hapsburg lands
- Spanish Hapsburg lands
- Swedish possessions
- Venetian possessions
- Ottoman Empire

.... Boundary of the Holy
        Roman Empire

■ Battle sites

Approximate division line
between Puritans
and Cavaliers in England,
May 1643

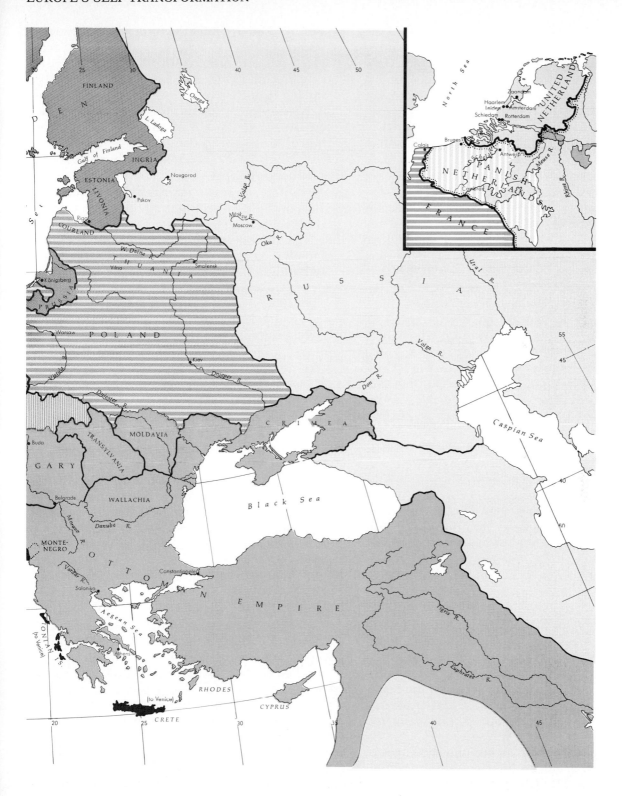

FINLAND

L. Ladoga

Gulf of Finland

INGRIA

ESTONIA

Novgorod

LIVONIA

Pskov

Riga

COURLAND

W. Dvina R.

LITHUANIA

Vilna

Smolensk

Königsberg

Volga R.

Moskva R.

Moscow

Oka R.

PRUSSIA

Warsaw

POLAND

Kiev

RUSSIA

Vistula R.

Dnieper R.

Ural R.

Dniester R.

MOLDAVIA

Don R.

CRIMEA

Buda

TRANSYLVANIA

Volga R.

GARY

Belgrade

WALLACHIA

Danube R.

Caspian Sea

MONTE-NEGRO

Morava R.

Vardar R.

Black Sea

Salonika

OTTOMAN

Constantinople

EMPIRE

Aegean Sea

Tigris R.

IONIAN IS.
(to Venice)

Athens

Euphrates R.

RHODES

(to Venice)

CYPRUS

CRETE

North Sea

Zaandam

Haarlem

Leiden

Amsterdam

Schiedam

Rotterdam

UNITED NETHERLAND

Bruges

Antwerp

Calais

Meuse R.

Rhine R.

SPANISH NETHERLAND

Cambrai

FRANCE

ited period of time. The Estates represented the nobles, clergy, and townspeople who paid taxes or helped to collect them from the peasants. Only in Italy did governments have standing professional armies and a large enough income to pay salaries to civilian officials.

By 1650 in Spain, France, Italy, and the Germanies, rulers generally had become absolute monarchs. This did not mean that they could do anything they wanted to do. It did mean that they did not have to consult representative bodies before collecting taxes or before spending tax income for whatever purposes the ruler and his personal advisers thought good. The religious wars in France, the Thirty Years' War in Germany, the Counter-Reformation in Italy, and the suppression of internal revolts in Spain had led to this result.

In fact, European rulers kept the interests of their subjects constantly in mind. They knew very well that their power depended on being able to supply their armies with guns and ammunition, food, clothes, and all the other things soldiers need. Equipping an army depended on industry and on trade. It meant trying to collect as much ready money inside the kingdom as possible, so as to be able to buy whatever might be needed. It meant, in short, close cooperation with bankers and businessmen.

One important European government did not follow this policy. The Spanish rulers actually persecuted townsfolk who were not good Catholics, and they banished Jews and Moriscos (converted Moslems) from the country. These latter two groups had been among the most active businessmen of Spain, and their departure helped to bring on the economic decay from which Spain began to suffer after 1600. In general, the Spanish government fostered the interests of the Church and of the clergy more than of any other group in the population. The policy was successful in uniting Spain under the king and gave the Spaniards a cause for which to fight. But it weakened Spain economically, and other kings were not eager to follow such a policy.

The countries that lay around the edges of Europe's center did not become absolute monarchies before 1650, although England came close to it under the Tudors (1485–1603). Parliament became almost a rubber stamp for Henry VIII

and Elizabeth I. Under the Stuart kings, who succeeded Elizabeth, however, Parliament reasserted its claim to a controlling voice in royal policies and, as we shall see in Chapter 4, civil war led to the establishment of full-blown parliamentary government after 1688. The nobility of Portugal, Ireland, Scotland, and Sweden continued to be able to defy their respective kings with armed force when it suited them. In Poland and Hungary the nobles kept sovereign political and military power in their own hands, for elected kings of these two countries had no administrative machinery to make their will effective.

Scattered through the heartland of Europe were the remnants of medieval city-states. In the Dutch Republic and in Switzerland, cities managed to create powerful and important new confederations. The Dutch, in fact, became the leading sea power of the world and handled the big business interests of all of Europe. The Swiss were famous soldiers and mercenaries. The Swiss Confederation was dominated by self-governing cities, such as Geneva, Zurich, and Berne, just as the Dutch Republic was dominated by Amsterdam and lesser cities. Venice, in Italy, and a score or so of imperial free cities in Germany carried on medieval traditions of republican self-government; but in these old-fashioned city-states, political power nearly always lodged in the hands of a privileged and wealthy upper class.

Only a few religious radicals supposed that the people had the right to govern themselves. It seemed self-evident that God had created separate social classes or, as they were usually called, Estates. Some were peasants, some were artisans; other were kings or nobles. Society was like a body. It needed a head, but it also needed feet and hands. Each class, or Estate, had its appropriate part to play. If any class refused to fulfill its proper function, then the body politic was diseased. Nothing would go right until the disorder ended. The gap between rich and poor, educated and uneducated, peasant and master, was very great. Differences in clothing showed at a glance who was who. Manners and the way a person walked and talked showed his or her class as well as where he or she had come from. Each rank had its duties as well as its rights, and there was always the possibility of rising through government service, since the king or prince could issue patents of nobility to anyone he chose. A rich businessman could buy such titles or a civilian official might be rewarded for faithful service with a title to nobility.

On top of the whole system stood kings and princes, who recognized no superior but God. They held their positions by God's choice. Hence they ruled by divine right, just as their subjects served and obeyed by doing whatever they were born to do, according to God's will. Revolution, by such standards, was always wrong. Any injustices of this world would be corrected in the next. Only false religion, which might keep souls from Heaven, could justify rebellion. Hence, it is not really surprising that the wars and revolts, of which the century and a half between 1500 and 1650 was unusually full, were justified in religious terms by the combatants.

A glaring gap in this social theory was that no rules or limits applied to the relations of one ruler with another. Each ruler claimed absolute sovereignty within his own territory. Each claimed the right to make war or peace with any or all neighbors. Scholars tried to find a natural law that would instruct and guide rulers in their dealings with one another. A Dutchman, Hugo Grotius (1583–1645), wrote a famous book entitled *On the Law of War and Peace* with this purpose in mind. But kings and princes followed Grotius' rules only when it pleased them.

In effect, the problem that had troubled Europe since feudal times—how to maintain public peace—was simply shifted to a different level. Rulers who succeeded in suppressing the war-making power of the nobility brought a higher level of peace and order to their kingdoms than Europe had known since the days of the Roman Empire. But they used the same military force that kept peace at home to attack one another—with results that could be disastrous, as the Thirty Years' War showed.

THE REALM OF THOUGHT

The basic fact in Europe's intellectual history in these years was the breadth and depth of uncertainty that became apparent everywhere. The Reformation made the question of authority in matters of religion acute for everyone. Discoveries made by European explorers proved that the classical authors of antiquity had often been wrong about geography and knew nothing about the plants and animals of the New World. A series of important inventions, starting just before 1600, also allowed experts to see and measure things far more accurately than ever before. The microscope (invented *c.* 1590), the pendulum clock (invented *c.* 1656), the thermometer (invented *c.* 1607), the telescope (invented *c.* 1608), and the barometer (invented *c.* 1643)—all sharpened human senses and extended the range of observation as dramatically as the explorations a century earlier had done. Discovery of microorganisms in drops of water was no less surprising than the moons of Jupiter. Things of which no one had ever dreamed suddenly became obvious. But such new knowledge discredited old authorities. Who and what should be believed? Was the Bible really infallible?

The Search for Certainty

Europeans responded to the tremendous uncertainty of the years 1500–1650 in two contradictory ways. Some, probably the majority, tried desperately to mend the chinks in their world view by finding a total and complete answer to all important questions through an act of faith. Calvin and his fellow Protestants, for example, made one basic assumption: God had told human beings all they needed to know in the Bible. Careful study of the Scriptures would, therefore, answer all important questions. Anything omitted from the Scriptures was by definition unimportant, and the only things that really mattered were the issues of salvation and righteousness with which the Scriptures dealt. The appeal of Calvinism rested largely on the logical simplicity of this assumption and on the skill with which Calvin was able to find answers from Scripture for the burning issues of the day. Roman Catholics, when stirred again to action by the Protestant challenge, also offered a complete system of belief. The more complicated origins of canon law and Catholic theology (based upon the Church Fathers, upon natural reason, upon Roman law, and upon decrees of the popes and coun-

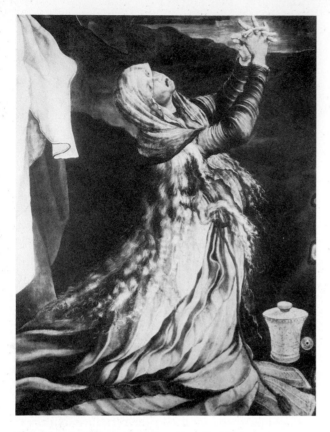

The Agony of Uncertainty This detail from an altarpiece showing the Crucifixion was painted in 1526, on the very eve of the Reformation, by Matthias Grunewald at Isenheim, Alsace. It portrays Mary Magdalene at the foot of the Cross, despairing at Christ's impending death. Her hands are especially eloquent of the agony of uncertainty—an agony felt by Christ's followers who had expected the Messiah to restore the Kingdom of David in Jerusalem and felt, almost as acutely, by those who followed Luther in denouncing the Pope for leading Christians away from the true path of salvation. This painting suggests the intensity of religious feeling and anxiety that the Lutheran movement tapped in Germany; and in fact the artist did associate with Lutherans in his later life.

cils, as well as upon the Holy Scriptures) were counterbalanced by the greater completeness of the intellectual system and the detailed rules for conduct that Catholic priests could offer the faithful in nearly every circumstance.

The effort to find an authoritative answer for every important question was shared also by

the great philosopher of the age, René Descartes (1596–1650). Descartes was a Frenchman, Jesuit-trained. He had a powerful bent for mathematics and invented analytic geometry by combining the ideas and techniques of algebra and geometry. Descartes believed that mathematical reasoning could arrive at truths that everyone who understood the argument would have to accept. Each step followed logically and necessarily from the one before. A handful of simple self-evident assumptions were all that mathematicians needed to arrive at surprising and useful results. Why not, therefore, try the same thing with the age-old questions of theology and philosophy, about which everyone was quarreling so bitterly?

Descartes eagerly set out and found that he could logically doubt everything except the fact of his own existence. "I think, therefore I am," was his famous phrase. From this slender assumption he then set out to answer all important questions by logical deduction. The existence of God; the nature of the soul; how the world machine, sun, moon, and stars worked; and how animal bodies functioned could all be demonstrated, according to Descartes, by careful reasoning.

The trouble, of course, was that the biblical, the Catholic, and the mathematical answers did not agree with each other. No one of them, even if complete and persuasive by itself, could command the acceptance of all Europeans. This indeed was what all the argument was about and what gave rise to so much persecution and bloodshed.

A few thinkers responded to this distressing situation by concentrating attention on whatever happened to interest them, leaving the big questions unanswered. In this way separate sciences and branches of a study made great progress. Sometimes, indeed, scientific progress upset some old idea that had been made part of official Church doctrine. In such cases the difference in outlook came clear between specialists who cared for detail and accuracy and others who felt that overall certainty was the only thing that really mattered. Calvin, no less than the papal Inquisition that condemned Galileo's astronomical discoveries, could not let specialists pull down sacred doctrine. But the specialists had a way of winning in the end because they based their work on more and more exact observation, measurement, and experiment.

The Development of Science

The scientists who took such pains to observe and measure and calculate had special reasons for doing so. Two great theories about the world were in conflict: One was based on Aristotle's logic and other writings while the other, mystical and mathematical, looked back to Plato. Aristotle's way of thinking had been skillfully worked into a Christian mold by the great medieval scholastics, chief of whom was St. Thomas Aquinas. Aristotle's physics and astronomy, revised in the light of more recent information, had also been well worked out before 1500. There was nothing important left to discover along these lines, a fact that made it all the easier for the Roman Catholic church to accept Aristotelian science as part of official doctrine.

During the Renaissance, however, men had rediscovered Plato and ancient "Pythagorean" writers. During his student days at the University of Padua in Italy, for example, Nicolaus Copernicus (1473–1543) accepted Pythagorean ideas about the mystical power and special qualities of numbers. He later argued that the earth revolved around the sun because a circular path for the planets was more "perfect" than the complicated movements required by the Ptolemaic-Aristotelian theory that made sun, moon, and planets revolve around the earth. Johannes Kepler (1571–1630) corrected Copernicus' theory by discovering that the path of the planets around the sun was not circular but elliptical. This required exact observation and measurement of the positions of the planets. It also required, or at least was inspired by Kepler's conviction, that mathematical ratios between the orbits of the different planets created the "music of the spheres" of which Plato and Pythagoras had written.

In medicine, too, an extraordinary character, who called himself Paracelsus (1493–1541), challenged the authority of Galen on mystical grounds. Only then did careful surgeons, such as Andreas Vesalius (1514–1564), discover errors that resulted from the fact that Galen had used pigs instead of human corpses for dissection. Once Galen's authority had been shaken by such discoveries, doctors began to experiment with new drugs and treatments for disease—often, perhaps, more to the injury than to the benefit of their patients. All the same, knowledge increased. William Harvey (1575–1657), for example, laid the foundation for modern physiology by figuring out that the heart was a pump and that it circulated blood throughout the body by means of the arteries and veins. He was led to this theory, however, by the same complex of Platonic-Pythagorean lore that treated the human body as a microcosm of the universe, and the heart as equivalent to the sun around which, by the new Copernican theory, everything else revolved.

The thought of Francis Bacon (1561–1626) and of Galileo Galilei (1564–1642), like that of their contemporary René Descartes, marked the coming of age of a new era in European science. Francis Bacon was a successful English lawyer, but in his spare time he set out to invent a new sort of logic that would improve on Aristotle's. He believed that if people would only stop arguing about abstract matters and instead use their senses to observe nature and keep careful count of what they saw, all sorts of new and useful information could be discovered. Bacon was no scientist himself, nor was he, like Descartes, a great mathematician. His ideas remained apart from the mainstream of scientific development; and, in fact, no one ever really followed his inductive method of scientific discovery in arriving at important new ideas and theories. Yet Bacon put a new challenge to old Aristotelian ideas in the field and helped to give English thought its own distinct character, more concrete and down to earth than the theories that had greater appeal on the continent of Europe.

Galileo, on the contrary, was a great practical inventor and discoverer, as well as a theorist. Unlike Descartes, he did not try to use mathematical reasoning to construct a complete system of knowledge. Galileo merely found ways to measure exactly how physical bodies moved, and put his results into mathematical form. He never tried to answer every question the way Descartes did. Instead he stuck to a limited range—to what we call physics and astronomy today. He was an ingenious experimenter and pioneered the use of

New Sciences Galileo was born in Pisa and started his career by lecturing on mathematics at the University of Pisa, within sight of the cathedral bell tower pictured above. The bell tower leans because of faulty foundations and was already famous in Galileo's day for its tilt. After Galileo discovered that falling bodies accelerate uniformly, regardless of their weight—a proposition that refuted a doctrine of Aristotelian physics—someone invented the story that he proved his point by dropping different sized cannon balls from this tower. But by the time Galileo worked out his new mathematical physics, he was far away at Padua and never returned to his native city for any such demonstration. Below, Rembrandt's painting, 'The Anatomy Lesson' illustrates another side of European science—resort to exact observation and the use of drawings to record what had been discovered. Human anatomy became far more accurately known through such methods—an advance of intense interest to artists as well as to medical students, like those being instructed here.

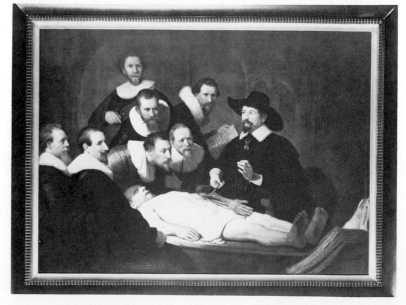

the telescope, discovering not only Jupiter's moons and Saturn's rings, but sunspots as well—thus, incidentally, disproving one of Aristotle's principles about the perfection of heavenly bodies.

More than any other single person, Galileo can be considered the founder of modern science. He tested theories by observation and experiment, and he argued for his own discoveries and theories with unusual literary skill. Near the end of Galileo's life, the papal Inquisition compelled him to state publicly that some of his astronomical theories were wrong. Galileo submitted in order to keep out of trouble, but in private he made it quite clear that his opinions had not changed just because some officials of the Church made him say he had been in error.

Overall, the tensions and points of friction between those who tried to find complete answers to all questions in a total system of belief and those who kept searching for new information and knowledge in detail proved extraordinarily fruitful. Neither the one nor the other could long relax and assume that there was nothing more to find out, or no new point to defend.

Europeans pursued truth along many different lines. Sometimes, perhaps, the yawning uncertainties seemed dreadfully frightening. But the effort to do something about uncertainties meant rapid increases in knowledge and a restless testing of every idea and belief. The birth of modern science, with all the consequences that it had in later times, was the unexpected result. Human minds had never engaged in more fruitful or more fateful endeavor. The society and technology, the ideas and beliefs, and the power and the risks of our own age arise largely from the continued development and practical applications of science as pioneered in the age of Galileo, Bacon, and Descartes.

THE PURSUIT OF BEAUTY

The efforts Europeans made to discover truth were matched by almost equally fruitful efforts to give expression to their sense of beauty. In literature, the century and a half from 1500 to 1650 was the time when most of the existing literary languages of western Europe achieved their definition. Miguel de Cervantes (1547–1616) in *Don Quixote* mocked medieval romances and created modern Spanish. French owed its literary definition largely to John Calvin, who wrote a version of his *Institutes of the Christian Religion* in that language. Luther's Bible defined modern German. The King James Bible (1611), together with William Shakespeare (1564–1616) and other Elizabethan poets, established modern English.

Latin remained the usual language for scholarship and science. It was also used for literary expression by men of letters such as Desiderius Erasmus (1466–1536) and Thomas More (1478–1535). In *Utopia*, More indirectly criticized injustices of the England of his day by describing a never-never land where people behaved rationally.

In the field of art, the force of Italian example was very strong. Especially in Catholic Europe, a more elaborate art style, called baroque, spread from Italy over southern Germany and eastward into the Austrian lands and Poland. The same style took root in the New World, where great baroque churches attested to the power of the clergy to organize the labor and loyalty of the Amerindians.

Distinct national schools of painting arose in Germany, Spain, and the Low Countries. Painters such as the German Albrecht Durer (1471–1528), the Spaniard Diego Velásquez (1599–1660), the Fleming Pieter Brueghel (1525–1569), and the Dutchman Rembrandt van Rijn (1606–1669) were each able to express something of the distinct national character of their homelands.

In Italy, the great days of Renaissance art ended with the disastrous wars that began with the French invasion of 1494. Particularly after the sack of Rome by Charles V's soldiers in 1527, one of the main centers of patronage for art was gone. The Catholic Reformation was less friendly than before to artists and to secular pursuits in general. Nevertheless, in Venice a school of painters carried on, including many well-known artists among its followers—Titian (1490–1576), Tintoretto (1512–1594) and Paolo Veronese (1528–1588) being the most famous.

Differing local traditions of art were sometimes mingled in the work of a single artist. The

Middle Class Comfort Despite all the religious and political conflict in Europe, town life flourished in the 16th and 17th centuries and a growing number of private families began to enjoy new standards of domestic comfort. This painting by Jan Vermeer (1632–1675) shows some of the things a private family could expect to possess: glass windows to let in light and keep out the weather, for instance, together with table and chair, silverware for serving food and drink, a map hanging on the wall, and varied kinds of cloth covering the table, draped over the back of the chair and, of course, used also for clothing. Vermeer's wife suffered bankruptcy after his death and he may have ranked as a poor man in his native town of Delft; but his pictures breathe an atmosphere of quiet comfort and tranquility that was enjoyed by the more prosperous citizens of the age. (Source: The Metropolitan Museum of Art. Gift of Henry G. Marquand, 1889.)

career of Domenico Theotocópuli (1541–1614)—born in Crete, trained in Italy, and active during his mature years in Spain, where he was commonly called El Greco (the Greek)—clearly showed the influence of all three of the environments he inhabited, allowing him to create a style that was distinctly his own.

In northern Europe (particularly in the Dutch provinces), artists took on new roles in society. Paintings intended for private display in homes could be bought and sold like other luxuries. This contrasted with older ideas about art, displayed in churches and other public places and intended to edify and instruct as well as to please the viewers.

In accordance with their new social role, a distinct Dutch school of artists came into existence which, along with Venetian, Spanish, and German schools, added greatly to the variety of European painting. But all these separate schools belonged together in some fundamental ways. They all accepted the techniques of perspective

that had first been worked out in Italy about 1440, and all agreed that a good painting should create an illusion of three-dimensional reality. These areas of agreement corresponded to the larger fact that Europe continued to have a loose but very real cultural unity throughout this age of sharp transition, despite all the fighting and quarreling in which Europeans continued to indulge.

Music, also, began to broaden. Systematic notation made possible more formal compositions. Court rituals and military parades gave new occasions for musical performances. Improved instruments opened new possibilities for harmony and rhythm. Singing and accompaniments became more closely linked to each other. In Italy the beginnings of opera date from before 1650. Congregational singing was a prominent part of Protestant services. Musical culture spread with Luther's hymns and Calvinist singing of psalms, as well as with the more stately and elaborate organ music that the Roman Catholic church permitted after the composer Giovanni

Palestrina (1525–1594) showed what could be done by combining choral voices with organ music.

Europe's artistic life was thus vigorous and varied, open to new ways of doing things. Patterns of thought and patterns of art and literature that had been created in the Middle Ages were not treated reverently, as though they were models that could not be tampered with. Even the ancients, who had been held up as models by the humanists of the Italian Renaissance, were found to be in error on important points. People were thrown back on their own resources—to pick and choose from the past and from what they could find in the world around them.

Such an open situation positively invited experiment and a more or less free personal invention in the fields of art, as well as in thought. In both these fields, Europeans responded to their opportunity much as they were doing in practical lines of activity, that is, with extraordinary energy, imagination, and creativity.

CONCLUSION

The common denominator of all the confusing changes that came to Europe between 1500 and 1650 was this: Western Europeans learned how to expand and intensify the energies they could bring to bear in almost every sphere of human activity. Overall, this meant a great increase in the power of the civilization both at home and abroad in contacts with other cultural traditions.

New kinds of organization allowed larger numbers to cooperate in peaceable and in warlike undertakings. The joint stock company, for example, was perfected just after 1600. Under a legal charter, it allowed the shared ownership of a company through the purchase of stock. The joint owners were liable in case of bankruptcy for only the amount of money each of them had invested. And, of course, as long as the company prospered, a joint owner could sell his share, sometimes at a price higher than he paid for it. Modern corporations are built on the same principles. What this kind of business organization did was allow thousands of persons to work to-

gether over long periods of time for goals defined by a small group of managers. Savings could be pooled, risks spread out, and special skills put to fuller use by this kind of organization than was possible with family businesses or partnerships.

In politics, nothing quite so dramatic as the joint stock company was invented. Bureaucracy and standing armies were not new. But they became much more efficient and took charge of more and more activities. Local self-help and the authority of separate town governments suffered; so did the rights of noble lords over their peasants. Simultaneously, it became easier for merchants to buy or sell anywhere within the kingdom without having to submit to local guild rules. Royal and princely governments also learned how to mobilize a larger proportion of the resources of their subjects for public purposes. Everything became more complicated as it assumed a larger scale. A handful of knights, supported by local peasants, no longer had any value on the battlefield. Instead, by the end of the period, dozens of cannon and thousands of muskets were what mattered, along with men carefully trained to use these weapons effectively. Skilled artisans, financiers, miners, smelters, wagon train drivers, riverboat captains and crews of seagoing vessels, tax collectors, army officers, drillmasters, and literally thousands of other specialists were needed to create and maintain such armies. But the cooperation of so many specialists produced more effective armies. Every new invention or improvement that worked spread rapidly, for no government could long afford to be without an armed force that could hold its own against neighboring states.

In thought and in culture, too, Europeans were able to find many new ways to mobilize greater energies. Sale of printed books, for example, allowed a man such as Erasmus to make a living as an author and scholar without having to take a post in a university or with the Church. The theater, too, by charging admission, created a livelihood for actors and playwrights such as William Shakespeare. Together, these changes gave secular literature a wider scope than before. The printing press also had great importance in spreading new ideas more rapidly and more accurately than previously. Luther's pamphlets, for example, made it practicable for anyone in Germany to learn the full details of his challenge to the papacy from Luther's own words—and to hear the arguments of his opponents, as well. In less controversial fields, too, the printing press made exchange of information far more efficient. Travelers' reports of new lands, woodcuts portraying newly discovered objects, maps drawn according to the latest news, anatomical and botanical drawings, mathematical proofs, philosophical or theological arguments—any sort of information, in fact—could be made public through printing. This meant that those who cared about any particular line of inquiry could secure the latest and best data or theory much more easily than before, even when they happened to live far away from the place where a new invention or where new information had first been discovered. Once again, human energies over wider areas could be mobilized more efficiently: Each new idea or new bit of knowledge that entered European learning gave people more things to think about. And just as the best-supplied and best-organized armies usually won battles, so also the best-informed and most experienced minds usually won arguments—and in doing so, enriched, enlarged, and expanded the intellectual inheritance of Europe as a whole.

Nowhere else in the world were these centuries nearly so full of fundamental novelties and departures from old ways. The appearance of well-armed European vessels along the shores of Asia did not make much difference to the old civilizations of that part of the world. Moslems, Hindus, Chinese, and Japanese were interested in keeping what they had and in keeping any necessary changes to a minimum. Only Europeans found it possible and necessary to question the assumptions of their ancestors so drastically—and so fruitfully. As a result, Europeans slowly but surely began to leave other peoples behind.

Chapter 17

THE WORLD BEYOND EUROPE

1500 to 1700

The pattern of communication created by the conquest of the world's oceans by European seafarers just before and just after 1500 did not upset the age-old balance among the major civilizations of Eurasia all at once. Both the Moslem and Chinese worlds continued to expand their territory very successfully until after 1700. Even the Hindus, although subjected to Moslem rule, gained new self-consciousness and energy through religious revival.

Outside of western Europe itself, the really radical changes during the centuries 1500–1700 were limited to the Americas, where the arrival of Europeans had immediate and disastrous impact on Amerindian peoples. Africa remained apart, although the slave trade brought throngs of Africans to the New World. On the other hand, Australia and Oceania were scarcely affected by European seafaring before 1700.

The new age that began about 1500 favored civilized peoples. This was dramatically evident in Asia and in eastern Europe, where the development of guns gave civilized infantry a growing military superiority over nomad steppe cavalry. As a result, by 1700 Chinese and Russian armies had divided almost the entire Eurasian steppe between them. The eclipse of the nomads as a serious element in the military balance of Eurasia made land frontiers upon the steppe less and less critical, while the importance of seaboard regions, where European ships arrived and departed with growing frequency, became correspondingly greater for all the world's peoples.

Yet the challenges that European ideas and techniques offered to other civilized communities were not so pressing that they could not be disregarded, when it seemed easier to do so. Between 1500 and 1700, each of the Asian civilizations chose to take this path. It was especially tempting because the spread of heavy artillery to all parts of the civilized world allowed great imperial states to consolidate their hold over wide territories. Vast and mighty empires seemed in no

danger from the occasional visits of European (or any other kind of) ships to their port cities.

Continuities are therefore more evident than revolutionary change in the history of the Asian civilizations during the first 200 years of European overseas expansion. Only in Japan, where an independent style of civilization was still comparatively new, and in Russia, where western Europe's pressure was felt more sharply because the distances were less, did far-reaching and drastic internal changes come to older patterns of life between 1500 and 1700.

THE WORLD OF ISLAM

In 1500 Moslems had no reason to doubt that the tide of world history was running with them, as it had done ever since the prophet Mohammed first proclaimed his revelation of God's truth in Mecca, centuries before. To be sure, the political unity of Islam lay in ruins, and civil war was constant. But this was nothing new. However reluctantly, Moslem thinkers had already come to terms with these political failures.

Moslem Territorial Advances

They could find reason to console themselves by considering the frontier successes that continued to come to Moslem warriors and to Moslem missionaries. In Africa and Southeast Asia, Islam continued to expand throughout the two centuries that we are concerned with here. No single great event led to this result. Rather, Islam spread through a series of local conversions—sometimes of a city, of a tribal leader, or just of individuals—until they constituted a majority of the politically powerful persons in the region. Moreover, conversion to Islam was a gradual matter. Reverence for Sufi mystics led to acquaintance with the Ko-

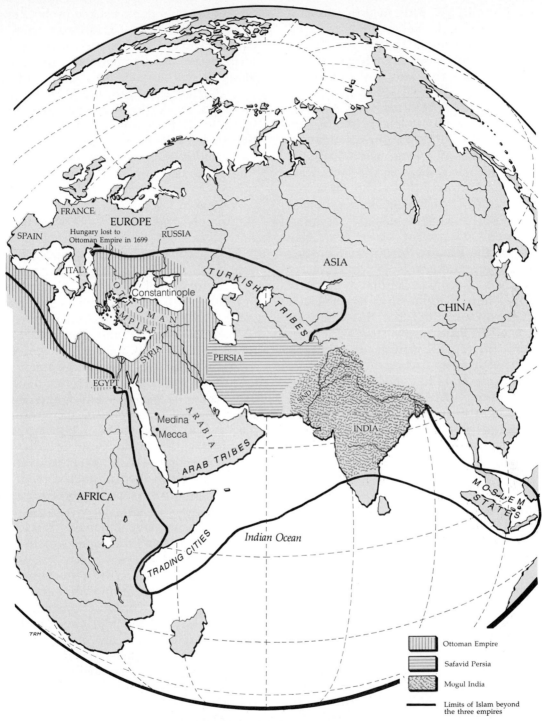

The Realm of Islam, ca. 1700

ran and the Sacred Law. This in turn was pro-
logue to familiarity with the entire cultural inheritance of Islam. Mastery of the Koran required
a knowledge of Arabic, and knowledge of that
language opened wide the door to the treasures
of Moslem learning.

On the battlefield, Moslem arms also did
well. All of India came under Moslem domination
after 1565, when the Hindu Empire of Vijayan-
agar fell to a coalition of local Moslem rulers.
Java became Moslem by 1526 in the same way.
Against Christian Europe, Ottoman arms reached
their high-water mark in 1683. The long naval
duel in the Mediterranean between the Turks and
the Spaniards ended with Turkish success. They
kept control of the eastern Mediterranean Sea
and excluded the Spaniards from North Africa,
except for a small foothold at Ceuta, just opposite
Gibraltar. By land, Ottoman armies extended
their power all around the Black Sea and, year
after year, kept up a generally successful local
frontier war with the Hapsburgs. In 1683 the
Turkish imperial army again besieged Vienna, as
in the days of Suleiman the Lawgiver, and again
failed to take the city. The long war that followed
ended in 1699 with the first really serious defeat
the Turks had ever suffered in Europe. By the
Treaty of Karlowitz, which ended the war, the
Turks had to yield most of Hungary to the Hapsburgs.

Moslem Setbacks on the Steppe

This was not the first really serious territorial loss
that the Moslems had suffered at Christian hands.
In 1552 the Russian Czar, Ivan the Terrible,
(reigned 1533–1584), conquered the khanate of
Kazan. Four years later he also took Astrakhan
at the mouth of the Volga River, thus opening the
whole of that river to Russian settlement and
trade. These victories added tremendous new territories to the Russian state; and the old masters
of Russia, the Golden Horde, passed permanently
from political existence. Not long afterward, Russian pioneers crossed the Ural Mountains. By
1588 they destroyed the khanate of Sibir and took
control of the headwaters of the Ob River. Here,
in the central regions of the steppe, Moslem states
and peoples began to topple like ninepins in the

face of Russian guns, backed up by Russian settlers. The reversal of relations between steppe
cavalry and civilized infantry was nowhere demonstrated more emphatically, or earlier, than
along Russia's eastern and southern frontiers.

Farther east, also, the Moslems suffered a
serious setback. By 1515 a new tribal confederation, the Uzbeks, conquered the Amu Darya and
Syr Darya valleys. In doing so, they dislodged
bands of Persianized Turks who ruled the region.
The Turks fled southward into India, and there
in time erected the Mogul Empire.

This sort of domino action was age-old and
completely traditional. What was different this
time, however, was that the region, which the
Uzbeks vacated when they moved southward,
was taken over by a pagan tribe known as Kalmucks. Instead of becoming Moslem, as the Uzbeks and their predecessors in that part of the
steppe had done, the Kalmucks preferred La-
maistic Buddhism. The same faith spread also
among the Mongols and held its own among the
Tibetans, who had created it in the first place.

Thus, a distinct nomad religious community
came into existence in eastern and central Asia,
holding itself consciously apart from Islam as
well as from China. In the end it was the Chinese,
not the Moslems, who conquered these communities, although China's victory was not complete
until 1757 when the Kalmuck confederacy, ravaged by smallpox as well as by Chinese guns and
cavalry, finally broke up. With this defeat, the
last significant steppe cavalry force dissolved.
The history of east Europe and Northern Asia had
definitely entered a new phase.

These setbacks on the steppe did not provoke
any sustained countermove on the part of the
civilized states of the Moslem world. The steppe
was in itself poor and unpromising ground. With
the opening of the ocean route between Europe
and the Far East, trade caravans, which had formerly crossed the steppe between China and the
west, lost much of their importance. Animal packtrains could not compete with ship transport.

Moreover, the steppe route was soon outflanked on the north also. Russian pioneers
quickly mastered the art of traveling through the
northern forests. They traveled in summer by
boat and in winter by sleigh along the rivers that
made a series of natural highways. Relatively

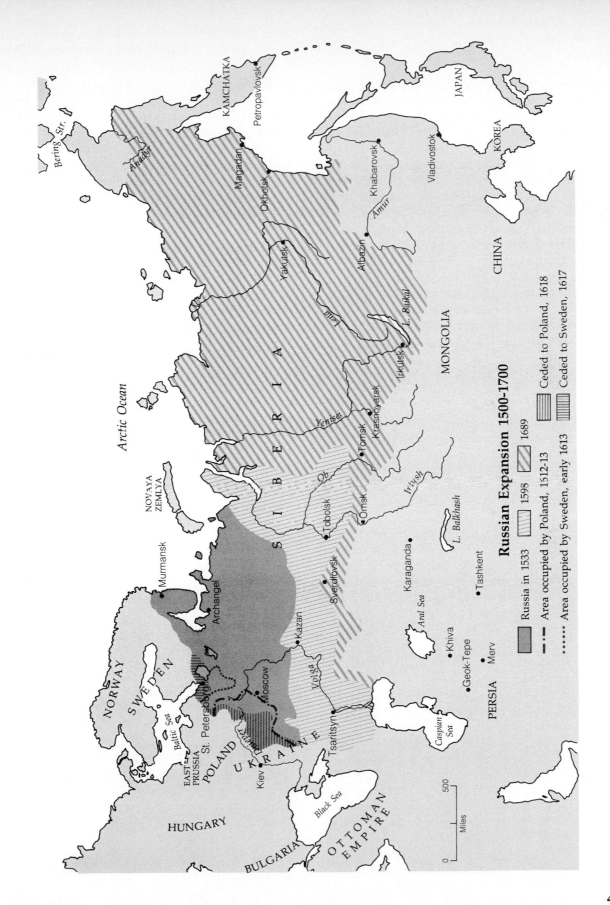

Russian Expansion 1500-1700

Russia in 1533
Area occupied by Poland, 1512-13
Area occupied by Sweden, early 1613

1598
1689

Ceded to Poland, 1618
Ceded to Sweden, 1617

Arctic Ocean

Bering Str.

KAMCHATKA

Petropavlovsk

Anadyr

Magadan

Okhotsk

Khabarovsk

Vladivostok

JAPAN

KOREA

Amur

Albazin

L. Baikal

Irkutsk

Yakutsk

Lena

MONGOLIA

CHINA

Yenisei

Krasnoyarsk

Tomsk

Ob

Tobolsk

Omsk

Irtysh

L. Balkhash

NOVAYA
ZEMLYA

S I B E R I A

Murmansk

Sverdlovsk

Karaganda

Tashkent

Archangel

Kazan

Aral Sea

Khiva

Geok-Tepe

Merv

NORWAY

SWEDEN

Baltic Sea

St. Petersburg

Moscow

Volga

Tsaritsyn

Caspian Sea

PERSIA

EAST PRUSSIA

POLAND

Dnieper

U K R A I N E

Kiev

Black Sea

HUNGARY

BULGARIA

OTTOMAN
EMPIRE

500

Miles

0

short and easy portages connected one river system with the next, and the native inhabitants—simple hunters and fishers for the most part—offered no resistance to Russian backwoodsmen who carried guns as part of their normal equipment. Hence, by 1638 Russian explorers reached the Pacific Ocean at present-day Okhotsk. They were attracted by furs, which they forced the local peoples to collect for them as a form of tribute. These furs were exported both to China and to Europe, where they were in great demand. Tea and other Chinese goods were then carried back to Russia along the same river route.

Thus, the loss of the central portions of the steppe seemed no great matter to the men who controlled the great Moslem empires.

The Rise of the Safavid State

Far more significant from the Moslem point of view was the great religious and political upheaval that came into the open in 1501, when Ismail Safavi openly proclaimed himself the descendant of the seventh Imam and therefore the true and only legitimate leader of the Moslem community. Ismail was a Shia. That is to say, he belonged to one of the sects of Islam that refused to recognize the legitimacy of the Omayyad caliphs and claimed instead that only descendants of Ali, Mohammed's son-in-law, could legitimately lead the community of the Faithful. The Safavid sect had been in existence for many years and a secret propaganda had spread its ideas far and wide over Iran and eastern Anatolia. Ismail's Turkish soldiers were organized tribally, just as Mohammed's soldiers had been in the first days of Islam. The fanatical spirit of the Shia movement was also similar to the spirit that had kept the original Moslem community together.

As a result, Ismail won a series of rapid victories. In 1502 he took Tabriz in Iran and crowned himself shah. He captured Baghdad and Mesopotamia in 1508 and defeated the Uzbeks in 1510. In 1514 a widespread rising of Ismail's sympathizers took place in Anatolia against the Ottoman sultan. Selim the Grim had to mobilize the whole strength of his imperial army to suppress the Shia rebels. When he had drowned the uprising in blood, Selim drove ahead toward Tabriz

to try to stamp out the source of the infection. He was able to defeat Ismail's troops in battle, thanks largely to the Ottoman artillery; but he could not capture Tabriz or destroy his rival.

Instead, Selim decided to eliminate any possible allies Shah Ismail might be able to find within the heartlands of Islam by conquering Syria, Palestine, Egypt, and the part of Arabia where the holy cities of Mecca and Medina were located. This he did in two years' campaigning, 1515–1517. But Iran was just too far away from Constantinople to allow the Ottoman armies to conquer it. The Turkish cavalry had to return to their estates after each campaigning season, and the sultan had to get back to his capital to assert his personal control over the central government. Hence the Ottoman armies operated within definite limits. Vienna lay at one extreme of the Turks' effective campaigning range, Tabriz at the other. Neither city could be captured, given the methods of transport and military organization available to the Ottoman Empire.

The Religious Issue: Shia vs. *Sunni*   Shah Ismail's claim to be the only legitimate political and religious leader of Islam was profoundly troublesome to all other Moslem rulers. It opened up again all the difficult problems of righteousness in social and political matters. What claim, indeed, did Turkish upstarts like the Ottoman sultans have to rule Moslems? Who was the rightful successor to the Prophet? What was the true and proper basis of religious and political authority?

These questions were strikingly similar to the issue of authority in matters of religion that was raised by the Protestant Reformation in Europe at almost exactly the same time. In Europe, Luther's challenge to papal authority provoked centuries of argument and a strenuous reexamination of biblical and early Christian texts. No universally accepted conclusion was reached, of course; but in the struggle for an answer, the depth and breadth of European knowledge and scholarship were greatly increased.

The Sunni Moslems of the Ottoman Empire responded to the Shia challenge differently. The pattern was defined under Sultan Suleiman (ruled 1520–1566), whom Europeans called "the Magnificent" but who was called "the Lawgiver" by his own people. Suleiman put the full weight

Persian Pomp and Splendor Court life at the three great Moslem empires of the sixteenth and seventeenth centuries achieved remarkable elaboration. Traces survive through works of art, like the carpet on the left and the painting on the right. Carpets like the one illustrated here served rulers and other powerful men as floor coverings both in private living quarters and also in rooms for public ceremonies, such as that portrayed on the right where one sees Shah Tahmasp (ruled 1524–1576) of Iran receiving an embassy sent by one of the early Mogul rulers of India. Tahmasp was the son of Ismail Safavi and inherited his father's claim to be the only legitimate Moslem ruler. This made diplomatic relations with other Moslem rulers delicate. But political differences could be somewhat softened by diplomatic ritual and courtly entertainments, like the professionalized music and dancing illustrated here. (Source: The Metropolitan Museum of Art. Bequest of Benjamin Altman, 1913. [14.40.721], *left*/Art Resource, *right*)

---

of his government behind Sunni orthodoxy. Schools for training experts in Sunni law were set up; and a carefully controlled hierarchy of religious officials, much resembling the hierarchy of the Orthodox church, was established in every Ottoman town. Unorthodox dervish communities were not usually persecuted. Rather, the Ottoman government allowed them to set up special *tekkes* (that is, monasteries of a sort). These were often out in the country, where the dervishes could pursue the mystic vision of God in their own way, without dangerously exciting the religious sentiments of the people as a whole.

Suleiman's efforts to reorganize and reinvigorate Sunni Islam worked. Revolt did not break out afresh. Shia believers went underground, pretended to accept the official form of Islam, and passed on their doctrine only to small, secret, initiated groups. This was as before. What was new was the official organization and control of the teachers and lawgivers of Sunni Islam— an intervention on the part of the state in the affairs of religion of which earlier Moslem empires never dreamed.

Ottoman success in controlling Shia heresy was made easier by the fact that the raw religious excitement of Shah Ismail's time faded rapidly. Ismail's heirs soon quarrelled with Shia experts in the Sacred Law, who were called ayatollahs. The shahs claimed God-given, absolute power; the ayatollahs wanted to subordinate the shah's government to their own interpretation of God's will. Both did agree, however, that all traces of other forms of Islam should be destroyed.

Accordingly, the Safavid government launched a great effort to make all the shah's subjects into true believers according to the doctrines of the so-called Twelver* sect of Shia Islam. Special catechisms and schools taught the people what to believe. The former tolerance of religious variety and even of skepticism—a spirit very much in evidence in some late Persian poetry—abruptly disappeared. Persian culture took on a new, intolerant Shia coloring. The change that came to Iran under the Safavids was therefore similar to the change that came to Italy under the influence of the Counter-Reformation. In both countries, religious uniformity was achieved at the cost of cultural creativity.

The Moslem rulers of India also had to come to terms with the Safavid claim to universal authority over all true believers. Both Baber (ruled 1526–1530), the founder of the Mogul Empire, and his successor, Humayun (ruled 1530–1556), publicly accepted the Shia faith at times when they badly needed help from the Safavids; but both renounced their Shiism when they were not in need of help. Akbar (ruled 1556–1605), who first put the Mogul Empire on a stable basis, tantalized everyone by experimenting with all sorts of religious views. Christian missionaries who came to his court were sure that he was about to become Christian; in fact he probably thought of himself as the head of his own religious community, experimenting with truth, seeking answers to all sorts of ultimate questions with a more or less open mind.

*Twelvers were those who recognized twelve legitimate successors to Mohammed before the line of Ali's descendants came to an end. Other Shia sects recognized different lines of descent from Ali and fewer legitimate successors to the Prophet.

Akbar's successors adopted orthodox Sunni Islam, and the emperor Aurangzeb (ruled 1658–1707) tried to suppress both Hindu idolatry and Shia error. In doing so, he conquered previously independent Shia states in southern India and expanded the Mogul Empire to its greatest extent. But he also aroused Hindu hostility. Guerrilla actions against the Moguls, which started in Aurangzeb's lifetime, quickly undermined the power of the central government in the years that followed his death.

The Splendor of Moslem Art

Moslem art entered upon a particularly splendid period with the development of the Ottoman, Safavid, and Mogul empires. The Safavid Shah Abbas I the Great (reigned 1587–1629), for example, created a new capital for himself at Isfahan and made it one of the architectural wonders of the world. The Taj Mahal in India, built for the Mogul emperor Shah Jahan (reigned 1628–1657), was erected only a little later. Persian miniature painting also attained its highest point in these centuries, when expert craftsmen were gathered together at court and given every facility for their work. Traces of Chinese and European techniques are easy to find, but the gemlike coloring and minute detail of the Persian miniatures make them one of the world's great art traditions.

In India a similar and closely related style of painting developed around the Mogul court. Hindu painters used Persian technique to portray scenes from Hindu mythology, creating what is called the Rajput school of art. Other arts, like carpet weaving, furniture design, and jewelers' work, also attained a very high refinement in the imperial workshops, where only the very best could please.

Moslem Thought and Literature

Intellectually, however, Islam showed far less energy. Formulas inherited from the first centuries of Islam were simply reasserted, memorized, and repeated. New thoughts were actively discouraged, perhaps because they threatened always to uncover once again the raw wound created by the Safavid challenge to political and religious

Two Mosques On the left is the dome of a mosque built outside Cairo by a mamluke ruler of Egypt, Qait Bey, between 1472 and 1474. It was intended to serve as his tomb. On the right is a mosque built on top of the highest hill of Istanbul by Suleiman the Lawgiver between 1550 and 1557. It also housed a school for students of the Sacred Law. Each of these buildings celebrated the power of the rulers who commissioned them; but Suleiman's mosque had a further significance. In size and elegance it surpassed the famous Byzantine church of Sancta Sofia that Emperor Justinian had constructed almost a millennium earlier in the same city, and thereby proclaimed the superiority of Islam to Christianity and of the Ottoman empire to its predecessors. Both of these buildings are elegantly precise in their proportions and decoration. Religious prohibition of images in human form had stimulated Islamic architects to perfect a distinctive and delightful style of geometric decoration, as Qait Bey's mosque shows. The two buildings thus expressed a self confidence and vigor in Islamic civilization that was entirely unaffected by the achievements of a few European sailors and adventurers in the early modern era.

legitimacy. Even such subjects as geography, in which Moslems had long taken a special interest, failed to respond to the stimulus of the European discoveries. Pious Moslems refused to read Christian authors, and so the new geographical knowledge that flowed into Europe was disregarded.

Literature escaped stagnation only by calling new literary languages into being at both the Ottoman and the Mogul courts—Turkish at Constantinople and Urdu at Delhi. Turkish and Urdu writers drew heavily upon Persian literary models, for the great Persian poets of the Middle Ages continued to command the admiration of all Sunni Islam. But they were banished from their homeland, for the Shia religious teachers could not abide the delicate ambiguities of religious doubt upon which classical Persian poetry depended for much of its effect.

Weaknesses of Islamic Societies

Despite its brilliant success, Moslem civilization had an important weakness. In almost every part of the Moslem world, just a tiny minority of rulers and landowners really shared in Islamic high culture. Peasants were left out, and of course they were the great majority. Poor townspeople, too, had little in common with the lords and governors who employed some of them to build splendid mosques or tombs or to work in the luxury trades. Western Europe was, by comparison, much more coarse and vulgar. Even peasants entered the market. Refinement in western Europe may have been less, but what there was spread further down the social scale than in the Moslem lands.

In the Ottoman Empire, an important new circumstance arose from the fact that after 1638 the Turks stopped taking children from the Christian villages of the Balkans and training them to become soldiers and administrators of the empire. Instead, new members of the sultan's slave household came to be recruited from among the sons of those who already served the sultan. The result was to cut off what had been an important link between the Ottoman government and the Christian peasantry of the Balkans. As long as the high administrators of the Ottoman Empire had begun life as ordinary villagers, they could never lose a certain underlying sympathy with the communities from which they had come. When, however, officials came to be mainly sons of officials, all sympathy with the peasants disappeared. Discontented peasant boys, who in an earlier time might have become soldiers and administrators of the empire, became outlawed brigands instead.

This change weakened Ottoman society. So did the decay of trade and manufactures, which became noticeable about 1650. Perhaps what happened was that the businessmen of the Ottoman Empire turned away from trade and used their funds instead to buy the right from government to collect taxes from a district, a town, or even from an entire province. This practice is known as tax-farming. It allowed the tax-farmers to make a handsome profit by collecting more from the public than they had paid for the right to fleece them. On the other hand, funds invested in this way were not economically productive; indeed, it probably became dangerous to invest in trade and manufacturing, for anyone who did make money from such activities was a natural target for the tax collectors. At any rate, the foreign trade of the Ottoman Empire passed almost entirely into the hands of French, Dutch, and English merchants, who took raw materials from Turkey and brought woolen cloth and other manufactured goods into the empire in exchange.

In the Indian Ocean also, the arrival of Dutch and English traders after 1600 began to cut into Moslem sea trade as the Portuguese had never done. The Dutch and English put great effort into developing trade between Asian ports, for their own manufactures were difficult to sell in India. The Dutch East India Company (organized 1602) took on the task of managing the agriculture of Java and adjacent islands, forcing local rulers to make their subjects plant whatever crops the Dutch judged would command the best sale in world markets. The English East India Company, organized in 1600, developed a flourishing trade in Indian cotton cloth. English agents made cash advances to Indian weavers and told them what kind of cloth to produce. In this way the English were able to take on the management of cloth production and sale throughout the whole Indian Ocean area.

The increasingly active and dominant role played by European traders in the economic affairs of the Moslem empires was a sign of things to come. But in 1700 no one could have foreseen that the English East India Company would become the successor to the Mogul emperors as rulers of India, or that the might of the Ottoman sultans would crumble before European interlopers. Moslem rulers cared next to nothing about who carried the trade from their ports or planned and controlled cotton manufacturing in their dominions. Such activities were the concern of humble folk who, as long as they paid their taxes and kept quiet, did not interest the rulers of the Moslem world in the slightest. The care most European governments (except Spain) took to foster trade and manufactures differed sharply from the attitudes of Moslem rulers and reflected the greater sympathy between rulers and townspeople in Europe. Thus, the economic history of Moslem lands also reflects the fundamental weakness of Moslem society arising from the wide gap between the rulers and the rest of society.

This gap was nothing new. On the contrary, it was as old as civilization itself in the Middle East. Only the comparison with Europe made the weakness potentially dangerous. Indeed, by every standard except the standard set by Europe's contemporary development, Islam was in a flourishing condition between 1500 and 1700. Moslem dismay, when after 1700 they discovered they had been left behind, was correspondingly profound.

HINDU REVIVAL

The fact that after 1565 no independent Hindu state survived anywhere except in the remote island of Bali did not paralyze Hindu culture. On the contrary, Hinduism entered upon a new stage of development that gave it the ability to withstand Moslem and, later, Christian missionary efforts with ease. What happened was that two great poets and a famous holy man gave a new focus to Hinduism. The holy man was named Chaitanya (d. 1527). He was born a Brahman but in early manhood began to experience intense mystic experiences, during which his followers believed he actually became the great god Krishna.

A god incarnate was no ordinary thing, even in India. A religious sect soon developed around Chaitanya, important particularly in Bengal, where Chaitanya himself lived. His followers eliminated all caste distinctions. This undercut the main attraction of Islam for Indian minds. Until Chaitanya's time, members of the lower castes, especially in Bengal, had often become Moslem. After the new sect had come into existence, conversion to Islam almost ceased. The emotional conviction felt by Chaitanya's followers found expression in warm manifestations of common feeling expressed through public ceremonies. This proved far more attractive than Islam, even in Sufi form.

The two great Hindu poets Sur Das (d. 1563) and Tulsi Das (d. 1623) took stories from the two great Hindu epics, the *Mahabharata* and the *Ramayana*, and put them into the common language of northern India. The effect was comparable to what happened when Protestants translated the Bible into the everyday languages of western Europe. Ordinary people memorized long passages from the two poets. Schoolboys studied them. The lessons of piety and good manners their poems emphasized became standard. Hindu self-consciousness and religious uniformity increased.

Of the two, Sur Das was the less influential. He chose to celebrate the deeds of Krishna, and in later life he was admitted to Akbar's court. His poems have a Persian touch about them. Tulsi Das, on the other hand, concentrated his religious devotion upon Rama and escaped all taint of foreignness. Tulsi's poems entered very deeply into all later Hindu religious and cultural life. They emphasized Rama's role as both god and man and expressed intense personal devotion to him.

This was, indeed, the effect of all three men's work. Worshippers identified themselves with one single figure, who was both god and man at the same time. Other deities and myths in the Hindu tradition were not rejected outright. But in practice each devotee focused his attention on a single god-man. The result was to create something rather like different sects in Hinduism—some preferring the worship of Krishna, others concentrating upon Rama. But both these deities were held to be incarnations of Vishnu, so there was no ultimate conflict between their worshipers.

Devotion to Shiva, the other great god of earlier Hinduism, tended to fade somewhat. So did the crude magic of Tantrism. On the other hand, the most ancient layer of Hinduism—the Sanskrit rituals based on the Vedas and administered by Brahman priests—continued to be necessary for all ordinary crises of human existence. The Brahmans, with their unintelligible Sanskrit chants, had to be called in for birth, coming of age, marriage, and death. Only the followers of Chaitanya refused to honor Brahmans because they upheld caste and distinctions based upon caste.

In the practical sense, too, Hindus continued to play an important part in the Mogul Empire. Emperor Akbar relied very much upon Hindu administrators and tax collectors, and his successors continued to do the same. Many Hindus continued to possess large estates and served in the Mogul army as warriors alongside the Persian-speaking Turks who constituted the core of Mogul power. The Hindu upper classes tended to take on much of the secular culture of their Moslem rulers. They, for example, were the patrons for whom Rajput painting was produced.

The overwhelming majority of the population of India remained Hindu. They treated the thin layer of foreigners who held the Mogul Empire together as a sort of caste—to be lived with but not to be imitated or listened to, or regarded as anything but what it was: an alien body in the midst of Indian society.

The missionary force of Islam was blunted by such attitudes. Hinduism had found a popular, emotional appeal through Chaitanya and the poets. There was no need to wrestle with Moslem accusations of idolatry any longer. Except in the extreme south, Hindu temples had been destroyed. The new forms of worship took place in public places out of doors and did not focus on idols but on hymns and prayers and congregational rejoicing. Hindus readily believed that the tremendous antiquity of their sacred texts made them superior to the Koran or, for that matter, to the Christian Bible. Hinduism, in other words, had nothing to fear from outside, being rooted securely in the feelings of the Indian people as a whole.

In Java, however, Hinduism crumbled before Islam, as we have already seen. On the mainland of southeast Asia and in Ceylon, Buddhism remained vigorous, partly, at least, because it allowed the Burmese, Siamese, Vietnamese, and Singhalese peoples to preserve their national identities in the face of Islamic and other foreign pressures.

THE CELESTIAL EMPIRE OF CHINA

When the first Portuguese reached the coast of southern China in 1513, the Ming Dynasty was already beginning to suffer from the signs of decay that had often before afflicted Chinese dynasties. Heavily taxed peasants were ready for revolt. Unruly generals intrigued for power. Tax income ceased to flow smoothly to the imperial court, and the nomads along the northern and western frontiers were restless.

In addition, the Ming government had to cope with piratical attacks from the sea that soon assumed a serious scale. The majority of the pirates were Japanese. By 1555, they were strong and numerous enough to sail up the Yangtze River as far as Nanking to besiege that great city. Nothing in Chinese experience had prepared the Ming rulers for this kind of attack. Efforts to organize a Chinese navy that could police the seas and suppress piracy were sometimes successful, but the emperors always decided to economize and disband the naval force when it had done its work. The result was that discharged sailors often joined up with pirate crews—confirming the court's worst suspicions about sailors, and at the same time making it necessary to organize a fresh campaign to clear the seas of pirates once again.

The Portuguese fitted into this disorderly picture with no difficulty at all. The Chinese soon recognized the fighting qualities of Portuguese ships and made a sort of informal alliance with them. In return for allowing the Portuguese to trade from Macao, near Canton, the Chinese got a promise of Portuguese help against the Japanese pirates (1557). On the other hand, when it suited them, the Portuguese turned to piracy themselves.

In 1592, the Japanese warlord, Hideyoshi, attempted to cap his victorious career (See p. 414) by attacking and conquering China. He sent a large Japanese army to Korea, where the Ming armies fought a long, hard campaign against the invaders. The struggle was undecided when Hideyoshi died in 1598. His successors simply withdrew. In an effort to stabilize political conditions at home, the new rulers of Japan, the Tokugawa shoguns, first restricted and then completely closed Japan to contact with foreigners. Strict laws prohibited Japanese ships from sailing to other countries from Japanese ports. Foreigners were also, of course, refused the right to sail into Japanese harbors. The result was to remove the main pirate threat. The Chinese were therefore spared having to do anything about improving sea defenses—a situation that cost them dearly

Palace and Castle in China and Japan On the left is the gateway to the enclosure where Chinese emperors lived between 1431 to 1911 and from whence they conducted the imperial government. The tourists seen here flocking toward it would not have been admitted when this, the so-called "Forbidden City," served its original purpose. Then, only persons who had business to transact with the government were allowed to enter; but what kept unwanted visitors out was the order and discipline of Chinese society, not fortification. The fact that the Chinese made no effort to guard the imperial palace from cannon fire is especially striking; for in the century that followed the original laying out of the Forbidden City, a revolution in warfare gave heavy guns the power to break down all older forms of local defense. In Japan, this military revolution had drastic consequences, as the White Heron Castle, shown on the right, suggests. Built by Hideyoshi, an upstart warlord, in 1581 to hold down the southern part of Honshu, it perches on top of heavy stone fortification, carefully sloped so as to absorb cannon fire without crumbling. Yet Japan's long-standing connection with Chinese civilized traditions still rises above the heavy presence of new-fangled fortification, as indicated by the resemblance of roof lines in these photographs.

two centuries later when European gunboats began to demand access to Chinese ports.

THE MANCHU CONQUEST

Neglect of the sea frontier reflected the fact that the Ming were under increasingly dangerous attack from the north and could not stop rebellion from within. In 1615, Manchurian horsemen formed a powerful confederation and began nibbling away at Chinese territories. Then, in 1644 the commander of the Manchu confederation entered Peking, supposedly as a supporter of a Ming general who was trying to put down rebellion. Once inside Peking, however, the Manchus ceased pretending to serve the Ming emperor and instead proclaimed a new dynasty. Manchu forces soon overran the rest of China; but the island of Taiwan held out until 1683, when it, too, submitted to the new rulers of China.

Like many steppe conquerors before them, the Manchus tried to keep their own people separate from the Chinese. Special garrisons of Manchu soldiers were set up at strategic places, mostly outside big cities, and high military command was rigorously reserved for Manchus. The civil administration, nevertheless, remained entirely Chinese. Indeed, the Manchus were already half won over to Chinese culture before they invaded the country and had none of the Lamaist foreign taint that made the Mongols so unpopular among the Chinese. However, many Mongols were recruited into the ranks of the Manchu army, for there were not enough Manchus to overawe all of China. Some Chinese also served as soldiers, but they always remained in subordinate posts.

The new emperors busily set out to improve defenses against the steppe peoples to the west and met with such solid success that by 1755 the danger from the steppe was forever destroyed. Incidentally, the Chinese Empire as we know it today was created by the Manchu annexation of Tibet, Sinkiang, Mongolia, and, of course, Manchuria too. The territory administered by the Chinese emperor almost doubled as a result. Traditional China acquired a fringe of half-empty borderlands in which to expand. The process is still under way today.

The Manchus also cultivated Neo-Confucian learning and conformed gladly to Chinese imperial precedents in all matters affecting the internal administration of the country. Population grew rapidly, both because of an improved level of internal peace and because introduction of the sweet potato and other American food crops allowed the Chinese to cultivate hilly lands, especially in the south where rice paddies could not be created.

Christian Missions to China

All foreigners were barbarians in Chinese eyes. They became worthy of courteous attention only when they had taken the pains to learn Chinese and become gentlemen. The first European to accomplish this feat was Matteo Ricci, a Jesuit missionary, who hoped to convert China to Christianity by winning over the emperor and his court. In 1601 Ricci gained permission to travel to Peking, where his mastery of Chinese learning made him acceptable to the officials and scholars who governed China.

Other Jesuits followed Ricci and soon proved that they had more accurate knowledge of astronomy and calendar making than the official court astronomer did. A Jesuit accordingly was appointed to this office, giving the mission an official status from which it could not easily be removed. Correct calculation of the calendar was thought to be of great importance, since lucky

and unlucky days for undertaking new enterprises depended on having a calendar that accorded correctly with the motions of the heavenly bodies.

The Chinese also found European geographical knowledge interesting and delighted in mechanical toys and pendulum clocks that the Jesuits imported from Europe. But these were trifles. Educated Chinese felt sure that everything important was already well taken care of by traditional Confucian wisdom. Jesuit efforts to convince the Chinese of the truth of Christianity therefore fell on deaf ears, though poor children and others who were helped by the missionaries with food or medical service did sometimes become Christian.

The missionaries themselves faced an interesting dilemma. How could the technical terms of Christian theology be translated into Chinese? Or, put in another way, how did Chinese religious ideas and terminology fit into a Christian framework? Was ancestor worship idolatrous? Or was this only a family ceremony, honoring but not worshiping the dead? The Jesuits, after some hesitation, decided that ancestor worship was not worship at all, but simply a civil ceremony. They also decided that the Chinese word "Tien," usually translated "Heaven," was a suitable equivalent for the Christian word "God." These decisions meant that the Jesuits could point out to a Confucian scholar that he was already half-Christian and did not need to change family custom to become fully Christian by admitting the truth of divine revelation as recorded in the Bible and interpreted by Catholic tradition.

Such arguments did not convince many Chinese, and they profoundly shocked other Christians who had come to the Far East to convert the heathen and wished to have no truck with pagan ways. Serious controversy began in 1628 and dragged on until 1742. The Jesuits, of course, tried to defend their policies, and in doing so wrote extensive accounts of Chinese society and civilization. Learned Europeans in this way acquired a remarkably full, often idealized stock of information about China.

As a result, appreciation for Chinese art and admiration for Chinese principles of government found a considerable lodgment in Europe. Even more important, quite a few Europeans tried to understand Chinese civilization as a whole and in itself, apart from their own inherited prejudices and opinions. This marked a new kind of relationship between different civilizations. Nothing could stand in sharper contrast to the sublime self-satisfaction of the Chinese educated class, who continued to believe that nothing of value could come from the Europeans, whom they called "south sea barbarians."

China's Cultural Conservatism

Given such attitudes, little really new could arise in Chinese culture. Scholars became more and more rigorous and set out to scrape away Buddhist and Taoist ideas in order to get back to the authentic Confucian point of view. Paintings and poetry continued to be produced in quantity, for every cultivated man had to be able to paint and write good verse. But all this fell into well-worn, thoroughly traditional patterns. Experts agree that the works of the writers and artists of the Ming and Manchu periods were inferior to earlier paintings and poems. Prose tales, smelling of the street, did get printed for the first time, and a new dimension to Chinese culture thus entered the literary record. But that is about all that changed.

Chinese social structure remained what it had been ever since Sung times. Growth of manufacturing and trade was matched by the increase in agriculture that resulted from the intensified use of American food plants. Merchants and businessmen accepted the low social station to which Confucian doctrine assigned them. As soon as they could, they escaped by buying land and sending their sons to school to become gentlemen. Upward social mobility fed energetic and capable men into government and strengthened the existing social order at the same time.

Thus the Manchus brought stability within a busy, prosperous, and extremely successful traditional order. Confucian ideals asked for nothing else. In 1700, reality came closer to matching the universally accepted principles of Chinese society than at most times before or any time since.

JAPAN'S SHARP SHIFTS OF POLICY

The Japanese welcomed the first Europeans to visit their shores more warmly and with a livelier interest in what the strangers had to offer than any other Asian people. St. Francis Xavier arrived in Japan in 1549, only six or seven years after the first Portuguese adventurers had come. His proud and imperious bearing impressed the Japanese. The Jesuit mission he inaugurated soon met solid success. Japan lacked any national religion of its own. Its religious loyalty was divided among Buddhist sects, Neo-Confucianism, and the still undeveloped imperial cult of Shinto. This undoubtedly helped the progress of Christianity.

Another contributing factor was the political division of the country. Local lords found it very much to their advantage to welcome missionaries. Missionaries could attract European ships to the ports where they were well treated and could warn them away from places where Christian preaching was not permitted.

European ships were important in two ways. They had guns for sale, and a European cannon or two could knock down castle walls with ease. This often made all the difference in the local wars that had long been chronic in Japan. In addition, the Chinese government officially prohibited trade with Japan because Japanese pirates were raiding the Chinese coast all the time. But a Japanese gentleman needed silks and other elegancies from China. The Portuguese were able to import such commodities and carried Japanese silver to China in exchange. Portuguese merchants profited handsomely from this trade and cooperated closely with Christian missionaries to make sure that both silk and guns were channeled into friendly Japanese hands.

Unification of Japan

Nevertheless, only a minority of the Japanese nation accepted Christianity, and the missionaries suffered, as well as profited, from their involvement in politics. This became obvious when, after a series of more and more violent wars, the whole of Japan came under the control of a successful warlord, Toyotomi Hideyoshi (1537–1598). Hideyoshi started out as a stableboy, but his ruthlessness and ability carried him to supreme power by 1590. He viewed foreign missionaries as political rivals and in 1587 issued a decree banishing them from the country. Yet, strangely enough, he did not enforce his own decree. Perhaps he was afraid that if he acted too harshly against the missionaries, the Portuguese would break off trade relations just when he was eager to build up his armaments for the invasion of China.

In 1592 Hideyoshi launched his great adventure on the Asian mainland by invading Korea. Early victories were followed by a long and difficult stalemate; and when Hideyoshi died in 1598, the Japanese forces were quickly withdrawn. The reason was that his followers soon quarreled. Each lord wanted all of his troops on hand at home. In a great battle fought in 1600, one of Hideyoshi's lieutenants, Ieyasu Tokugawa, came out on top.

Icyasu Tokugawa was a much more cautious man than Hideyoshi. After his victory, he sought only to keep what he had won by making his new position as secure as possible. He made Tokyo his capital and planted reliable family retainers as fief holders in most of Japan. In outlying regions, however, he permitted independent "outside lords" to retain their possessions. Ieyasu kept careful watch on all fief holders and required each ruling family to leave hostages in Tokyo to guarantee good behavior. In addition, the shoguns suppressed the use and manufacture of guns that had done so much to upset older Japanese society. By making skilled sword play the decisive factor in battle once again, the old samurai class of professional warriors could and did reclaim social primacy; and the shogun's power, backed by his faithful followers, was safe from upstarts armed with new weapons like those the Europeans had first brought into the country.

The imperial family and court continued to exist at Kyoto, but the Tokugawa family made sure that the emperors had as little to do with the realities of power as possible. The new system of government is referred to as the Tokugawa shogunate because the head of the ruling Tokugawa family took the title *shogun* (commander

of the imperial army). The regime lasted until 1867. Succession rested within the Tokugawa family, regulated by private rules. But the family possessions were so extensive that what amounted to a bureaucracy of officials had to be invented to administer the lands held by members of the Tokugawa family. Hence, while old feudal forms survived, something quite different grew up underneath.

The Closing of Japan by the Tokugawa Shoguns

During the first decades of Tokugawa rule, the family was deathly afraid of renewed struggles for power among the warrior class. Hideyoshi's son, for example, was killed in 1615 to eliminate a possible rival. A code of conduct for warriors, emphasizing loyalty to the feudal superior, was formally published in 1615. Active persecution of Christians began in 1617. When a body of Japanese Christians revolted in 1637, the shogun reacted by stamping out every trace of the foreign religion he could discover. Since the Japanese Christian community had reached a quarter of a million or more, this involved large-scale violence and much bloodshed. All foreign missionaries were killed. Japanese Christians who refused to renounce their religion were also executed, with great cruelty.

At the same time, the shoguns established a new policy of total isolation from the rest of the world. In 1636 Japanese were forbidden to leave the home islands. Anyone who did so was refused the right to return. In 1638 Portuguese traders were driven from Japan. Three years later arrangements were made with the Dutch whereby a single ship was allowed to come to Nagasaki once a year. Even then, it could only dock at an island in the middle of the harbor. In this way the shogun felt that foreign intrigues could be prevented and supplies needed from abroad could be carefully controlled.

Intervention in Japanese political-military affairs, which had allowed the first Christian missionaries to attain such important successes, thus backfired after less than a century, to the bitter cost of their converts. At the same time, Japan lost an opportunity to create a sea empire in the

TALE OF THE FORTY-SEVEN RONIN

Kira, the shogun's secretary, was a proud and haughty man. He mocked the clumsiness of Asano, a country noble who did not know the proper rituals for court behavior. One day, when Kira commanded Asano to fasten his shoe and then criticized the way the bow had been tied, Asano grew angry, drew his sword, and slashed the secretary's arm.

Great was the dismay at court. Not only had Asano wounded the shogun's secretary, he had also defied court ritual—for no one was allowed to draw his sword in anger at court. Asano's only honorable course was suicide, which he performed in the traditional manner (hara-kiri) by cutting his abdomen open with the same sharp sword.

But this was not the end. Asano had forty-seven faithful followers, his *ronin*. They were fighting men with no fiefs of their own, who depended on the gifts of their lord for a livelihood. Now, thanks to Kira, Asano was dead. The ronin's duty was plain: revenge! But Kira was crafty and strong. He had his own ronin to protect him; and after Asano's death they were all especially alert, expecting some effort at revenge.

Asano's forty-seven ronin therefore decided to wait. They pretended to forget their lord and went in for drunken brawling. Then, when two years had passed and Kira's men were lulled into carelessness, the forty-seven ronin assembled one night and attacked the secretary's palace, killed his bodyguard, and cut off Kira's head. The revenge was sure; but, as before, court ritual had been broken. What to do?

To escape being treated like criminals, the forty-seven ronin followed their master's example and each committed hara-kiri. Thus they lived up to the Japanese warriors' code, faithful even unto death.

Far East similar to the Japanese Empire created during World War II, for the shogun's policy of isolation compelled Japanese mariners to stay home and stop raiding and trading across the seas surrounding Japan which they had begun to dominate.

Divergent Forms of Japanese Culture

A time of such profound political shifts might be expected to create important new forms of cultural expression. That was, in fact, the case. Hi-deyoshi's age was a time for bigness and brashness. Hideyoshi himself was a great egoist, a religious skeptic, and flamboyant in everything he did. He built a bigger palace than had ever been seen before in Japan; and when he invaded Korea, he announced that his aim was the conquest of the whole world, beginning with China.

Japanese artisan skills developed rapidly in Hideyoshi's time. Chinese and Korean captives established or expanded new industries in Japan, such as fine pottery manufacture and silk weaving. Eager efforts to imitate European gunsmiths were also successful, though shortages of iron always hampered Japan's armament. City life developed with the new wealth that came from overseas ventures, as well as from trading within Japan.

The Tokugawa regime was tamer and much more conservative. In 1608 Ieyasu made Neo-Confucianism official. His successors continued to patronize this Chinese school of learning, since its emphasis upon deference toward superiors could be made to justify the Tokugawa system of government. Yet the active, unruly life of the cities, which had taken such a spurt of growth in the age of the civil wars, did not disappear with the end of political disorder. On the contrary, peace provided still greater opportunities for trade within the Japanese islands.

The merchant class and other city dwellers, therefore, continued to support the popular, vigorous, and, at least occasionally, crude and sensuous culture that had come to the fore in Hideyoshi's time. In strong contrast to this tradition, the samurai class cultivated a heroic ideal, from which all forms of self-indulgence were banished. Loyalty and courage, even to the sacrifice of personal life and fortune, were the supreme virtues. Suicide by hara-kiri was an accepted and admired solution for any personal failure to live up to the warrior ideal. In the realm of art, this ideal found its own appropriate expression in the manufacture of magnificent swords and in such spare entertainments as the "tea ceremony" or the art of flower arrangement.

Japan therefore developed a curiously double face under the Tokugawa regime. Officially all was controlled, traditional, and strongly colored by Chinese models. But underneath, in the cities particularly, a sharply different cultural tone prevailed. Friction between these two worlds could not be avoided. Constant tension mirrored political strains, never entirely suppressed, between the Tokugawa family and the outside lords, and between the shogun and the emperor.

This situation kept Japanese minds open to new thoughts in a way that was not true to China. In China practice and theory matched one another so closely, after the Manchu conquest had again established a strong imperial authority, that no one could doubt the essential rightness of China's inherited wisdom and skills. The Japanese, on the contrary, had plenty of reason to

wonder about a system that valued warrior skills above all others yet gave the samurai no chance to use their skills—and which officially put merchants at the bottom of the social scale but in practice allowed them to grow richer than any warrior. Such disproportions between theory and practice meant that the Tokugawa government was like a corset for Japanese society, enclosing something quite at odds with, and very difficult to fit inside of, the official framework.

RISE OF THE RUSSIAN AUTOCRACY

The effectiveness of firearms, together with the furious energy of war captains such as Hideyoshi, united Japan. Russia's dramatic expansion over all of northern Asia was likewise the direct result of the revolution in warfare that came with the spread of gunpowder weapons.

For more than 200 years, Moscow and other Russian towns, except for Novgorod far in the north, paid tribute to the heirs of Genghis Khan, rulers of the Golden Horde, who made Kazan their capital. When Ivan III, the grand duke of Moscow, repudiated his subjection to Kazan in 1480, he continued to collect tributes that had once been forwarded to the Golden Horde. Ivan simply used them to support his own army and his own set of officials. This made Moscow by far the most powerful of Russian cities. But the Muscovites found themselves militarily inferior to their western neighbors, the Swedes and Poles, whose wealth and armament, commercial development, and level of culture were all superior to those existing in the Russian lands.

This presented Ivan IV (ruled 1547–1584) and his successors with a difficult problem. Constant effort was needed to keep their western neighbors from taking over Russian lands. Russia required large and well-equipped armies, but the government could not afford to pay for everything that was needed. The solution that Ivan IV adopted was a violent revolution from the top which earned him the nickname "Ivan the Terrible." He seized the lands of most of the old, noble families of Russia and assigned them to his

Cathedral of St. Basil, Moscow This extraordinary church was built by Czar Ivan the Terrible to celebrate victories over the Tartars of Kazan and Astrakhan between 1552 and 1556. Byzantine, Persian, and Italian architectural traditions all contributed to this splendidly colorful and strangely effective array of domes and towers; but the dominant element in the design was authentically Russian, for medieval churchmen had learned to build elaborate churches of wood, complete with domes and arches like those Ivan's architects translated into stone when they constructed this church. This architectural monument gave an enduring expression to the remarkable political achievement by which Ivan and his predecessors pressed Tartar and European foreigners into the service of the Muscovite state, using their skills to exalt the autocratic power of the czar. The way foreign art traditions were here mingled with and subordinated to an inherited Russian style exactly matches the way foreign military and administrative skills were adopted and adapted by the rulers of Russia to serve Russian purposes and increase the power of the state.

own personal followers. These men were then required to serve the czar (literally Caesar or emperor), as Ivan started to call himself. To make their lands worthwhile, peasants had to cultivate them and pay rents. To assure the necessary labor power, the Russian government passed laws that made it more and more difficult for peasants to run off into the woods or southward to the open steppe. In this way, a burdensome form of serfdom, approaching slavery, was fastened upon the Russian peasantry.

In theory, there was a rough sort of justice in the system. The peasants served their lords, who in turn served the czar; and the czar served God by protecting the Russian lands and the Orthodox faith from foreign encroachment. Moreover, the system worked, though not without difficulty. As long as Ivan IV lived, he kept his western enemies more or less in check, losing only minor border territories to them. Meanwhile, as we have seen, Russia profited enormously by expansion south and east at the expense of the steppe nomads. But Ivan left an incapable son to succeed him, and the son died without a direct heir. A confused "Time of Troubles" followed. Poles invaded and occupied Moscow for a couple of years and claimed the crown for the king of Poland. The Swedes also overran important new territories inland from the Baltic coast.

The Time of Troubles

Inside Russia, the greatest confusion reigned. Old noble families were interested in getting power back into their own hands. Far to the south, a rude, democratic Cossack community of warriors had arisen in the steppe. The Cossacks joined the fray, opposing the nobles and sympathizing with the peasants, but also robbing them as they marched to and fro across the countryside. The new "service nobility" that Ivan the Terrible had created lacked cohesion and leadership, once the legitimate line of czars died out. Several pretenders, each claiming to be the son of Ivan the Terrible, only added to the confusion.

In this situation, merchants and townspeople, together with the leaders of the Orthodox church, played a critical role. The Poles were Catholic, and their invasion of Russia was partly a crusade to bring that land under the pope. In 1595 the pope agreed to permit the eastern churches to continue to conduct services in Church Slavonic and to keep some other peculiarities of ritual—making the sign of the cross with three fingers instead of two, for example. These concessions persuaded the high clergy of the Ukraine to accept the papal claim to headship of the entire Christian church. Those who followed them were known as Uniates, and the branch of the Roman Catholic church that thus came into existence was commonly referred to as the Uniate Church.

Russian national feeling, however, was deeply committed to the idea that the one true Orthodox Christian faith had found refuge in Russia after the fall of Constantinople. To admit that the pope's claims to rule the Church were right seemed a dreadful heresy to most Russians. Hence it was not difficult for the head of the Russian church, the patriarch of Moscow, to rally widespread popular feeling against the invaders. He was aided by the merchants and townspeople, who in turn rallied Ivan's new service nobility and peasant sentiment behind a movement to throw the Poles out and to reestablish a Russian czar to defend the true Orthodox faith.

In 1613 a national assembly representing different classes of the Russian state chose a new czar, Michael Romanov, the son of the patriarch of Moscow. Reorganized Russian forces soon drove back the Polish invaders and reestablished the autocracy. The Romanovs, like the Tokugawas, were cautious rulers and adopted a policy of keeping strangers at a distance, as far as possible. Japan could close itself off completely, being an island. Russia had more difficulty in isolating itself because of its long, open land frontiers. All the same, the first Romanovs reduced communication with the outside world. Foreign traders were required to live in special ghetto quarters in the towns, for example, and contact with them was reduced to a minimum.

Church Reform

But pressure from the west was unrelenting. In particular, Jesuit missionaries, who had been extremely successful in eliminating Protestantism from Poland, kept up a telling assault upon Orthodox "errors." The trouble was that the Russian church books were full of mistakes that had crept in through scribal errors of translation or of copying. Jesuit scholars delighted to point these out, and some of them were so obvious that they could scarcely be denied. Yet Russian clerics could not admit that the Jesuits were right without seeming to endanger their whole claim to Orthodoxy.

In 1667 a new and masterful patriarch, Nikon, decided to take the bull by the horns. He set out to revise the Russian prayer books and service manuals by going back to the Greek originals and correcting whatever errors had accumulated over the centuries. Since the Greek church was undeniably older than the Roman church, the appeal to Greek church books seemed like an effective reply to Catholic propaganda.

On the other hand, any change in the familiar phrases of the church services shocked many Russians. An important party, known as "Old Believers," refused to accept Nikon's reforms and, indeed, accused him of being Antichrist. The czar soon quarreled with Nikon, but even after deposing him, maintained the policy of church reform. What to do with those persons who refused to accept the revised forms of church ritual then became a serious problem. The czar resorted to persecution, but this simply drove religious dissent underground.

Communities of Old Believers spread over Russia and became particularly numerous in the fringe areas, where the power of the state was weak. Some groups developed extreme doctrines, expecting the end of the world at any minute and seeing in the acts of the czar fulfillment of the prophecies in the book of Revelation.

Costs and Gains of Russia's First Encounter with the West

Russian society thus came to be sharply divided. The upper class accepted the restored czardom and the revised forms of church worship. But they ruled over a "dark and deaf" peasantry who felt that their masters had betrayed true religion as well as elementary social justice. Peasant revolts expressed the anger of the lower class, but the uprisings always failed. Such experiences merely confirmed the Old Believers in thinking that Antichrist was on the march and that the end of the world was truly at hand. Expecting God to set right the injustice from which they suffered, they remained, for the most part, sullen but passive when Czar Peter the Great (ruled 1689–1725), undertook still another revolution from the top to bring Russia more fully into touch with the western European world. But since Peter did not begin his reform until 1698, we shall wait until a later chapter to consider his career and its importance for Russia and the world.

One point, however, deserves emphasis here. The very real and profound troubles that Russia had in coping with the west and in keeping the Poles and Swedes in check had the effect of making the Russians extremely successful in their dealings with the peoples to the south and east. Thus, the time when Russia's problems with the west were especially acute was also the time when the vast Russian Empire took shape. Siberia and the Russian Far East in the Amur Valley were occupied under the first Romanovs. Even more important, the Ukraine was annexed to Russia in 1667.

Russia in fact became, with China, the principal gainer from the gunpowder revolution that undermined the battle effectiveness of steppe cavalrymen. In 1689, after minor collisions in the Amur Valley, the two powers signed the Treaty of Nerchinsk, defining boundaries and regulating trade between them. By this treaty, a buffer zone, including Mongolia and the lands around the Ili River, was declared off limits for both China and Russia. But by thus delimiting the zone of nomad life, the two great agricultural empires of northern Asia were also signing the death warrant of independent nomad power.

However costly in themselves, Russia's troubles in adjusting inherited ways so as to repel western attacks therefore paid off handsomely across Russia's other frontiers.

THE NEW WORLD

The Amerindians, like the Russians, had to change their ways drastically between 1500 and 1700 to adjust to the presence and activity of western Europeans. Moreover, the gap between Amerindian and European society was too great to allow the inhabitants of the New World to gather the same kind of compensation that came to the Russians. Instead, wherever they came into close contact with Europeans, Amerindian communities suffered cruel disruption and soon lost all effective independence.

Spanish Empire in the Americas

In the most highly developed regions of the New World—Mexico and Peru—Spanish policy was to convert the Indians to Christianity but otherwise to leave the traditional institutions of their village communities in place. Nevertheless, as new diseases cut into the native population, the Spaniards and their descendants needed to use a large proportion of the remaining Indian manpower to keep their mines and other economic enterprises going. Ways were found of breaking into the Indian villages despite the legal protections that Spanish law gave the natives.

In particular, Indians might become debtors and then could legally be required to work off the debt. So, in practice, it was easy for Spanish ranchers to keep their Indians constantly in debt and thus assure themselves of a steady supply of labor. The mine owners had more difficulty, for their labor needs were much greater. Labor shortage, however, promoted labor-saving improvements. As a result, the Mexican mines became among the most technically advanced in the world. After about 1650 the tremendous destruction of population by disease came to a halt. But by then the population of central Mexico had been reduced from between 11 and 20 million persons to a mere 1.5 million. Recovery was slow at first, for death rates remained high.

Despite the drastic depletion of the Indian population, Spanish America, before 1700, became the seat of a flourishing provincial version of Spanish Catholic civilization. Mexico City and Lima were great cities by European standards—far larger and more impressive than anything yet established by English or French colonists. Universities were founded to train the priests and lawyers needed by the Spanish regime. The universities kept up close connections with the European world of learning and imported such novelties as the philosophical speculations of

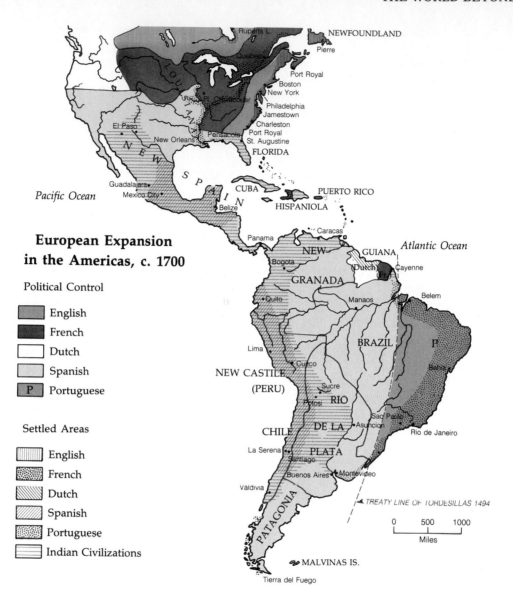

European Expansion in the Americas, c. 1700

Political Control

- English
- French
- Dutch
- Spanish
- P Portuguese

Settled Areas

- English
- French
- Dutch
- Spanish
- Portuguese
- Indian Civilizations

Descartes soon after they burst upon the European intellectual scene.

Not only were the Indians excluded from such activity, but their own cultural traditions were shattered beyond repair. Only simple village crafts—basketmaking, weaving, or the like—survived. Everything else disappeared with the overthrow of the priests and rulers who had governed the Amerindian civilizations. Thus, Spanish power and Spanish culture were secure and unchallenged in the New World, even though only a few persons of Spanish birth or descent shared in them fully.

Portuguese Brazil

In Brazil, the Portuguese settlers created a much more complicated and disorderly society by importing large numbers of slaves from Africa to work the sugar plantations, upon which the prosperity of the colony soon came to depend. Since few Portuguese women left home, Portuguese men married African or Indian wives and recognized their children as legitimate. A gradation of racial mixtures therefore emerged in Brazil that was more complex than the Spanish-Indian blend. Moreover, since the African slaves brought their own cultural traditions with them to the New World, African elements blended into the Indian and Portuguese cultural traditions to make the Brazilian heritage unique.

Brazil's political history was also more complex than the bureaucratic regularity that prevailed in the Spanish Empire. First the French and then the Dutch tried to take over Brazil, but they were driven out by the colonists themselves. A bold buccaneering spirit led the Brazilians to penetrate deep into the Amazon forests looking for slaves for the sugar mills and, later, also for gold and diamonds, which were discovered in the interior of the continent. Recurrent friction with Jesuit missionaries who controlled the Guarani Indians of Paraguay and with Spaniards who settled along the Rio de la Plata gave local bands of Brazilians an excuse to raid and plunder far and wide. By doing so they extended the boundaries of their colony at a rapid rate.

French and British Colonies in North America

By comparison with the Spanish Empire and even with Brazil, the British and French colonies in North America were still poor and undeveloped in 1700. Nowhere had settlement penetrated far from the coast. Colonial society was, for the most part, a crude, simplified version of the English and French model. Permanent settlement began at Jamestown in 1607 and at Quebec in the following year. But the infant colonies grew slowly at first. The easy wealth the first settlers expected was not to be found. Conditions were hard, food short, the climate unfamiliar. The arrival of religious dissenters (Puritans) in Massachusetts, beginning in 1620, added a new strain to the English settlement of the New World. The Puritans became a body of hard-working, disciplined people, ready to undertake the heavy labor of cultivating even the stony soils of New England.

Like the Spaniards, the French put great emphasis upon converting the Indians to Christianity and tried to protect them from unscrupulous traders. But European diseases proved fatal, even when communicated by well-meaning priests. As a result, only a few of the Indians of Canada and the northeastern United States survived contact with the strangers.

The French in Canada soon developed a profitable trade in furs. Explorers learned how to travel by canoe along the waterways of the continental interior. By going up the St. Lawrence River to the Great Lakes and then portaging from Lake Michigan to the Mississippi River, the French outflanked the English colonists, who were blocked from the deeper interior by the Appalachian Mountains. The government of New France (the possessions of France in North America) was closely controlled from Paris. Governors, appointed by the king, managed all important affairs.

The English colonies were much more varied. Virginia and Massachusetts had both been founded by companies chartered by the king of England. New York was acquired from the Dutch in 1664 by conquest, having, however, already been granted to the king's brother, the duke of York. Pennsylvania was founded on the strength of a royal grant to William Penn, and many of the other colonies started through grants to other proprietors.

Between 1640 and 1660, England was troubled by civil wars. In 1688 the mother country suffered another revolution and then plunged into European wars that lasted until 1714. During most of this time the colonies were allowed to go their own way with only occasional efforts at supervision from England. Moreover, efforts to centralize control in London met with strong local resistance. When the royal charters for Virginia and Massachusetts were canceled, for example, and governors were sent out from England to conduct the public affairs of the colonies, they found themselves face to face with representative assemblies whose members were used to running their own affairs. Hence nothing like the orderly dignity and systematic thoroughness of Spanish or even of French administration ever prevailed in the English colonies. Instead, they became a refuge for religious dissenters (Catholic, Quaker, and Puritan) as well as for other misfits of English society.

Relations with the Indians were left largely to local decision. The settlers early found that they could not make the Indians work for them.

They sometimes tried to treat the Indians fairly. William Penn was the chief exemplar of this policy. But in general, the settlers trampled on Indian rights and took what they wanted or could use without troubling themselves about what their actions might do to the Indians.

The fact was that the Indians could not defend themselves or make their wishes effective politically except by trying to play off the French against the English. Even with French guns and diplomatic encouragement, desperate acts of violence against the encroaching English could not restore Indian lands. Such attacks, however, convinced almost all the colonists that the Indians were cruel and dangerous enemies who could not be trusted.

Everywhere along the frontier where Indian communities were confronted by the newcomers, the Indians withered and drew back, unable to offer much resistance. Disease was always a factor. In addition, the Europeans had vastly superior knowledge and skills that put the Indians at a disadvantage they could never overcome.

AFRICA AND OCEANIA

The improvement of transportation, which resulted from the opening of the world's oceans by European explorers just before and immediately after 1500, meant that all the simpler societies of the earth that lay within easy reach of a coastline were in the same sort of danger as the Indians of North America. There were obstacles of distance which it took time to overcome, especially in the Pacific, where the smaller islands were, in general, not explored or disturbed by European sailors until after 1700. Australia, too, remained effectively isolated behind the Great Barrier Reef that made approach from the north difficult for sailing ships. The coastlands of the Arctic were but slightly disturbed by the activities of English traders in Hudson Bay (from 1670) or in the White Sea (from 1553). In these parts of the world, age-old hunting and collecting societies continued to live in their accustomed ways, without noticeable disturbance from outside.

Africa and the Slave Trade

The African continent was much more complicated. Ships could not penetrate far into Africa except along the Nile because rapids near the mouths of all the African rivers interrupted navigation. Even more important, tropical diseases like yellow fever, malaria, and sleeping sickness made it dangerous for outsiders to reside in sub-Saharan Africa. Local populations grew up exposed to these and other infections and developed resistances to them that newcomers lacked. Exactly the opposite condition prevailed in the Americas, where the native inhabitants lacked resistances to diseases Europeans and Africans brought into the New World and so suffered drastic die-offs in the first century and a half after contacts with the newcomers started.

This disease difference was fundamental to the history of Africa from earliest times. It meant that strangers and intruders from north of the Sahara could not take over from disease-experienced local inhabitants, even when the local peoples, to begin with, were less well organized and less well equipped than the outsiders. As a result, Africa remained African, in full charge of its own fate and pattern of historical development in a way that the Americas did not.

To be sure, the heavy disease burden carried by African populations was a handicap as well as a protection. People carrying malarial parasites in their bodies could not work as hard as healthy persons, for example, and productivity inevitably suffered. Nevertheless, by the time the Portuguese began to sail along the West African coast, West and East African kingdoms had about a thousand years of history behind them, and of course North Africa was the site of one of the earliest of all human civilizations in Egypt. In the rest of the continent, trade was intensifying, kingdoms were arising, and contacts with the outside world were increasing in the decades when the Portuguese were exploring the entire length of the west coast, 1418–1486.

After the Portuguese rounded Africa in 1499, their main attention was fastened on the fabled wealth of the Indies because the African coast had less to attract them. Nevertheless, they set up a series of shore stations (some on off-shore islands)

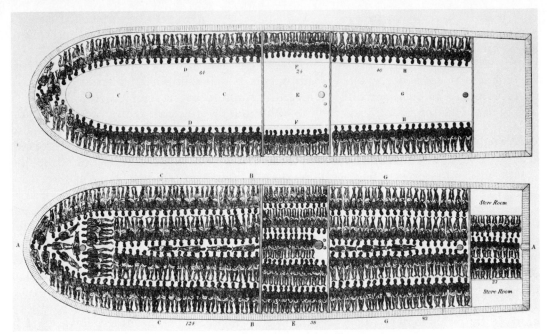

Slave Ship Plan This woodcut shows how African slaves were crammed onto the lower decks of specially designed vessels for crossing the Atlantic. Trade winds made sailing easy but crowded conditions such as these and the mingling of human beings on board from different parts of Africa, resulted in much disease and many deaths. Millions of Africans crossed the ocean between the 1520s, when the slave trade began, and the 1830s, when it was suppressed and all of them suffered under conditions like those illustrated here. In these centuries, African arrivals outnumbered European immigrants to the Americas by four or five to one. Moreover, well over half of the Europeans who crossed the ocean arrived as indentured servants, and were herded onto ships almost as brutally as were the African slaves. Obviously, the repopulation of the New World from the Old was carried through more by compulsion than by free choice.

where they traded with local peoples and tried to convert them to Christianity. This established a new cultural frontier of African-European encounter. It ran all the way from the Straits of Gibraltar to about half way up the east coast.

This new frontier supplemented a far older zone of encounter between Africans and Moslems. Even in Mohammed's lifetime (d. 632), converts to the new faith appeared in Africa as well as in Arabia proper. The whole of North Africa became an integral part of the realm of Islam by 700, and Moslem traders began to operate along the coast of East Africa at about the same time. In ensuing centuries, contacts between the Moslem world

and the African interior gradually increased in importance. A major landmark was the conquest of Ghana in West Africa by Moslems from Morocco in 1076. Thereafter the rulers of most of the West African kingdoms were Moslems, and trans-Saharan caravans maintained close connections between West Africa and the heartlands of the Moslem world.

Another powerful current of migration and cultural influence came across the open savanna lands that lie south of the Sahara. After the collapse of the Christian kingdoms of Nubia (1504), nomadic tribesmen, moving from east to west, brought the grasslands firmly under Moslem control, all the way from the Horn of Africa to the Atlantic coast. By contrast, the savanna lands of East Africa remained beyond the reach of Moslem traders and conquerors, partly because the tsetse fly and the sleeping sickness it carried created very effective barriers to penetration from the coast. Beyond the range of the tsetse fly, at Zimbabwe in southern Africa, powerful kingdoms arose after about 1100. The rulers of Zimbabwe exported gold and ivory to Moslem cities on the east coast but, unlike the situation in West Africa, retained their own pagan religion.

Elsewhere in the interior of Africa far less is known about the rise of states and of the trade and warfare that supported royal courts and officials. Yet when the Portuguese showed up at the mouth of the Congo River in 1483, they discovered several powerful kingdoms in the region, some of which were probably of quite recent creation. Further south, racially different peoples called San (Bushmen) and Khoikhoi (Hottentots) followed hunting and pastoral ways of life. They had been in retreat before the advance of Bantu-speaking black Africans for many centuries. The Bantus were farmers and herders and knew how to make iron tools. Some of them had become skilled miners as well and could build impressive stone fortifications, as they did at Zimbabwe.

During the early centuries of Africa's contacts with the outside world, the continent was famous for its exports of gold, ivory, salt, and slaves. But it was the slave trade that flourished most vigorously after 1500 and became indelibly associated with Africa in European (and American) consciousness. The trade was very old. Black Africans were valued as household servants throughout the Moslem world, sometimes holding key posts—for example, as guardians of the Ottoman sultan's harem. But African slavery took on new scale and significance in the course of the sixteenth century when European settlers in the New World discovered how to grow sugar in Brazil and the Caribbean Islands. Sugar required heavy labor for harvesting and processing the juice of the canes into crystalline form for transport to distant markets. The vulnerability of Amerindians to European diseases meant that efforts to compel them to work on sugar plantations were destined to failure. But Africans were inured

to diseases and proved to be far more resistant than Europeans, who could not easily endure the tropical infections that soon crossed the Atlantic from Africa. As a result, beginning in the 1520s, Europeans began to import African slaves to work on sugar plantations in the New World.

Numbers were small at first, but with each passing decade the scale of sugar production and the numbers of Africans brought across the ocean to labor in the New World increased. In time, the majority of the inhabitants of the Caribbean Islands and of the sugar-growing regions of Brazil came to be descendants of black Africans who had come to the New World as slaves. Later, tobacco and cotton planters on the mainland of North America also started to rely on black slave labor, bringing a substantial black population into the southern British colonies. The trans-Atlantic slave trade therefore carried African populations to vast new regions of the earth, in tandem with the expansion of European settlement across the ocean.

African slaves in the New World were always baptized to make them Christians, since saving souls was one justification Europeans used to defend the slave trade from its critics. But baptism could not erase the cultural heritages the slaves brought with them. Consequently, African as well as European and Amerindian heritages entered into the mix of cultures and peoples that arose in the Americas after 1492.

In sub-Saharan Africa itself, the effect of the slave trade was sometimes destructive. Raiders, often based in coastal cities, penetrated far inland seeking captives, and many of their victims died in chains while traveling to the coast or on shipboard afterward. Slave raiders ravaged innumerable villages and brought previously isolated communities into sudden contact with the outside world. But for the continent as a whole there is no reason to think that depopulation resulted, even though perhaps as many as 1.9 million Africans had been shipped away as slaves by 1700. (Incidentally, the export of slaves to the Moslem world also seems to have increased after 1500. In Moslem lands, however, household slaves were not allowed to marry and have children, and so they failed to establish a black population like that which arose in the New World.)

One reason why the mounting intensity of the slave trade did not reduce African populations was that new crops from America allowed African farmers to raise more food than before. Maize was by far the most valuable of the new crops, and it eventually became a staple of African agriculture, although peanuts and sweet potatoes were also important, especially in West Africa. No one knows for sure just when the new crops spread from the coastlands to the interior, and it is quite impossible to balance the growth of population permitted by the increased food supply against the losses of the slave trade. All one can say is that the spread of the more productive American food crops tended to sustain African populations at the same time that slave raiders were destroying it. One therefore counteracted the other, allowing the various African peoples to survive and maintain their own ways of life in the general context of an increasingly militarized and commercialized society.

Since Europeans (and Asians) could not long survive in the African interior owing to their vulnerability to tropical diseases, the actual conduct of the slave trade remained always in African hands. Rulers and merchants imported cloth, iron, and guns from Europe in exchange for slaves. Access to guns transformed the prevailing techniques of African warfare and slave raiding, although old-fashioned armored cavalry long survived, partly for ceremonial reasons, at a court like that of Oyo in what is today western Nigeria.

The various states and peoples who thus entered more and more vigorously into the expanding trade nets that criss-crossed the continent maintained traditions and skills unique to Africa. Even those who became Moslem or Christian retained local customs that marked them off from the rest of the world. African art is the most obvious evidence of the continuity of local traditions and skills. Masks and sculpture, presenting distorted haunting images of human and animal forms, had religious and ceremonial uses that cannot be shared by modern museum-goers; but this does not prevent such objects from arousing a powerful aesthetic response. Styles varied greatly in pagan Africa and merged into standard forms of Islamic art in those parts of Africa most firmly attached to the Moslem world. This reflects the fact that by 1500 North Africa, the savanna lands of West Africa, and the coasts of East Africa were well established parts of the world of Islam. Moslem traders regularly doubled as missionaries of their faith; and as trade connections multiplied, conversions to Islam continued to occur over wide regions of the continent. By comparison, efforts of Christian missionaries met with rather modest success, although they, too, made some converts close to the western coasts where European influence concentrated.

Only in the extreme north and south of the continent, where cooler climates inhibited tropical diseases, did European settlement prove viable. As a result, when the Dutch established a shore station at Cape Town at the southernmost tip of Africa in 1652, it took root and eventually began to flourish. By 1700 Dutch farmers and herders had begun to move inland, displacing local Khoikhoi pastorialists by force. Elsewhere the population of Africa remained entirely African until French settlers started to establish themselves in Algeria after 1830.

Overall, between 1500 and 1700 Africa began both to enjoy and to suffer from its growingly intimate contact with the rest of the world. After the European voyages of discovery, Africans in effect found themselves caught between an expanding Moslem world to the north and east and an expanding European-managed world in the Americas and the Indian Ocean. Beginning about 1520 the trans-Atlantic slave trade carried large black populations to the tropical and subtropical parts of the Americas. In Africa itself, during the next two centuries, long-distance contacts multiplied, social change accelerated, American food crops transformed agriculture, and the expansion of Islam continued. Africa, of course, had never been entirely isolated from the rest of the world, but after 1500 it was bound more and more closely into a worldwide economic system. Yet, protected by tropical diseases, African peoples remained in charge of their own affairs, building kingdoms, conducting trade, and dealing with outsiders pretty much on their own terms. Africa, in short, remained fully and uniquely itself, whereas the Americas, owing to their new trans-Atlantic immigrant populations, experienced drastic demographic and cultural discontinuity.

CONCLUSION

The appearance of European sailors, soldiers, and settlers in the Americas disrupted and, in time, destroyed the earlier Amerindian societies. Nowhere else, however, did the opening of the oceans to European ships have anything like such drastic consequences. In the civilized ports of Asia, mixing of peoples from different parts of the world was already quite familiar. European skills and knowledge did not persuade Moslems, Hindus, or Chinese to abandon familiar ways. There seemed to be no good reason why the Asians should not cling to what seemed good to them and leave the Europeans to do the same.

Yet the world did not stand still. The opening of the oceans led to the spread of American food crops, to population increase, and to a price revolution that affected all the civilized world, as we saw in Chapter 1. These changes had long-range consequences of the greatest importance. Within the 200 years from 1500 to 1700 another fundamental change took place within the Eurasian continent, when the age-old superiority of cavalry to infantry came to an end. This was the result of the development of guns and muskets, which allowed foot soldiers to fire volleys that could break up an ordinary cavalry charge.

In Eurasia, consequently, the advantages that steppe nomads had enjoyed ever since about 700 B.C., when attacking farming peoples, ceased to exist. Rapid expansion of civilized control over the steppe regions resulted. Nevertheless, before that happened both India and China underwent one final conquest from the steppes. In India the conquest led to the establishment of the Mogul Empire, beginning in 1526, and in China to the establishment of the Manchu Dynasty that ruled from 1644 to 1912.

The development of guns and muskets also meant, in all civilized countries, that central governments had growing advantages over more local authorities. Cannon could knock holes even in well-defended castles and city walls. But siege guns were expensive and conspicuous, which made it easy for a central authority to monopolize them. Local leaders, accordingly, had to submit far more completely than had been customary.

Everywhere in the civilized world, therefore, the size of political units and the effectiveness with which a single ruler could impose his will on distant parts increased sharply between 1500 and 1700. Almost all the buffer zones between the separate civilized communities of Eurasia were rapidly gobbled up by one or another civilized government. Russia and China were the two powers that gained most from this situation; their territorial expansion in fact paralleled Spain's empire-building in the Americas both in time and geographic scale.

Improved communication among all the coastlines of the world increased the pace of social change everywhere. Many small and weak communities disappeared completely. In fact, only in Africa (and perhaps in New Zealand) were local peoples able to withstand and, in time, react successfully to the challenges that sudden exposure to alien styles of civilization presented to previously isolated peoples.

These changes in world relationships were fundamental and vastly important for human history. Yet it would be wrong to emphasize the novelties too much. Each of the major civilized traditions of the Old World continued along familiar and well-worn paths. Moslems continued to win converts along almost every frontier. Hindus underwent a religious revival that assured the continued vitality of that cultural tradition despite political subjection to Moslem rulers. The Chinese underwent the crisis of going from the rule of one dynasty to another in a completely traditional fashion. They did so rather more quickly and painlessly than had often been the case in earlier centuries and emerged so strong and prosperous as to arouse the admiration of many Europeans when they learned how the Chinese governed their "Celestial Empire."

The western European world, to be sure, showed signs of its growing expansive power. European settlement of the Americas began to make inroads upon the continental vastnesses of North and South America. Until long after 1700, most of the New World was not occupied by settlers of European origin; but it was clear enough, all the same, that Amerindian populations could not stop westward expansion across North America, nor prevent occupation of the temperate parts of South America.

On Europe's eastern flank, Russia became more and more closely tied to the west. The relationship irritated the Russians, for they wished to keep their Orthodox faith and defend their cultural independence from western Europe. But they did so by borrowing western skills, importing western workers, and becoming more like the western nations of Europe. Russia's experience between 1500 and 1700 was thus a foretaste of the dilemmas other civilized peoples confronted later on when Europe's power compelled Moslems, Indians, Chinese, and Japanese to pay attention to what had happened in that remote peninsula of Asia called Europe.

The Use of Plants and Animals in Agriculture

SLASH AND BURN

For slash-and-burn farmers, leafy forests are the only kind of terrain suitable for farming. They slash the bark to kill the trees; a few years later they burn the dead tree trunks and branches and use the ashes as a fertilizer. Slash-and-burn methods were first used in the Middle East before 7000 B.C.

1. For this kind of agriculture, farmers used land with thick and leafy forest growing on it. Such land produced a good grain crop.

2. To kill the trees, farmers slashed the bark all around the tree trunk. Sunlight reached the ground, filtering through the dead trunks.

3. Farmers raked away dried leaves to expose soft loam underneath. They scattered seeds on the loam and covered these with loose soil.

4. At first no competing plants existed in newly cleared forest patches, so only desired food-producing grasses could grow.

5. When the grain ripened, farmers harvested it with sickles and stored seeds in jars or baskets.

6. After a few years of cultivation in this way, farmers burned the dead tree trunks and scattered the ashes as fertilizer.

7. Each year more airborne seeds came onto the cleared land. These grew into plants that competed with planted seeds, until a satisfactory crop could no longer be raised.

8. Slash-and-burn farmers then moved on and found a new patch of forest land where they could repeat the whole cycle.

Crops   Wild grain reseeds itself by allowing the ripe kernels to break off from the spike and fall to the ground. When people began to harvest grain, only kernels with tougher spikes could reach the storage area without being shaken to the ground and lost. And only kernels that reached the storage area were available for seed next season. This meant a very rapid seed selection for kernels that had tough spikes. New types of grain arose with spikes so tough that they could not seed themselves without human help. People, too, soon came to depend on these kinds of grains for food.

Highlights   The significance of slash-and-burn agriculture is that

> Human beings brought seed-bearing grasses into regions in which they did not naturally grow and eliminated the mixture of plants found in nature.
>
> Slash-and-burn farmers created food for themselves instead of finding or killing what grew naturally, as hunters did.
>
> A new interdependence arose as human communities came to depend on plants, while the plants in question came to depend on human action for their biological existence.

IRRIGATION

Irrigation is the process of channeling water onto dry land to make arid soil fertile. This was the basis for Middle Eastern river valley civilizations along the Tigris-Euphrates, Nile, and Indus rivers, beginning 3500–2500 B.C.

1. Rivers, like the Tigris and Euphrates, that start in high mountains and flow through plains cut into the land in their upper reaches but drop gravel, sand, and silt as they flow more slowly across the plains.

2. In spring the river floods; and as it rises above its normal banks, it widens out, flows more slowly, and leaves large deposits at the edges of its usual bed. This creates natural levees.

3. When the flood subsides, the river returns to its bed, trapped between the levees. It continues to deposit gravel and sand. In time, therefore, it flows above the level of the surrounding plain.

4. When the flood subsides, stagnant water lies in shallow pools and swamps outside the levee on both sides of the river. As the year

passes, these swampy pools evaporate until the annual flood comes to fill them again.

5. When the swamp water gets low, a channel cut through the natural levee can allow river water to reach the lower land lying on each side of the stream.

6. With construction of bigger channels, diked on each side to direct the flow of water, wide regions can be irrigated by following the contour of the land downstream. This is known as arterial irrigation.

7. Irrigation along the Nile differs. The lower Nile carries only fine silt which sinks too slowly to form natural levees.

8. The Nile flood comes slowly and gently, so that dikes can channel the flow of water onto the land and from field to field. This is called basin irrigation.

Highlights The use of irrigation is important because

As long as floods occurred, the same fields could be cultivated year after year. Comparatively large populations could then live in a relatively small space.

The operation of an arterial irrigation system required much human labor for construction and maintenance. Centralized control and planning were needed as canals became longer and deeper and irrigated more land.

Massed human labor, responding to centralized organization, created the material basis for the first civilizations.

FIELD AND FALLOW

Field and fallow is a method of farming in which a piece of land is plowed and sown with seed during one growing season, then plowed and allowed to remain idle during the next. It was probably first developed in Middle Eastern river valleys a little before 3000 B.C.

1. Field-and-fallow farmers used animals to pull a simple plow through the soil. This allowed them to cultivate more ground than when human muscles alone supplied digging power.

2. This method effectively kept down weeds by plowing the fallow field in summer time, killing competing plants before they formed seeds.

3. As a result, the former grain field, left fallow, was cleared of weeds by being plowed.

4. By plowing and planting the grain field at the start of the growing season, then plowing the fallow field, then harvesting the ripened grain, labor was spread more evenly through the year.

Crops and Draft Animals The main crops of early field-and-fallow farming were the same as for slash-and-burn: wheat and barley. The big change was the use of animal power. Castrated bulls, called oxen, were used for plowing because of their strength and tameness, acquired at the expense of their normal biological power of reproduction. (Compare this to changes in domesticated grain crops.) Oxen also had horns to which it was easy to attach a simple plow.

The scratch plow had three essential

Slash and burn agriculture, Venezuela.

parts: a beam or rope which attached the plow to the oxen, a share that dragged through the soil, and a handle which plowmen used to "steer" the share through the soil. The scratch plow had to be light enough for a man to steer, so it did not work well in heavy clay soil.

Highlights   The field-and-fallow style of farming meant that

> Effective weed control and cultivation of more land allowed an ordinary farmer to harvest more grain than his family could eat.
>
> This surplus grain could support a class which did not produce its own food but worked at other things. Such specialists created the earliest civilizations.
>
> Farming had been women's work until the invention of the plow brought men into the fields with their animals. This made men, as in the hunting days, the main providers of food within families and assured male dominance in society at large.

VEGETATIVE ROOT

In vegetative root farming, roots were cultivated for food, sometimes on flooded areas of land. Vegetative root agriculture probably began somewhere in southeast Asia. The date of origin is quite uncertain. It may have begun as early as 13,000–9000 B.C., before slash-and-burn agriculture got started.

1. Vegetative root farming probably started near the edge of rivers or lakes where fishermen had settled in permanent villages.
2. A live shoot from the parent plant was partly buried in the moist or flooded ground so that it would take root.
3. In tropical climates all stages of growth may be found on a single patch of land at any given time.

Crops   Many different kinds of crops were grown in vegetative root agriculture. Taros, yams, and manioc have large tuberous roots that store large amounts of starch. They were cultivated very early because they were easy to use. A single root makes a meal for two or three people. Such roots can be fried, boiled, or baked. They can also be made into a soup, a paste, or a cake; and manioc is processed to produce tapioca.

Highlights   Vegetative root farming is significant because

> Vegetative root agriculture solved the weed problem by raising a few individually large plants. Weeds could simply be pulled out by hand.
>
> Since staple root crops provide mostly starch, fish or some other food source was necessary for the human diet.
>
> This type of cultivation flourished mainly in tropical climates where plants can ripen at all times of the year, since the roots are not easily stored.

RICE PADDY

Rice paddy cultivation requires the land to be under water while the rice plants grow, but at harvest time fields are drained dry. This procedure causes competing plants to be either drowned or baked out, thus keeping weeds down. Rice paddy cultivation began somewhere in China or southeast Asia, perhaps about 3000–2500 B.C.

1. Since rice paddy land must be perfectly level, farmers have to cut down the higher portion and fill in lower parts of a field until water will stand at a uniform depth.
2. Only regulated amounts of water are wanted on the field. A rice paddy must therefore be surrounded by waterproof dikes with sluices and channels to control water flow.
3. After this preparation, fields are plowed and planted with seedlings sprouted in a special nursery. The water which flows gently into the fields prevents the growth of weeds that live on land, carries dissolved minerals, and supports a complex interaction of organisms that keep the soil fertile.

4. When the rice is ready to ripen, the farmer stops the water from flowing into the paddy, and it dries out. This kills weeds that flourish in water.

5. The rice is harvested with sickles; and if water remains available, a second crop of rice can be planted in the same growing season.

Crops   Rice has the enormous advantage of producing more food per acre than any other crop, particularly when double-cropping is possible. This allows a very dense population to come into existence. The high food yield from rice paddies, in turn, supports the abundant labor force needed to construct and maintain paddy fields with the elaborate conduit system that brings water into fields and keeps it there as long as it is needed. The rice plant requires a mean temperature of 70° F., a good deal warmer than wheat.

Highlights   The importance of the rice paddy is that

The alternation between flooding and draining achieves both weed control and fertilization of the soil.

The labor required to build rice paddies ties the farmers to the land permanently. Nowhere else can they hope to secure as much food for their labor.

Dense population depending on rice paddy cultivation can be compelled to support distant governments, since farmers cannot leave the land nor hide the harvest from tax collectors. This makes state-building easy.

MOLDBOARD PLOW

The moldboard plow turns the soil over in furrows instead of merely breaking it up into loose bits as the scratch plow does. The moldboard plow came into existence in the moist climate of northwestern Europe about A.D. 100; but it came into general use slowly, between A.D. 500 and 1000.

An Egyptian shadoof for irrigation.

Harvesting flax.

1. **Construction of the Moldboard Plow.** The moldboard plow has a share and a beam essentially the same as the scratch plow.

Two new parts were added to this. A colter that slices vertically through the earth from above runs just ahead of the tip of the share. A moldboard, lying behind the share, turns the furrow, cut from the earth by the combined action of the colter and plowshare.

2. Use of the Moldboard Plow. Four to six oxen were needed to pull the moldboard plow, and such a team cannot turn quickly or easily. Long, narrow fields were, therefore, the only efficient shape for cultivation.

The moldboard turns the furrow to one side only. As the plow comes and goes the length of the field, it turns the slices toward a center furrow, or ridge.

On a field plowed year after year in the same way, this builds up ridges in the centers and makes shallow ditches called balks on each side. The plow thus creates a drainage system on flat, water-logged fields.

Highlights   The moldboard plow changed farming methods because

Moldboard plow agriculture opened the flat, abundantly watered plains of northwestern Europe to cultivation on a large scale for the first time.

With the moldboard plow, a rotating three-field system with winter crop, spring crop, and fallow could be used. In northwestern Europe, the soil could be plowed with the moldboard plow at any time of the year. A single farmer could therefore cultivate more land and raise more food than in lands where plowing was seasonal. This helps to account for the rapid rise of Latin Christendom after A.D. 1000.

ELIMINATION OF FALLOW

Between 1600 and 1750, Dutch and English farmers discovered that they could plant certain valuable new crops on land previously left fallow, and still keep down weeds or even increase and improve the soil's fertility. These new crops were used mainly for animal feed.

1. One way to use the fallow productively was to plant a fast-sprouting cover crop, like clo-

ver, alfalfa, or vetch, that can get started early in the growing season and smother competing plants.

2. A second way of using fallow was to plant crops in rows, and then cultivate between the rows often enough to destroy weeds.

3. Agricultural "improvers" used manure and other materials to fertilize their fields: chalk, lime, seaweed, ashes, even soot and sometimes sand were tried with good results.

Crops   New crops came into use with the elimination of fallow. Nitrogen-fixing bacteria flourish in the roots of clover, alfalfa, and vetch. When the top part of these plants had been used for cattle food, the roots remained with

Two photos showing rice cultivation in Java.

extra nitrogen that the bacterial action had taken from the air and made into plant protein. This assured a noticeable improvement in the field's fertility. Turnips were the most important row crop; cabbages, beets, and later potatoes were also raised in this way.

Highlights   The elimination of fallow meant that

> The new crops, suitable for fields formerly left fallow, were mainly used for animal feed. This allowed a vast increase in pigs, cattle, and sheep and an improvement of the human diet.
>
> The nitrogen-fixing crops incidentally improved fertility for grain raising, thus increasing cereal yields also.
>
> With more and better fodder, farmers could develop specialized breeds of dairy, meat, and draft animals.

SCIENTIFIC AGRICULTURE

During the nineteenth century, the application of science and technology to agriculture became conscious and widespread. From western Europe and North America, scientific efforts to improve agriculture spread throughout the world.

Crops and Farming Methods   Fertilizers and food additives supply chemicals needed for plant and animal growth. A German professor, Justus von Liebig (1803–1873) was the first to analyze plants chemically and experiment with artificial fertilizers. Scientific study of animal nutrition began only in the twentieth century with the discovery of vitamins.

Geneticists can alter plants and animals to suit human uses. Mendelian theories of inheritance (named after Gregor Mendel, whose ideas were published in 1866 but forgotten until 1900) enabled experimenters to create strains of hybrid corn in the 1920s that greatly increased U.S. farm yields. In the 1960s other experimenters invented new kinds of rice, giv-

ing Asians a chance to increase their food production very greatly.

Machinery allows farmers to plow, plant, and harvest large areas quickly. Farmers had always used simple machines, from the digging stick on up. But only with the industrial revolution could big, complicated, factory-made machinery come to the fields. The first practically successful factory-made farm machine was the McCormick reaper, patented in 1834.

Food storage and distribution were also altered by the application of science. Canning depends on heat to sterilize food and prevent decay. It was discovered in France in 1809, but

The moldboard plow at work. An illumination from the Duc de Berry's *Book of Hours*.

came into common use in the United States only with the Civil War, 1861–1865. Freezing, another important method of preserving food, became common after World War II.

Highlights　　The significance of scientific agriculture is that

> Fewer hands produce more food in less time. As a result, in the parts of the world where scientific agriculture has spread, most people eat food produced by others. Until about 100 years ago, most human beings worked as farmers. Now a majority live in cities and work at other tasks.

AMERICAN CROP MIGRATION

With the opening of the world's oceans to shipping (1500–1600), the Old World received several important new food crops from recently discovered lands.

Maize　　The center for early domestication was probably in Mexico and Central America. Corn was taken to Europe by Spanish explorers in the sixteenth century, and from there it reached the Middle East. The Portuguese are credited with introducing corn into Africa and India. Magellan is supposed to have brought it to the East Indies via the Pacific Ocean.

Potatoes　　Potatoes were native to the Andes in South America and were first domesticated by the ancient Peruvians. They were introduced into Europe twice: first by Spanish sailors and a second time by Sir Francis Drake after his circumnavigation of the globe in 1580. From western Europe, potatoes were introduced to the North American colonies, central and eastern Europe, and the Middle East. As was the case with corn, the potato came to Africa with the Portuguese and to southeast Asia and China by way of the Pacific.

Sweet Potatoes　　Sweet potatoes probably originated as a cultivated crop in the Caribbean region. Spanish explorers brought them back to Europe before white potatoes arrived from the more distant coasts of Peru. Sweet potatoes never became very important in Europe. But in southern China, the sweet potato, introduced across the Pacific in the sixteenth century, became a crop of basic importance. In parts of Africa, too, sweet potatoes rivaled corn in importance.

EURASIAN CROP MIGRATION

As food crops were introduced into Europe, Asia, and Africa from the New World, the crops and agricultural methods of the Old World also spread to the newly explored areas.

In many parts of the world, European settlers brought with them the equipment of agriculture that was familiar to them in their homelands. They simply displaced the peoples they found living there, as in most of North America and in Australia.

In some parts of the world, however, older forms of agriculture were little affected by the skills and knowledge that opening the oceans diffused around the world. This was the case with rice paddy cultivation, which continued unchanged and spread slowly in southeast Asia and to some Pacific islands.

In between were regions where new crops or domesticated animals radically altered older lifestyles. An example was the rise of Plains Indian cultures in North America after they learned to use the horse, introduced by Spaniards.

The American and Eurasian crop migration had several effects:

> Efficient crops and techniques of cultivation spread all around the globe into vast new regions climatically suited to them.

> Human food supplies increased in amount and in many places there was an improvement in quality as well.

> The diffusion of agricultural techniques caused by regular oceanic movements of people, plants, and ideas tended to equalize the level of development within each climate zone all around the globe.

The Harvesters, by Pieter Brueghel. (Metropolitan Museum of Art, Rogers Fund, 1919)

Modern harvesting done by machine.

Chapter 18

EUROPE'S OLD REGIME
1650 to 1789

Between 1648, when the Peace of Westphalia ended the Thirty Years' War, and 1789, when the French Revolution began, Europe passed through a period of calm. But it was a calm and quiet time only by comparison with the storms that had gone before and those that came after. Wars did not cease, but they were conducted by professional armies with a decent respect for the fact that an enemy province might change hands at the peace table—and who wanted to acquire a smoking ruin? Challenging new ideas did not cease to arise in Europe; but they were advanced by professional writers and scientists who did not feel they had to go out and make their ideas come true, without delay, in the way the religious reformers of an earlier age and the political reformers of the age that was to come tried to do.

It was an age of moderation and compromise. People agreed to disagree on many matters and found, somewhat to their surprise, that they could do so and still get along with one another. An elaborate code of manners made this possible by cushioning collisions among individuals and between classes. Good manners often required men and women to disguise their feelings and betray their private characters by acting out a role. But individuals did in some degree become what they pretended to be—noble king or humble servant as the case might be; and the web of pretenses imposed by good manners did smooth over difficulties and helped to keep violence in check.

The restless energies that had helped to tear Europe apart in the age of religious wars was turned outward. The result was an enormous expansion of European empires in the Americas, in India, and throughout the forest and steppe zones of Eurasia. What had been a strictly west European civilization ceased to be so, when both Russian nobles and American settlers in the foothills of the Appalachians came to share the culture and tradition that continued to have its center and main focus in northwestern Europe. European civilization, in short, became Western civilization, no longer tied to its original geographical cradleland.

Calm did not involve inactivity or the end of rapid change. It meant, instead, that innumerable small groups of professionals were able to go ahead and work along their own lines without bothering too much about how their ideas or actions would fit into the overall picture. Intellectual pace-setters gave up the effort to find an absolute, universal truth and to fit the whole of society into its mold. This had been the great ambition of the Reformation age; but after about 1650 people more and more gave up the attempt, having seen too much violence and cruelty mobilized in the name of too many kinds of religious doctrines, each claiming to be the one and only truth.

Kings and princes organized violence more effectively than ever before by maintaining professional standing armies. Most rulers claimed absolute power within their frontiers. But so-called absolute monarchs faced all sorts of practical limits to their power. Many local groups possessed traditional rights and privileges that had come down from medieval times. In addition, the soldiers and officials, who made royal absolutism effective, acquired a vested interest in maintaining their own special rights and roles. As such they resisted unwanted changes, even when those changes were decreed by a ruler who in theory held absolute power.

Absolutism was also counterbalanced by the development of communication networks that ran across political boundaries among people with similar interests or pursuits. Priests, bankers, and merchants had maintained such networks for centuries. What happened during the Old Regime was that scientists, writers, musicians, agriculturists, and others developed regular means of exchanging professional information about new discoveries and achievements. Thus, by one of the contradictory compromises characteristic of the Old Regime, Europe was divided into hundreds of separate states, each in theory completely independent of all the others. Yet it was also more united in matters of culture than before (when religious barriers had divided Europe into hostile parts) or after (when national differences did the same).

SOCIAL AND ECONOMIC CHANGES

Europe met with extraordinary success under the Old Regime. This showed up most dramatically in the way European settlers, merchants, and monarchs extended their reach into new regions of the earth. Expansion abroad was matched at home by stepping up the pace and intensity of economic activity so that larger populations lived better at the end of the Old Regime than at its beginning and had some important new commodities at their disposal.

Population Growth

Population growth was fundamental. In the eighteenth century every part of Europe began to undergo such growth. Epidemic diseases became less common and less severe. The last important outbreak of bubonic plague in Europe raged sporadically between 1663 and 1684. Thereafter, one of the factors that in earlier times had kept down population ceased to affect western Europe, and the modern population explosion started, averaging a growth rate of about 1 percent per year.

Medical science had little to do with the first stages of this change, for doctors knew too little about the causes of disease to be very effective in stopping it. Quarantine of ships and of travelers from foreign parts may have been helpful sometimes (although often the fleas or rats or other carriers of disease were left alone because no one knew they were dangerous). Not until 1796 was the first successful inoculation against smallpox discovered by an English doctor, Edward Jenner (1749–1823); and several decades passed before his idea of deliberately infecting people with a weak form of the disease became an accepted practice.

The Agricultural Revolution

Improved methods of agriculture were more important than medical science in forwarding population growth. Two valuable American food crops, potatoes and maize, slowly but surely came into their own in Europe during the Old Regime. Maize became important in southeastern Europe; potatoes in the north and west, where cooler climate and sandy soils were particularly favorable to them. In such regions, potatoes could produce nearly four times as many calories per acre as oats or rye, the only cereals that would ripen in Europe's less favored regions. Nearly four times as many people could therefore find nourishment by eating potatoes instead of oatmeal or rye bread. Only in Ireland did an almost total shift occur. Elsewhere, potatoes and maize supplemented bread in a significant way, but never entirely drove the older staples from the diet of even the poorest classes.

In addition to new crops for human nourishment, European farmers learned how to farm much more efficiently. By planting clover, alfalfa, or hay on grainfields, it became possible to do without fallowing. In medieval times, about a third of the arable land had to be left fallow each year to allow the extermination of weeds and recovery of fertility after two successive crops of grain. But by planting such fields with clover or alfalfa, the soil was restored, thanks to the activity of nitrogen-fixing bacteria that infest the roots of these plants; and at the same time, good winter fodder for horses and cows could be produced.

Better winter food meant larger and stronger animals. Improved plows, carefully designed to do the work with the least effort, could be pulled by a single team of horses, where four to six oxen had been needed in medieval times. Another crop, turnips, when planted in rows, allowed a careful farmer to cultivate his land repeatedly during the growing season and thus cut down on weeds while still getting a valuable fodder crop from the land. Drainage and flood control works, systematic experiment with a wide variety of fertilizers, and improved designs for such things as farm wagons, scythes, spades, and plows all increased yields or reduced the cost of production. In either case, the effect was to create a larger food supply with which the growing city populations could be fed.

Significance of Agricultural Advances   Holland and England were in the forefront of agricultural improvement. Other parts of Europe lagged behind, and in some regions there was almost no change at all. Nevertheless, the agricultural improvers of the seventeenth and eighteenth centuries showed that great increases in yields and profits could be secured by using new methods, new crops, and new implements of cultivation. Improving farmers pioneered the idea of systematic experimentation. They tested results by keeping accurate records of how much seed, how much labor, and how much yield per acre were involved in using a new technique. And they communicated their results to other interested landowners through agricultural journals and newsletters, so that any really valuable discovery could spread rapidly and widely.

Always before, agriculture had been in the hands of persons who assumed that what their predecessors had done was the only way things could be done. Disproving this notion was one of the most fundamental breakthroughs of modern times. Simple as it may seem today, the idea that farming methods could be improved directly challenged age-old ways of life that tied the overwhelming majority of humankind to a fixed routine. And when a majority of the members of any society begin to alter their ways in important respects, then the scope and pace of historical change may enormously increase. This, of course, is exactly what has happened in modern times.

Looking backward, it is clear that an agricultural revolution had to come ahead of the better-known Industrial Revolution, which has been reshaping European and world society during the past 200 years. Without far-reaching changes on the land, Europe's industrial development could not have advanced as it did; for the Industrial Revolution required both food and labor to come from the countryside—and in ever-growing quantities. What permitted this to happen was the systematic application of the experimental method to techniques of farming, pioneered by a few hundred improving farmers, landlords, and scientists in England and Holland, beginning soon after 1650.

Trade and Finance

Growing populations and improved agriculture sustained and were, in turn, sustained by a rising curve of commerce. Important improvements in transportation made it easier to carry goods to market. Canals, for example, linked the major rivers of France. All-weather roads, smooth enough to allow wheeled vehicles to pass at any time of year, came slowly into existence as road builders learned how to drain the roadbed, cover the surface with gravel, and fill in holes before they got too big. Regular stagecoach connections between major cities were established so that anyone able to pay the price could travel scores or hundreds of miles at will and be more or less sure of arriving on schedule. The net importance of these improvements is difficult for us to imagine. But if you try to think of what life would be like without wintertime roads and without public transportation, the significance of these improvements for everyday life will become apparent.

Trade and commerce and all other economic enterprise were also stimulated by improvements in banking methods. Devices were found for assembling larger and larger quantities of capital. This capital was used to organize larger and more expensive undertakings. The effect was to allow Europeans to mobilize goods and manpower for common enterprises on an ever-larger scale. War was always their biggest undertaking; and Europeans learned how to fight wars on credit, thereby mobilizing more and more of their resources in the pursuit of victory and empire.

The Idea of a National Debt   The decisive invention here was the concept of a national debt. Until about 1700, bankers and rulers tended to treat government borrowing as the personal debt of the reigning monarch. The new king or prince did not always feel obliged to pay off what his predecessor had borrowed. High interest rates were one consequence, and lending money to rulers remained a highly speculative business. In England, however, as we shall soon see, the king's powers over government were sharply reduced after 1689; and succession to the throne passed from one Stuart heir to another until it lodged in the House of Hanover in 1714. The result was that bankers began to make a clear distinction between the king's personal debts and the public debt.

The Bank of England was organized in 1694, in large part to manage the public debt. Its "bank notes," that is, promises to pay a given sum in metallic currency on demand, soon became standard currency for large transactions. And, most important of all, anyone could buy a government bond and collect interest on it, secure in the knowledge that the Bank of England and the whole financial community of London would see to it that the interest would be paid on schedule. In this way, the spare cash of a large proportion of the English public (and foreigners too) could be used in time of emergency to help finance unusual public expenditures. Interest rates for government borrowing became much lower when the risk of repudiation no longer worried investors. As a result, financial and material resources could be mobilized more efficiently than ever before.

Other governments lagged behind England in developing an efficient central bank and establishing public debts—but not by much, for the advantages of such a system for waging war were enormous.

Techniques of Manufacture

Expenditures for war went, very largely, into the hands of merchants and manufacturers who supplied Europe's armed forces with the hundreds of items they required. New and expanded industries and transport systems resulted, some of which could be put to ordinary peacetime uses with little or no adjustment.

Between about 1650 and 1750, western Europeans faced a growing crisis as a result of the rapid disappearance of forests. Timber, fuel, and rough pasturage traditionally had come from Europe's forests. But as more and more people put greater demands upon the forests, big trees became scarce. The consequences of this scarcity

for shipbuilding and metallurgy—both industries requiring large quantities of wood—were particularly important. The only solution for shipbuilding was to import timber, either from northern Europe—Sweden or Russia—or from the Americas. But English ironmasters discovered a far more effective way to solve their difficulty in getting enough fuel for their smelters by discovering how to make a new form of fuel—coke.

Ordinary coal, which existed abundantly in parts of western Europe, was useless for smelting iron ore. It had too many chemical impurities to be capable of producing a usable iron or steel. Even a trace of phosphorous, for example, if allowed to penetrate the molten iron, would make a brittle and generally useless product. As a result, iron ore had always been smelted with charcoal; and to produce enough charcoal for Europe's iron smelters required enormous amounts of wood. For several decades in the early eighteenth century, therefore, Sweden and Russia had a special advantage in the iron and steel industries, since they still had enough forests to fuel the forges.

As early as 1709, an English ironmaster, Abraham Darby, discovered that he could purify coal of the objectional chemicals by burning it part way, just as wood had long been partly burnt to make charcoal. The coke that resulted from this could then smelt iron ore just as charcoal could. For a long time, the Darby ironworks kept the method for making coke secret, and consequently the new technique did not come into general use until after 1750. When it did, coal, which was already an important fuel in western Europe for heating houses and for various industrial processes, acquired a much greater significance than before.

New Sources of Power   Steam engines, which converted the energy of coal into mechanical motion, were invented as early as 1710 to drive pumps needed to lift water from coal mines. But the first such engines were extremely inefficient. Only when James Watt (1736–1819) invented an engine that did not have to be cooled to make the steam condense (1769) did steam power become really significant. Even then, the problem of making pistons and cylinders fit closely was very difficult

Naval War Professional standing armies and navies altered European warfare after 1650 in far-reaching ways. The scene shown here is of a battle off the port of Vigo, in northwestern Spain in 1702. English and Dutch ships in the foreground are bombarding the fortifications on shore and have set fire to a Spanish vessel inside the harbor. Ships like these, each carrying scores of heavy guns, could bring overwhelming firepower to bear across enormous distances. Moreover, captains and crews nearly always obeyed orders from their home governments, and did so without question even when the order had to come half way around the world. This gave European governments a hitherto unmatched capacity to support their commercial and political interests forcibly, thus assuring the continuation of rapid expansion overseas. Disciplined standing armies produced the same result overland. Europe's resulting expansion across every frontier helped to sustain the comparative quiet at home that characterized the Old Regime.

to overcome, so that the age of steam and power-driven machinery scarcely got started before 1789.

Watermills, windmills, and larger and better-designed ships were far more important sources of power than steam in the days of the Old Regime. Because horse power remained the fundamental source of power for agriculture and land transportation, the most weighty improvement of all was the increased size and strength of horses; and horse power multiplied as improved agricultural methods provided more and better fodder.

Overall, new techniques increased the amount of power—both muscular and mechanical—at the disposal of Europeans several times over between 1650 and 1789. This progress was fundamental. It opened all sorts of new possibilities for everyday activity.

Precision Tools and Luxury Crafts   In other directions, too, European skills reached new levels during the Old Regime. Clockmakers, gunsmiths, lens grinders, glass blowers, jewel cutters, die-makers learned how to shape metal and other hard materials very precisely. One of the great triumphs of Europe's technology was the invention of a clock so accurate and so insensitive to the pitching motion of a ship at sea that it could keep time within a few seconds for months on end. This invention, in turn, allowed ships' captains to calculate longitude. The first chronometer (as such clocks were called) accurate enough to measure longitude was invented in 1761 by an Englishman named John Harrison (1693–1776). He built upon a long tradition of mechanical ingenuity going back to the Middle Ages when the first mechanical clocks were built in church steeples to keep time for a whole town.

European artisans and inventors were also eager to borrow, and even improve upon, foreign skills when they found them useful. Two noteworthy examples were the discovery of how to make porcelain in imitation of the Chinese, who long kept the process secret, and the establishment of cotton manufacture in Europe in competition with Indian artisans. Since Indian weavers lived more cheaply than European workers could afford to live in the harsher climate of the north, it was only by inventing labor-saving devices that European manufacturers could come close to rivaling Indian production costs. They began to do so, with startling success, from about 1770; but, as in the case of the steam engine, the main impact of the new technology in textiles came later.

Luxury trades in the age of the Old Regime actually introduced much of the everyday equipment of an ordinary U.S. household of the twentieth century. Light, strong, and handsome furniture, "china" dishes, big windows filled with transparent glass, and printed wallpaper were among the new household items introduced between 1648 and 1789. Taken together, they made a more comfortable, cleaner, and attractive life possible—at first only for the upper classes and then, with mass production, for larger and larger numbers of people.

Territorial Expansion

The advance of European settlement in North America is a familiar part of our national history. By the time the English colonies won their independence, they numbered about 4 million inhabitants—nearly half the population of England at the time. The frontier of settlement reached and, in places, had even crossed the Appalachian Mountain barrier. Far in advance of settlement, fur traders had explored the American west as far as the Rocky Mountains and the Mackenzie River, while Russians and Spaniards competed along the Pacific coast of North America. Claims overlapped, but in practice a gap remained between Russian and Spanish spheres of influence, for Russian fur traders never were active south of Vancouver Island, while San Francisco remained the northernmost regular Spanish settlement.

In Latin America, the decline of the Amerindian population reached its low point about 1650, after which a slow and then more and more rapid growth of population set in. Settlement in the Rio de la Plata region and in the interior of Brazil resembled what was happening at the same time in North America. In the La Plata region, ranching was more important than farming; in Brazil the discovery of gold and diamonds (c. 1695) far in the interior sparked the exploration and partial settlement of the vast Amazon basin. The Brazilian coast and the islands of the Caribbean supported profitable sugar plantations, worked by slaves brought across the Atlantic Ocean from Africa. The importance of the sugar islands in international trade was extraordinary. Indeed, in 1763 the French preferred to give up all of Canada in order to keep the island of Martinique; and as late as 1773, British records show that trade with the Caribbean Islands was more valuable than trade with the mainland North American colonies.

Despite weakness at home, the Spanish and Portuguese empires survived all the wars of the seventeenth and eighteenth centuries, at least partly because yellow fever, to which local inhabitants of the Caribbean had become accustomed after about 1670 when the disease arrived from Africa, had a way of destroying British and French forces sent into the region. A few weeks ashore within reach of the mosquitoes that carried the yellow fever virus was enough to defeat any expedition from Europe. This meant that even slender garrisons ashore could easily defend fortified places long enough for the fever to paralyze vastly superior invading forces.

After 1750, Spanish power and wealth in the new world began to recover from the depression that had set in with the radical decay of Amerindian populations. Demographic turnaround about 1650 gave way to rapid population growth a century later. Mestizos, whose ancestors were partly white, partly Indian, outnumbered any other group in most parts of the Spanish Empire; and in Brazil and the Caribbean lowlands, a black element was also prominent in the mixture of races that was emerging. Increased population

North America and the Caribbean, 1763

sustained a rising curve of trade and manufacture; this in turn supported urban populations that kept in touch with new currents of thought in Europe. In this way, ideas of the French Enlightenment took root in parts of the Spanish Empire; and when the English colonies of North America became independent in 1776, a few restless spirits in lands to the south began to think that they ought to follow the North American example by rebelling against Spain.

The Eastward Movement in Eurasia   Overseas expansion in the Americas was matched by eastward expansion in Eurasia. The Austrians and Hungarians, for example, conquered a thinly settled land from the Turks in 1699; and for seventy-five years thereafter, the Austrian government and Hungarian nobles shared the task of planting settlers on the grasslands of central Hungary. Farther east it was principally the Russians who took over the task of occupying the steppelands north of the Black Sea and bringing them into cultivation. Other settlers crossed the Ural Mountains into Siberia or traveled down the Volga River toward the Caspian Sea. It is impossible to know how many pioneers took part in this eastward movement, but the number was probably as great as or greater than the number of settlers and slaves who crossed the Atlantic.

Characteristics of Frontier Society   On the frontier, whether in the New World or in eastern Europe, society was simpler than near the centers of European civilization. Population was scant in proportion to land and other resources, and all the different levels and ranks, into which European nations divided, tended to break down. Two alternatives presented themselves. The first was for individuals and families to go off, more or less on their own, even though this meant giving up many of the advantages of civilized life—since schoolteachers, professionals, and other specialists could not support themselves in such a poor, crude, free-and-equal environment. The American frontier and parts of Siberia were, in fact, populated in this way. This produced a lawless, rough, half-barbarous frontier population, with a great ability to help itself and a fierce unwillingness to submit to anyone who was, or claimed to be in any way superior.

The other alternative was to maintain some sort of social subordination by using force. In Europe, the poor had to work for the rich to be able to eat. On the frontier, the only way to make some people work for others was to enslave them. Slavery and other forms of forced labor, such as peonage and bonded servitude, played a big role in the New World. Such legal devices permitted a few plantation owners to remain far more cultured than was possible where rude equality prevailed. The same pattern dominated the eastward movement, where the legal powers of landowners over their serfs expanded throughout the period when settlement on new ground was most rapid

From European to Western Civilization These two buildings symbolize the
way the United States and Russia, one far to the west and the other far to the
east of the main center of European civilization, both became part of what
must henceforth be called Western rather than European civilization, since
its seat was no longer limited to Europe. On the left is Independence Hall,
Philadelphia, where the Declaration of Independence was proclaimed on July
4, 1776 and where the first seat of the new government was established. On
the right is a view of the square in front of the Winter Palace in Leningrad,
completed in 1784 during the reign of Catherine II. The buildings on this
square housed some but not all of the officials who governed Russia in the
eighteenth century. The difference in scale between what the Americans and
Russians needed for housing their respective governments reflected the different structure of the two frontier societies that had arisen on the flanks of old
Europe. In the one, freedom and equality were greater, whereas subordination and control went much further than was customary in western Europe
in the other. But the fundamental connection of America and of official Russia with Europe is clearly attested by the so-called 'classical' style of architecture evident in both photographs.

and labor shortages were most critical. From the
point of view of the Russian government, no other
policy was possible. Landlords were needed to
staff the government and to fill the officer ranks
in the army. A strong and efficient army was
needed to fend off attackers from the west and
to overpower rivals in the south and east. The
looser, freer, and more individualistic type of society that flourished in the English colonies of
North America could and did arise only because
the colonists never had to support a trained and
well-equipped army in order to defeat the Indians. Serious quarrels among the European states
over possession of lands in the New World did of
course arise; but they were fought out between
England, France, and Spain mainly with soldiers

Hapsburg lands
Prussia

KINGDOM OF SWEDEN

KINGDOM OF DENMARK AND NORWAY

North Sea

Baltic Sea

Volga R.

RUSSIAN EMPIRE

HANOVER

UNITED NETHERLANDS

KINGDOM OF GREAT BRITAIN AND IRELAND

HOLY

KINGDOM OF PRUSSIA

BRANDENBURG

KINGDOM OF POLAND

Dnieper R.

AUSTRIAN NETHERLANDS

ROMAN EMPIRE

SAXONY

SILESIA

BAVARIA

Atlantic Ocean

KINGDOM OF FRANCE

NEUCHATEL

Saône R.

Loire R.

Rhône R.

SAVOY

GENOA

MILAN

VENETIAN REPUBLIC

MODENA

LUCCA

TUSCANY

PAPAL STATES

KINGDOM OF HUNGARY

Save R.

Danube R.

Black Sea

MONTENEGRO

RAGUSA

KINGDOM OF PORTUGAL

Tagus R.

KINGDOM OF SPAIN

MONACO

CORSICA

SARDINIA

KINGDOM OF THE TWO SICILIES

OTTOMAN EMPIRE

Mediterranean Sea

FEZ AND MOROCCO

ALGERIA

TUNIS

0 100 200 300
Miles

Europe in 1789

NORTH AMERICA

FURS

EUROPE

FURS

ASIA

Pacific Ocean

FISH

TIMBER

MANUFACTURES

TOBACCO

BULLION

Atlantic Ocean

MANUFACTURES

BENGAL

Pacific Ocean

PHILIPPINE IS.

SLAVES

PORT. GUINEA

AFRICA

CEYLON

MOZAMBIQUE

SPICES

COFFEE

TEA

ANGOLA

TEXTILES

BULLION

SILK

Indian Ocean

AUSTRALIA

CAPE COLONY

SOUTH AMERICA

European Expansion Overland and Overseas, 1650–1789

Europe in 1492   European Trade Routes after 1500

European Empires in 1763

British   Dutch   Russian   Portuguese   Spanish trained, equipped, and paid for by the home governments. This tipped the balance in favor of freedom and equality on the North American frontier.

POLITICS AND WAR

Intensification and expansion also dominated the politics of Europe. Until 1715 France held the center of the stage and led all other European states in developing an efficient army and bureaucracy. Between them, French soldiers and French officials were able to call on far greater resources—whether to fight a war or to build a palace at Versailles worthy of Louis XIV, the Sun King (reigned 1643–1715)—than any other state in Europe could do.

French Territorial Expansion

Early in Louis' long reign an armed uprising nicknamed the *Fronde* (French for "sling") broke out (1648–1653). Louis was thoroughly frightened when armed men struggled in his bedroom for

The Sun King and His Palace at Versailles Louis XIV, who reigned in France from 1643 to 1715, took his duties as King very seriously. Convinced that God had personally and specifically chosen him to rule, Louis consciously worked at the task of behaving like a king. This meant playing a part from morning to night, imposing his will and presence upon everyone he met, not only by issuing orders and making decisions (which he did with great faithfulness), but also by looking and acting majestically. This portrait, painted in 1701 when the king was fifty three years old and at the height of his powers, expresses the theatrical image Louis shaped for himself. To play the royal role effectively, Louis needed an audience. Accordingly, he attached hundreds of noblemen to his court, encountering them in stately levees each day, where his gracious word or carefully directed snub made everyone's standing rise and fall according to the King's good pleasure. To house the court, Louis built an enormous new palace at Versailles, shown on the left. Thousands of persons lived here, for each nobleman needed a train of servants to maintain him in the high style required for life at court, celebrating the greatness of the king.

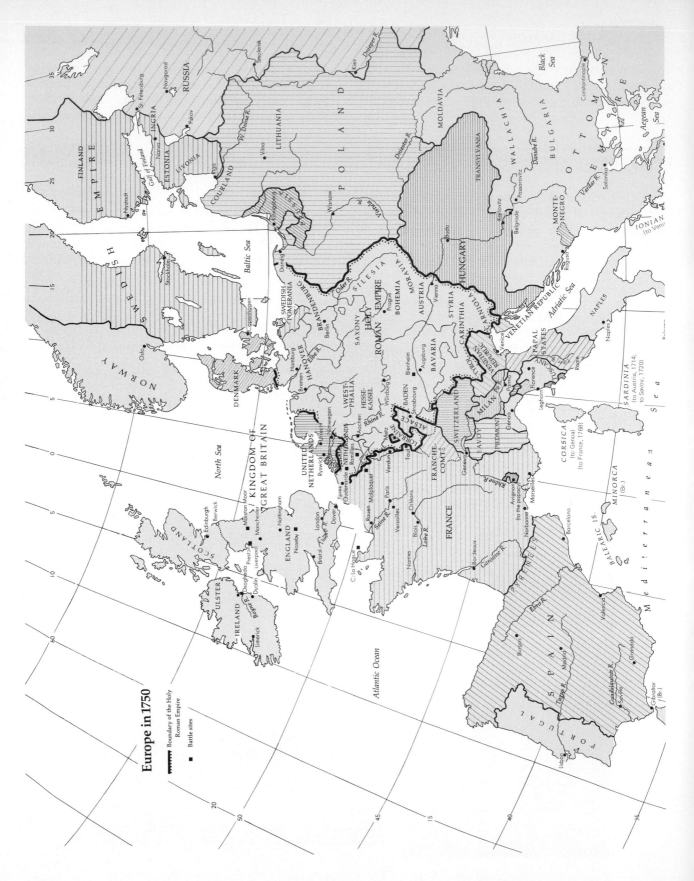

Europe in 1750

~~~~~~~~ Boundary of the Holy
          Roman Empire

■ Battle sites

control of the boy king, and when he grew up and took power into his own hands, he decided to permit absolutely no rivals within France. This required him to maintain an armed force, year in and year out, far superior to anything his own nobles or any foreign ruler could bring against him. Louis was able to keep such a standing army because France was a rich land, and ever since the Hundred Years' War the king had been legally entitled to collect taxes as he saw fit.

Louis XIV was a serious and hard-working monarch. He chose ministers who tried to develop French resources in every way possible. In particular, the controller general of finance, Jean Baptiste Colbert (in office 1662–1683), encouraged new industries, regulated old ones, adjusted taxes to make them more uniform and easier to collect, and always tried to make the king of France as rich and powerful as possible. The royal government and administration thus took over many functions that in earlier times had rested with guilds in separate towns or with other local authorities. The result, with Colbert's careful management of finances, was spectacular, for Louis XIV became able to maintain the greatest army and the most splendid court Europe had yet seen.

The king set himself the task of extending his kingdom to its natural frontiers, that is, to the Pyrenees, the Alps, and the Rhine. In 1659 he signed a treaty with Spain that drew the frontier line along the watershed of the Pyrenees. During the rest of his reign Louis tried to reach the Rhine, but his efforts were checked by the Dutch and after 1689 by the English and Dutch together. In 1700 Louis undertook the last great venture of his reign, for in that year the king of Spain died without direct heirs and left a will assigning his kingdom to one of Louis XIV's grandsons, Philip of Anjou. When the French tried to make good the claim to the Spanish throne, a general war broke out. England, Holland, the Austrian Hapsburgs, and many other rulers of Europe joined in a Grand Alliance to stop the French. The war was hard fought and strained French resources to the limit. In the end a compromise was agreed to by the Treaties of Utrecht and Rastatt (1713, 1714). Philip's claim to the Spanish throne was recognized by all concerned, but Spanish possessions in Italy and the Low Countries (present-day Bel-

gium) were transferred to Austria; while the British, as their part of the bargain, acquired Gibraltar from Spain, and Nova Scotia and Newfoundland from the French.

The result of the War of the Spanish Succession showed that the Austrian Hapsburgs and the British government had both caught up with the French when it came to waging war and managing the state. The power of the Dutch, by comparison, faded; so did the power of France's traditional allies—the Swedes, the Poles, and the Turks. From 1715 onward, the French advantage over neighboring states was gone. Instead, governments closer to the expanding edge of European civilization gained the advantage. By bringing new territory under their control, they could add to their resources, while the French were stopped by one or another coalition of enemies from doing anything similar themselves.

British Territorial Expansion

In the west, the country that benefited from these new possibilities was Great Britain. Great Britain was itself a new creation resulting from the union of England, Scotland, and Ireland in 1707. Britain's main expansion took place overseas in the Americas and in India. Each time the English fought the French in Europe, the struggle extended across the oceans of the earth and into the colonies. Sometimes fighting in the colonies began before war started in Europe. The most important instance of this came in 1754, when the French and Indian War began in North America two years before a full-scale war was joined in Europe between France and Great Britain. The upshot of this so-called Seven Years' War (1756–1763) was British victory in both America and India. By the Peace of Paris (1763), the French surrendered Canada and India to the British.

To be sure, the Spanish, Portuguese, and Dutch empires still existed. But the British had secured the right to trade with the Spanish colonies as part of the Peace of Utrecht in 1713, and they actually controlled much of the trade with South and Central America. Ever since 1689 when William of Orange, a Dutchman, became king of England, cooperation between the Dutch and British had become close and habitual. The same was true of British relations with Portugal. Hence British trade and British naval supremacy seemed unchallenged overseas after 1763.

Yet when quarrels between the government of George III (1760–1820) and thirteen of the British colonies of North America led to open warfare in 1776, not only the French but also the Spanish and even the Russian governments challenged Britain's predominance at sea, either by engaging in outright war or by an "armed neutrality" aimed against British naval power. Eventually the British had to yield. Through a second Peace of Paris in 1783, they agreed to the independence of their former American colonies and saw French power reestablished in North America in the Louisiana territory—a land that seemed much more promising than the snowy wastes of Canada to statesmen interested in sugar and other tropical products.

Despite this setback, British overseas trade and the empire built around that trade continued to be the largest in the world. British power and wealth increased with great rapidity. British business methods and parliamentary government, which had taken fresh hold on England after the "Glorious Revolution" of 1688, also began to arouse admiration among some Frenchmen who came to think that the successes of the British government—and the failures of their own after 1715—resulted from the superiority of the British constitution.

Eastern European Expansion

In eastern Europe, expansion overland matched western expansion overseas. Not one but three new empires rose to greatness at the expense of older and less well organized states. The rising powers were the Austrian Hapsburgs, based in the Danube Valley; the kingdom of Prussia, based in the eastern reaches of the north German plain; and the Russian Empire, based far to the north and east.

Russian Agricultural Expansion   Of the three, Russia had the most favorable position, being situated like Britain at the outermost edge of the European world where expansion into new and

vast territories was quite easy. Yet Russia had special problems, too. Agriculture was inefficient. Peasants who worked as serfs for masters they disliked could not be made to work efficiently. In addition, Russia had inherited a civilization and style of life from medieval times that derived in part from Byzantium and remained always a little different from the life of western Europe. After the Time of Troubles (1610–1613), when Polish armies seized Moscow for a short time, the Russian government tried to safeguard the national tradition by holding Westerners at arm's length.

The policy worked pretty well. In particular, after a long competition with the Poles, the czars of Moscow took over the Ukraine (1667) and thereby added a broad and fertile agricultural land to their dominions. The problem, however, was to find settlers to cultivate its empty expanses, and then to find markets for the grain it could produce. Not until 1774 were these two problems really solved; for in that year, after a successful war against the Turks, the Russians made a treaty that gave them the right to send ships through the straits at the mouth of the Black Sea. Thereafter, a great boom came to the Ukraine, and the Russian government began to profit from its rich new agricultural base.

The Western Ways of Peter the Great   Long before then, Russia's upper classes had accepted many West European ways. This was the result of deliberate policy on the part of Czar Peter I, the Great (reigned 1682–1725). Not until 1698, when he returned from a visit to western Europe, did Peter try to revolutionize his country. But once started he never rested. He forced every courtier to cut off his beard and put on Western clothes. He tried to teach the Russian court ladies to behave like French women. He also required every man of noble rank to serve the state in one capacity or another. Some acted as civil administrators, but most served in the army or navy. To equip his armed forces, Peter built factories to make all the things soldiers and sailors required, from cannon to uniform cloth and gaiter buttons.

The overriding goal Peter sought was military strength. He achieved it. After a long and difficult war, he compelled the Swedes to give up important territories along the Baltic Sea (1721).

Without waiting for the peace, Peter built a new capital city on the newly acquired coast and named it St. Petersburg. Here he had a "window on the West" through which French governesses and German tutors soon swarmed to educate the children of the nobility in European manners and ideas.

One of the reasons that Peter could achieve such a sharp break from the Russian past was that many, perhaps most, peasants regarded him as Antichrist. In their eyes, therefore, it did not matter how wicked his actions might be. Each new shock simply seemed another sign that the end of the world was at hand, when God could be counted on to right all wrongs. The great conservative mass of the Russian people therefore remained remarkably passive while their ruler ordered them and their noble masters about. Even when Peter laid hands on the Holy Orthodox church itself, deposed the patriarch of Moscow, and put the church under the administration of ordinary state officials, there was no outcry. The

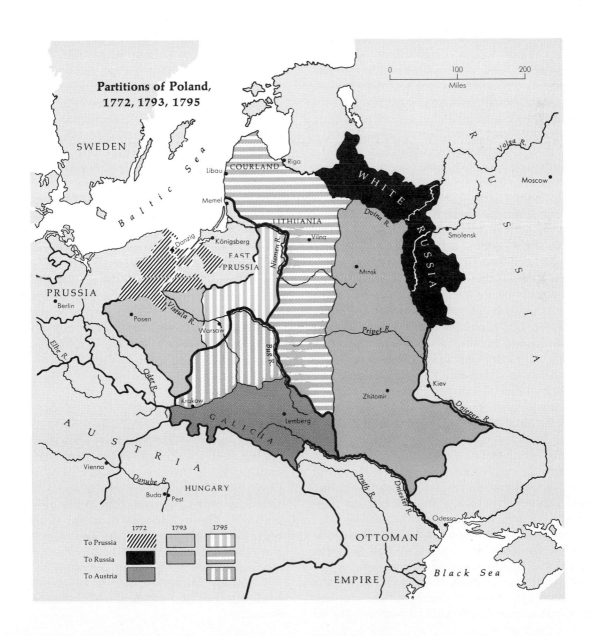

Partitions of Poland, 1772, 1793, 1795

Russian church had already lost its hold on popular religious feeling due to Nikon's reforms of the preceding generation.

The other secret of Peter's success lay in the way he trained the nobles to serve him. He required noblemen's sons to serve as privates in special "Guards" regiments. There they learned all the newfangled ways of court. Those who caught the ruler's eye or had any unusual qualities were sent off to perform any of hundreds of special jobs for the impatient czar. Diplomats, factory managers, governors of a province, commanders of a fleet—any or every job might open; and for those who did well, wealth and power came with the job. Nor was noble birth the only path to advancement. Peter was always short of skilled subordinates. He welcomed foreigners, roughnecks, adventurers of any background, into his service. They could go as far as luck and their own abilities would carry them. This policy created a nobility almost completely alienated from the rest of Russian society and correspondingly dependent on the czar.

The Greatness of Russia Under Catherine   Peter's successors, mostly women, had to rule over the Russian lands by keeping on good terms with the nobility. Catherine the Great (reigned 1762–1796) had the least claim to the throne yet was by far the most successful. A German princess by birth, Catherine came to power when a clique of courtiers murdered her husband, Czar Peter III. She lived to see Russia become a European power of the first rank. By intervening in Swedish politics, she made Sweden a dependency and nearly conquered Turkey. She destroyed Poland by arranging three successive partitions of that country among its neighbors—Russia, Austria, and Prussia.

Nearly all of the nobles and officials, army officers and tax collectors, who served the Russian state in Catherine's time believed that what they did was worthwhile. They opened up new land to agriculture, built new towns, and in general made Russia more powerful, modern, up-to-date. As for the common folk, they had to work for their noble masters and for the benefit of the state—if need be, against their will. The gain seemed worth the cost to nearly all the nobles. Russia's future greatness and its superiority to

the pygmy states of western Europe seemed assured.

Austrian Expansion

The other growing states of eastern Europe were Austria and Prussia. Austria was ruled by the Hapsburg family, whose claim to the title of Holy Roman Emperor had become traditional. But the real strength of their state rested on the Hapsburg hereditary lands of Austria and Bohemia. From this core, Austrian power expanded eastward and southward by driving back the Turks, beginning with victory in a long war (1683–1699). After 1714, when the Hapsburg rulers added the former Spanish possessions in Italy and the Low Countries to their other territories, the great power status of the Hapsburg Empire was assured. But it never achieved administrative unification. Each separate duchy, principality, or kingdom kept its own forms of government and administration. To be sure, the empress Maria Theresa (ruled 1740–1780) and her son Joseph II (ruled 1780–1790) tried hard to make the same laws and rules apply everywhere in their dominions. Yet they fell far short of success. The Austrian lands, like Germany and Italy generally, remained divided by all sorts of local differences. This weakened the empire and made it impossible to bring anything like the full resources of the various Hapsburg lands to bear on any common enterprise as the French, British, and Russians were increasingly able to do.

Prussian Expansion

Prussia, on the other hand, was the most strictly centralized and carefully adminstered state in Europe. From the time of Frederick William, the Great Elector (ruled 1640–1688), everything was subordinated to making the army as strong as possible. The result was to make Prussia a far more powerful state than its sandy soil and scant population could otherwise have supported. A symbol of Prussia's rising importance came in 1701 when Frederick, whose highest title had been Elector of Brandenburg, became king in Prussia.

MARIA THERESA
AND THE HUNGARIAN DIET

In 1740 a young queen, Maria Theresa, succeeded to the throne of the Hapsburgs. Her father had spent years trying to get his various subjects to promise to obey his daughter, but the Hungarians were stubborn. According to their ancient constitution, the Diet had to approve a new king; how could they accept a woman as their ruler? A king was supposed to command in battle; no woman could do that. Nevertheless, in 1723, seventeen years before she actually came to the throne, the Diet had reluctantly voted to accept Maria Theresa as heir.

The question of what the Hungarians would do became acute soon after Maria Theresa's reign began. Prussia attacked the Hapsburg lands, backed by France and Bavaria. An army had to be raised and Hungarian help was required. Maria Theresa journeyed to Pressburg (called Bratislava today), where the Hungarian Diet was meeting. She appeared before the assembled nobles, carrying her infant son in her arms, and appealed for help.

In a sudden burst of enthusiasm, the Hungarians promised to fight for her cause and did in fact take the field against the invaders with considerable success. The Hapsburg power was saved, although Maria Theresa did lose the valuable province of Silesia to the Prussians. For the rest of her long reign, Maria Theresa remained grateful to the Hungarians for coming to her help in time of need. She therefore did nothing to hurt the interests of the nobles or to alter the ancient Hungarian constitution that protected the nobles' privileges.

In the War of the Austrian Succession (1740–1748) and again during the Seven Years' War (1756–1763), Prussian soldiers proved their mettle to all Europe. In the first of these wars, Frederick II, the Great, king of Prussia (ruled 1740–1786), seized the province of Silesia from Austria and made his conquest stick. In the Seven Years' War he faced a far more dangerous coalition, for the French and Austrians, rivals for centuries, combined forces against the Prussians, and the Russians also joined them. Nevertheless, with help from Great Britain in the form of money and supplies, the Prussian army staved off defeat until Russia changed sides (1762), and the French and Austrians at length gave up the struggle and made peace. Prussia thus escaped from what had seemed overwhelming odds, and—as we have seen—Frederick II lived to divide Poland with his former enemies, Austria and Russia, making his state greater still.

NEW CHALLENGES
TO ROYAL ABSOLUTISM

Prussia under Frederick the Great, Austria under Joseph II, and Russia under Catherine the Great—all were ruled by monarchs who claimed

The Third Estate From medieval times, European society had been divided into three legally different classes: nobles, who fought; clergy, who prayed; and the rest, who worked. But under the Old Regime this inherited structure twisted out of shape. Most nobles no longer fought: that was entrusted to professional soldiers. The high clergy were too busy with administration to have much time for prayer. But the biggest change came in the so-called Third Estate, where new ideas and new wealth changed older ways profoundly. Above a painting of a French peasant family, made in the seventeenth century, celebrates the satisfactions of rest from work, food, and a sort of simple abundance, despite the bare feet and drab clothes appropriate to their humble status. Peasants were, always, the great majority in Old Regime Europe. Slow changes in their level of life sustained the far more conspicuous changes in town life, one of which is illustrated below. The etching of Denis Diderot (1713–1784), pen in hand, registers the new role played by writers and intellectuals in eighteenth century France. Diderot's most important achievement was editing the *Encyclopedie*, published between 1752 and 1772. This famous work publicized new ideas about science and society and the possibility of improvement by deliberate reasoning.

D. DIDEROT.

to be absolute and also "enlightened." This meant, first of all, that they were not believers in traditional Christianity. It also meant that they tried, or talked about trying, to use the state to promote wealth and well-being among the people as a whole. It meant, too, administrative cen-

tralization and concentration of authority in the hands of officials who were themselves told what to do by the ruler or by his ministers. These political principles worked rather well in eastern Europe in the eighteenth century. But in western Europe, royal absolutism failed to cope successfully with the more complex societies that prevailed in France, England, and Holland.

France

In France, which had once been the model of efficient government for the rest of Europe, all sorts of vested interests prevented the king and his ministers from changing established ways of doing things. Many key government officials bought their offices. As a result, they could not be shifted around by the king. Under these conditions the administration lost its flexibility. French taxes ceased to produce enough money to keep the French government in funds. The army and navy suffered, and the French had to endure humiliating defeats at the hands of the British and Prussians. A growing number of writers were openly critical of the way things were run. In particular, professionals and business leaders were inclined to feel that they had too little voice in making governmental decisions. They began to look across the Channel toward Great Britain, where people like themselves played important roles in Parliament and helped run the government.

England

Britain's internal political development was almost exactly opposite to the French experience. When the Stuart kings first came to the throne in 1603, they tried to build an efficient royal government like the French. This soon got them into trouble with Parliament, a medieval institution that got in the way of efficient administration by refusing to grant needed taxes and by defending unruly groups that refused to obey the king in matters of religion and taxation. Indeed, in 1642 relations between Charles I and Parliament got so bad that civil war broke out. Parliament won, and in 1649 a special commission decided that King Charles should be executed for failing to keep his promises to Parliament. But cutting off Charles's head solved nothing and, in fact, shocked many Englishmen.

Legal quarrels over the rights of the king as against those of Parliament were only part of the dispute. Many Englishmen believed that the church needed to be reformed and purified along Calvinist, biblical lines. Called Puritans by their opponents, they dominated both Parliament and the army that Parliament raised to fight against the king. But victory in the field presented Parliament with the difficult task of deciding how church and state should be reorganized. The members of Parliament could not agree. When the army made Oliver Cromwell—Parliament's greatest general—Lord Protector, a military dictatorship was fastened on England. But this soon became unpopular and indeed violated Cromwell's own convictions.

When Cromwell died (1658), the regime fell apart. Almost in desperation, a group of generals and other political figures called the Stuart heir to the throne. Charles II (reigned 1660–1685) had grown up in France and had no wish to be exiled again. In general, he kept on reasonably good terms with Parliament. Nevertheless, King Charles tried to escape Parliament's financial control by making a secret arrangement with Louis XIV, whereby the French paid a considerable sum of money to Charles. In return Charles agreed to keep England quiet while Louis attacked his neighbors in order to make the Rhine his frontier.

When James II came to the English throne in 1685, suspicion between king and Parliament caused a crisis once more. James was a Roman Catholic, and Parliament suspected that he wanted to make England Catholic again. They also suspected treasonable relations with France. In 1688, therefore, a coup d'état was organized. William of Orange came from Holland and claimed the throne jointly with his wife, Mary, who was the daughter of James II. The coup was successful, but Parliament made the new monarchs agree to a Declaration of Rights that defined the limits of royal power in a sense favorable to Parliament. Thereafter, the kings of England reigned but did not rule. Taxes had to be authorized by Parliament before they could be collected legally. No royal standing army could be maintained in England; the army's allegiance was to Parliament.

William was a vigorous king, but he was mainly interested in wars against Louis XIV on the continent. As long as his new kingdom supported such wars, he was well content to leave the government in the hands of ministers agreeable to Parliament. Queen Anne (reigned 1702–1714), George I of Hanover (reigned 1714–1727), and George II (reigned 1727–1760) followed the same policy. The first Hanoverian kings found it simpler to govern by choosing ministers who could get support for their policies in Parliament. Neither George I or George II could speak English easily and stayed away from most of the meetings of the ministers at which government policy was discussed. They were satisfied to give the responsibility for choosing ministers to Robert Walpole, an ordinary member of Parliament who was able to win the confidence of both the monarch and of a majority in Parliament. In common speech he came to be called prime minister, and the group of ministers he selected were referred to as the cabinet.

Rules and traditions of parliamentary and cabinet government were not perfectly defined until after George III (reigned 1760–1820) tried to take a personal hand in governing his kingdom. He was able to get personal supporters elected to Parliament and to choose his own ministers. But the king roused opposition when his plan to bring the American colonies under tighter control led only to rebellion and a disastrous war with France. The fact that George III soon afterward became intermittently insane hurt the king's cause even more and gave control of the British government back to Parliament and parliamentary leaders.

The advantages of the British system of government as it developed under the Old Regime were real. Members of Parliament represented the major propertied interests of the country. The election process allowed rising new interests to make themselves heard in Parliament at the expense of other groups whose importance was declining. In this way a rough match between political decision-making and the balance of British society as a whole could maintain itself, as it were, automatically. Moreover, closer partnership between government and the upper classes made support for government policies more reliable than was the case in a country like France.

The result was that an awkward representative assembly that in 1600 had looked like an outmoded survival from medieval times became, by 1700, the sovereign body controlling one of Europe's greatest and most rapidly growing states. The brilliant successes that came to the British government and nation in the decades that followed made parliamentary and cabinet government a model for all those on the European continent who disliked their own royal, absolute governments.

Autocratic Russia, where society was divided between nobles and serfs and where the military model dominated all administration, stood on one flank of Europe and, with Prussia, represented one extreme of social and political organization. Great Britain, where the middle classes were more powerful than in any other great state and where religious and other kinds of pluralism were more widespread than in most other parts of Europe, stood at the other extreme. The rest of Europe fell somewhere between.

Thus we see how Europe's enormous success under the Old Regime—and the territorial expansion that registered that success—meant the inclusion, within the circle of Western civilization, of greater variation, socially and economically as well as politically, than in earlier ages.

EUROPEAN CULTURE

Pluralism and internal variety also characterized Europe's culture under the Old Regime. Different social classes and different nations, not to mention different professions and different cliques and parties, tended to develop their own distinct styles of thought and behavior. General patterns existed, but only vaguely and never in a way that prevented individuals and small groups from following their own particular bent.

French art and literature won a leading place in all Europe, particularly after the Polish and Russian upper classes in Catherine's time came under the influence of French culture. But there was also a Spanish-Italian-Austrian sphere of influence, built around the Hapsburg Dynasty and carrying on the traditions of the Catholic Counter-Reformation into the eighteenth century. Finally, the English and Dutch made up a circle of their own; and by 1770 romantic poets had declared Germany's cultural independence of France as energetically as they knew how.

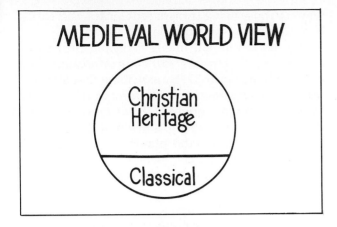

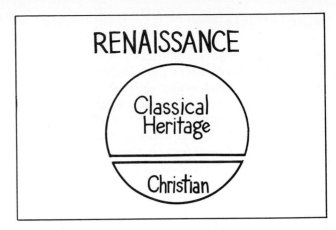

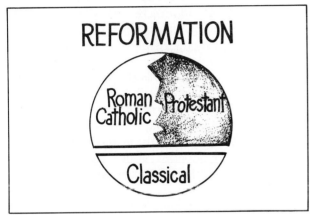

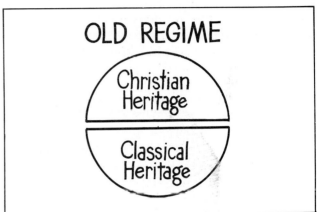

How European Civilization Changed between 1200 and 1800. These four diagrams offer a schematic way of thinking about how the different elements of European civilization split apart and rearranged themselves between 1200 and 1800.

Science remained much more international, though French followers of Descartes clashed with English Newtonians; and the German Leibniz also quarreled with Newton on grounds that were at least partly nationalistic. However, in scientific matters, observation and measurement offered a means for settling most disputes quite quickly; whereas in fields where taste was the only thing to go by, preferences based on language, religion, personal whim, or local connections tended to create and support a number of separate cultural circles.

The leading characteristic of the culture of the Old Regime was growing professionalism. Writers became able to live from the sale of their work, creating a new, independent profession apart from both church and government. Painters and musicians still depended, usually, on noble patronage or on a church appointment. Scientists sometimes held university posts, and sometimes governments competed for their services. The Swiss mathematician Leonhard Euler (1707–1783), for example, took a job as professor at the University of St. Petersburg when only twenty-three years of age; then, at Frederick the Great's call, he moved to Berlin in 1741, but he returned to St. Petersburg in 1766. The prestige of scientists rose very high. Isaac Newton (1642–1727), the great English mathematician and physicist, was treated as a public monument during his own lifetime and, when he died, was buried in Westminster Abbey with England's kings and queens.

Natural Science

Modern science got an enormous new energy after 1650. The task of observing, recording, and classifying all the plants and animals of the world was immense. In addition, with new instruments like the microscope and telescope, thermometer, barometer, sextant, and marine chronometer, Europeans had the tools to observe and record facts far more exactly than ever before. This great task of assembling information and arranging it in some sort of order was what kept most scientists busy and gave the whole enterprise of science such excitement. Everybody could understand what was being done, and no one could doubt any longer that Europe's knowledge far outstripped other peoples' knowledge, or even what the ancients had known. Making useful, workable classifications was, of course, the big problem. The two most successful classifiers were the Swede Linnaeus (1707–1778), who invented the system for classifying plants by genus and species that is still used today, and the French naturalist Georges Louis Leclerc de Buffon (1707–1788), who wrote a forty-four-volume *Natural History* in which he dealt with both animals and plants.

The Newtonian Era

But the aspect of scientific discovery that mattered most for later ages was more mathematical and abstract. The key figure was Isaac Newton, born in the year that Galileo died and, in a real sense, Galileo's intellectual successor. Newton was a great mathematician who, among other things, developed calculus. A German, Gottfried Wilhelm Leibniz (1646–1716), also invented calculus and developed the kind of notation used today. Later, a nasty quarrel broke out between followers of the two great men over the question whether Leibniz had gotten his original idea from Newton or not.

Newton's greatest work was, however, in physics and astronomy. He experimented with sunlight and discovered that he could split it up into the colors of the rainbow and then recombine it into white light by use of prisms. He invented a reflecting telescope that was superior in some ways to those using transparent lenses. But Newton's fame rests mainly on the theory of gravitation, as developed in his *Principia* (full title, *Philosophiae Naturalis Principia Mathematica*), first published in 1687. By assuming that all bodies attract one another with a force that varies inversely with the square of the distance between them, Newton was able to show that the motions of the moon and of the planets, as well as the motion of falling objects near the surface of the earth, obeyed exactly the same laws. He put these laws in mathematical form, so that when appropriate data as to mass, distance, and velocity could be supplied, motions could be predictably calculated and could also be projected back into the past.

The marvelously simple world machine that Newton's theory revealed struck contemporaries with the force of a new revelation. The motions of the heavenly bodies suddenly fitted in with everyday things like the curving path of a thrown ball or the arc of a falling apple. Everything could be explained with a few simple mathematical formulas. Some wondered about the mysterious nature of "gravitational force" that could work invisibly at a distance; others feared the mechanical, impersonal nature of Newton's vision of the universe. But when innumerable observations backed up his theories, and when planets and cannonballs kept on behaving as Newton's formulas predicted, who could doubt the essential accuracy of the new theory? Many felt, in the words of the poet Alexander Pope, "God said, 'Let Newton be,' and all was light!"

Scores of other ingenious experimenters and mathematical minds of the first rank surrounded Newton, in England and also on the continent. The scientific community founded special societies, the most famous of which was the Royal Society of London, where gentlemen interested in natural science could meet and exchange ideas. These societies corresponded with one another and published records of their meetings and of papers submitted to them from a distance. As a result, a lively network of communication among scientists and scholars came into existence, running from London to St. Petersburg, and from Florence and Rome to Stockholm. A distant outsider like Benjamin Franklin (1706–1790) could communicate the results of his experiments with lightning and win recognition throughout the European world for proving lightning to be a form of electricity. The existence of such a network for communicating scientific results guaranteed the continued flow of data and ideas and made science a truly international enterprise.

No theoretical breakthroughs comparable to the importance of Newton's work came until after 1789. Chemistry, however, achieved a new precision with the work of Antoine Lavoisier (1743–1794). He measured the weight of matter entering into and coming out of chemical reactions with greater accuracy than ever before. On the basis of such measurements he was able to explain what happened in an ordinary fire, for he detected and measured the consumption of oxygen from the air and the discharge of carbon dioxide and other gases into the air. Lavoisier also kept clear the distinction between an element and a chemical compound and introduced many of the names used still by chemists (for example, *oxygen*). As a result of such work, chemistry was poised, by the close of the Old Regime, for all the technical and practical triumphs that came in the nineteenth century.

Social Theory

Newtonianism changed Europeans' view of the world in fundamental ways. It was difficult to believe that God stood ready to intervene at a moment's notice in human affairs when the vast spaces of the universe all obeyed the same laws of motion. God seemed to be a master mathematician and craftsman who created the world in accordance with natural laws. He could not be expected to spoil his own handiwork or admit its imperfection by intervening to work a miracle. Thus, the whole world view of the Reformation era was called into question.

As prevailing views of God and his way of controlling the universe changed, political theory had to be readjusted. The idea that God personally chose kings to rule and intervened in everyday affairs to reward and punish his people by sending them good and bad rulers seemed less and less convincing. But if God did not choose kings, what right had they to rule? The best answer theorists could find was to suppose that a

contract, implied rather than real, between ruler and ruled gave kings their right to govern. But the practical force of any such theory depended entirely on the terms of the contract. Thomas Hobbes (1588–1678), for example, argued that individuals, fearing one another, made a contract that transferred absolute power to their rulers. John Locke (1632–1704), on the contrary, asserted that subjects had the right to overthrow a ruler who broke the terms of the contract by endangering their lives, liberty, or property, since the only purpose for submitting to a ruler's authority in the first place was to assure the protection of these natural rights. Jean-Jacques Rousseau (1712–1778) carried the argument to its democratic extreme by arguing that the social contract requires kings or other rulers to obey the "general will" of the people. If rulers failed to do so, it was a duty as well as a right to overthrow them.

Others concentrated their attention on economics and tried to find natural laws that governed human behavior in the marketplace. Two Scots, John Law (1671–1729) and Adam Smith (1723–1790), were particularly bold in their speculations. Law had a chance to put his theory of bank credit and currency management into practice in France, where his policies provoked a speculative boom and bust that discredited his ideas—perhaps unjustly—as well as his practice. Adam Smith was content to be a professor at Glasgow; but his treatise entitled *The Wealth of Nations*, published in 1776, became fundamental to all later economic theory. Smith's view was like Newton's in an important sense. He believed that if individuals were left alone to follow their private preferences in economic matters, enlightened self-interest would, in fact, create the best possible pattern of production and exchange. Just as gravitation kept the planets in their orbits, so Adam Smith believed private calculation of personal advantage was a universal force that operated behind all particular choices and made the economic machine work as it did.

Philosophy and Literature

Formal philosophy underwent a remarkable deflation during the Old Regime. At its beginning, René Descartes (1596–1650), Baruch Spinoza

(1632–1677), and Gottfried Leibniz (1646–1716) still hoped to use mathematical rigor to reason out a complete system of truth that would explain everything in the whole world. Their disagreements focused attention on the question of how anyone can know anything at all. The more carefully critics considered this matter, the more uncertain knowledge of any kind seemed. John Locke (1632–1704), George Berkeley (1685–1753), and David Hume (1711–1776) made it increasingly difficult to believe that human minds could ever really know anything about the nature of things. Immanuel Kant (1724–1804) rescued philosophy from this dead end by pointing out that, even if the nature of things was forever unknowable, still the nature of the knowing mind could be explored. And since nothing that did not fit in with the capacities of the mind could ever be known, to understand the qualities and capacities of the mind, in fact, allowed a philosopher to know the character and limits of all that could be known.

Such abstract ideas interested only a few; but there were others who called themselves "philosophers" and who wrote about social and political problems and often sought to reform the world around them. These philosophers were closely connected with the world of literature. They used novels, plays, or poems to convey their ideas more effectively to the audience they wanted to interest. The main center for this kind of "philosopher" was in France where, especially after 1715, there seemed much to criticize in government and society.

Charles-Louis de Secondat, Baron de Montesquieu (1689–1755), was among the first to voice dissatisfaction with the French government. He wanted the nobles to play a larger part and argued that good government required the separation of legislative, executive, and judicial functions. His ideas, together with those of John Locke, were particularly influential among the men who wrote the Constitution of the United States.

The most famous of the French "philosophers," however, was Voltaire (real name, François-Marie Arouet, 1694–1778). Voltaire wrote plays, poems, histories, as well as pamphlets and books. His central idea was that reason and good sense would show people how to behave—if only priests and others who had a vested interest in appealing to human fears and superstitions would let the light of reason shine forth freely. He set himself, therefore, to attack religious superstition and to spread the light of reason. Everything he wrote contributed in one way or another to this general aim.

Voltaire and others like him believed they were helping humanity by spreading science and truth. The task of enlightening others, although immense, seemed very much worthwhile. Progress and social improvement could only come through the spread of reason and knowledge. One of the most powerful ways to spread knowledge was the preparation of a great encyclopedia. The articles, arranged alphabetically, dealt with almost everything under the sun. The main figure responsible for producing the French encyclopedia, published between 1751 and 1772, was Denis Diderot (1713–1784). Similar works were soon produced also in English and German. Like ordinary dictionaries, which also were first compiled in the Old Regime, this sort of reference work allowed anyone to look things up accurately and rapidly as never before.

This is not the place to try to describe the literary work of Europe's major writers in any detail. Poetry and drama—both tragedy and comedy—remained vigorous in France and in England too. The three great "classical" dramatists of France flourished under Louis XIV: Pierre Corneille (1606–1684), Molière, whose real name was Jean Baptiste Poquelin (1622–1673), and Jean Racine (1639–1699). John Milton (1608–1674) and Alexander Pope (1688–1744) were perhaps the two most important English poets of their age. England also saw the birth of the modern novel with the works of Samuel Richardson (1689–1761) and Henry Fielding (1707–1754). Other countries of Europe failed to produce writers of Europe-wide reputation, until a brilliant group of Germans emerged toward the end of this period. Chief among them were Gotthold Ephraim Lessing (1729–1781), Johann Christoph Friedrich von Schiller (1759–1805), and Johann Wolfgang von Goethe (1749–1832).

These German writers and important British literary figures like Robert Burns (1759–1796) and William Wordsworth (1770–1850) tended to seek inspiration from everyday language of the people. They declared that personal emotion and self-expression were the key to great art. Such "romantic" ideas stood in self-conscious opposition to the "classical" rules of correctness that had been fashionable in earlier times. Like the criticism of the "philosophers" and the smoke of the new steam factories, the "romantic" movement pointed ahead toward the age which was to follow the overthrow of the Old Regime.

Art and Music

The Old Regime was not an age of major departures in the visual arts, but during that time European music evolved rapidly toward "classical" form.

Palaces, like that built for Louis XIV at Versailles, were designed for grandeur and perfection. Size and formal balance of doors, windows, and decorative elements were the ways in which architects chose to achieve these goals. Soon after 1700 a lighter, more graceful style called rococo came in, and exact balance of each part was deliberately abandoned. Then, toward the close of the eighteenth century, a reaction toward more "classical" simplicity and geometric regularity took place.

These shifts of style spread over most of Europe from France, where taste was, for the most part, defined. In painting there was somewhat greater variety. Antoine Watteau (1684–1721) in France, Thomas Gainsborough (1727–1788) in England, Francisco Goya (1746–1828) in Spain, and Meindert Hobbema (1638–1709) in Holland—each embodied different national traditions. Yet differences, though real, were slight. The ideal of painting that had been defined so brilliantly in Italy, during the Renaissance, continued to be the norm for all of Europe.

What happened to European music between 1648 and 1789 was rather like what had happened to painting about two and a half centuries before. European musicians, first of all, had new or newly perfected instruments at their disposal. The violin and harpsichord were the most important. The scientific study of sound opened a better theoretical understanding of musical pitch, scales, and timbre. All this gave musicians the tools of their trade, just as Italian painters in Renaissance times had developed oil paints and canvas easels as the basic tools of theirs.

Using the new tools, a series of great composers created musical forms and works that still are performed regularly. Johann Sebastian Bach (1685–1750), George Frederick Handel (1685–1759), Wolfgang Amadeus Mozart (1756–1791), and Franz Joseph Haydn (1732–1809) are the most famous and familiar. Two general remarks about their achievement must suffice here. First, instrumental music became central and singing secondary, although, of course, all sorts of combinations of instruments and voices were experimented with. Few other musical traditions have given such prominence to instrumental music, but then few other musical styles have had instruments so flexible and various to put through their paces.

Second, secular music—opera, symphonies, and so forth—became as elaborate as, and perhaps even more important than, church music. This reflected musicians' roles as entertainers at royal courts and great noble houses. The fact that they were classed just above the rank of servants explains the relatively low social status held by Mozart and Haydn. Fuller recognition of music among the arts had to wait for the development of concert halls open to the public and supported by the purchase of tickets. This did not become usual until after 1789. Until musicians had a way of making a living by public performance, they had to exist either on the patronage of the rich or by holding church positions (as, for example, Bach did).

Religion and the Churches

Any brief survey of the cultural life of an age is likely to stress what was new and different and leave out the things that remained more or less the same. This is misleading, for most people are more influenced by the stable, old, and familiar ideas and styles of thought than they are by anything new, however attractive it may seem.

Eighteenth Century Aristocrats These two portraits, oddly, resemble one another, although one
comes from France and portrays Madame de Pom-
padour, mistress to Louis XV (above), while the
other comes from China and portrays an unnamed
lady from another and quite different court (below).
Both were painted in the mid-eighteenth century, at
a time when admiration for chinoiserie had become
something of a vogue in Europe. François Boucher,
the painter on the left, was among those affected by
chinoiserie. The resemblance perhaps arises from
that fact. European admiration for aspects of Chinese civilization in the eighteenth century was a departure from the disdain for heathen ways that had
dominated contacts between bearers of different civilizations up to that time. Incipient cosmopolitanism
set in, reflecting a real resemblance that existed between the decorative courtly roles each of these ladies played at opposite ends of Eurasia.

This is particularly true in the period we have been considering, when so many radical new ideas were put before the European public yet affected only small minorities in most cases.

We may be sure that nearly all Europeans remained Christian in some sense or other. The official churches, supported by the different governments of Europe, all continued to claim that their own version of Christian doctrine offered the one and only true path to salvation. Children were taught the catechism in school or at their mother's knee, and even those who in later life rejected some or all of what they had been taught in childhood remained deeply influenced by their religious training. Most people never really made up their minds between the traditional doctrines of Christianity and the impersonal "deist" view that portrayed God as the creator of the universe, who then abandoned his handiwork to let it run itself like a great machine. Many, particularly in the lower classes, never heard deist views expressed and thus remained loyal to traditional Christian ways of understanding the world. Still others reacted strongly against the new scientific vision of reality and consciously reaffirmed their faith in a personal and immediate relationship between God and individual human beings.

The powerful new religious movements of the age were all of this sort. In England, George Fox (1624–1691) founded the Society of Friends (or Quakers) on the strength of his own personal experience of God and of commanding visions that ordered him to preach to the public. The sect he founded had no clergy at all and put great emphasis upon following one's own "inner light." Occasional persecution only hardened Quaker convictions. In the following century, John Wesley (1703–1791) took up a career as traveling evangelist after he, too, experienced a conversion and felt his "heart strangely warmed within him." His followers were known as Methodists. Both Quakers and Methodists became important in the English colonies of North America, where established churches were weaker than in England itself.

On the continent, Philipp Spener (1635–1705) founded Pietism. This was a religious movement that flourished within the Lutheran and Calvinist churches of Germany. Details of doctrine seemed unimportant to Spener and his followers. What mattered was direct personal experience of God, to be had through meditation and prayer and Bible study, conducted privately or within the family, as well as in public. German Pietism influenced Wesley and nearly all of Protestant Germany.

The Roman Catholic Church was disturbed by Quietism and Jansenism, both of which were eventually judged to be heretical and were therefore suppressed. Quietism was founded by a Spanish priest, Miguel de Molinos (1640–1697). He was a mystic and taught that the soul should wait quietly for God to come. Jansenism was named for a Dutch priest, Cornelis Jansen (1585–1638), but the main leader of the movement was a Frenchman, Antoine Arnauld (1612–1694). The Jansenists wanted to go back to St. Augustine's teachings, putting much stress on predestination and personal piety. They came into sharp controversy with the Jesuits, and for some years France was divided between those who sympathized with the Jansenists and others who went along with the Jesuits. The pope ruled against the Jansenists in 1713, and their center, Port Royal, just outside Paris, was closed down. But the Jesuit victory left them many enemies in France. They also fell into disfavor with the rulers of Spain and Portugal for refusing to submit to royal decrees; and the combined pressure of the governments of Spain, Portugal, and France persuaded the pope to suppress the order in 1773. The Jesuits survived, however, by taking refuge in Russia and Prussia, until in 1814 the papacy recognized their order once again.

Movements like these and the reaction all over Europe to Louis XIV's suppression of Huguenots in France (1685) showed the continuing hold Christianity had on the minds of men and women. Europe's other religion, Judaism, began to undergo a fundamental transformation toward the end of the Old Regime, when the longstanding isolation of Jews from gentiles in German towns began to break down a bit, and individual Jews ventured out into the wider worlds of business, literature, and the arts. Moses Mendelssohn (1729–1786) was the main pioneer in opening intellectual communication between Jews and other Germans.

CONCLUSION

Even from this brief survey, it should be clear that Europe acquired knowledge and power at a faster rate than ever before during the Old Regime. Expansion on all fronts continued without halt; and with expansion went intensification, increasing variety, complexity, and an ever faster rate of change. The political and social balance that had been struck after the religious wars was never rigid and unchallenged. But by 1789 industrialism, arising primarily in England, and democratic political ideas, at home mainly in France and in America, had both begun to challenge the old order. Breakdown came with the French Revolution and the quarter century of war that the Revolution provoked.

Yet the eagerness with which later generations attacked the remnants of the Old Regime that survived the revolutionary struggles should not blind us—their descendants—to the positive achievements which that phase of Europe's long history had to its credit. No earlier age had been more brilliant or successful; the painful break with Europe's medieval frame, which had been the business of the Renaissance and Reformation, really paid off during the Old Regime when relative calm at home allowed Europe to take on the world—and to try to understand and appreciate, as well as trade and fight with, peoples of every kind. The impact Europeans had on the rest of the world will be the theme of the next chapter.

Chapter 19

WORLD REACTIONS TO EUROPE'S EXPANSION

1700 to 1850

Between 1500 and 1700, European merchants, explorers, soldiers, missionaries, and other adventurers had made their presence felt along almost every habitable coast. When first the newcomers appeared, local peoples often greeted them with curiosity and sometimes with hospitality, although both Moslems and Chinese were suspicious and aloof from the start. As soon as Europeans in any way threatened, or seemed to threaten, things that local peoples held dear, rulers reacted by trying to break off relations and withdraw from what had become a disturbing contact. The increasing power that Europeans acquired during the Old Regime meant that they threatened more and more to upset other people's ways. Almost everywhere, except in Russia, the response was to cut off or to cut down on contact with the source of the trouble. This was the policy of Asian and African peoples and states from 1700 to 1850.

WITHDRAWAL FROM CONTACT WITH EUROPEANS

Stronger and more remote peoples could insulate themselves from Europe's influence successfully, but weaker or less favorably situated peoples could not. Thus, each of the great Asian civilized societies was able to cut off effective communication with Europeans, even when—as in the case of Moslems of India and of the Ottoman Empire—they had to endure the physical presence of foreigners in their midst. Their policy was to pay no attention to anything the Europeans had to say and to adhere to old tradition and patterns of behavior in the hope of seeing the intruders go away after a while. The Japanese and Siamese carried this policy to its logical extreme by completely prohibiting contacts with Europeans. The Chinese confined trade to a single port, Canton, and entrusted the task of dealing with foreigners to a special group of merchants, the Co-hong.

In other parts of the world, however, weaker and simpler societies were not always able to withdraw. This was the fate of the Amerindians, for example, and of peoples of the Pacific Islands, of Australia, and of South Africa. In all of these regions, Europeans or people of European descent and culture kept pursuing the retreating natives, taking their land for farms or ranches, spreading diseases, and destroying traditional social discipline by defying it without punishment.

In the African interior, tropical diseases and comparatively well-organized kingdoms blocked European penetration. The simple geographical fact that sub-Saharan Africa's rivers have falls near their mouths created a barrier to inland travel. By requiring any traveler to come ashore and walk, the river falls exposed strangers to local human hostility and to mosquito-borne infections. As a result, the interior of Africa remained proof against European penetration until after 1850, although the slave trade left almost no part of the continent unaffected.

Taking the world as a whole, the cost of withdrawal from disturbing contacts with Europeans was heavy. Closed minds, fearful of having to face awkward facts, could only repeat what had been thought and done in earlier ages. That was no way to cope with Europe's eager acquisition of new skills and knowledge. As a result, the gap between European accomplishments and the achievements of the rest of the world widened rapidly.

By the years 1850–1860, the great civilizations of Asia found themselves helpless in the face of Western superiority, which by then had become literally overwhelming. Hence, the effort to hold fast to old tradition and familiar ways of doing things backfired in the long run by requiring the non-Western peoples of the world to suffer an extremely painful and prolonged breakdown of their various styles of life after 1850. But between 1700 and 1850, no one could foresee what was coming; and in the Far East particularly, the policy of withdrawal and insulation seemed to work fairly well.

Population Growth

Another dimension of the worldwide scene between 1700 and 1850 made the "stand pat" policy easy in the short run and dangerous in the long run. This was the upsurge of population that set in among civilized peoples at a rate seldom equaled before. Japan was an exception, for the custom of allowing unwanted newborn children to die from exposure—usually in some remote and unfrequented spot—kept Japan's population almost constant. But in China, in India, and in at least parts of the Moslem world, population spurted upward.

Three worldwide factors contributed to the remarkable growth of population. One factor was the fading away of epidemic diseases. A second factor was that American food crops enhanced the food-producing capacity of heavily populated parts of the world. Sweet potatoes in south China, maize in Africa and southeastern Europe, the potato in northern Europe and Russia, came into their own between 1700 and 1850. Many millions of people came to depend on these crops.

A third factor was that the development of artillery allowed a few centers of political authority to control larger empires more effectively than in earlier ages. Thus, the Manchus in China established a higher level of peace and order over a larger territory and for a longer time than the world had ever seen before. In other parts of the world, kingdoms and empires were less majestic in scale. Nevertheless, rulers in Europe and Asia were in a better position than ever before to suppress banditry and small-scale raiding. In all probability, therefore, loss of life through local violence lessened at a time when deaths from disease were decreasing and food supplies were increasing.

In the short run, as long as fresh land lay uncultivated or more intensive tillage allowed food production to keep pace with growth of population, things went along smoothly and traditional ways of life were strengthened rather than weakened by growth in numbers. But when limits to traditional methods were reached, population did not stop growing. Mass desperation on the part of the peasantry, on a scale that traditional political methods could not cope with, was an inevitable result.

The world still finds itself affected by this crisis. It set in at different times in different parts of the earth, beginning, for example, about 1775 in China and about the same time in some of the European provinces of the Ottoman Empire. From the point of view of the great civilizations of Asia, therefore, this development meant that European pressures from outside became irresistible after 1850, at a time when fundamental internal problems were building up toward massive peasant revolt. Only Japan, where population was harshly and deliberately kept in check, escaped this difficulty.

With the benefit of hindsight we can see clearly how non-Western peoples eventually paid a heavy price for putting off fundamental transformation at home to take account of new things the restless Europeans kept on discovering. But at the time, when Europe was not yet equipped with the additional force that developed with the Industrial Revolution, the policy of withdrawal and conservative loyalty to traditional ways seemed adequate for coping with the situation that faced Moslem, Chinese, and Hindu peoples. A policy that was able to keep expectation and reality more or less in touch with each other during a century and a half should not be hastily condemned.

THE WORLD OF ISLAM

From the time of the prophet Mohammed until about 1700, the general course of history conformed to Moslem expectations. In spite of some serious defeats and disasters—such as the breakdown of political unity among Moslems, dating from A.D. 750, or the Mongol sack of Baghdad in A.D. 1258, Moslem missionaries and conquerors kept on adding new lands to the realm of Islam. No large or important territories had been lost by Mohammed's followers. Border wars with the

Retreat of Moslem Power, 1699-1856

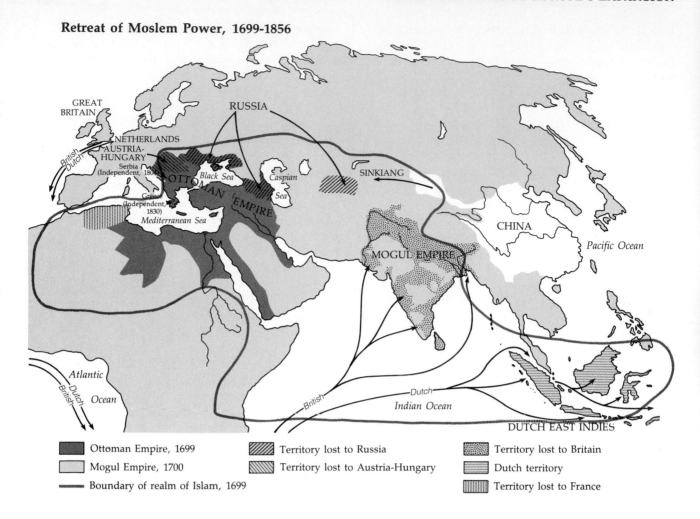

Ottoman Empire, 1699

Mogul Empire, 1700

Boundary of realm of Islam, 1699

Territory lost to Russia

Territory lost to Austria-Hungary

Territory lost to Britain

Dutch territory

Territory lost to France

Christians in Europe and against Hindus and other unbelievers in Asia and Africa tended for more than a thousand years to favor the Moslem cause. Who, then, could seriously doubt that Allah continued to favor his people as he had in the days of the Prophet and the first caliphs?

Moslem Military Power Fades

It was, therefore, a tremendous blow to Moslems when the political and military balance rather suddenly reversed itself after 1700. In 1699 the Ottoman Empire was forced to make a humiliating peace with the Austrian Hapsburgs, surrendering most of Hungary. This was the first time the Ottoman Turks had been compelled to retreat before Christian arms.

Immediately thereafter, the Mogul Empire in India began to founder. Aurangzeb died in 1707, leaving his empire distracted by revolt. Mogul power never recovered. Exactly half a century later, British traders emerged as the strongest military power in all of India. The East India Company made the Mogul Emperor its puppet, but everyone knew that Moslems no longer really ruled India.

The third great Islamic empire was the Safavid, based in Iran and Azerbaijan. It, too, suffered a breakdown, beginning in 1709 with an Afghan revolt. Drastic political disorder invited the intervention of Russian, Chinese, and even

British agents. Old-fashioned Moslem cavalry continued to charge across the landscape, brave and bold as ever; but their defeats and victories more and more depended on supplies of powder and shot that came from foreign, usually Christian, sources. The old independence and power were irremediably gone.

The overthrow of steppe warriors as a major force in the Eurasian balance of power lay behind these dramatic military-political setbacks. More than any other civilization, the Moslems had opened themselves up to the steppe. Their victories in India and in Europe had depended in large part on migration of steppe warriors from central Asia to the frontiers, where holy war against infidels promised booty. But when cavalry ceased to be decisive on the battlefield, the whole military-political tradition of the great Moslem empires became outmoded.

The Janissary Corps   Only the Ottoman Empire made a serious effort to develop an efficient infantry equipped with guns. But the Janissary corps, which won many famous victories by its discipline and firepower in the age of Suleiman the Lawgiver, fell behind European troops from the time when its members ceased to be recruited from the Christian villages of the Balkans. Village boys, pulled up by the roots from their places of origin, could be kept under a severe discipline and, as slaves of the sultan, were trained to serve him well. But after 1634, the corps came to be recruited instead from sons of Janissaries, and the character of the troops changed quickly. Because the sultan found it difficult to pay his soldiers a living wage, the Janissaries worked at various artisan trades during the winter when they were not in the field.

This soon resulted in merging the Janissaries with the Moslem artisans of the towns. By 1700 or 1750 most Moslem artisans in the European provinces of the empire held appointments in the corps. Positions were bought and sold freely, and little check was kept on whether or not the purchasers had military training or would submit to discipline. The efficiency of the corps could not survive such practices; the Janissaries nevertheless had the sultan and his ministers at their mercy. To protect their own privileges and traditions, they were ready to riot and revolt. They absolutely refused to allow any new body of troops to come into existence that might challenge their power at home.

The Indian Armies   Such experiences did not encourage other Moslem rulers to try to build up infantry forces that could make firepower really effective in battle. Neither the Mogul nor the Safavid rulers actually tried. The Mogul armies were poorly equipped, poorly trained, and poorly led by comparison with European armies of the Old Regime. But with European guns, uniforms, and drillmasters, Indian soldiers proved quite effective. Ironically, it was this that made it possible for the English East India Company to dominate India so easily. A mere handful of company employees from the British Isles were able to train *sepoy* (that is, native Indian) troops in the European manner—and thus by 1763 created what was by far the most efficient army in India.

Hindu rebels in central India, called Marathas, also weakened the Mogul power. Sikhs, too, made good their independence in the northwest. Local governors, who in theory owed their position to the emperor's appointment, became independent in all but name. Invaders from the north, first Nadir Shah from Iran and then Afghan raiders, crossed the mountains and plundered northern India.

Many Moslem princes, faced with Hindu unrest at home and the danger of Afghan raids from the north, fell back on British protection. The East India Company adopted the policy of "indirect rule." Existing states and tax systems were allowed to stand as long as a British resident at court was kept informed and allowed to give advice, which, in most cases, had to be followed. This cost the Company less, opened the doors to trade, kept the peace, and aroused a minimum of local hostility.

However, the iron hand within the velvet glove appeared from time to time. In 1818, for example, British troops put down the last Maratha bid for genuine independence. And in the years 1839–1842, a British army invaded Afghanistan, across India's northwest frontier, to enforce the Company's will. By that time the mighty Mogul Empire had become a shadow and

ALI PASHA OF JANINA

Ali Pasha of Janina (1740–1822) was one of several upstarts who took control of outlying regions of the Ottoman Empire just before and after 1800. Ali's power centered in the wild mountains of the western Balkans, where Greece and Albania meet.

In some ways Ali was thoroughly old-fashioned. He was an Albanian chieftain's son; but when he was about fourteen years old, his father was killed by a neighboring tribe. Ali and his mother had to flee for their lives into the barren mountains of southern Albania. Soon a group of outlaws gathered around them, and Ali's mother led the band until her son became old enough to take command.

As soon as he could, Ali set out to revenge himself. Eventually he succeeded in destroying all those who had taken part in killing his father. But this was only a start. By hook and by crook—and by applying a good deal of simple violence—Ali extended his domain over most of what is today Albania and much of western and northern Greece. He built up a private army and ruled as a complete despot. As he rode through the streets of his capital, Janina, or traveled in the country round about, he often would order his bodyguard to kill on the spot a man whom he accused, rightly or wrongly, of misdoing. Ali never learned to read. He also never learned to trust anyone. He administered his government entirely on the basis of his memory of faces, names, and places.

All of this was quite traditional. But there was another side to Ali's career that made him very different from any earlier Albanian or Moslem despot. His power reached its peak during the disturbed era of the French Revolution, when French, Austrian, English, and Russian diplomats and secret agents were unusually active in the Ottoman Empire, as well as elsewhere. Therefore

Moslem rule over India had become a hollow pretence. Moslem princes and their hangers-on had to submit. The Hindu majority was indifferent and politically inert, seeing little difference between one kind of foreign master and another. As long as the discipline of their Indian troops held, the British position in India was unshakable.

The Growth of Russian Power

In central Asia and the former Safavid lands, Afghans, Uzbeks, Persians, Kazaks, Kalmucks, and Azerbaijani Turks engaged in a general melee.

Successful captains like Nadir Shah (1736–1747) built vast empires that crumbled as fast as they had been constructed. Until after 1750, the power that made the greatest gains in this confused situation was China. A series of successful military campaigns extended China's northern and western borders to their present limits.

After that date the southward advance of Russian power became the most significant result of the continuing upheaval. Long leaps forward, such as that which brought Peter the Great's authority to the southern shore of the Caspian in 1723, were sometimes followed by withdrawal. But shifts back and forth usually tended to favor

Ali frequently played host to rival representatives of the European great powers, trying always to get promises of support and supplies of arms from them.

Ali also was interested in ideas, and he could not help wondering what it was that allowed revolutionary France to defeat its enemies so often. It was difficult for French agents to explain the power of the slogan "Liberty, Equality, Fraternity" to a man like Ali, who assumed that French successes in battle must be due to supernatural help. When he discovered that some of the revolutionaries were deists and did not accept Christianity, he was delighted. Ali's own religious background was a heretical form of Islam, which taught that traditional Islam and Christianity were both in error. Consequently, Ali felt that his religious opinions and those of the latest thinkers of Paris were really in agreement. If only he could find out the rituals through which the French got in touch with their God, then his armies, too, might be as successful as Napoleon's.

Ali never gave up this hope. Near the end of his life he entered into negotiations with a secret revolutionary society that helped to start the Greek War of Independence in 1821. To be sure, he was looking for help against the sultan in Constantinople, who had resolved to destroy Ali's power. The Greek revolt did not save Ali. Instead, he helped the Greeks because the Turks decided to concentrate on overthrowing him first. This allowed the Greeks to set themselves up solidly in the south. The eventual success of their revolution was made possible by the long siege of Janina that was required before Ali's power collapsed in 1822.

Clearly, the effort to build a bridge between the world of an Albanian tribal chieftain and that of democratic French revolutionary thinkers was not a success. Yet, since Ali's time, many others have made a similar attempt to bridge the gap between their own traditional ideas and those of the Western world. In this sense, the despotic, old-fashioned, religious heretic of Janina was a forerunner of our own age.

Russia because Russian armies and administration, tempered by participation in Europe's rivalries, were generally superior to anything the Moslems of central Asia could create.

Major landmarks of Russia's advance were the annexation of Georgia in 1800 and occupation of the Amu Darya Valley, south of the Aral Sea, in 1849. The net result, shortly after 1850, was to bring the Russians up against the Chinese frontiers in central Asia, while Afghanistan and Persia (Iran) constituted a buffer zone, separating the Russian frontiers from the outposts of British power in India's northwest provinces. These two countries suffered from continual intrigues and violence as local chieftains tried to play off Russian against British agents. The old tribal life survived, but what had once been the crossroads of the world had by 1850 become a backwater, bypassed by everything that really mattered.

Ottoman Retreat   The case of the Ottoman Empire was more complex. It, too, had to keep on retreating. Loss of Hungary in 1699 was followed by further losses to Austria in the Balkans in 1718, but the military tide was temporarily reversed in 1739–1740 when the Turks won several battles against Austrian commanders who had acted rashly. This victory came at an unfortunate time

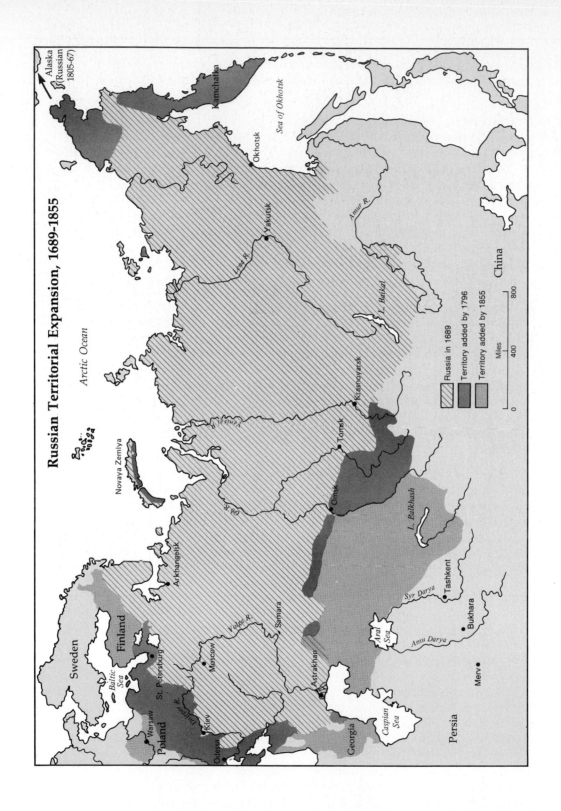

Russian Territorial Expansion, 1689–1855

Alaska (Russian 1805–67)

Arctic Ocean

Sea of Okhotsk

Kamchatka

Okhotsk

Yakutsk

Lena R.

Amur R.

L. Baikal

China

Krasnoyarsk

Yenisei R.

Tomsk

Ob R.

Omsk

L. Balkhash

Novaya Zemlya

Arkhangelsk

Volga R.

Samara

Astrakhan

Syr Darya

Tashkent

Aral Sea

Amu Darya

Bukhara

Merv

Sweden

Finland

Baltic Sea

St. Petersburg

Moscow

Dnieper R.

Warsaw

Poland

Kiev

Odessa

Caspian Sea

Georgia

Persia

Russia in 1689

Territory added by 1796

Territory added by 1855

Miles

0   400   800

How to Borrow from Europe, Ottoman Style On the left a portrait of Selim III (1789–1807), the Ottoman Sultan who started to train a new infantry army in the European fashion. He paid for it with his life when the Janissaries of Istanbul revolted against the threat to their privileges. The fact that he allowed his portrait to be painted was itself an act of impiety; the further fact that the cloak he wears imitates the dress of European kings indicates departure from strict Islamic precedent. Yet his cross-legged posture is that of an Islamic ruler holding court. Selim, after all, was not prepared to borrow very much from Europeans. On the right the upstart ruler of Egypt, Mohammed Ali (ruled 1805–1849), is shown conferring with French engineers who were, presumably, in charge of the industrial plant partly visible through the window. Mohammed Ali not only succeeded in building an army along European lines but also tried to develop a tax base for his government by employing Napoleonic veterans to expand irrigation, improve transport, and establish factories. Yet Mohammed Ali remained traditional in dress and mentality and kept his distance from the French who served him, as we see here. He borrowed to become strong and rich so he could maintain the old ways. It paid off for a while. Mohammed Ali was on the verge of overthrowing his nominal overlord, the Ottoman sultan, in 1840 when a British fleet intervened and compelled him to withdraw to Egypt. He and his successors did not recover effective independence until the late twentieth century.

for the Turks because it convinced them that with only minor adjustments their old military establishment could cope with European arms. Hence, for the following quarter century, the Turks dropped efforts at military reform. Therefore, when the Russian armies, rested from their campaigns of the Seven Years' War, invaded the Ottoman Empire in 1768, the Turks found themselves woefully unprepared. Russian soldiers were completely successful and dictated a peace, at Kuchuk Kainarji in 1774, that gave them control of the Black Sea and the right to pass freely through the straits.

Turkish response to this blow was ineffective. Some thought the situation called for military reform along European lines, but preliminary efforts in that direction were stopped in their tracks by Janissary revolts. Local governors became independent in all but name. Serbs, Greeks, and Arabs rose in revolt. It looked as though the last days of the Ottman Empire were at hand.

What saved Ottoman power until 1918 was the diplomatic intervention by the great powers of Europe. First the French and then the British came to Turkey's aid—sometimes with diplomatic notes, sometimes with a fleet, and sometimes with military instructors and advisers who tried to make the Turkish armies able once again to cope with the empire's defense. Success was only partial. Outlying parts of the empire became independent (Egypt from 1809, Greece in 1830) or autonomous (Serbia from 1815, Romania from 1828). Algeria, which had never been administered regularly from Constantinople, was annexed by the French in 1830. On the other hand, the sultan's administration became stronger in the parts of the empire left to him. The unruly Janissary corps was destroyed in 1826 and a new Turkish army took shape. Efforts to reform the law and administration in accordance with European ideas never achieved success, although sweeping proclamations to that effect were issued in 1839.

The Moslem Reform Movement

Most Moslems felt deep doubts about trying to imitate the West. To do so ran against their deepest prejudices. It meant admitting, in effect, that Islam was not the true faith, for Islam was embodied in the Sacred Law, and the Sacred Law did not allow good Moslems to imitate European laws and customs. If Allah ruled the world and if he had revealed his will to Mohammed, as every Moslem believed, then it was folly to abandon the ancient ways. No doubt, shortcomings on the part of the faithful had angered Allah and persuaded him to withdraw his favor from the Moslem community. The answer, clearly, was to go

back to the rigor of the Prophet's day, to follow every jot and tittle of the Sacred Law and wait patiently until Allah's favor was restored.

Wahhabi Reform   In different parts of the Islamic world many Moslems drew this conclusion. Efforts to get back to the purity of the original Islam created disturbances in China, in Java, and in parts of Africa; but the most successful and influential reform movement, appropriately enough, started in Arabia itself. The spokesman of reform was Mohammed ibn-Abdul-Wahhab (1703–1792), whose followers are often referred to as Wahhabis. A local chieftain of the Saud family became the military leader of the movement and spread its power through most of Arabia. This brought on a collision with the Ottoman sultan, who claimed possession of the two sacred cities, Mecca and Medina. In 1818 Mohammed Ali, pasha of Egypt and only nominally subordinate to the sultan, sent troops, trained in European style, against the Wahhabis and defeated them with ease.

Yet this setback did not destroy the reform movement. On the contrary, Moslems in India and other parts of the Islamic world became interested in the Wahhabi reform only after it ceased to be identified with a strictly Arab military cause. The essence of Abdul-Wahhab's message was simple. He wanted an exact and faithful obedience to the Koran and the Sacred Law— and the ruthless discard of all the Sufi incrustation that had grown up in Moslem practice since the prophet Mohammed's day. The movement had a strong puritanical element in it. In particular, the prohibition of wine was taken in the strictest sense, as were all the other injunctions of the Koran. The Wahhabi reform remains to the present day a great force within Islam and affects the conduct of millions of Moslems even beyond the borders of Saudi Arabia, where it is still the official form of religion.

Moslems unaffected by the Wahhabi movement remained passive for the most part. After all, other disasters had come and gone. This one, too, would finally pass. Allah would show his power only when it pleased him to do so. The wise do not demand reasons for God's acts. Such arguments pressed to their logical extreme seemed to prove that efforts at reform were futile and meaningless, since everything had to wait for Allah.

Only a tiny minority took seriously the idea of borrowing Western skills. Even when such individuals held high positions in government, they could not make their will effective. Until the twentieth century, no Moslem ruler was able to create a clique of administrators whose careers depended on continuance of radical reform, as Peter the Great had done in Russia. Hence, efforts to borrow Western ways always flagged. Too few believed in such a program to make it work.

Art and Literature

Under the circumstances no one would expect to find important new art or literature arising within the Islamic world. Even the effort to stay safely within old forms fell short, for political upheaval meant that steady royal patronage for artists, architects, and poets could not be depended on. Yet the breakdown of these traditional patterns had a negative virtue, since it opened the way for new beginnings. Ottoman Turkish, for example, was cast into new and simpler literary molds, far closer to everyday speech, by Akif Pasha (1787–1845). His literary efforts did not win much admiration, but his deliberate act of cutting Persian and Arabic words out of written Turkish created the literary language used in Turkey today.

Moslem Missionary Work

The bad fortune that came to the Moslem heartlands between 1700 and 1850 was scarcely compensated for by the fact that in Africa and southeast Asia, conversion to Islam continued to advance as it had for centuries. Individuals and small groups, especially those who began to take part in trade, found Islamic law useful. Acceptance of Islam offered a convenient way of entering into the great world at large. Arabs from Oman, in southern Arabia, became active in the slave trade of East Africa, operating mainly from the island base of Zanzibar. European commercial activity in that part of the world was unimportant. On the other side of the Indian Ocean,

Malay pirates and traders sailed the South China Sea and traded with the islands nearby—Mindanao, Borneo, and points between. These traders acted as missionaries of Islam, as their predecessors had done for centuries. But conversions in these regions were a poor substitute for the dominion over the entire Indian Ocean, which had once rested in Moslem hands. On the sea, as on the land, Moslem fortunes were at a low ebb indeed.

HINDU AND BUDDHIST ASIA

Hindus and Buddhists of Southeast Asia found the presence of Europeans far less hard to take than the Moslems did. Both Hindus and Buddhists had already been forced to subordinate themselves to Moslem strangers, who expected to rule and to trade and who were ready to use force, when needed, to get their way. The European trading companies behaved in the same way.

From the Hindu point of view, habits that had been developed to deal with the Moslems worked perfectly well when applied to Europeans. The intruders were treated as another caste, and appropriate rituals were at hand to remove any defilement that might come to a pious Hindu from having to deal with them. Hindu religion was strong and vibrant and therefore could easily resist Christian missionary efforts. Since religion and the entire way of life were intimately bound together, this meant, in effect, that Hindus were not inclined to inquire into European ideas or, indeed, into any other aspect of their civilization.

Hindu-European Cultural Interaction

The British, however, were curious. Until 1837 the language of administration in India remained Urdu, the mixed Persian-Turkish speech used by the Moguls. This meant that British officials and the Hindu clerks who worked for them both had to learn Urdu. As a result, the British tended to view India through a more or less Moslem pair of spectacles. But a few individuals became interested in the other languages of India. The greatest pioneer was Sir William Jones (1746–1794), who translated works from Persian, Arabic, and Sanskrit and founded the Asiatic Society of Bengal. He noticed the relationship between Sanskrit and European languages, a discovery that excited much attention in European learned circles and started quite a vogue for the study of Sanskrit. Enthusiastic scholars assumed that, as the oldest recorded form of Indo-European speech, Sanskrit must be closer to the original thought and language of their own ancestors.

European scholarly interest in Sanskrit studies was also fanned by the attraction many Europeans felt for Hindu philosophy and mystical doctrines. Filled with doubts about the truth of Christian dogma, yet repelled by the mechanical emptiness of a Newtonian universe, many sensitive Europeans became interested in Hindu doctrines that emphasized the illusory nature of the world of sense. Interest in India became, in fact, a trait of the romantic movement, especially in Germany.

Christian Missions   Christian missionaries provided a second and quite different channel for interaction between Hindu and European worlds. To be sure, until 1813 the East India Company carefully excluded Christian missionaries from its trading posts. The theory was that any attack upon local religious customs would damage trade and endanger the Company's position. In 1813, however, Parliament required the Company to admit missionaries freely. Once on the spot, the missionaries decided to put their message in the local vernacular language and, for the purpose, had to develop printing presses and standards of literary usage. The modern written Bengali language got its start in this fashion, though it was soon taken over by Hindu writers for their own purposes. Mission schools were also set up, in which secular subjects were taught as well as Christian doctrine, thus bringing Indian minds into contact with the European intellectual world.

Rammohun Roy   Neither Hindus nor Moslems were much attracted to the doctrines of Christianity. Indeed, in one famous case, a Christian missionary lost his own faith after arguing with learned Hindus and emerged a Unitarian, convinced that all the great religions of the world conveyed essentially the same message. This was also the conclusion arrived at by the first Indian who studied and tried to understand the cultural world of Europe. His name was Rammohun Roy. Born a Brahman, he first learned Urdu in order

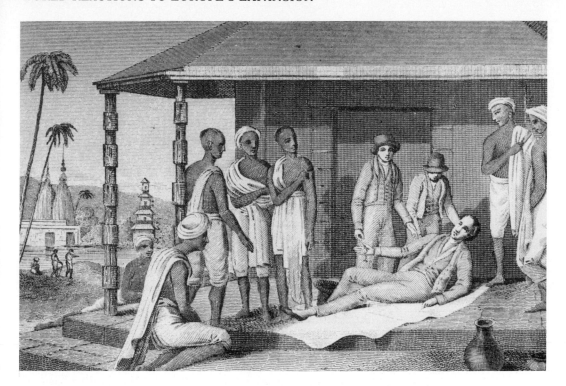

The British in India On the left a miniature painting by an Indian artist shows an agent of the British East India Company taking his ease in private, attended by two Indian servants. The Englishman obviously lives between two different worlds: dressed in European garb, he looks awkward on the settee, since sitting cross-legged did not come easily. Yet he is smoking a hookah (water pipe) and his servants and the furniture of the room are all thoroughly Indian. In the eighteenth century, when this miniature was painted, agents of the India Company often went over to elegant Indian styles of living, finding them better attuned to the climate. In the nineteenth century, however, when steam ships shortened the trip to India and made it safer, more strenuous efforts to impose European standards on India set in. The scene on the right shows a Christian missionary dying of fever in a village, far from the luxuries of upper class urban living preferred by the man on the left. His dress and that of his two European assistants, suggest that the missionary had made no concessions to Indian ways. Liability to unfamiliar diseases remained a serious barrier to European penetration of tropical countries until after 1850.

to qualify for a government job. He then learned English. This led to Greek and Latin, and soon his Bible studies required him to acquire a smattering of Hebrew also. As soon as he could afford to do so, Rammohun Roy resigned from his government job to devote himself more fully to religious studies. From Christianity he turned to the study of Islam, and the comparison of both with his inherited Hindu faith convinced him that all three religions needed to be revised in the light of modern knowledge. The truth conveyed by each of the world's great religions boiled down, he thought, to a simple belief in one God. Unitarians in England and America were much impressed by Rammohun Roy's message, which he brought to England just before his death in 1833. His efforts to reform Hinduism were not very successful. Yet he did persuade the British authorities to prohibit the custom of *suttee*, according to which a widow had been required to sacrifice herself on her husband's funeral pyre.

Rammohun Roy was the first of a long line of prominent Indians who learned English, and through English became acquainted with European civilization. In 1835 the East India Company set up schools to teach English and other European subjects. This opened the door wide for later generations of Indians to straddle two cultural worlds—one English and official, the other Hindu and private.

By and large, Indian Moslems stayed away from the new schools, leaving the pursuit of government clerkships to Hindus. Schooling in India was often defective, and graduates were usually more interested in getting a job in a government office than in interpreting Western civilization to their own people or in reforming Hindu customs in the light of European ideas or examples. Yet, for all its defects, the schools and administration of India began a process of interaction between Hindu and European civilizations on a scale and with an intimacy that was not achieved elsewhere until much later.

Buddhist Retreat and Isolationism

Nothing of this sort bridged the gap between the Buddhist peoples of southeast Asia and the outside world before 1850. These people lived in Ceylon, Burma, Thailand, Laos, Cambodia, and Vietnam. All of these kingdoms found themselves squeezed between the vigorous and expanding land power of China on the north and an aggressive European, primarily British, seapower. The Chinese emperor claimed a vague traditional lordship over all of Southeast Asia, as well as over the British and other European traders who visited Chinese ports. In the years 1766–1769 the Chinese sent an army into Burma to try to enforce Peking's authority, but without lasting success.

British seapower was more difficult for these states to deal with. In 1802, for example, the kingdom of Kandy in Ceylon submitted to British guns. The Burmese had to give up part of their coastlands after a short war (1824–1826), and Thailand lost control of Malaya when local Moslem rulers shifted allegiance from the king of Siam to the East India Company's agents at various times between 1768 and 1824.

However disagreeable, neither Chinese nor British pressure persuaded the Buddhists of southeast Asia to do anything drastic to change their traditional ways. Like the Moslems of Afghanistan and Iran, these peoples and kingdoms were far enough off the beaten track so they could afford to hold fast to old-fashioned ways, although their power of self-defense was clearly inadequate to keep European intruders away.

CHINA'S REVERSAL OF ROLES

China prospered under two exceptionally long reigns. The K'ang-hsi emperor occupied the imperial throne from 1662–1722 and made the Manchu Dynasty secure for the first time. The Ch'ien Lung emperor ascended the throne in 1736 and abdicated in 1795 so as not to reign longer than his famous predecessor; in fact, he continued to fulfill the emperor's role until his death in 1798. The Chinese ideal of stability and decorum was almost perfectly summed up in these two reigns. Virtue as defined by Confucius flourished. Scholarship was vigorous. Imperial patronage of pottery works produced the finest porcelains ever manufactured in China. Painting and poetry flowed from thousands upon thousands of brushes.

Peace prevailed at home; and along the distant frontiers of central Asia, Chinese armies overthrew the last nomad power that dared to defy the celestial emperor's will. Russia, by the Treaty of Kiakhta (1727), recognized the forward movement of Chinese frontiers to include Mongolia and Chinese Turkistan. Having made the northern border secure, the Chinese turned attention to the south and invaded, with varying success, Tibet (1751), Burma (1766), and Nepal (1792).

Population grew rapidly from about 150 million in 1700 to about 430 million in 1850. An increase in artisan manufactures and exports no doubt provided employment for a small part of the new population of China, but the great ma-

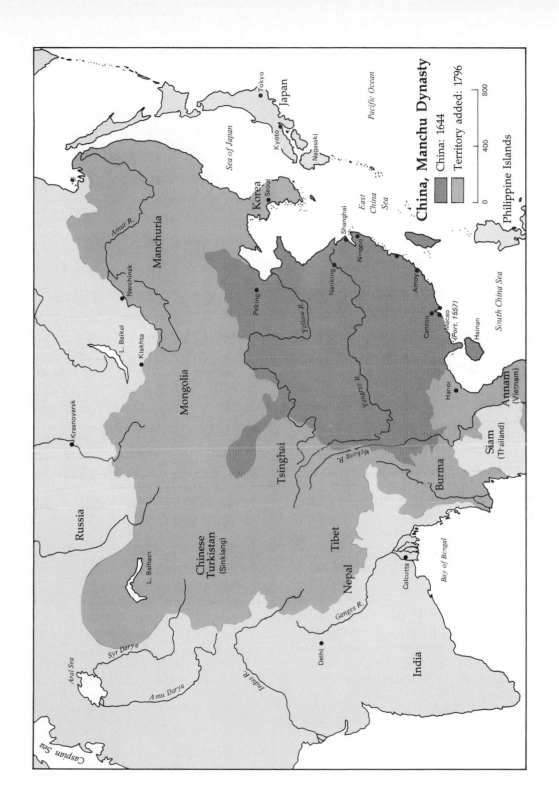

China, Manchu Dynasty

China: 1644
Territory added: 1796

| | 0 | 400 | 800 |

Philippine Islands

Pacific Ocean

Tokyo
Japan
Kyoto
Nagasaki

Sea of Japan

Korea
Seoul

East China Sea

Shanghai
Ningpo
Nanking
Amoy
Peking
Yellow R.
Canton
Macao (Port. 1557)
Hainan

South China Sea

Yangtze R.

Mekong R.
Hanoi
Annam (Vietnam)

Manchuria
Amur R.
Nerchinsk

L. Baikal
Kiakhta

Mongolia

Krasnoyarsk

Tsinghai

Siam (Thailand)
Burma

Russia

Chinese Turkistan (Sinkiang)
L. Baihash

Tibet
Nepal
Calcutta

Bay of Bengal

Syr Darya

Aral Sea

Amu Darya
Indus R.
Ganges R.
Delhi
India

Caspian Sea

jority lived in the villages where rice lands were close at hand.

China's Confucian Mold

Until about 1775 all seemed well. More people simply increased China's vast bulk. New land could be found for cultivation by moving higher up the hill slopes or deeper into swamps and other marginal lands. Everyone who worked hard enough could eat, and the peasants asked for nothing more than that. Their increasing numbers supported many landlords, whose sons studied the Confucian classics, sat for the imperial examinations, and, if they worked hard enough, could hope to pass the necessary tests and get jobs in the government. Since government jobs meant a chance to accumulate wealth, as well as the enjoyment of power and prestige, competition for appointments was intense.

The investment of time and energy in study was correspondingly immense. Study of the classics began in earliest youth and was often pursued day in and day out until middle age, since failure the first time did not mean that a student could not try the examinations again. The extraordinary effort required to pass the tests molded the rulers and leaders of Chinese society to the Confucian ideal and completely closed their minds to anything not tested in the examinations.

The government also patronized scholars directly. Men, famous for their learning, were assigned the task of editing ancient texts and compiling reference works of the most diverse sorts, such as bibliographies, familiar quotations, dictionaries, encyclopedias, lists of "best books," and the like. The grandiose scale of these labors is hard for us to believe. In 1726, for example, a famous encyclopedia of 5020 volumes was completed (although it should be pointed out that a Chinese volume was smaller than those European printers usually produced). By comparison with the bulk of such labors, however, really new work was hard to find. The attention of China's rulers was firmly fixed upon the past. It seemed self-evident that the more ancient anything was, the more valuable it must be.

Of course, not everyone passed the examinations, and among those who did not make it a

more self-indulgent cultural underworld came into existence. Novels or romances, the most famous of which is *The Dream of the Red Chamber* by Ts'ao Hsueh-Chan (d. 1764), reflected the life of such leisured but ineffective individuals. Since this sort of writing was regarded as unworthy of a scholar, the book was never published in the author's lifetime. It portrays the inner life of a large Chinese family with an intimacy modern readers find delightful but which seemed like undressing in public to Ts'ao Hsueh-Chan's contemporaries.

Christianity Discredited   As for European ideas and skills, Chinese scholars and officials had no time for such trifles. Until 1715, to be sure, the emperor often found it useful to employ Jesuit missionaries on various technical tasks at which they excelled, such as casting cannon and making a map of China with reference points established by astronomic observations. But in 1715, after years of bitter quarreling, the pope decided that the Jesuit view of Confucian rites was in error. This was a deep insult to the emperor, who only a few years before had come to the exactly opposite conclusion. Since a key point at issue was how the word "God" should be translated into Chinese, it seemed, to indignant Chinese, that the pope was trying to tell them how to use their own language. No greater insult could have been offered to an emperor who prided himself on his scholarship.

Thereafter, the Christian mission was completely discredited at court. The Jesuits were allowed to stay because they knew how to keep the calendar correctly, but they were forbidden to make converts. Christian missions, as far as they continued to operate at all, had to do so in defiance of the law. Limited underground preaching appealed mainly to poor and discontented groups in the cities. But in the eyes of the scholar class, this only discredited European ideas that much more.

The Peasant Revolt

In 1774 a peasant revolt disturbed the peace of China. It was put down, but secret societies, such as the White Lotus, which was associated with

Old and New in Eighteenth Century China Both these paintings are the work of Joseph Castiglione (1688–1766), a Jesuit missionary in China who brought the full array of European painting techniques to China for the first time. Painting was an important accomplishment for Chinese gentlemen. As a result, the novelty of Castiglione's use of bright color and mathematically accurate perspective attracted a good deal of attention at the court, where the Jesuit mission resided. How far toying with foreign novelties could go is illustrated on the left where one of the Emperor's concubines is pictured in European armor. Yet court routines remained thoroughly traditional, as we see on the right, where the Emperor is shown observing archery, an exercise befitting gentlemen according to Confucius. Chinese painters soon decided that bright color was vulgar, while reliance on a single disappearing point in the European manner seemed unduly restrictive for scroll painting. European novelties were thus dismissed as unworthy of further consideration. Accordingly, Chinese court and society continued faithful to ancient models until the 1840s and beyond.

this revolt, kept on multiplying. The reason was that poor peasants no longer could live in traditional ways in those parts of the country where the growing population had begun to press on the supply of cultivable land. If loans to peasants to tide them over a bad season could not be repaid, creditors could acquire whatever land the debtors had once possessed. This soon created an angry, landless class ready for revolt. The result, therefore, was a series of disturbances—some small, others more serious—that kept the imperial authority on the defensive. The government's long success in maintaining peace and prosperity thus began to backfire after 1775 in a most distressing way.

Trade Problems Lead to War

At almost the same time, China's foreign trade began to present a serious problem too. In 1757 the emperor had decreed that Canton should be the only port at which foreign ships might put in. China's main European trading partner was the East India Company, which enjoyed a legal monopoly of Britain's trade with China. Dutch, French, and, after 1784, U.S. ships also put in at Canton occasionally; but the Chinese were able to keep them all under control by giving an association of merchants, the Co-hong, a monopoly of all dealings with strangers.

From the European point of view, the great problem was to find something the Chinese wanted to import. Chinese-made goods commanded a lively market in Europe and elsewhere, but about the only thing the Chinese wanted in exchange was silver. Europeans were reluctant to see their good silver disappear into China, and it was not until a brisk market for opium developed in China that the Europeans discovered a commodity they could offer instead. Opium was produced cheaply in India, and it gave the English just what they needed to make the China trade really profitable for the first time.

In 1834 the British government canceled the legal monopoly the East India Company had long enjoyed and tried to put trade with China on the same basis as trade with any other part of the world. A swarm of private traders therefore descended on Canton, eager to get in on the profits to be made from the opium trade.

The Chinese imperial authorities soon took alarm at the spread of the opium habit. They forbade the production or sale of the drug, but this simply drove the trade underground. European merchants began dealing with all sorts of shady characters and smuggling became a large-scale, organized gangster affair. In 1839 the Chinese decided to crack down. A special commissioner came from Peking with instructions to break up the illegal trade. He seized 30,000 chests of opium within a few months and seemed on the point of cleaning up the whole mess when he collided with British authority.

The Opium War   The point at issue was trifling. Some English sailors had engaged in a brawl at Canton and killed a Chinese. The Chinese demanded that one of the sailors be handed over to them to be executed. From a Chinese point of view, this was only common justice and an ordinary assertion of sovereignty. From the British point of view, however, handing over a man to be executed without trial and without any proof of his guilt was an appalling miscarriage of justice. The British ship's captain therefore refused. He was backed up by a commissioner of trade, appointed by the British crown. When the Chinese then tried to use force, the British government decided to send a detachment of the Royal Navy to the scene.

British naval vessels and marine landing parties found the Chinese coast almost completely at their mercy. Chinese ports lacked harbor defenses, and Chinese troops could not move rapidly enough from one threatened place to another. When clashes did take place, the Chinese soldiers proved far inferior to the British detachments. In 1842 the bewildered and indignant Chinese had to make peace. By the Treaty of Nanking they opened four additional ports to British trade, agreed to levy a uniform 5 percent tariff on imports, ceded Hong Kong to the British, and officially recognized that Queen Victoria was not—as the Chinese had always before pretended—paying tribute to the emperor when British ships put in at Chinese ports.

Unequal Treaties   The French and American governments soon made similar and even more advantageous treaties with China. In 1844, the

Americans secured the right of extraterritoriality. This meant that American citizens would be tried by American law, even on Chinese soil, and before American consuls. In the same year, the French secured official toleration of Christianity and of missionary activity in the port cities. By the principle of the "most favored nation clause," which was inserted into each of these treaties, any concession to one foreign power became a concession to all. Thus, a mere five years from the time when the clash had begun, China found itself the victim of unequal treaties and unable to stave off the intruding foreigners.

The shock to Chinese feelings was immense. The Celestial Kingdom, to which all barbarians ought to pay tribute, had suddenly ceased to occupy the center of the world. New and strange powers, unknown to Confucius, had burst upon the scene. The ancients offered no rules for how to cope with such a situation. Stunned surprise and utter dismay were all that Chinese scholars and officials could feel at first; and in their state of shock they had no time to turn toward more constructive action before a new and violent civil war flamed up, the Taiping Rebellion, which for fifteen years (1850–1864) tore at the vitals of the empire.

The suddenness of China's fall needs to be emphasized. Until 1839 the internal troubles of the country remained marginal. Tried-and-true Confucian patterns of conduct seemed to be working well, and China's superiority over the barbarian world was completely taken for granted by every educated Chinese. The intellectual class, in other words, had been so homogenized that no one had any idea of how to deal with the crisis that burst so suddenly. The great bulk of China sprawled helpless, blind, angry—completely unprepared for the reversal of roles that events had thrust upon the nation.

THE LAND
OF THE RISING SUN

Japan's history from 1700 to 1850 was in almost every respect the exact opposite of China's. While China fought a series of victorious frontier wars, Japan remained at peace. While China's population nearly tripled, Japan's population remained almost constant. While Chinese scholars fixed their gaze upon their own past to the exclusion of everything else in the world, Japanese intellectuals explored several different kinds of learning and paid considerable attention to what was going on in Europe, even though the official policy of isolation remained rigidly in force.

Political Insecurity
of the Shogun's Power

From the beginning, the Tokugawa shoguns had to face some awkward problems that refused to go away. Nothing like China's smug self-satisfaction could, therefore, arise in Japan, since both the ruling clique of the Tokugawa family and the "outside lords," who had been excluded from any part in the central government, realized that the whole system might fall apart again. Only the bitter memory of Japan's long civil wars and the political watchfulness of the shoguns kept the peace. But memories of a time when the Tokugawa family was just the equal, not the superior, of other noble families never died; nor could the Japanese forget that the emperor, kept in seclusion by the shoguns, was in theory supreme. No doctoring of the historical record could hide the fact that the shoguns' power was a usurpation.

Economic Disbalance
between Warriors and Merchants

Another difficult problem arose from the success with which the shoguns kept the peace. The warrior class had no occupation when there was no war. It was a matter of policy (as established by Ieyasu Tokugawa in 1603) to require all important lords to spend part of the year in the capital, Tokyo, where they would be directly under the eye of the shogun; and when they were not in residence they were required to leave hostages behind in the form of sons and other close relatives. Hence, all of the fief holders had to keep houses in the capital, where they had nothing much to do.

Two consequences followed. First, fief holders had to convert at least a part of their income, which was in rice, into money that could be used in the capital to keep up the family establishment. This required merchants to buy surplus rice in the countryside and sell it in the cities, above all in Tokyo, the new magnet to which population and other resources flowed. Second, the merchants who organized the distribution of rice and other necessary commodities grew rich; whereas the fief holders had to sell at the merchants' price and buy at the merchants' price and therefore grew poor. At least they found themselves too poor to live up to the standard of luxury that rapidly developed in Tokyo and other cities. Special amusement quarters catered to the taste of rich merchants for song and dance, good food and company. Warriors, whiling away their time idly in town, could not resist such attractions; and when they could not afford them, they ran recklessly into debt.

The result was a sharp discrepancy between what was and what most Japanese felt ought to be. The warriors and rulers were poorer than the merchants, who, according to Confucian ideas, were social parasites and pests, ranking, by rights, below hard-working peasants. The fief holders and the peasants agreed in deploring what had happened and tried all sorts of ways to remedy the injustice. Sometimes the government resorted to outright confiscation of merchant fortunes. More often a repudiation of debts was decreed, in whole or in part; or the currency was debased to make repayment of debts easier. All such measures failed. The merchants quickly made good their losses by charging more for services rendered. As long as the fief holders were not allowed to remain all year round on their lands, the merchants' services were literally indispensable, and they were, therefore, always able to regain the upper hand economically.

Toward the end of the period, some of the fief holders tried to solve their economic problem by developing mining and other enterprises on their holdings. New crops and skills spread—particularly the cultivation of silk worms. Japan, for the first time, became self-sufficient in silk. Another practice was to marry into a merchant family, thus refreshing the depleted fortunes of the noble warrior stock and endowing the merchant with a new respectability. Blurring of class lines in this fashion was forbidden by the warrior code

of behavior, but the temptation was great on both sides and instances multiplied.

Official Ideology

The shoguns' policy in face of these difficulties was to sit tight and hope for the best. Neo-Confucianism was official. Study of other schools of thought was formally prohibited. Great emphasis was put upon loyalty; and the code of approved conduct for the warrior class was spelled out exactly, both in formal decree and in literature and drama. Yet, the more the official line stressed loyalty to superiors, the more awkward it became to justify the shoguns' own disloyalty to the emperor. Public demonstrations of loyalty to the emperor thus became a way of expressing dissatisfaction with the shogun. But the government found it impossible to suppress sentiments that were outwardly so correct and proper.

The Development of Shinto   Accordingly, a school of thought arose that stressed the divine origin and descent of the imperial house. By degrees experts elaborated rites and ceremonies to celebrate the great events recounted in Japanese legend. These practices, referred to as *Shinto*, evolved rapidly to the level of an organized religion—complete with priests, different sects, and rituals for everyday human emergencies of birth, marriage, and death. Borrowing from Christian and Buddhist rituals seems to have gone into the development of Shinto. An even stronger element was preference for an authentic Japanese, instead of a borrowed Chinese, doctrine.

The development of Shinto cults among the Japanese public at large was matched by the labors of a handful of scholars who set out to learn about Western thought. The medium was Dutch, for a single Dutch ship was permitted to put into Nagasaki harbor each year and to carry on a carefully supervised trade. Foreign books were smuggled into Japan by this route, and a few persons learned how to read them and even made Japanese translations or adaptations of some medical and mathematical texts.

Admirers of Dutch learning and those who cultivated Japanese tradition got along with one another quite well. Both opposed the official Neo-

Japan and the Europeans In 1638 the Japanese government limited foreign contact by allowing only a single Dutch ship to dock at an island in Nagasaki harbor each year. This law remained in force until 1854. On the left a Japanese artist recorded the outlandish appearance of a Dutch merchant of the early eighteenth century. The mingling of European and Asian cultures that intensifying trade relations provoked is clearly apparent, for the Dutchman carries a clay pipe from Holland and has a mongrel dog for company, while he wears a coat of Indonesian batik cloth, tailored in European style, and takes shelter from the sun beneath an enormous umbrella (of Indian provenance) held aloft by an Indonesian servant. Such isolated, rather comical visitors scarcely seemed threatening, which is why they were allowed to come ashore. Yet in fact European capabilities were building up throughout Japan's period of isolation to become as dangerous as the great wave, portrayed on the left by a famous Japanese woodcut artist, Katsushika Hokusai (1760–1849). As the wave inundates the fishing boats in the foreground and even overtops the snow capped peak of Mt. Fuji that rises east of Tokyo, so European and American influence broke upon Japan immediately after Hokusai's death.

Confucian orthodoxy of the shogun's government; both were supported more or less secretly by the "outside lords," who never quite gave up their jealousy of the Tokugawa family; and both were looking for alternative lines of action for their country. Hence, when foreign pressures did persuade the shogun to open Japan again to foreign trade (1854), a few individuals in Japan were already familiar with some of the basic characteristics of Western civilization.

The Life of the Arts

Japan's remarkable social structure was reflected in the arts. On the one hand, official culture conformed closely to Chinese models. Japanese painters, whose work can scarcely be distinguished from the work of Chinese masters, flourished at court. Literary scholarship along Chinese lines was brought to bear on the Japanese past. Chinese characters were used to write Japanese, and Chinese words were imported wholesale into the Japanese language to carry the proper Confucian distinctions. All this Chinese influence made Japan seem little more than a provincial variant of Chinese civilization.

On the other hand, there was a vigorously vulgar artistic life in the amusement sections of Tokyo and other cities, designed to appeal to the taste of merchants and other uneducated persons. Kabuki plays and the arts of geisha girls were examples of this sort of cultural tradition. In addition, artists produced cheap, multicolored prints that have since won the admiration of art critics and historians. They allow lively glimpses of the delights of city life as known in old Japan. In addition, novels and tales of adventure which were produced at this time gave literary expression to the same lifestyle.

Toward the end of the Tokugawa period, blurring of the distinctions between paintings done in the Chinese manner and the more popular styles faithfully mirrors the breaking down of the distinctions between merchant and warrior classes. Japan, therefore, saw the emergence of a more varied, complex, and pluralist society and culture—in a small way similar to the expanding pluralism of Western civilization—immediately before the nation plunged into new complexities

by opening itself wide to imitation of and borrowings from the West in 1854.

THE WORLD'S LESS-DEVELOPED REGIONS

The largest human population that remained on the fringes of civilized life lived in sub-Saharan Africa. Actually, the peoples of that continent were much involved with the larger world, but without knowing much about the rest of the world, or themselves being known by it.

Effects of the Trade in African Slaves

Black Africans experienced two powerful, contradictory changes between 1700 and 1850. Throughout the eighteenth century and until about 1810, the slave trade, which went into high gear after about 1650, grew in scale and importance. Decade after decade, more captives were hunted down and shipped across the ocean. The demand for more and more slaves meant that slave hunting spread throughout almost all parts of the African continent. Slave raiders began to work inland from the east coast as well as from the west, where slaving had concentrated at first. But as the slave trade mounted in intensity, critical voices arose in England and France. After decades of agitation, in 1807 antislavery reformers prevailed upon the British Parliament to pass a law making the slave trade illegal. When the British ceased to be preoccupied by fighting Napoleon, the Royal Navy assigned some of its vessels to the task of preventing slave ships from carrying their human cargoes across the ocean. As a result, after about 1810 the number of slaves leaving Africa began to shrink very fast, and by 1850 only the sultan of Zanzibar in East Africa and a few Portuguese slavers moving between Angola and Brazil kept the trade alive.

The steady intensification and then sudden slackening of the slave trade had disruptive effects on African life. Weak and exposed village populations were ruthlessly assaulted by slave raiders, but local devastation seems not to have led to any general or widespread depopulation. Presumably, the productivity of crops derived from the New World improved African food supply so much that more children survived and thus counterbalanced the losses due to slave raiding. But no one really knows because exact statistics cannot be discovered.

On the other hand, historians do now know a good deal about the number of slaves who crossed the ocean because the trade was conducted by specialized ships, whose arrivals and departures were recorded at their ports of call, and whose carrying capacity can be figured out pretty accurately. On this basis, historians now believe that a total of about 11.3 million Africans were shipped across the ocean. Two-thirds of them—7.5 million—crossed between 1700 and 1810; and despite British and French efforts to suppress the slave trade after that date, another 1.9 million left Africa before the trade finally came to a halt about 1880.

These are enormous numbers. Four to five times as many Africans as Europeans reached the New World by 1800; but as long as new slaves fresh from Africa were easy to get, not many of them were able to raise children. The establishment of a self-sustaining population of African descent in the New World came mostly after 1810, when the British navy began to intercept slave ships and compel them to return their captives to Africa. Slave owners in the New World then found it cheaper to encourage their slaves to reproduce themselves instead of buying replacements as before. Not long thereafter, slavery was abolished throughout the French (1815) and British (1832) empires. Slavery survived in the United States until 1863, in Cuba until 1886, and in Brazil (the last important country to abolish it) until 1889. Emancipation made ex-slaves of African descent the largest element in the population wherever sugar plantations had prevailed. The burden of slavery thus resulted in the establishment of large black populations overseas, most notably in Brazil, the Caribbean Islands, and the United States of America.

Within Africa itself, the dwindling of the slave trade after 1810 had mixed consequences. Africa's political and economic system had been built around the slave trade to a very considerable

degree, so when that trade suddenly slacked off, the shock was correspondingly great. States that had drawn power and income from slaving raids had to find a new basis or crumble. Some survived and even flourished, like the Ashanti federation that had risen to power in the northern part of Ghana in the eighteenth century. In that part of Africa, other forms of economic production and trade had long existed; and the Ashanti federation maintained its power because West African society was able to shift from exporting slaves to exporting palm oil and other agricultural commodities.

In other parts of Africa the collapse of the slave trade had different and even destructive consequences. This was most apparent in southern Africa, where a series of wars between advancing whites and black farmers and herdsmen started in 1779 and achieved new intensity after 1836, when several thousand Boers, descendants of the original Dutch settlers at the Cape of Good Hope, migrated northward, across the Orange and Fish rivers. They did so to escape the British, who had replaced the Dutch at the Cape in 1815 as part of the peace settlement after the Napoleonic wars. In 1834, the British governors set out to abolish slavery in South Africa in accordance with Parliament's decree. A great many of the Boers objected; and in an effort to preserve their own way of life, which depended in considerable degree on using African labor for nasty jobs around the farm under conditions that amounted to slavery, they embarked on a Great Trek northward and eventually (1853–1854) set up two new republics of their own in the African interior.

The Boers had rifles and used them freely against Africans who tried to oppose them. Local tribesmen, armed only with spears, could not resist successfully. But in Natal, to the north and east of the Boer republics, an extraordinary military revolution was carried through by Shaka, who became chief of a small Zulu clan in 1816 and was assassinated by his half-brothers just twelve years later in 1828. In that short time, Shaka created a new and terrible form of warfare by training warriors to march in close order and fight hand to hand with short spears. Earlier, South African warfare had been a matter of individual combat, featuring javelins thrown from a distance; and fighting was habitually broken off after a few champions had been killed or wounded. Shaka, however, fought to win. His soldiers killed everyone who resisted them on the field of battle. Defeated tribes were compelled either to flee or to submit by sending their young men to serve in the Zulu units. Shaka's forces therefore grew very rapidly, and the range of their operations expanded every year.

The result was catastrophic. In the twelve years of Shaka's rule, his ever-victorious army devastated much of southern Africa and provoked flights and migrations that extended as far north as the Great Lakes and as far south as the borders of Cape colony. The political upheaval Shaka's bloodthirsty victories created actually helped the Boers to advance. The Zulu army had disrupted the tribal societies that might otherwise have opposed the Boers more successfully than was possible under the conditions that prevailed after Shaka's death, when the Zulu army lacked the will to do more than maintain itself amidst the chaos Shaka had created.

In other parts of Africa, the breakup of traditional political and economic patterns was not so sudden and violent as in the south. Yet there are signs that African states and peoples in all their variety were facing something of a general crisis about 1850. The rise of a number of Moslem reform movements, aimed at restoring true religion, was one sign of distress and dissatisfaction. As a result, efforts to achieve religious reform by military action kept much of West Africa in uproar, both before and after 1850.

In most of Africa, established ways of life were already under unusual strain at the time when the age-old disease barrier that had previously protected the continent from outsiders began to break down. The great breakthroughs of scientific medicine lay still in the future, but after about 1850 Europeans did become able to keep malaria at bay, and malaria had been the most common cause of the fevers that killed strangers in Africa. Europeans protected themselves from malaria by taking preventive doses of quinine, a drug derived from the bark of a tree native to Peru. Although they had known about quinine since the sixteenth century, Europeans secured a regular supply only after Dutch entrepreneurs took seeds from wild-growing (and relatively rare) trees in Peru and developed plan-

tations of them in Indonesia. Regular and dependable supplies of quinine became available in Europe just about mid-century. As a result, exploration of Africa became far safer, even though other tropical diseases continued to endanger outsiders who lacked childhood exposure and inherited resistances to them.

Under these circumstances, European efforts to explore the interior of Africa became more and more systematic and successful. Geographical societies in London and elsewhere financed expeditions to find the source of the Nile, for example, or to explore the courses of the Niger and Congo rivers. Until the 1880s, important features of the African interior remained unknown to outsiders; but the main mysteries of what Europeans had dubbed the Dark Continent were solved between the 1840s and the 1870s. Commercial, missionary, and military penetration of Africa swiftly followed, fueled by European rivalries and facilitated by the disorganization of African states and peoples that was reaching crisis proportions by about mid-century.

Thus, the special position of Africans in the world—exposed to contact with both the Moslem and European heartlands but safeguarded by the outsiders' vulnerability to tropical diseases—came to an end at a time when Europe's power and technical advantages over other peoples were reaching a climax. The suddenness with which almost all of the African continent came under European political and economic domination after 1850 was the natural, even if surprising, result.

Explorations of the Pacific

The lands of the Pacific were thinly occupied by comparison with Africa. After the first few years of oceanic discovery, European ships stopped exploring for a long time. The reason was that nothing worthwhile attracted ships to the barren coasts of such lands as Australia, where the native inhabitants were hunters and gatherers and had nothing to offer Europeans in trade. In addition, there were serious problems for European vessels that wished to sail for long distances across an ocean so vast as the Pacific. Until an accurate marine chronometer had been invented (1761), the longitude of a small island could not be meas-

SHAKA, THE ZULU CHIEF

Shaka was the son of a Zulu chief, born about 1787 in Natal. His birth was scandalous because both his parents belonged to the same clan and marriage within the clan was prohibited by Zulu custom. As a result, when he was six years old his mother took him back to her homeland, where he grew up fatherless and despised as a bastard. When he was about fifteen, he and his mother fled from the persecution they suffered, taking refuge in land controlled by a rising new military empire, headed by the paramount chief of the Mtetwa people.

When Shaka finally came of age, he proved to be a man of fierce energy and found release for some of his pent-up anger by becoming a warrior in the Mtetwa army. For six years he served in the ranks, distinguishing himself for his bravery and skill. Then, in 1816, the paramount chief sent him to take over command of the Zulus, who were then a small tribe, part of the confederation of tribes headed by the Mtetwa.

Returning to his father's people in this way meant that Shaka had to overcome the disgrace of his illegitimate birth. He did so by dint of personality and ready resort to instant execution of anyone who opposed him. But what really confirmed Shaka's authority was a reform of military tactics and training that he inaugurated. Instead of relying on individual combat, as had been customary, he armed his warriors with short spears and formed them into units that maneuvered on the battle field so as to take the enemy in flank and rear while simultaneously pinning the foe down by an intense frontal attack.

Close order drill had the same effect on Zulu warriors that it had once had on Spartan hoplites and Roman legionaries. Young men, trained to move together on the battlefield, achieved an intense esprit de corps that bound them together and separated them from the rest of society. As a result, Shaka created a professional army that easily defeated all rivals. He displaced the Mtetwa paramount chief in 1817 and rapidly extended his power in every direction. Conquered tribes were compelled to send their young men to join Shaka's regiments, where the psychological effect of close order drill made them over into proud Zulu warriors. In this way the Zulus rapidly became a numerous and powerful people, able to dominate a wide region of southern and central Africa.

Then in 1827 Shaka's mother died. His grief was bitter, and Shaka decreed that no crops should be planted and no children born for a year of mourning. He even ordered pregnant women and cows to be slaughtered so that everyone would know the greatness of his loss. He also ordered his army to keep fighting without the usual season's rest for the harvest season.

This was the last straw, and two of his half brothers murdered him in 1828. But in twelve short years Shaka had built a Zulu nation. Even after British riflemen showed the limits of hand-to-hand combat by defeating Zulu regiments in battle in 1879, the Zulus continued to be a proud and powerful people and memories of Shaka's extraordinary career remain alive even today.

ured. Hence, the chance of returning to the same speck of land in the vastnesses of the open Pacific was slight. Moreover, on long voyages the crew suffered from scurvy—a serious disease brought on by lack of vitamins. No ship's captain could therefore afford to cruise around looking for an island that ought to be somewhere in the general area where the ship was, but whose exact location no one could tell for sure.

In the eighteenth century, organized European navies took over the work of exploration, and within a short time they had charted the coastlines of nearly the whole Pacific Ocean. The first official explorer was Captain Vitus Bering of the Russian navy. He made two voyages, in 1728 and 1741, and discovered the straits that bear his name, the Aleutians, and the Alaskan mainland. Russian fur traders soon followed in Bering's wake and set up trading posts on the American side of the straits. The French sent Captain Louis Antoine de Bougainville to cruise in the Pacific, 1767–1769; the British countered with Captain James Cook, who made three voyages to the same regions between 1768 and 1779. Captain Cook carried with him the first really successful marine chronometer and was able, therefore, to plot the longitude as well as the latitude of the coasts and islands he explored. The first usefully accurate maps of the Pacific region resulted from his careful labors. He also required his sailors to eat sauerkraut in order to protect them from scurvy by providing a supply of vitamin C in their diet. Later the British navy discovered that lime juice was even more effective as a protection against scurvy, whence the nickname "Limey" for British sailors.

Settlement Patterns in the Pacific Area   Whalers soon followed the explorers, with the result that Tahiti and Hawaii and other less-famous islands of the Pacific had to put up with boisterous whalers and other sailors who put ashore for a bit of relief from the cramped quarters of their ships and from the smell of whale oil. Diseases brought to the Polynesians by the mariners had the usual effect of spreading devastating epidemics, from which the old island life never recovered.

Around the shores of the Pacific, too, European settlers and traders began to leave their mark before 1850. Spanish missions moved north

to Nootka to counter the Russian advance into Alaska. But the imposing Spanish Empire in the Americas began to break up after 1808 as local revolts gained headway. Not long after Mexico became independent of Spain (1821), the United States attacked (1846) and took over California. Almost immediately, the discovery of gold (1848) started a rush into that remote land.

Across the Pacific, in Australia, European settlement dated from 1788, when the British government sent the first shiploads of convicts there to make a new life for themselves on the other side of the world. Beginning in 1793, free settlers began to arrive. The effects of the arrival of the newcomers upon the Australian aborigines were drastic. They were driven toward the northern parts of the continent, where deserts and heat made the land unattractive to the English. New plants and animals introduced by the Europeans upset the existing balance of nature in dramatic ways, so that, for instance, a plague of rabbits resulted from the absence of the natural predators.

The last important area of European settlement was New Zealand, where British colonists arrived for the first time in 1840. The Maori tribes, who lived in New Zealand, were more able to cope with the shock of contact with Western civilization than were the native Australians. As a result, after the usual losses from disease and social disorganization, the Maoris, with the help of the new food resource supplied by the potato, made an astonishing recovery. In recent years Maoris have entered freely into the public life of New Zealand and now enjoy ordinary citizen rights.

Amerindian Retreat

The fate of the Amerindians differed from that of the Maoris. Some tribes were utterly destroyed, but many survived, often only as a shattered remnant. As late as 1890, some of the Plains Indians in North America attempted armed resistance to the white settlers, but this was the last flicker of a century or more of hopelessly one-sided struggles. Repeatedly, Indians were assigned lands by treaty arrangements, only to see white settlers press into the areas supposedly reserved for the

Indians. Only poor and unpromising land, which the white settlers did not want, was allowed to remain in Indian possession. In South America, too, the last flicker of warlike resistance to advancing settlement came between 1841 and 1871, when the Araucanian Indians met defeat at the hands of Chileans who proceeded to extend their frontiers to the southernmost tip of South America.

By far the largest number of Amerindians lived in Peru, Mexico, and adjacent regions where they served the Spaniards and mestizo populations in various humble capacities. When revolution broke out among the whites of Spanish America (after 1808), it did not make much difference for the Indians. Until after 1850, the Indian element among the peoples in Spanish America remained passive politically. They continued to submit quietly to the demands imposed upon them by persons of Spanish descent.

Only in the remoter recesses of the Amazon jungles and in parts of the frozen Arctic did life continue unaffected, or almost unaffected, by the presence in the New World of persons who shared the skills and ideas of Western civilization. Civilized ways had a remarkable reach. For example, metal hatchets, traded from hand to hand, often penetrated far beyond any face-to-face encounter between European traders and the people who ultimately put the hatchet to use. Moreover, even

simple tools sometimes transformed life patterns in surprising ways. In this sense, we can be sure that by 1850 no part of the inhabited globe was immune to the impact of civilization; and the regions where isolated, simple societies still survived were shrinking faster than ever before.

CONCLUSION

By comparison to the state of the world in our own time, the globe remained a relatively spacious place in 1850. It took months for persons, goods, or news to move from one side of the earth to the other. What occurred in China had no immediate impact upon what happened in Europe, Africa, or America. A lag in reaction time and defects in communication gave local peoples room to maneuver without immediately attracting the attention and intervention of world powers. The Industrial Revolution, already well launched in Europe, soon took care of this lag in communication, inaugurating a new age which we will consider in the last part of this book.

Before we do so, however, we must return to Europe and the West for a closer look at the two great movements that were to transform the world in the period after 1850: the Democratic and the Industrial revolutions.

Chapter 20

THE DEMOCRATIC AND INDUSTRIAL REVOLUTIONS

1776 to 1850

In 1776 the states of western Europe were threatened by the giant power of Russia. Vast resources and an enormous population had been organized by the despotic government of Catherine the Great to support an immense army, which was as well trained and equipped as any in Europe. Moreover, Russian power was on the move. Poland lost its eastern provinces to Russia in 1772; Turkey had been humbled in 1774; Catherine was laying plans to create a new, dependent Greek empire on the ruins of the Ottoman state; and only a royal coup d'état in Sweden in 1772 prevented that country from becoming a province or protectorate of the Russian Empire. Joseph II of Austria judged it better to cooperate with the Russians against the Turks than try to oppose them. The Prussians, unable to find any allies to help them stop the Russian advance, came to the same conclusion and joined with Russia and Austria three separate times—in 1772, in 1793, and in 1795—in successive partitions of Poland. When an independent Poland had thus been completely erased, the Russian frontier and the eastern boundaries of Prussia and Austria coincided, leaving no buffer zone between.

Three-quarters of a century had shown how rapidly the Russians could learn all they needed to know about Western military skills and organization. By 1775 they had come abreast of western European states in these respects, with the result that Russia's size was no longer a handicap but an immense advantage. The Germanies, divided among more than 300 sovereign states under the shadowy leadership of the Holy Roman Emperor, were clearly in no position to check Russian power. Even a one-time giant such as France seemed dwarfed by Russia's size and resources—quite apart from the fact that rivalry with England and frictions among the different classes at home made it impossible for the French government to devote more than passing attention to the rise of Russia.

EMERGENCE OF EUROPE'S NEW REGIME

Three-quarters of a century later, the aspect of Europe was strikingly different. By 1850, Russia was definitely old-fashioned. The czar's empire had fallen behind western Europe once again, in military matters as well as in industrial and political organization. The restless drive to expand Russian power in every direction, which had been so much in evidence in Catherine's reign, had given way to a conservative policy aimed at keeping things as they were. Internal difficulties were beginning to trouble the Russian state, which was still built upon serfdom for the majority and privilege for the few.

The fundamental difference between the situation in 1775 and the situation in 1850 was that the peoples of western Europe had been able to raise themselves again to a new and higher level of wealth and power, and in doing so outstripped Russia and the rest of the world. Thus western Europeans postponed by a century having to face up to states as large as Russia and as well organized as they were themselves.

This remarkable reassertion of the primacy of western Europe was carried through on two fronts. No one planned it; no one foresaw the result. France took the lead in politics; Britain took the lead in economics. Between them, they revolutionized the life of Europe and moved that continent from the Old to the New Regime. The change in politics was simple in principle. Government and people came into closer partnership than before. As a result, the energies of a larger proportion of the total population could be brought to bear upon common, deliberately chosen goals. Routines of local life, particularly of village life, were broken in upon; service to the nation in war became the duty of every male citizen simply because the government was now "his" government and not the king's. Where the Old Regime had settled for political passivity on the part of the lower classes, the New Regime allowed and expected activity. The power, wealth, and energy at the disposal of governments that succeeded in taking their peoples into this kind of active partnership increased far beyond the limits imaginable to Louis XIV or Catherine the Great.

This "Democratic Revolution" gained much of its success from the fact that it got under way at the same time as the Industrial Revolution. The essence of the Industrial Revolution was the discovery of new ways to use mechanical power for producing useful goods. In particular, steam engines were used to drive textile and other kinds of machinery. Increased supply of power permitted the design of larger machines and new processes. As more and cheaper goods were produced, consumption increased. Then transportation and communication were revolutionized by the use of steam and electricity. As a result industrialized nations became able to draw food and raw materials from all over the world to feed themselves and their factories. The pioneers of industrialization reaped enormous wealth. Some of the new wealth became available for state purposes, with the result that western Europeans could be both strong and rich at the same time. When total production leaped upward every decade, harsh and difficult choices between private and public, civilian and military, use of resources did not have to be made.

Europe's power and wealth under the Old Regime had also expanded rapidly. What happened from the 1770s on, therefore, was nothing new, although the pace of economic and technical change increased decade by decade. Internal balances between industry and agriculture and between the middle class and the aristocracy shifted sharply in favor of the former. This led to political transformations which gave the middle classes the leading role in public life because they, more than any other segment of society, were able to voice the public opinion to which the new governments of Europe paid attention.

Thus the New Regime that emerged by 1815 from the upheavals and wars of the French Revolution was, in a sense, a middle-class regime. Business people and professionals took over roles formerly reserved for nobles. High social status, wealth, and office were often earned by individual skill, luck, education, or personal characteristics. Such flexibility, in turn, allowed abrupt shifts of social energies into new activities—whenever they became profitable or seemed important for some other reason.

All the characteristics of the Old Regime that had distinguished Europe from other civilizations thus emerged from the crucible of the Democratic and Industrial revolutions in exaggerated form. In changing itself once again, western Europe remained true to its changeable past and became, more emphatically than before, the dominating center of the entire world.

THE AMERICAN REVOLUTION

As long as the English colonies in North America had to contend with unfriendly Indians and with French rivals in Canada and Louisiana, differences of opinion with the British government—intense enough at times—were always settled short of an open break. The British navy and, in time of war, British soldiers were necessary for the colonists' protection so it was not safe to quarrel too much with the mother country. After 1763, however, French power no longer existed in North America. This meant that the colonists no longer had anything to fear from their neighbors. The Spaniards were weak and distant; and without the French to arm them, the Indians could not hope to put up much resistance either.

The government of George III felt that the colonists had become too independent. In particular, British ministers in London thought the colonies should help to pay for the war that had just been won by submitting to taxes imposed by Parliament. The colonists objected. They had not been consulted and were not represented in the English Parliament. As the colonists saw matters, Englishmen had fought the Civil War of 1642–1649 to win the right of paying only those taxes agreed to by their elected representatives. They concluded that the sacred rights of Englishmen were endangered by the tyranny of King George, who was, in any case, trying to manipulate elections to Parliament in order to make it a rubber stamp for his own royal will.

Many people in England agreed with the colonists' arguments. Even when the dispute led to public violence and then to war, a party in Parliament criticized the king and sympathized openly with the rebellious colonists' cause. On the other hand, some people in the colonies believed that nothing justified open resistance to the king. Argument was fierce; and when fighting broke out, the patriot cause tended to become more radical. Not merely the "rights of Englishmen" but the "Rights of Man" were called upon to justify resistance to the British government. The theory that government derived its just powers only from the consent of the governed was formally proclaimed by the colonists in the Declaration of Independence (1776). Liberty and equality became the watchwords of the patriot group, although few of them took liberty and equality to mean the abolition of slavery or equalization of property. The words had, instead, a limited political meaning: The right of ordinary men of sound mind and modest wealth to take part in choosing representatives to shape governmental policy.

France Supports the Revolution

The French were fascinated by the American uprising. The theoretical debate about political rights thrilled the ears of some, for their own position as subjects of an absolute monarch displeased many Frenchmen. In addition, by helping the colonists the French government could hope to undo the disasters of the Seven Years' War. Even if their own colonial possessions could not be recovered, at least the British position overseas would be weakened if the rebels won their independence.

After helping the Americans in unofficial ways, the French finally went to war in 1778. French soldiers joined the ragged forces under General George Washington's command with such effect that, when the British surrendered at Yorktown (1781), more French than Americans were on hand to witness the victory. Moreover, the French fleet made things extremely uncomfortable for the British at sea, and French diplo-macy also brought the Spaniards and the Dutch into the war against King George. When the Russians, too, began to organize a diplomatic offensive against the British among all the Baltic powers, Great Britain was almost completely isolated. In 1783, therefore, King George made peace, recognizing the independence of the rebellious colonies and ceding Florida to Spain.

American Constitutional Government

Victory in war presented the colonists with the problem of governing themselves effectively. During the war, the Articles of Confederation (1777) had been agreed to by each of the colonies. This document committed them to a permanent union to be called The United States of America. But the separate colonies or states kept control of taxation with the result that the central authorities suffered from a crippling lack of income. The experience of the immediate postwar years did not solve the problem, although the decision made in 1785 to transfer control over the western lands to the federal government meant an important increase in its powers. In 1787, on the initiative of the state of Virginia and with the endorsement of the Congress of the United States, a new constitutional convention assembled. After four months of discussion, the delegates agreed upon a constitution that gave greater powers to the federal government. Having been ratified by two-thirds of the separate states, the new system of government began operation in May 1789.

Such a rational way of setting up a new government, after discussion and deliberation on the part of representatives of the people at large, seemed an extraordinary demonstration of political wisdom to many Europeans of the day. The rude and simple Americans had proved able to make a government according to reasonable principles and along lines to suit themselves. To be sure, there were skeptics who waited confidently for the arrangements embodied in the Constitution to fall apart. Aristocrats found it impossible to believe that the passions of common people would not upset orderly government. After all, the political experience of centuries seemed to show that republican government could only succeed in small city-states, and that monarchy was required to keep a large, sprawling country together.

The Impact of the American Revolution   But whether they looked hopefully and with sympathy upon the American experiment in rational self-government or waited, instead, for its failure to prove the folly of trying to subordinate the operation of government to popular approval, no European interested in political questions could remain indifferent. Theories of the rights of man and of the citizen had been talked about for decades in French drawing rooms and all over Europe. Now the Americans had been bold enough to act on them. The more successful the Americans seemed, the more restless Europeans felt in finding themselves subject to the authority of rulers they had no part in choosing, and over whose actions they had no legal control. The United States of America, in other words, became a shining beacon, proving to those who wished to believe it that reasonable citizens could govern themselves without any need for kings, nobles, or priests.

The idea that government is, in fact, a human creation and can be changed by human wills is accepted everywhere today. It is therefore difficult for us to realize how new and exciting such an idea seemed in 1789. Nearly all of Europe was then ruled by kings and emperors who claimed to have been entrusted with their power by God. They ruled with the help of nobles and officials. These were privileged classes in the sense that different laws applied to them than to commoners. Differences of clothes and of manners also distinguished the privileged classes from the rest of society. They expected to be treated as superior beings by the common people.

The old idea that society was a great organism, requiring some at the head to do the thinking, while others were the hands and had to do the work, no longer convinced people of the middle class that they should remain in the walk of life to which they had been born. Too many of their superiors were clearly incompetent. Too many individuals had, in fact, changed status. Legal theory and practical fact were too far apart. To such persons the simple truths, acted on by the Americans, alone seemed worthy of free and rational minds. Government that failed to win the consent of the governed had no rightful claim to exist and should be changed. Or so it seemed to a vocal and energetic minority, especially in France, where the failures and rigidities of the government were not redeemed by the victory against the British in 1783.

THE FRENCH REVOLUTION

The widespread dissatisfaction with the way France was run became critical when Louis XVI (reigned 1774–1792) found himself in serious financial difficulties. The war with Britain (1778–1783) had cost a lot of money, and the French tax system could not produce the extra amounts needed to keep the government from bankruptcy. In theory, of course, Louis XVI was an absolute monarch and needed only to decree a new tax to make it legal. In practice, however, the bureaucracy that was supposed to serve the king had developed a will of its own. Many official posts were sold at auction. Those who purchased an office naturally felt that they owned what they had paid for and refused to change the way things were done unless the change was somehow clearly to their own advantage. In particular, high courts had the right to "register" the king's decrees. Originally, these courts were merely supposed to make sure that if any new decree contradicted some other law, the conflict would be drawn to the king's attention. Then, if the king wished, the new law was entered in the statute books or, on second thought, might be modified to avoid unnecessary confusion in the administration of justice. When, however, the high court of Paris refused to register new taxes decreed by the king, the judges became great popular heroes. The king's ministers decided that they could not afford to push through new taxes in the teeth of such opposition.

The royal government next tried calling together an assembly of notables (1787) in the hope that the great and powerful men of the realm would agree to accept a new tax law. But the notables were unwilling to agree to anything that might require them to pay larger taxes. The king next tried to revive the medieval institution of the Estates-General. This was a body rather like the English Parliament. Its members represented each of the three "estates" into which medieval political theory divided the country: Clergy being the First Estate, nobility constituting the Second Estate, and commoners—everybody else—making up the Third Estate. The Estates-General had been called for the first time in 1302, when King Philip IV wanted to get support in his quarrel with Pope Boniface VIII, and had met for the last time in 1614 at the beginning of the reign of Louis XIII.

The Meeting of the Estates-General

The Estates-General had been a gathering of representatives from the whole kingdom of France. But in 1789 great uncertainties existed as to how to choose representatives from each of the three estates. Even more critical was the question as to how the Estates-General would vote. If the representatives from each estate met separately and voted separately, conservatively minded clergy and nobles would control the Estates-General. If, however, all three estates met together, individual nobles and many of the clergy could be expected to sympathize with reform-minded representatives of the Third Estate who wanted to assure that in the future the king and his ministers would consult representatives of the nation regularly.

These uncertainties provoked a burst of political debate in France. The case was argued in numerous pamphlets. Each electoral district was invited to instruct its representatives in writing; consequently all sorts of complaints and programs for reform were put on paper, with the result that even those who had not felt especially aggrieved before became aware of serious political injustices. A great many people, therefore, expected drastic reform when the Estates-General met in May 1789.

Revolt of the Third Estate   King Louis and his ministers agreed that, up to a point, reform was needed. New taxes certainly were necessary, but Louis XVI never decided what else ought to be done. The king was a well-meaning man but weak-willed. In the spring of 1789, he failed to decide how the Estates-General should sit and vote; and even after the first ceremonial meetings had taken place, he hesitated. Then, in June, he decided to order each estate to meet and vote separately. Before he got round to announcing his decision, however, someone locked the doors of the room where the Third Estate had been accustomed to assemble. The representatives reacted by jumping to the conclusion that a plot was afoot to dismiss them entirely. On June 20, 1789, they moved to a tennis court nearby and amid great excitement solemnly swore an oath that they would never disband until they had made a constitution for France.

Such an act was revolutionary. The representatives of the Third Estate, in effect, had announced their intention of curbing royal absolutism. Yet King Louis reacted mildly. He first went ahead and announced his decision that the representatives should sit and vote separately by estates. The Third Estate refused to accept his ruling. In the next few days, a growing number of clergy and nobles began to attend the meetings of the Third Estate. A week later the king yielded and ordered the representatives of all three estates to meet together and to vote individually. The Estates-General thus became the National Assembly, committed to making a written constitution for France just as the Americans had recently done for the United States.

The National Assembly

Excitement ran high all over France. Louis XVI was by no means sure that the National Assembly could be trusted, and some of his advisers wanted him to call up soldiers and dismiss the troublesome representatives by a show of force. Troop movements stirred the people of Paris to action. They set up their own revolutionary authority, the Commune, to control the city; and on July 14, 1789, a great crowd attacked the Bastille—a royal fortress in the heart of Paris—and captured it. In later times this event was celebrated as the birthday of the French Revolution. It brought a new element into action—the people of Paris, who in the years that followed often demonstrated in favor of radical measures and on several critical occasions were able to silence the opposition.

The example of Paris proved infectious. Radical-minded reformers took control of other cities. Peasants, too, took the law into their own hands and began to attack their lords' houses. Often they set out to burn the charters that listed the obligations they owed their lords in the belief that if the documents were destroyed, the lords would never again be able to collect the rents and services listed in them.

The National Assembly responded by "abolishing feudalism" in the course of a hectic night, August 4–5, 1789, when, one after another, excited representatives renounced special rights and privileges. From that time onward, all Frenchmen were, at least in theory, equal before the law. All were citizens, owing the same duties and obligations to the state and enjoying the same rights and protection from it. Legally separate classes or estates and privileged corporations had been abolished. Liberty and equality had dawned. Before long, a third slogan was added to the revolutionary program: fraternity, meaning the brotherhood that ought to exist among free and equal citizens. These three ideals stirred enthusiasm not only in France but in other parts of Europe. The English poet, William Wordsworth wrote:

"Bliss was it in that dawn to be alive"

—and many young men in Germany and Italy, as well as in England, felt the same.

Financial Problems   Events, however, refused to stand still in order to allow the National Assembly to draw up a constitution for France. In particular, the government's financial problem would not wait. As a stopgap, the Assembly decided to issue paper currency that would be redeemed by the sale of Church lands. But issuing paper currency proved such an attractive solution that more and more "assignats," as the bills were called, were printed to meet pressing government obligations. Even when in addition to the Church lands, the property of runaway nobles and the royal domains were put up for sale, the face value of assignats far exceeded the value of the lands that were sold. As a result, the paper currency could not be retired as intended. Inflation and a rapid rise in prices resulted; wage earners suffered, but some businessmen and borrowers benefited.

The National Assembly's decision to sell Church lands and reorganize the Church as a branch of the state, by paying salaries to priests and bishops, was flatly condemned by the pope. This made the first great split in the revolutionary ranks. The many Frenchmen and women who remained good Catholics could not support the Assembly in opposition to the pope. Louis XVI was among those who refused to accept the drastic reorganization of the Church. But for the time being, he was helpless. His secret appeals for assistance sent to the other monarchs of Europe produced no result, although when discovered later, they proved that the king had become a traitor to the Revolution.

The Constitution of 1791

By the summer of 1791 the new constitution was finally ready. It made France a limited monarchy. Supreme authority was conferred upon an elected legislative assembly. It controlled taxation, exercised supreme judicial authority, and had the power to call royal ministers to account. Essential sovereign rights, in other words, were transferred from the king to the elected representatives of the French people. The king, nevertheless, kept important powers, such as the right to choose his ministers and to appoint army officers and diplomats, as well as a veto on legislation, which could, however, be overridden by the Legislative Assembly.

These provisions did not last, but the reorganization of local government written into the Constitution of 1791 proved durable. All France was divided into departments of about the same size. Church dioceses, judicial districts, and department boundaries were all made to coincide. All sorts of monopolies and special privileges were swept away. Simple, uniform administration, linking the individual private citizen with the government directly, was made to prevail all over France.

The effect of these changes was that in time

of crisis the central government could demand more from each citizen than the government of the Old Regime had ever dreamed of doing. The thick tissue of privileged bodies that had grown up during the Old Regime meant that the king's ministers had seldom been able to touch citizens individually, but had always to deal with guilds, town governments, high courts, provincial assemblies, and the like. Thus, the overthrow of privilege and the dawn of liberty, of which the revolutionaries were so proud, turned out to have a meaning they did not expect. Liberty, equality, and fraternity meant equal (and unlimited) service to the state—whether as a conscripted soldier or as a taxpayer.

The fatal flaw in the Constitution of 1791 was that Louis XVI, who no longer had the slightest sympathy for the Revolution, could not be trusted with the powers assigned to him. In June 1791, the king tried to flee abroad in disguise. But the royal party was recognized and compelled to return. The National Assembly was not prepared to do without a king. Outright republicanism was almost unthinkable still. All the same, when the new Legislative Assembly met in October 1791, suspicion of the king's good faith in accepting the Constitution ran deep.

Matters came to a crisis as a result of the outbreak of war against Prussia and Austria. King Louis and a circle of conservative "aristocrats" had tried to get these rulers to intervene against the Revolution for months and so welcomed war when it came in April 1792. Oddly enough, the most extreme radical faction represented in the Legislative Assembly also welcomed the war. An organized party of enthusiasts for the Revolution—called Girondins because some of their most conspicuous spokesmen came from one of the new departments in southern France, known as Gironde—were eager to bring liberty, equality, and fraternity to the other peoples of Europe. They also believed that foreign war would compel French citizens to rally to the cause of the Revolution and would help to silence internal frictions that were threatening civil war.

The expectations of the Girondins turned out to be as false as those of the king. Revolutionary enthusiasm was not enough to win battles, and when the Austrians and Prussians began to advance into France, rumors that King Louis was in treasonable correspondence with the enemy roused the Paris crowds to fresh action. Under the leadership of Georges Jacques Danton, they surrounded the legislators and demanded that they suspend the king. Reluctantly, the Legislative Assembly obeyed and organized new elections for a convention to revise the Constitution once again.

The Radical Phase: The Convention

Opinion shifted rapidly in the days of crisis that followed. To be sure, in September 1792 French armies turned the tide and a few weeks later started to march into the Austrian Netherlands (Belgium), where they were received as liberators. The Prussians also retreated, so that soon after the National Convention met in September 1792, French armies stood victoriously on the banks of the Rhine. But Louis' treasonable correspondence with the Austrians and the Prussians had been discovered. Accordingly, when the National Convention met, its first act was to abolish royalty and declare France a republic. In the following months, "Citizen Louis Capet" (Louis XVI) was brought to trial before the Convention, condemned for treason, and beheaded (January 1793).

This event shocked all of Europe. Kings and nobles everywhere felt threatened, and even those who had sympathized with the first stages of the French Revolution found it hard to justify the acts of the Convention. Britain, Holland, Sardinia, and Spain promptly joined Austria and Prussia in war against France. Discontent inside France became widespread, and the threat of revolt and civil war hung over the deliberations of the Convention.

The National Convention was also hampered by bitter factional fights within its own ranks. The Girondins, who had been the radicals of the year before, were challenged by a new faction, known as Jacobins, whose principal spokesman was Maximilien Robespierre. The Jacobins were or became leaders for the Paris crowds, and part of their power depended on being able to summon Parisians for a mass demonstration to back up their policies. The Girondins, in reaction,

Two Faces of the French Revolution Both of these works of art were made by Jacques-Louis David (1749–1825). He became official artistic director of the French Revolution, entrusted with planning revolutionary celebrations like the "Festival of the Supreme Being" in Notre Dame cathedral (1794) and commemorating the great events of the revolution on canvas. Above is a painting of the Oath of the Tennis Court (1789) when representatives of the Third Estate swore not to disperse until they had made a constitution for France. Below, a sketch of Queen Marie Antoinette, arms tied behind her back, as carried through the streets of Paris to the public square where she was beheaded (1793). The Oath of the Tennis Court is not accurate to the event for David was not present and the painting was made long afterward. But the heroic posturing of the deputies does capture the enthusiasm of the moment and the solidarity of all those who sought reform of France in 1789. Yet David's personal commitment of the revolution did not prevent him from capturing Marie Antoinette's disdainful defiance of her enemies, even in the face of death. Her humble dress, bringing her to the level of an ordinary Parisian housewife, does not disguise the fierceness with which she and other defenders of the Old Regime opposed the revolution.

tended to become identified with the provinces, where, on the whole, less radical views prevailed. Danton tried to stand above party and, as a result, alienated both sides. Many delegates to the Convention belonged to neither faction, but swung back and forth as the emergency of the moment seemed to require.

In the summer of 1793 it looked as though the Revolution would go down in defeat. The most successful French general, Charles François Dumouriez, with part of his army, went over to the enemy. In the south the British besieged Toulon, and the Prussians advanced across the Rhine toward French soil. A rash of revolts spread through France, particularly after the Girondins had been excluded from the Convention in June, leaving the Jacobin party in full control.

The Reign of Terror

The crisis roused the Jacobins, supported by the people of Paris, to heroic effort. Executive power was concentrated in the hands of a Committee of Public Safety, of which Maximilien Robespierre became the leading spirit. A "Reign of Terror" began. Hasty trials of anyone suspected of disloyalty to the Revolution led to mass executions.

Universal military service for all male citizens was decreed. Frantic efforts to assemble and equip vast new armies quickly bore fruit. By the fall of 1793 the revolutionary forces were once more on the offensive, and the most dangerous internal uprisings had been suppressed.

The effort to turn back the danger required strong, centralized control. Special "representatives on mission" carried the authority of the Convention to the provinces. Local dignitaries and officials were summarily executed if they seemed disloyal or merely inefficient. Jacobin societies sprang up in all important towns. These societies carried on a vigorous correspondence with the Jacobin club in Paris and, in effect, served as local propaganda agencies to spread enthusiasm for the latest policy decreed from Paris. The Jacobin societies also made it their business to oversee the activities of local officials. If they detected any lack of zeal, a letter to the Jacobin club in Paris would lead to prompt dismissal or even to the execution of the accused. The same system worked inside the army to keep check on the officers.

In this fashion, something close to total mobilization of the French nation was achieved. Close mutual support between "the people," organized into the Jacobin societies, and their government achieved amazing results. The massed forces of the European Old Regime could not stand against the revolutionary armies. Everywhere the French took the offensive. The Revolution was once more secure.

Success in battle did not, however, solve the question of how France should be governed. Robespierre talked of a "Republic of Virtue." This frightened many delegates to the Convention, who were not sure they were virtuous enough to satisfy Robespierre. The Paris populace, on the other hand, wanted to extend equality to economics. In particular, the Parisians were angry at the rise of food prices, believing that greedy bakers, or grain dealers perhaps, were responsible. Robespierre hesitated and eventually refused to go along with the Paris crowd. He tried to eliminate awkward criticism by executing the leaders of the Paris Commune in March 1794, and Danton in April 1794. His own turn was not long delayed. In July of the same year, some of his colleagues on the Committee of Public Safety ar-

rested him. When news spread through Paris, a group of Robespierre's admirers tried to free him, but Paris, as a whole, did not rise. In the confusion which his supporters created, the man who had become identified with revolutionary extremism was shot, dying a few hours later (1794).

Reaction and Consolidation

The politicians who conspired against Robespierre did not intend to end the Reign of Terror or to change policy in any important way. But Robespierre's overthrow sparked a sharp reaction all over France. Summary revolutionary justice was halted. Soon the Jacobin hold on the National Convention was broken; their meeting place was closed in November and the surviving Girondin deputies were recalled. When a new constitution was drafted and approved in October 1795, the Convention ended its sessions.

Government by the Directory   The new government was headed by five Directors. Stability at home and victory abroad was the Directory's policy. With the help of brilliant young generals such as Napoleon Bonaparte, who led a ragged army into Italy and utterly defeated the Austrian forces there (1796–1797), the Directory at first met with general success. Prussia and then Austria made peace. According to the resulting treaties, revolutionary France, in a few short years, had achieved Louis XIV's ambition of extending French territory to the Rhine. Moreover, a client state in Holland, the Batavian Republic, and another in northern Italy, the Cisalpine Republic, extended French influence and revolutionary principles even further into Europe. Plans for fundamental reorganization of the Germanies were left undefined; but France, Prussia, and Austria all were eager to get rid of the hundreds of separate sovereign states into which Germany had been divided ever since 1648.

Great Britain remained a problem. The British navy guarded England's shores, and no French superiority on land could force the British government to make peace or recognize the territorial gains won by revolutionary arms. In 1798 Napoleon proposed to invade Egypt, as a way of threatening India and bringing pressure on the

Napoleon as Hero and as Oppressor On the left a painting of Napoleon at the Battle of Eylau, fought against the Russians in wintertime, 1807. The painter, Antoine-Jean Baron, exhibits Napoleon a little left of center, issuing orders from horseback, while in the distance the long thin lines of soldiers march against one another. This sort of official painting was meant both to record the event and to glorify the role of the French commander, Napoleon. Yet Eylau turned out to be an inconclusive battle and victory over the Russians had to wait until the following June. On the right, a painting by Francisco Goya shows Napoleon's soldiers executing citizens of Madrid who had tried to resist the French invasion of the city in 1808. Popular resistance to the French conquerors in Spain started the erosion of Napoleon's power; and when similar uprisings spread to other nations of Europe in 1812–1813, the French empire crumbled into dust. Yet the heroic image of Napoleon lingered, in France and beyond French borders as well. His victories had turned the Old Regime upside down across most of Europe; and those who benefited from all the legal and administrative changes the French had wrought remembered Napoleon as he is here portrayed, both as hero and as oppressor.

English to make peace. The Directors feared Napoleon's popularity and were glad to see him leave the country. They therefore promptly agreed with Napoleon's plan.

Soon afterward British diplomacy and subsidies raised a new coalition against the French. The Russians joined in, for the first time, with the Austrians and Prussians, and sent armies to fight in Italy and Holland. The French were driven out of Italy, and Russian armies even crossed the Alps but failed to invade France when supplies gave out. Napoleon's first victories in Egypt had been well publicized at home; later failures were overshadowed by the news of French defeats in Italy. Accordingly, when Napoleon suddenly appeared in France in November 1799, he seemed to be a savior and had little trouble arranging a

coup d'état that made him First Consul and the effective ruler of France.

Napoleonic Rule Napoleon soon restored French power in Italy. The Russians had already gone home, due to quarrels with the Austrians. After defeating the Austrians, consequently, Napoleon found himself in a position to make peace with all the enemies of France. He even negotiated an agreement with the papacy in 1801, by which the pope recognized the loss of the Church lands in France and made it possible for a Catholic once more to support the French government in good conscience. This was followed in 1802 by the Peace of Amiens whereby the British government gave up the struggle to undo the achievements of the French Revolution in Europe. Napoleon

NAPOLEON'S CORONATION

Napoleon Bonaparte was born in Corsica. As a boy he was both very poor and very proud, for his family claimed noble rank but had little money. When he went to France he felt like an outsider, for the Corsicans spoke a language more like Italian than French. Napoleon never lost the feeling of being an outsider, even when he rose to undisputed power over all of France and a large part of Europe.

In 1804 Napoleon was approaching the peak of his career. Only Britain opposed him in war. At home, most Frenchmen admired his victories. Napoleon decided that he should make his power hereditary. But Napoleon was also a son of the French Revolution, and the French revolutionaries had set out to overthrow the hereditary privileges of kings and nobles. How could the Corsican upstart become a monarch without betraying his principles—and those of his most devoted followers?

Napoleon's answer was to put the question to a vote. If the people of France wanted him to hold hereditary power, then his rule would be based not on empty tradition or ancient privilege but on the will of the people. The vote was taken, and the people overwhelmingly approved the proposal that Napoleon should become Emperor of the French.

From the time of Charlemagne, emperors had been crowned by the pope. Napoleon decided that his new title required a coronation, and he demanded that the pope come to Paris for the ceremony. After some hesitation, the pope agreed; and on December 2, 1804, the solemn ceremony took place in Notre Dame Cathedral at Paris.

But there was another difficulty for Napoleon. In the traditional ceremony, the pope put the imperial crown on the emperor's head. This seemed to say that the imperial crown was the pope's gift; and, again, Napoleon's revolutionary principles made any such idea unacceptable. For the French revolutionaries had also attacked the Church and denied that political rule came from the hand of God, or from any bishop, priest, or pope.

Napoleon solved this problem, too. As the ceremony of the coronation approached its climax, the imperial crown was carried forward. Just as the pope was about to pick it up and place it on Napoleon's head, the emperor himself leaned forward, seized the crown, and placed it on his own head. No one but Napoleon himself was going to crown the new Emperor of the French.

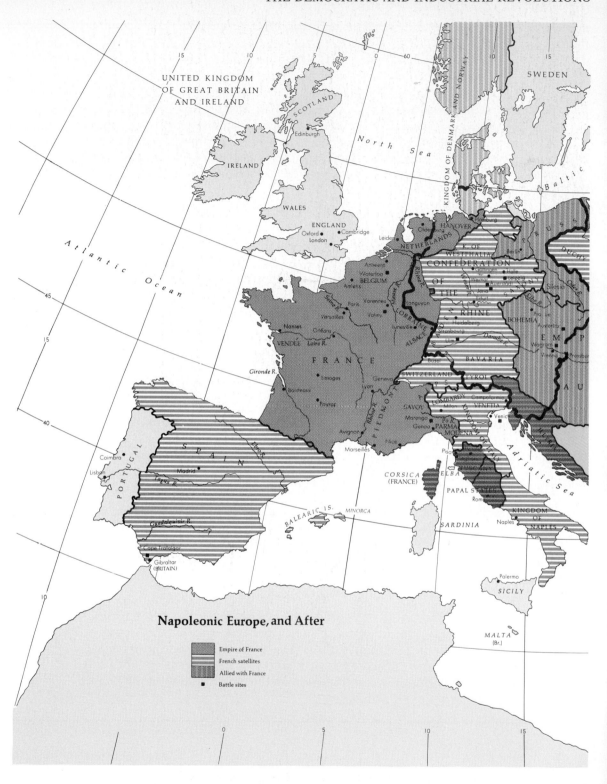

Napoleonic Europe, and After

Empire of France
French satellites
Allied with France
■   Battle sites

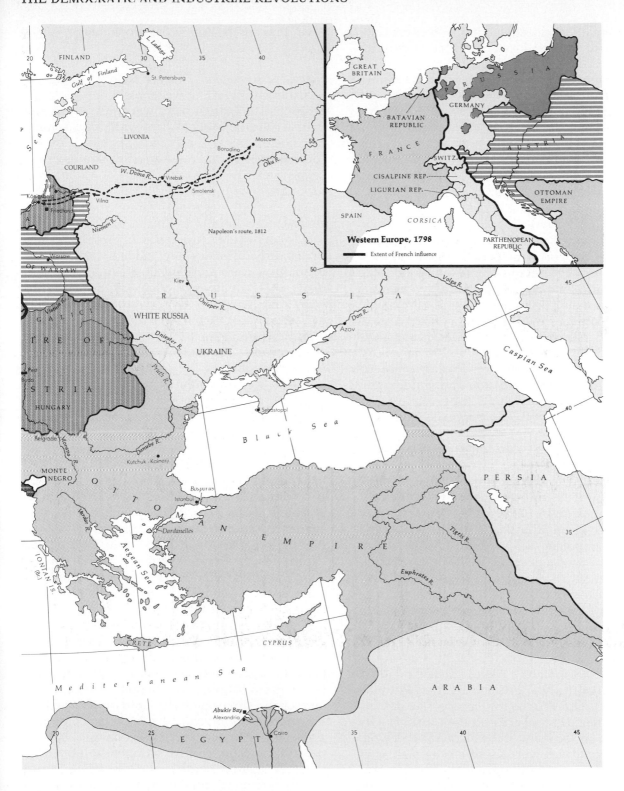

FINLAND
L. Ladoga
Gulf of Finland
St. Petersburg
LIVONIA
Moscow
Borodino
COURLAND
W. Dvina R.
Vitebsk
Königsberg
Smolensk
Friedland
Vilna
Niemen R.
Napoleon's route, 1812
OF WARSAW
Warsaw
GALICIA
R U S S I A
Kiev
RE OF
Dnieper R.
Pest
WHITE RUSSIA
Buda
STRIA
Dniester R.
HUNGARY
UKRAINE
Prut R.
Belgrade
Morava R.
Danube R.
Azov
Don R.
MONTE
NEGRO
Kutchuk - Kainarji
Sevastopol
O T T O M A N
Black Sea
Vardar R.
Bosporus
Istanbul
E M P I R E
Dardanelles
Aegean Sea
IONIAN IS.
(Br.)
Tigris R.
CRETE
CYPRUS
Euphrates R.
Mediterranean Sea
ARABIA
Abukir Bay
Alexandria
E G Y P T
Cairo

Volga R.
Caspian Sea
P E R S I A

GREAT
BRITAIN
P R U S S I A
R U S S I A
GERMANY
BATAVIAN
REPUBLIC
A U S T R I A
F R A N C E
SWITZ.
CISALPINE REP.
LIGURIAN REP.
OTTOMAN
EMPIRE
SPAIN
CORSICA
PARTHENOPEAN
REPUBLIC
Western Europe, 1798
Extent of French influence

was universally acclaimed at home, became consul for life in 1802 and, two years later assumed the title "Emperor of the French."

Thus monarchy had been restored to France; but Napoleon was at pains to refer every change in his regime to the vote of the people, and always claimed to rule only by virtue of the popular will. In large degree, the claim was justified. The French were proud of the greatness Napoleon thrust upon them and appreciated the peace and order he maintained at home.

The fundamental changes the Revolution had made were consolidated and written into law—the famous *Code Napoléon*—that gave exact definition to property and personal rights as they emerged from the revolutionary upheaval. Napoleon maintained a strictly centralized administration, appointing prefects over each department and mayors over all important towns. A special police kept track of suspects by means of a vast card file. Public opinion was managed by carefully controlled news releases. Discontent could not find open expression and, in fact, few French citizens felt anything but pride in what their nation, under Napoleon's leadership, was able to do.

Abroad, matters were different. The Peace of Amiens soon broke down, and Napoleon started a new war against Great Britain in 1803. Austria, Russia, and Sweden joined Britain against Napoleon in 1805; but the Austrians met crushing defeat at the Battle of Austerlitz. The next year Napoleon defeated the Prussians and, in 1807, arranged a peace at Tilsit with the young czar of Russia, Alexander I. When Austria resorted to arms again in 1809, Napoleon was victorious once more. By marrying the Austrian emperor's daughter, Marie Louise, in 1810, he entered the most select and exclusive ranks of European royalty.

In 1810 Napoleon's power reached its peak. He controlled Italy and Germany, having made both Austria and Prussia into second-rate powers and his allies. He had created the Grand Duchy of Warsaw on the ruins of the former Polish kingdom. His relatives were established on thrones in Spain, Italy, and Holland; and the Russian czar agreed to cut his country off from British trade as part of Napoleon's grand plan for bringing

Great Britain, the "nation of shopkeepers," to its knees by economic boycott.

Nationalist Resistance to French Rule   Nevertheless, there were serious weaknesses in Napoleon's position. The British navy was undefeated, and British subsidies were always available to foment resistance against the French anywhere on the continent. Overseas ambitions that Napoleon had briefly nourished after the Peace of Amiens had to be abandoned. Accordingly, he gladly sold Louisiana, recently acquired from Spain, to the United States in 1803. In Europe itself, the French provoked popular resistance in Spain. Soon a British expeditionary force added weight to the guerrilla warfare waged by the Spaniards. In Germany and Italy, many people asked themselves why France should be so powerful and their own nations so weak. National feeling, in other words, began to turn against the French and made the rising against Napoleon, when it came, strong and irreversible.

The breaking point occurred in 1812 when Czar Alexander quarreled with Napoleon and went over to the British side. Napoleon organized a great army to invade Russia and marched to Moscow. But winter closed in and Russian resistance did not end. The proud French army had to withdraw, suffering enormous losses from cold and hunger en route. News of this defeat set all Germany ablaze. The Prussians entered the war against Napoleon; soon the Austrians did the same. A great battle at Leipzig, in 1813, ended in allied victory. Napoleon faced defeat.

The allies found it difficult to agree among themselves; nevertheless, the alliance held until Napoleon surrendered in 1814. The victors exiled him to Elba, a small island off the coast of Italy. Then they set out to make peace, after the upheavals of twenty-three years of war. Scarcely had the peace conference met at Vienna when fierce quarrels broke out. Napoleon took advantage of the situation and secretly embarked for France. On his arrival, the French people and armies rallied once more to his banner, but the news of Napoleon's return brought the allies back together again. British and Prussian troops swiftly organized; and at Waterloo, in Belgium, not far from the French border, they met and defeated the French (1815). Napoleon surrendered once again, and this time he was shipped off to St. Helena, far away in the South Atlantic Ocean. He died there of cancer in 1821.

The Congress of Vienna

The Congress of Vienna resumed its task of restoring the balance of power in Europe. The Bourbon monarchy was restored in France, in the person of Louis XVIII, brother to Louis XVI. (According to royalist principles, Louis XVI's son counted as Louis XVII, even though he never reigned.) The restored king issued a constitutional decree, giving legislative power to elected assemblies. In general, he made little attempt to turn back the clock. The basic revolutionary idea that people and government could and should cooperate remained in force. To be sure, not all the people were allowed to vote in elections; only the wealthy and better educated were invited to assume that responsibility. But despite this limitation upon the democratic principle, the constitutional decree marked the restored Bourbon government of France as vaguely "liberal."

In Germany and Italy, where Napoleonic reforms had erased old boundaries, return to the Old Regime was equally impossible. Instead, Austria took over the task of guarding Italy against France and passed to Prussia the task of watching the Rhine frontier. The Prussians, therefore, annexed broad territories in the Rhineland in return for giving up Polish territories to Russia in the east.

By these and many other complicated deals a balance of power between the major states of Europe was carefully adjusted so that no one of them could dominate the rest. France, on the one side, and Russia, on the other, were the two chief threats—or so it seemed to Prince Metternich of Austria and to the British foreign minister, Lord Castlereagh, who, between them, arranged most of the important compromises. Czar Alexander was fond of thinking of himself as Europe's savior, and at different times he entertained various plans for establishing a new order. He toyed with the idea of uniting Germany and Italy in accordance with the will of their people. With himself

as king, he restored Poland. A great crusade against the Turks attracted him, too. But most of all, he pinned his hopes on a Holy Alliance of Christian monarchs who would work in harmony and consult with each other regularly in order to end the warfare that for too long had brought such havoc to Europe.

The French Revolution Overseas

The French Revolution provoked upheaval in the French and Spanish empires overseas. In 1791, for example, black slaves in Haiti, the largest of France's Caribbean colonies, responded to news of the revolution in France by proclaiming their own liberty and equality with whites and mulattoes. The National Convention eventually accepted the rebels' logic and prohibited slavery throughout the French Empire; but Napoleon tried to restore slavery, and it was permanently prohibited on French soil only in 1815.

When Napoleon sent an army to Haiti to reassert French authority in the island, he met with initial success. Toussaint L'Ouverture, who had led the slaves to freedom, surrendered; but soon yellow fever began to wreak havoc with the French soldiers, and in 1804 Napoleon had to withdraw the remnants of his army. Haiti became independent under black governance, for by then race war had almost eliminated the white and mulatto population.

The Spanish Empire in Mexico and South America also responded to the revolutionary ideals of liberty and equality. Rebellions aiming at independence began when Napoleon overthrew the Spanish king in 1808 and put his brother Joseph on the Spanish throne. This allowed local rebels to claim that they were loyal to the legitimate king, Ferdinand VII. But when Ferdinand regained the Spanish throne in 1815, he proved himself very much opposed to liberal principles and set out to restore imperial administration. As a result, all the first efforts at independence collapsed, except in Argentina.

Nevertheless, Ferdinand's efforts soon backfired. The white population of the Spanish colonies had become used to taking part in public policy making; and when new officials sent from

Europe after 1815

—— Boundary of German Confederation
■ Battle sites

SIMON BOLIVAR, THE LIBERATOR

Simon Bolivar was born in 1783 in what is today Venezuela. Of aristocratic descent, he went to Europe as a young man to pursue his education. There he was converted to radical and liberal ideas and conceived the ambition of freeing his native land and all of Spanish America from the power of the Church and of the Spanish monarchy that supported the Church while excluding men like himself, natives of America, from any share in the government of the empire.

Bolivar returned to Venezuela in time to take part in the earliest revolts against Spanish authority. He distinguished himself both for the radical nature of his aims and by his energy in war. Bolivar had many adventures during the early wars of liberation; but by 1814 the cause had failed and he had to flee to Jamaica and then to Haiti, where he was able to gather support for a renewal of the struggle. In 1817 he returned to Venezuela, organizing a guerrilla war from deep in the forests of the Orinoco River basin. Then in 1819 he conducted a spectacular march through the backwoods and captured Bogota, the capital of the Viceroyalty of New Granada. Bolivar renamed the country Colombia to symbolize the new era he hoped to inaugurate.

Thereafter, Bolivar went from success to success. In 1820 he established his authority in his native Venezuela; in 1824 he conquered Peru. Finally, in 1825 the last stronghold of the Spanish monarchy on the mainland capitulated to Bolivar's forces in Upper Peru, which was renamed Bolivia to commemorate its debt to the man who had been nicknamed "The Liberator" by admiring followers ever since 1812.

Bolivar found himself ruler of most of Spanish South America, being at one and the same time president both of Peru and of Gran Colombia—a federation of Venezuela, Ecuador, and Colombia. He had still grander visions of a United States of America that might embrace the entire New World, or at least would unite all the Latin American countries. But local quarrels among his followers soon broke out, and Bolivar's autocratic temperament alienated others. In an effort to hold Gran Colombia together, he assumed dictatorial powers in 1827 and narrowly escaped assassination when discontented liberals decided to take the law into their own hands.

By this time, Bolivar's health was broken. In 1829 Venezuela broke away from Colombia, thus shattering his dream of federation forever. He died the next year, profoundly disappointed at the failure of his hopes.

Spain disregarded them, revolts broke out afresh, and this time were successful. By 1825 all of Spanish South America had become independent, thanks to the leadership of Simon Bolivar, José de San Martin, and others.

In Mexico, independence came by a rather different route. In 1810 the early revolt against Spain attracted a substantial mestizo following. But when poor mestizos began to take the idea of liberty and equality seriously, white landlords and other members of the Mexican upper class took fright and were glad to see the movement collapse after 1815. But in 1820 Ferdinand's reactionary government provoked a new liberal revolution in Spain, whereupon the Mexican ruling elite decided to declare their country's independence (1821) in order to preserve their social position.

Self-government proved attractive to Brazilians also, and in 1822 that country followed the Spanish example by declaring its independence from Portugal. Brazil remained a monarchy, however, ruled by Pedro I, son of the Portuguese king. He soon proved himself a patriotic Brazilian, resisting his father's efforts to assert his authority over his son and over Brazil.

Cuba and Puerto Rico remained Spanish colonies until 1898; most of the other islands of the Caribbean also stayed under European rule until the late twentieth century. One reason was economic hard times due to the fact that after 1815 European nations depended less on imported sugar, having discovered how to supply themselves from sugar beets grown at home.

On the mainland, in contrast, increasing populations meant economic growth as new land came under cultivation and new urban occupations continued to open up. Development was slower than in the United States but still very rapid. Amerindians remained politically passive, many of them living in remote villages with few outside contacts of any kind. The new Latin American governments therefore presided over a split-level society. At the top were whites and some mestizos who took part in the world of politics and commerce. Underneath was an Indian population of subsistence farmers who sometimes paid rent or performed services for white landlords but otherwise had little to do with the rest of society.

Revolution *versus* Reaction in Europe

Meanwhile, in war-weary Europe, Tsar Alexander's vision of a Holy Alliance of Christian monarchs boiled down to no more than an agreement among the powers to meet at intervals in the future in order to agree upon joint action when any crisis required it. Congresses did meet until 1822, but after that date Great Britain withdrew and the system fell to the ground. In the meanwhile, Metternich had been able to persuade Alexander that a wicked conspiracy to spread "the revolution" existed in Europe. Instead of toying with liberal ideas, therefore, the czar became wholeheartedly reactionary. As a result, the three eastern monarchies of Austria, Prussia, and Russia became stalwart defenders of the status quo. France and Britain, on the contrary, were more sympathetic with revolutionary outbreaks and refused to agree to international intervention aimed at suppressing liberal revolutionary movements. This lineup became clear when Britain refused to go along with proposals to put down the Latin American revolutions that had broken out in the Spanish Empire of the New World. Britain, indeed, looked kindly upon President James Monroe's declaration (1823) that European intervention in the New World would be considered an unfriendly act by the United States. The Greek revolt against the Turks, which broke out in 1821, also commanded widespread sympathy in France and England. Russia, too, after Alexander's death (1825) could not refrain from supporting the rebels. The result in 1830 was an international guarantee of Greek independence.

In July of the same year, an almost bloodless revolution in France brought a new "citizen king," Louis Philippe, to the throne. Two years later, the Reform Bill of 1832 passed the British Parliament.

This bill reapportioned representation in Parliament so that it more nearly corresponded to the distribution of population and gave the vote to middle-class taxpayers. The result was to confirm the liberal character of these two states and make middle-class political leadership secure. Germany and Italy remained a dubious battle-

Revolutionary Romanticism The man who painted this picture, Eugene Delacroix, entitled it "Liberty Leading the People." It celebrates the Paris revolution of 1830 that put a new "Citizen King," Louis Philippe on the throne of France. The idea that an angry people had the right to take to the streets and overthrow an unpopular government was one of the heritages of the French revolution. Between 1789 and 1794 Parisian crowds had repeatedly launched mass demonstrations that changed the government of France and the same thing happened in 1830. Delacroix sympathized with the revolutionary cause and painted this picture immediately afterwards to glorify and commemorate the event. Liberty, personified as a woman, holds a red flag aloft, while middle class bourgeois and common laborers, clearly distinguished by their different modes of dress, risk death to follow her lead. This heroic vision of revolutionary direct action remains powerful down to the present, even though the development of urban police forces later in the nineteenth century made it far more difficult for a crowd to prevail, no matter how angry it might be.

ground where liberal and conservative principles clashed. Farther east, Austria and Russia alone remained opposed to the liberal idea that government should be responsible to the people.

In 1848, a fresh round of revolution, beginning in France, spread over most of Germany and Italy and into Austria as well. Metternich was overthrown, but the revolution failed to establish representative government in Germany or Italy because agreement on national unification could not be reached. By about 1850 among Germans and Italians most of the aspirations inherited from the great days of the French Revolution itself had been exhausted through repeated failures. Revolutionary enthusiasm was soon to find a new socialist form. As far as Europe was concerned, the era of the French Revolution had come to an end.

The change from 1789, however, was great. In all the western parts of Europe, a closer partnership between government and people had brought the urban middle classes actively into politics. Public opinion mattered as never before. Governments rose and fell on the strength of it; and when supported by the enthusiasm of their people, governments had proved able to reach deeper into society and bring greater energies to bear, both in war and in peace, than any governments of the Old Regime had been able to do. Problems were identified, discussed, and then acted upon in the light of public opinion that found its voice mainly through newspapers. This procedure allowed an extraordinary outpouring of energy. City folk, instead of being merely subjects, had become citizens, responsible for the conduct of public affairs in their own right and through their representatives. The farmers and peasants of the countryside remained quiet, generally, and did not take much part in political and public affairs. But then, the problems of the day, aside from war and diplomacy, all centered around the transformation of urban life that came with the Industrial Revolution.

THE INDUSTRIAL REVOLUTION

The term "Industrial Revolution" was popularized about 1880 by an English historian, Arnold Toynbee, who applied it to the reign of George III (1760–1820). At the time, however, what contemporaries noticed were the wars and political upheavals of the age. The fact that cotton manufacturers in Manchester were making money by building new machines in dark and unpleasant factories hardly attracted the attention of anyone who was not in the cotton business.

Yet from the vantage point of our own age, it seems clear that the changes in the ways factories made things in Manchester and other cities had great importance for the world's history. By harnessing inanimate forms of energy, ingenious inventors and manufacturers added a new dimension to human power over nature. The use of coal and steam, and later of electricity, was like the discovery of agriculture in Neolithic times, and a whole range of new possibilities opened up in both cases. Agriculture led to settled villages and then to cities and civilization. What power-driven machinery may lead to, we have still to find out. But it is already clear that where development of the new techniques has advanced most rapidly, human beings have been freed from the age-old round of the farmer's year. Instead of regulating our lives according to the simple necessities of planting and harvesting, industrialized societies have cut people loose from the soil and have enabled them to live in cities under conditions very different from those their ancestors knew. The immensity of the change in the everyday experience of ordinary people has not been fully explored even now, some 200 years after the critical breakthrough occurred.

Invention of Steam Engines

Improvements in spinning and weaving machinery had been made throughout the eighteenth century. But the fact that wool and linen production was firmly established as a cottage industry carried on in the homes of innumerable artisans—some of them part time—set limits upon the size such machines could attain. The first steam engine started operation in 1712. It was invented by Thomas Newcomen to pump water from a coal mine. Other engines were built for the same purpose in following years without making much difference to anyone.

But when James Watt improved Newcomen's engine by making it unnecessary to cool the cylinder to make the steam condense, the consumption of coal became much less extravagant. When he further designed simple ways to convert the back-and-forth motion of the piston in its cylinder into rotary motion that could be transmitted by gears or drive belts to other kinds of machines, the critical point in the Industrial Revolution had been achieved. Watt took out his first patents in 1769, but fully satisfactory performance of his engines came more slowly.

As soon as Watt tried to make large numbers of engines, he encountered new difficulties. The piston had to fit snugly into its cylinder or else the steam escaped around the edges, wasting energy. Filing down a piston by hand to make it fit a cylinder exactly required skill and patience in extraordinary degree. No two cylinders were ever alike; each fit had to be separately achieved. A few clumsy strokes of the file could spoil a piston entirely. This made large-scale production of steam engines impossible until a skilled mechanic, Henry Maudslay, in 1797 invented a lathe that could cut metal accurately within a thousandth of an inch.

The importance of this first "machine tool" can scarcely be exaggerated. It and others designed later for special purposes allowed skilled artisans to make parts for steam engines and other machines accurately. Eventually, instead of having to make each separate machine fit together by trial and error, standard parts could be assembled to make a standard machine that really worked. And even after temporary breakdown, standardized spare parts could be supplied, so that with relatively simple adjustments the whole machine would work again.

These things seem elementary to us, but it took time and skill to make such methods routine. For a long time, small adjustments with file and chisel had to be made by the skilled "engineer" who put the machine together or repaired it after breakdown. The first manufacturer who clearly worked out the theory of replaceable parts was Eli Whitney (1765–1825), an American; he was the inventor of the cotton gin and a manufacturer of muskets.

Labor in the Machine Age

A second problem raised by the new machines was human rather than mechanical. When steam power was turned on in a new factory, all the machines leaped to life; but if their attendants were not on hand, something could go wrong and serious damage might occur. This called for mass punctuality. But weavers and spinners, accustomed to working in their own cottages on their own time and when they felt like it, could not easily get used to living by a clock. As a result, owners and managers used very high-handed methods to force their workers to submit to the routine requirements of the new machines. Women and children were easier to control, and

were often strong enough to tend the new machines; but the conditions under which they lived and worked, the brutality of the methods by which overseers forced them to be punctual and careful, and the long hours they were required to stay at their machines seem shocking today. Wages were low, barely above starvation levels. Workers' unions were illegal in Great Britain after 1799. In France the National Assembly had prohibited them, too, along with guilds and other combinations in restraint of trade.

The problems of factory life were multiplied by the rapid growth of industrial towns on or near coal fields. Housing was miserable and high-priced. Family life often broke up. Especially when the factory work force was wholly or mainly female, as was the case in many textile plants, men had no satisfying role to play in the family. They could not live on their wives' earnings and keep their self-respect. In addition, elementary city services—water supply, garbage removal, and schools—did not exist, and at first no one thought it necessary to provide them.

Early Adjustments to Industrial Life   But human inventiveness, so active in creating new machines, was not absent in the social field either. Reformers began to demand legislation to protect the working people from oppressive hours and dangerous conditions in the factories. In Great Britain the first such laws did not get through Parliament until 1833, and effective inspection and enforcement came even later. Organization of city services and local governments in the new industrial towns became systematic only after 1832. British workers could hardly afford to wait that long, since the great boom in textiles and coal, in ironworks and related industries, started with the wars of the French Revolution (1792–1815). In Great Britain, therefore, two generations of industrialism passed before anything in the way of legislative regulation helped to improve human living conditions.

In the new factory and mining towns that began to deface the English countryside, the dreariness of working-class life was relieved in two meeting places: the church and the pub. Methodist chapels offered evangelical religion and elementary experience in self-government. A surprising number of later labor union leaders and labor politicians of Great Britain got their start as lay preachers in Methodist chapels, or were the sons of Methodist lay preachers. Pubs offered a different kind of assembly place, where alcohol helped to reconcile the laboring poor to their lot in life. In a later generation, labor unions and self-help societies such as the Rochdale Pioneers, from which the modern retail cooperative movement descends, also came into existence.

In Britain, therefore, the harshest impact of the new industrialism had become a thing of the past by 1850, through a combination of working-class self-help and regulation from Parliament. In other countries, adjustment was delayed. Without fail, the first stages of industrial development saw a widespread breakdown of older social patterns, with corresponding human distress. But as industrialism spread from Great Britain to the European continent, governmental and official regulation came faster and more sweepingly, leaving less to local makeshift and private initiative.

The Napoleonic Wars and the British Economy

Britain prospered enormously during the French wars (1792–1815). Government need for uniforms put special demands upon the textile trades. As a result, mechanization spread from cotton mills, where it had started, to woolen mills. In the 1780s cotton mills—because they engaged in a new manufacture in England—did not displace artisans, but opened new jobs for unskilled women and children. However, as soon as the extraordinary war demand ended, use of power machinery in woolen manufacture brought about the destruction of a great cottage industry in England. This involved much suffering on the part of poor weavers who could not compete with the price of mill-made cloth, but could not afford to pull up roots and leave their patch of land and little cottage either.

Military demand for guns and ships and all the equipment needed for land and naval forces had parallel consequences for the metal trades. New methods and larger-scale operations opened new uses for power-driven machinery. Mines went deeper, and more engines were needed for pumping. On every hand, fresh uses for steam power were found. The result was greater production and lower costs.

Sharp alternation between boom and bust hastened the transformation of the British economy. What made these alternations was the letting of massive government contracts for war supplies whenever the British government took on a new campaign or signed a treaty promising to supply the forces of one of their continental allies for war against the French. But whenever a campaign ended or an ally made peace with the ever-victorious French, such programs were canceled. Boom conditions then suddenly gave way to equally dramatic periods of depression. The effect of such conditions was to push and pull labor and resources into new industries and open the way for radically new techniques in periods of boom. Then in periods of depression, all the less efficient firms and old-fashioned methods had to be given up, since they could not compete with newer and more productive methods that had been pioneered in the boom times. The long-drawn-out Napoleonic wars therefore acted as both a whip and a carrot to reshape the British economy. It emerged in 1815 far more developed than any other in the world.

The Wars and the French Economy   Until about 1780, France kept pace with Great Britain in the development of new industrial methods. War stimulated some branches of the French economy, too; but France lacked extensive coal fields and was not in a good position to take advantage of the new steam power. Early steam engines were extremely wasteful of coal by comparison with those designed later. It was therefore much cheaper to bring labor and raw materials to the coal than to try to ship vast amounts of coal any distance from the place where it was mined. This handicapped the development of French industry during and after the war years of 1792–1815.

In addition, the vast conscription of manpower into the army and into government service drew human energy and inventiveness away from the grubby industrial process and into war and administration. Hundreds of thousands of Frenchmen spent the best years of their lives stationed in distant parts of Europe, either as garrison forces or simply marching to and fro. Many

Coal and Iron in the Industrial Revolution On the left, a painting of the pit-head of an English coal mine about 1820 shows the heavy and rather crude machinery for raising coal from below ground quite clearly; but the workings of the steam engine, fired by coal, that activated the ropes and pulleys remain unclear. The horses in the foreground show that animal power remained important long after steam engines began to change the industrial scene. On the right, the painting of a gun foundry illustrates one of the uses to which Europeans put their new technology. Iron had many uses, of course; but military requirements accelerated metallurgical development markedly in the early stages of the industrial revolution when the revolutionary wars (1792–1815) resulted in an urgent and enormously expanded demand for weapons.

died, and those who lived did not learn the habits of the new industrialism or become interested in its skills and opportunities. In 1815, therefore, the demobilized French soldiers went back home to small farms, small towns, and an economy not nearly as much transformed by the war as Britain's.

Other Parts of Europe Much the same was true of other parts of the European continent. The coal fields that run in a belt across Belgium, the Ruhr region of Germany, Saxony, and into Silesia, the Ukraine, and central Asia were a great treasure for the future; but until railroads opened up the continental interior, the cost of transporting bulky goods for more than a few miles overland made the industrial value of these coal fields almost nil. Coal fields and iron deposits, located on or near navigable water, were England's good fortune at a time when water transport was inexpensive and easy and transport overland was still prohibitively expensive. In Belgium, however, where many of Napoleon's cannon had been forged, coal beds close to navigable rivers provided the basis for rapid development of industry on the British model after 1830.

Postwar Industrial Progress

In the postwar period, to 1850, Britain kept the lead in industrial growth. The years 1815–1818 were difficult, for government spending decreased sharply and new markets were not immediately at hand to take up the slack. Overseas sales helped, for machine-made British goods were definitely less expensive and often better than handmade products. As a result, the Indian cotton industry was almost wiped out by the competition of British-made cloth, carried halfway round the world. The trade of Latin America also fell largely into British hands. British arms and diplomacy sometimes helped trade too, as we have seen in the case of China. After prolonged diplomatic conversations, the Ottoman Empire,

The Impact of Railroads Beginning in the 1840's railroads began to change the relation between town and country by cheapening transport and allowing peasants, like those shown in the painting on the left, to come to the city and return to their villages, all in a single day. The ancient gap between town and country, which had dominated all civilized history, began to narrow with this new mobility. Railroads also narrowed the gap between the European center of Western civilization and outlying lands like Russia and the United States. The construction of railroads enormously cheapened and accelerated travel and transport across the vast continental interiors of Asia and North America and linked them with world markets as never before. The photograph on the right was taken in 1867 when the first transcontinental railroad in North America was still under construction. It shows passengers leaving the train and getting into stage coaches for the completion of their trip. (Source: The Metropolitan Museum of Art, Bequest of Mrs. H. D. Havemeyer, 1929. The H. D. Havemeyer Collection.)

too, was opened freely to British goods in 1839, with the result that Ottoman artisans, for the first time, found themselves exposed to competition they could not meet.

The development of speedy, cheap mechanical transportation, in which the British pioneered, laid the groundwork for the later rise of Germany, the United States, and Russia to the first rank industrially. The key invention was the steam railroad. The first successful steam locomotive was built in 1804, but the first railroad was not built until 1825. Development was rapid thereafter, and by the 1840s railroad building spread to the continent of Europe.

Railroads speeded overland transportation and lessened costs enormously. People and goods could move scores or hundreds of miles in a few hours. Iron ore and coal, even when separated by long distances, could be brought together to provide the basis for iron and steel production; and they, in turn, provided the fundamental material

from which a larger and larger number of new machines were made. Railroads themselves became consumers of vast amounts of iron and steel. Bridges and steamships, storage tanks for the coal gas with which the cities were lighted, and literally thousands of other new uses for iron and steel developed, one after the other, between 1815 and 1850.

Some Key Inventions and Breakthroughs

The extraordinary development of the iron industry that dominated the European industrial scene between the 1780s and 1850 required the use of the new fuel—coke—for smelting ore. Throughout the eighteenth century, Europe's iron and steel production had been limited by the scarcity of charcoal, which was the traditional fuel used for smelting iron. How to make coke from coal became generally known in England after about 1750. The necessary fuel for the vast development of the iron industry thus became available.

As so often is the case with discoveries, the invention of coking involved useful by-products that changed European life in quite unforeseen ways. "Coal tars" left behind by the coking process provided important chemical raw materials for dyes, aspirin, and dozens of other products manufactured in the second half of the nineteenth century. Even before 1850, "coal gas"—produced by turning coal into coke—provided a cheap source of illumination for houses, streets, and public places of assembly. Inexpensive artificial light, in turn, opened all sorts of possibilities. Nineteenth-century theater and concert life, for example, would have been inconceivable without the utilization of artificial lighting for stage and concert hall.

Two other key inventions are worth mentioning here. In 1814 the first rotary press was installed in the printing office of the *London Times*. This made high-speed printing possible. Newspapers, in turn, created a link between government officials and other social leaders on the one hand and the public on the other. The flexibility and energy of nineteenth-century European society could not have been achieved without this sort of close linkage between the top and middle ranges of society.

A second key invention was the development in 1836 of a breech-loading handgun. The Prussian army was the first to adopt the new style of weapon. Superiority of the "needle gun," as it was called, was proven in 1866 when Prussian soldiers lay down on their bellies to fire at their Austrian foes, who had to stay on their feet to reload their muskets in the old fashion.

With this invention, therefore, the training of European armies had to be altered. Instead of standing close-massed in ranks, loading and firing on command, as had been necessary with muzzle-loading weapons, a far looser, open order became the key to success on the battlefield. New forms of discipline for the effective control of skirmish lines were called for, but it took European military experts a long time to adjust tactics to the requirements of breech-loading weapons.

Innumerable other inventions changed the character of human activity in less dramatic ways. The camera (1839), electric telegraph (1844), horse-drawn reaper (1834), screw propeller for ships (1836), revolver (1835/1836), bicycle (1839), and sewing machine (1846) are only a few of the new devices that were introduced or improved during these years. Invention became deliberate and expected. Ingenious inventors tinkered in their backyards or basements, hoping to make a fortune by some lucky patent. Few of them had much acquaintance with science or theory. Invention was still the province of the commonsense mechanic with a deft hand and three-dimensional imagination. Complicated mathematical calculations as well as academic physics and chemistry were largely irrelevant to the sorts of inventions that changed the texture of life in European cities between 1789 and 1850.

Rural Conservatism

In the countryside the impact of the new inventions was delayed. Even after Cyrus McCormick invented the horse-drawn reaper in 1834, farming went on much as before. In Europe, particularly, farms were often too small and peasants too poor and ignorant to take advantage of the reaper. Better transportation made it easier to get their produce to market, and growing city populations with ready money tended to push up farm prices in the more densely populated parts of Europe. More intensive cultivation, better seed, better tillage, and better rotations of crops all combined to increase Europe's food production sufficiently to keep pace with the rapid growth of its cities and population. Simplifying rights to particular parcels of land had been part of the legal reforms of the French Revolution, and this made agricultural progress much easier. Wherever the *Code Napoléon* applied, every particular piece of land was assigned to a single owner, and all overlapping and competing rights were abolished. In other words, the last remnant of manorial agriculture disappeared from western Europe; only in the Austrian and Russian empires did the older collective types of tillage survive until 1848 or even later.

Most Europeans remained on the land. Even in Britain, farming and occupations directly related to agriculture continued to engage a majority of the population until after 1850. This meant that European society as a whole could count on a generally stable and increasingly prosperous rural population. Farmers and peasants were, in general, willing to let city dwellers and their traditional superiors, the nobility or gentry, run political affairs, as long as the work on the land went on in familiar ways, and prices were not too bad.

Such basic stability, in turn, gave scope for city dwellers to push and pull against the conservative spirit of the landed element—lords and gentlemen, receivers of rents who were the traditional rulers of European society. In France, home of the Revolution, landed classes never recovered real political strength. Elsewhere in Europe, the balance varied with time and place; but in general it was the city people—rooted in industry and commerce, rising to new wealth and self-confidence with every successful new venture—who advanced and the landed conservative classes who retreated.

CONCLUSION

Between 1775 and 1850, western Europe developed two new and strikingly successful sources of power. One was political: the closer alliance between government and people (at least, the upper and middle classes), pioneered in the United States (1776–1789) and carried triumphantly forward by the French (1789–1815). Even the defeat of Napoleon in 1815 did not reverse this Democratic Revolution—for Napoleon's enemies were able to defeat him only by taking their own public into partnership in some degree or other, and the restored French monarchy continued to try to find public support among the same groups that had been most important in supporting the revolutionary regime.

Western Europe's second major innovation was technical: the Industrial Revolution, pioneered mainly in Great Britain. Here the central fact was that inventors found ways to use inanimate sources of power—coal and steam primarily—to drive all sorts of new machines and perform other services for humankind's convenience. Cheaper, sometimes better, and far more abundant goods were the first result; radically changed living conditions for urban dwellers were a second, sometimes less pleasant, by-product of the new forms of industry.

Thus, the manufacture of more and cheaper goods plus a closer cooperation between political leaders and the public at large combined to produce far greater disposable power for those countries and peoples who were successful in making these twin transformations take root in their midst. Great Britain led the way, but Belgium, Germany and the United States followed close behind. France lagged industrially, and so did all of Mediterranean and eastern Europe. Other civilizations fell even further behind and, by 1850, found themselves entirely incapable of resisting the new kinds of power that western Europeans were able to bring to bear against them—commercially, diplomatically, and militarily.

Such an upsurge in Europe's power set the stage for the collapse of other civilizations' effective independence. Improved communication and transport laid the technical basis for closer and closer interaction of all parts of the world. After about 1850, the separateness that allowed Chinese, Japanese, Indian, and Moslem peoples—not to mention the inhabitants of Africa, Australia, and the Americas—to maintain their own distinct ways of life no longer existed. Such a change in human relationships marks the end of one historic era and the beginning of a new, globally cosmopolitan age, in which we ourselves are living. The inauguration of this new age was the real significance of Europe's Democratic and Industrial revolutions.

Diseases and Their Effects on Human Societies

Disease has played a very big part in human history. In all modern wars, more soldiers died of disease than from enemy action until World War II. Whole societies have sometimes been destroyed by epidemics. Unfamiliar diseases prevented successful European settlement in many tropical lands. Elsewhere European diseases, spreading like wildfire among local peoples, often cleared the way for settlers.

This essay explores the way people and diseases have altered their relationships across the ages. Lack of exact information means that we have to guess details; but there are some general principles—for example, the difference between endemic and epidemic disease—that go far to explain what happened.

THE CASE OF THE VANISHING AMERICAN: 1519–1650

When Cortes invaded Mexico, the inhabitants of Montezuma's empire numbered 11 to 25 million persons. They lived close together in villages wherever good land for cornfields existed. They had never been exposed to Europe's "childhood" diseases: smallpox, chicken pox, measles, mumps, and whooping cough. One after another, these diseases spread among the Indians, killing adults as well as children. But the Spaniards, having almost always had such diseases in childhood, did not suffer. By 1650 the population of central Mexico, where Montezuma had once ruled, was about 1.5 million; at least 10 million persons had disappeared.

Why did so many Indians die of diseases the Spaniards and other Europeans did not find so very serious? The answer lies in the different disease history of the two populations. In Europe, smallpox, measles, and the rest had become *endemic*. This means that the disease was always around so that in the first years of life nearly everyone caught it. Natural immunities inherited from the parents made

recovery more likely. Many children died all the same, but they were quickly replaced by new births. In Mexico and the rest of the Americas, the new diseases became *epidemic*. This means that old and young alike fell ill. Because they lacked any sort of inherited immunities, many died. When a large proportion of adults died, all activity began to fail.

Highlights   The consequences of this disease pattern in the Americas were vast.

> A handful of Spanish conquistadors and missionaries easily controlled large populations. Their resistance to diseases that killed so many Indians seemed to prove that God was with them.
>
> In Massachusetts and Virginia, weaker Indian communities simply disappeared, leaving empty land for English settlers. Similar disease patterns often arose elsewhere. A population among whom a particular disease was endemic always had an advantage in any new encounter with another population among whom the disease was unknown.

HOW EUROPEANS ACQUIRED THEIR CHILDHOOD DISEASES

Medical records are too vague to allow us to know exactly what disease hit when. But general considerations tell us a good deal. We assume that different diseases first broke out in different parts of the earth and among separate human communities. In any one area, a new disease begins as an *epidemic*. Either it kills everybody, and the disease germ itself disappears, or enough people survive the first epidemic to raise children who inherit some immunity to the disease. If enough of them survive childhood exposure to be able to reproduce themselves, after four or five generations the new disease will become *endemic*.

The spread of disease endemic in one human community to another where it is not endemic depends on how far and how often people travel between the two communities. Most

The Bubonic Plague in Europe, ca. 14th century.

major changes in disease distribution ought, therefore, to take place when people change the pattern of their travel and communication in some important way. (The arrival of the Spaniards in Mexico was such a case.)

Our question then becomes: When did people *first* venture upon important new kinds of travel and communication? About 100 B.C. to A.D. 200, caravans regularly traveled across Asia along what Europeans called the Silk Road. During this period ships also sailed the southern seas, connecting the east Mediterranean lands with south China via India and Malaya.

The disease consequences are clear. Severe epidemics hit both the Han Empire of China and the Roman Empire of Europe in the first Christian centuries. Serious depopulation resulted. Depopulation eventually made trade unprofitable, until regular movement along the caravan routes almost petered out. This was probably the time when most of our familiar childhood diseases became endemic among all the civilized populations of Eurasia.

Highlights

The distribution of infectious diseases depends on the patterns of movement and contact among human populations.

Important changes in human travel are likely to trigger new patterns of disease distribution.

The epidemic impact of new diseases upon a dense population without immunities may destroy the conditions needed to sustain the trade and travel that triggered the epidemic in the first place.

This natural cycle had much to do with the decline and fall of classical civilization of the Han and Roman empires, though military and other factors also played a part in the collapse.

THE BLACK DEATH: A DIFFERENT DISEASE PATTERN

When infection passes direct from person to person, the transition from epidemic to endemic requires from four to five human generations. The pattern differs when there is another carrier for the disease. For example, the infectious organism for bubonic plague is carried by rats and is spread further by fleas. It is endemic among wild rats in parts of India and China. From time to time, the disease takes hold as an epidemic among the dense rat populations of cities. When enough rats die off, their fleas may try to live on humans, thus spreading the epidemic to humankind, too. Immunities do not build up, for the disease disappears among humans when an epidemic is over, only to emerge again from the regions where it is endemic among wild rats.

Why, then, did bubonic plague cease in western Europe after 1718? Probably because changes in the ways Europeans got along with rats and fleas checked the spread of the disease. First, public quarantine of ships, houses, or whole cities where plague broke out made it illegal for anyone to leave the quarantine area until after a fixed time—usually forty days—had elapsed without fresh outbreaks of the disease. Second, improve cleanliness made it harder for fleas to take up residence on human bodies. Third, with better housing people encountered rats less often. What really stopped bubonic plague were the changes in European habits that made contacts between human beings on the one hand and rats and fleas on the other less common than before. In Asia and other parts of the world where no such changes took place, bubonic plague continues to threaten fresh epidemics.

Highlights

Some epidemic human diseases are endemic among animal population.

In such cases, the natural shift from epidemic to endemic forms of disease does not occur as far as humans are concerned.

One method of protecting ourselves from the diseases carried by animals is to reduce human contacts with the animal carrier.

An Aztec warrior stricken with smallpox.

THE IMPACT OF SCIENTIFIC MEDICINE

During the past 150 years, scientists discovered how infectious diseases spread. With the identification of disease-causing bacteria and viruses, new methods of preventing disease became possible. Chief among them is inoculation with a weakened form of the disease-causing organism. This induces the human body to build up antibodies in the blood that make infection unlikely. In this way a long list of former killers, like smallpox and infantile paralysis, have become unimportant.

In other cases, chemicals have been discovered that check the disease within the human body. In this way malaria, pneumonia, syphilis, and other diseases have been brought under control. These artificial immunities have extended humankind's freedom from infectious disease enormously, increasing the average length of life by many years.

Today scientific medicine allows control of most infectious diseases. An enormous improvement in the quality and dependability of human life results. Yet there is another side. Less infectious disease means longer life. Babies that would have died in infancy grow up to have children of their own, and their children do the same. Very rapid growth of population results. One of the most distinctive

Smallpox vaccination in 1870.

characteristics of modern times is the runaway population explosion.

Growth of dense human populations created a fertile field for new infections, and several examples of recent disease transfers from animal populations to humans are known. Most of these were quickly eliminated by simple medical countermeasures. But one new virus, which interferes with the immune reaction of human bodies, has not been brought under control. The Acquired Immune Deficiency Syndrome (AIDS) epidemic results. Increasing numbers of people began to die of AIDS in the 1980s, despite efforts by medical scientists to find a cure.

Highlights

Between about 1650 and 1850, epidemic diseases ceased to be important killers. Modern communications spread diseases around the world, and the epidemic-to-endemic shift occured almost everywhere.

Since 1850 scientific medicine also brought the main endemic diseases under control.

Sustained population growth (about .1% per year) began about 1750 when epidemic diseases had been largely checked. Galloping population growth (up to 1.5% per year) took over as many of the important endemic diseases were also brought under control.

Disease and disease-control did not act alone. Increased quantity and quality of food supplies also contributed to modern population growth, and so did other changes in the condition of human life.

Because the causes of the bubonic plague were not fully understood, a variety of folk remedies were developed in an attempt to prevent infection.

THE STATE
OF THE WORLD
1850

From the time when civilizations first began until 1850, the world had been big enough to find room for a dozen or more different civilizations, as well as for literally thousands of other societies. Patterns of communication and transportation set definite limits to the size of states. The Ottoman Empire, for example, could not grow beyond the radius of a three months' march from Constantinople for the simple reason that, if he had to march more than three months to reach the scene of combat, the sultan could not bring his armies into the field for long enough to win a decisive victory. Comparable limits existed for other empires in other parts of the world. The limits of political dominion were only outward signs of the limits to other forms of communication. Such limitations defined the circles within which people could interact continuously with one another and thus create and maintain a single civilization.

EUROPE'S IRRESISTIBLE INVENTIONS

By 1850, however, these old limits upon human interaction had been broken through. European inventions made worldwide interaction possible. Railroads opened up the possibility of penetrating the continental interiors of all the world, making the most remote village no farther removed from the outside world than the nearest railroad station. The electric telegraph opened still more amazing horizons, for all that was needed was to string wires across the lands and oceans of the world to create instantaneous communication around the entire globe. Steamships had a less

revolutionary impact, for the oceans had already become highways for contact between the world's habitable coasts. Still, cheaper and faster ocean transport did make the worldwide net of communications and contacts so much the tighter.

In 1850 these new means of communication had been invented but had not yet been used outside of Europe and North America. Their global effect, therefore, lay still in the future. But Europeans clearly had both the will and the means to catch all the world in this new net of their devising. The Industrial Revolution had affected weapons, as well as transport and communications. The result was that European governments controlled ships, guns, and soldiers—all of which were so much superior to the forces any other people in the world could put into the field that armed resistance to Europeans had become all but impossible. The Chinese, to their surprise and dismay, discovered this fact in the Opium War of 1839–1842. The Turks learned that same lesson during the Napoleonic Wars, when French, British, and Russian forces took turns at being enemy or friend to the sultan but always enjoyed a clear upper hand when it came to military action. In India, British power was supreme by 1818. In central Asia, Russian advance was checked only by distances and the limited interest that the Russian czar felt in adding new deserts and barren steppelands to his domain. In the Americas there had been no contest from the time that the conquistadors first set foot in the New World. And the same was true in Australia. Of the inhabited continents, sub-Saharan Africa alone remained safe from European penetration, but the disease barrier that had long protected Africa from outsiders was shattered in the 1850s when Europeans learned how to protect themselves from malaria and other mosquito-borne infections.

LEADING ROLE OF EUROPE

Hence, after 1850 no part of the world could prevent Europeans from moving in if they wished to do so. Moreover, there was a second and no less powerful weapon in the European armory: cheap goods. With the help of machine production, it was possible for European factories to turn out a host of consumer goods—saws, hatchets, scythes, pocketknives, sewing machines, cooking pots, textiles, and hundreds of other items that were cheaper and better than anything which local artisans could produce by hand. European traders wished to sell such goods freely in order to get raw materials and other supplies they needed in return. Local peoples often welcomed the new goods. Local governments had little choice but to admit the Europeans. The futility of trying to prevent trade was sharply demonstrated by the Chinese defeat in the Opium War, and no other major civilized government ever again made the attempt.

But the availability of cheap machine-made goods, which could be supplied in almost any quantity if the demand was brisk enough, brought about a fundamental disruption of traditional society in all those parts of the world where artisan handicrafts had become important. Every civilized society, in other words, stood at Europe's mercy, for the disruption of handicrafts meant the breakdown of traditional city life, and cities were always and necessarily the centers of civilization.

The world had become one, in a way never known before. What happened in Peking, Delhi, Accra, or Constantinople depended on what was thought and done in London, Paris, New York, and Hamburg. The possibility of isolating one civilization from another had disappeared. All humankind had become part of a single worldwide interacting whole. Europeans played the lead role and, to begin with, enjoyed most of the advantages of this new world balance. The three major Asian civilizations suffered catastrophic breakdown, all at the same time and within a mere fifteen years, 1850–1865. During the same period, the less highly developed parts of the world felt the impact of European enterprise more forcibly than ever before; and disruption of tribal and other forms of local society became widespread, though not quite universal.

WORLD COSMOPOLITANISM

Europe and the Western world beyond Europe remained for a long time almost unaware of what was happening to the rest of humanity. From a Western point of view, it all looked like progress and the spread of Christian civilization, or the advance of science and technology. Inherited ways of thinking and doing, modified though they were by the Democratic and Industrial revolutions, provided a general framework for European life and thought that did not seem to need fundamental revision. How could it be otherwise when the world lay open to European curiosity and enterprise as never before, when everything seemed to work in Europe's favor, and when people of European culture could find nothing in the world that seemed equal, or nearly equal, to their own achievements?

Yet enough time has now passed since the end of the separateness of world civilizations and cultures to make it plain that the worldwide interactions that started to take on such intimacy after 1850 were not entirely one-sided. World cosmopolitanism required Westerners to get used to living with people of backgrounds different from their own, just as much as it required the rest of humankind to get used to the Westerners. The last part of this book will, therefore, explore this interaction, insofar as our present place in time and space allows us to understand what happened.

Chapter 21

THE DECISIVE YEARS
1850 to 1865

Interaction among the world's civilizations attained a new level of intensity between 1850 and 1865. During that short period of time, the impact of Europe's Industrial Revolution began to hit home in all parts of the globe. In particular, the great Asian civilizations found themselves unable to keep intrusive Europeans and/or Americans from doing more or less whatever they wanted to do, even on Chinese, Indian, Moslem, and (in much lesser degree) Japanese soil. This discredited old institutions, habits, and customs among more and more of the leaders of Asian opinion; but what to put in place of ancestral practices was difficult to agree upon. A time of troubles thus began, when almost everywhere outside the Western world people found themselves forced to experiment with new and unfamiliar ways of coping with daily emergencies. As a matter of fact, the world has not yet emerged from this time of troubles. We ought, therefore, to study the years 1850 to 1865 with particular attention if we want to understand how the world arrived at its present condition.

THE BREAKDOWN OF TRADITIONAL SOCIAL ORDER

The opening up of the world's oceans by European seafarers marked the start of modern times, not only for Europe but for all the world. The oceans ceased to be barriers to movement and became, instead, connecting links bringing individuals of diverse and different backgrounds into contact with one another, on a scale and with a regularity that had never been possible before. Within thirty years after Columbus' first voyage in 1492, the main breakthroughs took place: Vasco da Gama's voyage round Africa in 1497 and Magellan's circumnavigation of the globe, 1519–1522.

Just as sharp a break came when new techniques of transportation and communication allowed Europeans to penetrate the continental interiors of the earth more or less at will, beginning about 1850. In the next fifteen years the traditional civilizations of Asia collapsed, in the sense that their leaders no longer could follow customary ways, and instead more and more had to react to European initiatives.

To be sure, western Europe was not particularly affected, at least to begin with. Europeans were mightily reassured by the fact that their diplomats, armies, navies, missionaries, merchants, explorers, technicians, scientists, and settlers were able to break in upon almost every other human society on the face of the earth, without bothering about how their behavior might interfere with local customs or interests. This seemed to prove Europe's superiority beyond all doubt.

Indeed, by 1850 they were so sure of themselves that few Europeans really tried to understand the foreign peoples and different civilizations they met. In the 1700s, many Europeans were ready to admire the wisdom of Confucian sages, but the ways of the "heathen Chinee" struck their descendants of the 1800s as merely peculiar. Armed with such smugness, Europeans were not, therefore, particularly affected by the opening up of the continental interiors of the world, which took place during the fifteen years between 1850 and 1865.

But the rest of the world's peoples were deeply affected, for they found themselves plunged into a buzzing, blooming confusion where their forefathers' tried-and-true rules of conduct no longer worked. As a result, in the 1850s traditional political, social, and economic patterns of life broke down in China, Japan, India, and the Ottoman Empire. These breakdowns were by-products of the Opium War of 1839–1842, and of two other wars: the Crimean War of 1853–1856 and the Indian Mutiny of 1857–1858.

In the next decade both Russia and the United States entered upon a particularly painful transformation. In Russia the abolition of serfdom in 1861 gave legal expression to changes that ran from top to bottom of Russian society—changes that were triggered by the fact that Russia's Old Regime had failed in the Crimean War. In the United States the Civil War of 1861–1865 and the emancipation of the slaves in 1863 gave far more violent expression to the growing pains through which the American nation passed in these same years.

EUROPE'S IRRESISTIBLE IMPACT

This widespread and sudden breakup of traditional social orders had worldwide as well as local causes. For one thing, the impact of the Industrial Revolution (which had gotten under way one-half to three-quarters of a century earlier in Great Britain) began to be felt in the far parts of the world only after 1850. Being delayed, the impact, when it came, took a double form: one military, one economic. First of all, by 1850 European weapons and military organization had become overwhelmingly superior. Unprecedented mobility and firepower came easily to armies and navies equipped from Europe's new industrial workshops.

Secondly, after gunboats and marine landing parties had battered down political barriers, European merchants found themselves, in a position to supply goods at lower prices, and often of better quality, than could be produced locally. A flow of such goods quickly changed consumers' tastes and ruined local artisans. With their ruin, the traditional social structure of towns and cities was damaged beyond repair. This presented most of the world's peoples with a painful crisis. Societies and governments that lacked power machinery and factories had to find ways of creating them or else submit to foreign economic domination. The old routine of doing nothing in particular, and of paying no attention to what Europeans were up to, became quite impossible to follow when Europe's guns, and the will to use

them, opened the way for Europe's cheaply manufactured goods.

Industrialism was not the only factor causing change, of course. Europeans were far better organized than were the other peoples of the world. Standing armies and navies, well-equipped and carefully trained, could operate thousands of miles from home and still get reinforcements, supplies, and strategic directives—if not always when most needed, at least eventually. As for trade, corporations and other kinds of companies coordinated the efforts of scores or of hundreds (and sometimes of thousands) of individuals across as well as within national boundaries. As a result, common purposes could be carried out anywhere in the world and across decades or even longer periods of time. No other civilization could operate nearly so well at a distance.

In addition, Europeans were sure they were right: Adam Smith and others had proved that free trade was a good thing. If trade benefited Europeans more than others in the 1850s and 1860s, it merely proved how well thrift and a shrewd eye for business paid off. Moreover, the precious blessings of exposure to Christian civilization justified, in European eyes, the political subordination of peoples whose own past had kept them in heathen darkness.

A third piece of Europe's moral armament for its great venture of smashing the idols long held dear by other peoples of the earth was the value Europeans placed upon heroic achievement. Both as individuals and as representatives of the nation back home, Europeans valued deeds of daring and took risks most of us would shrink from. As in the days of the conquistadors, incredible expeditions carried tiny companies of adventurers into strange and hostile parts of the globe, blazing trails for the administrators who followed afterward. Nineteenth-century Europeans took their vision of heroism mainly from the Greek and Roman classics. Schoolboys read Plutarch, Livy, and Caesar and then tried to act on the model the ancient heroes offered them; and this was so whether the schoolboys pursued their activities in darkest Africa, in heathen Asia, or in desolate Australia—or whether, indeed, they were merely chasing a fox across the hedgerows of England.

The combination of such traits made the mid-nineteenth-century Europeans literally irresistible. As Thucydides said of the ancient Athenians: "They were born into the world to take no rest themselves and to give none to others."

Europe's Civilized Rivals

At the same time, we can point to special areas of weakness that afflicted Europe's civilized rivals, China and Islam in particular. Both these great civilizations had been psychologically on the defensive for centuries.

China   Ever since the Chinese had driven the Mongols out of their country (1368), the overriding aim of Chinese rulers and thinkers had been to keep themselves pure by preventing foreigners from again bringing in new and uncivilized habits. To be sure, the Manchu rulers were foreigners and the Chinese never quite forgave them for that. But at least the Manchus had the grace to accept Chinese civilization and tradition as fully and completely as any foreigners could. Foreigners who did not take the pains to meet the Chinese on their own terms by mastering the Confucian classics and the Chinese language were of no interest or concern to China's upper classes, except when they became unruly and had to be punished.

Such a policy worked very well indeed until about 1775, as we saw; it made China great and prosperous. But it had also allowed China to fall behind the European world in innumerable ways. Therefore, when military collision came, in the 1840s, Chinese minds and traditions were completely unprepared to face the crisis. Sticking to methods successful in the past seemed the only thing to do. It hurt dreadfully to acknowledge that foreigners had knowledge and skills that were actually superior to Chinese knowledge and skills. To admit such a thing was to admit that the whole policy of Confucian China had been a mistake. Indeed, the more obvious it became that something vital was lacking in traditional Chinese civilization, the more traitorous it became

to say so in public—up to the time when it was too late to avoid being trodden upon by European intruders.

Islam   Islam had a similar though different history. The great divide, as far as Moslem skills and knowledge went, came about 1500. In 1499 the Safavid Shah Ismail challenged the prevailing compromises of Islamic society. But in the Ottoman Empire, where Islam's main contact points with Europe lay, this revolutionary religious movement was kept under control by administrative devices and military force. Debate was hushed up. Official Sunni Islam became dependent on the administrative structure of the Ottoman Empire. As a result, the official guardians of truth and knowledge could no longer afford to think freely and seriously for themselves. It seemed safer and better to memorize the Koran and ancient commentaries upon it.

But this intellectual attitude also required Moslems to turn their attention away from the new thoughts evident all over Christian Europe in the age of the Renaissance and the Reformation and to pay no attention to anything outside the official canon of Sunni Islam. Consequently, all the dazzling new ideas and techniques that grew up right next door to the Ottoman Empire were deliberately disregarded by Ottoman and Islamic society until, once again, it was too late to catch up and keep pace with the restless Europeans. Territorial retreat became necessary instead. Only complicated diplomacy prevented complete collapse. Time, the will, and the means to catch up with Europe were as utterly lacking in Islamic lands as in China.

Japan and India   Japan and the Hindu communities of India were in a less awkward position. The Hindus already had been overrun by Moslems. The religious ideas and caste organization of Hindu society made it easier for them to get used to having Europeans—in this case the British—ruling them and interfering in their economic and political affairs. One foreign master was much like another, after all; and if Europeans offered jobs in the government to clerks who could learn how to get along in an English-speaking world, there were plenty of bright and ambitious young men who were eager to qualify themselves as soon as suitable schools had been set up.

Japan's case was almost the opposite. The Japanese had never been conquered. When Japan's rulers deliberately opened the country to contact with Europeans and Americans, they did so because they knew that their traditional military defenses against foreign attack were no longer effective in keeping the foreigners out. It seemed better, therefore, to learn the Westerners' secrets as quickly as possible. Only so could Japan be safe again from the danger of foreign conquest. After a shaky start, Japan's efforts along these lines proved remarkably successful. The nation was thus able to keep its traditional social structure and safeguard old values while working hard to modernize technology, the armed forces, and government along Western lines.

Everywhere else in the non-Western world, among civilized and uncivilized peoples alike, the collision between Western ways and local traditions led to the disruption of old patterns of leadership. This was painful and confusing enough, but the difficulty grew greater as new ideas, new ideals, and new leaders struggled to cope with the ever-present white foreigners, who were always wanting something and would never take No for an answer. A century of paralysis, or near-paralysis, resulted. Moslems, Indians, and Chinese, not to mention the other less numerous and less mighty peoples of the earth, all found themselves helpless, unable to act together effectively for any clear and attainable goal. Anger and frustration were inevitable. Occasional outbreaks of violence gave vent to such feelings but led only to new defeats at European hands. Dismay, despair, and passive retreat while waiting out the storm were the inevitable result. Few individuals were able to act constructively amid the chaos surrounding them as a result of the sudden collapse of traditional guidelines and landmarks in every walk of life.

Westerners, by contrast, had few or no hesitations before 1914. Some thinkers and artists did, indeed, foreshadow the collapse of Europe's New Regime—bourgeois, capitalist, parliamentary, reformist, progressive, and smug. But the great majority paid no attention. Westerners kept any doubts they may have had strictly to themselves when dealing with people who were less powerful than they were.

This extraordinary contrast dominated the history of the world from 1850 to about 1950. Then a new era set in. Western empires in Asia and Africa collapsed as local peoples reclaimed their independence, and Westerners' self-confidence suffered serious shock from the disasters of two world wars.

But for a century before 1950 our contemporary doubts about the uniqueness and superiority of Western civilization did not enter into the picture. Instead, triumphant Europeans asserted their power everywhere; and in a short fifteen years, between 1850 and 1865, old barriers to their supremacy everywhere crumbled.

THE CRIMEAN WAR AND ITS CONSEQUENCES

The Crimean War, 1853–1856, was one of the silliest wars ever fought; yet its consequences were extraordinarily important for Russia and for Europe as a whole, for the Ottoman Empire, and even for India. The struggle began with a quarrel between Roman Catholic and Orthodox Christian churchmen over control of the holy places in Palestine. The Ottoman Turks were nominally in charge; but when the French backed the Roman Catholics and the Russians backed Orthodox claims, the sultan found himself in a delicate position. Turkish fear of the Russians was deepseated. If the czar made good his claim to protect Orthodox interests in Palestine, the next step would be interference between the sultan and his Orthodox subjects in the Balkan Peninsula, where Serbs, Bulgars, and Greeks all belonged to the Orthodox Christian faith. English diplomats feared the same thing; and English journalists stirred up popular excitement in Great Britain by pointing with alarm to the consequences for the balance of power in Europe if the Russians should advance into the Balkans or, worse still, seize Constantinople and the Straits between the Black Sea and the Aegean Sea.

Hence, when Russian demands provoked the Turks to declare war on Russia, France and Britain came to the sultan's aid. Austria intervened by sending the Russians an ultimatum requiring them to withdraw from the provinces which later made up Romania or face the threat of Austrian attack. When the Russians did withdraw their troops from this territory, Austrian forces marched in. As a result, the Turks and Russians had no place to fight; and if British and French journalists had not been so bloodthirsty, the war might have ended before the French and British land forces even entered into action.

Instead, the French and British mounted an amphibious attack on the Crimea, hoping to eliminate the main Russian naval base at Sevastopol. A difficult campaign ensued, for both the Russian and the Allied forces had to operate at the end of very long supply lines. Supply and medical services were not set up to take full advantage of the new resources of science and industrial mass production; but the telegraph made it possible for journalists to send back daily news reports of everything that went wrong. Shortcomings revealed during the Crimean War made the British—and to a lesser degree the French also—realize the need for fundamental reorganization of their army supply systems and of their promotion policy for officers. Modern nursing started at this time, when Florence Nightingale organzied emergency measures to help the British wounded. The French and British, who had been rivals ever since 1688, even became accustomed to cooperating with each other; they soon extended the practice to China, as we shall see. After a winter's siege, Sevastopol surrendered and peace followed. The Russians were humiliated but made peace anyway because, after Czar Nicholas died in 1855, his successor, Alexander II, felt that far-reaching internal reforms had to come first, before revenge would be practicable.

As far as Europe was concerned, the most important consequence of the Crimean War was the bitter feeling that arose between Austria and Russia. The conservative alliance that had kept Russia, Austria, and Prussia together since 1815 broke up completely. The Russians felt that their help in 1849, when a Russian army had invaded Hungary to put down rebels against the Hapsburg authority, had been repaid with the basest ingratitude. Instead of backing the status quo against any efforts toward change, as the Russians had done for forty years, the new czar was unwilling to raise a finger in their support when Prussia challenged the traditional Hapsburg leadership of central Europe. The result was the unification of Germany under Prussia between 1866 and 1871. Much of the world's history since then hinges upon German efforts to make up for the lateness of their arrival upon the European scene as a united nation, but it seems best to postpone exploration of this by-product of the Crimean War until the next chapter.

Here we are concerned with the consequences of the Crimean War for Russia and the Ottoman Empire and with the echo that the Turks' victory over Russia had in India.

Russian Reaction to Defeat

Russia's reaction to the defeats that the czar's armies suffered in the Crimea was confused and not very successful. The whole system of government had been built around the army, which had shown itself unable to defend Russian soil. Something was obviously wrong. Russia had again fallen behind the Western powers, and heroic efforts to catch up, as in the days of Peter the Great, seemed called for. But agreement on what had to be done and how to do it was never reached.

At first "liberals" had the upper hand in trying to meet the difficulty. The great problem, as they saw matters, was the absence of real freedom in Russia. What was needed was to unleash individual initiative by changing laws that made most Russians serfs. Accordingly, in 1861 the government abolished serfdom and divided legal ownership of the land between landlords and their former serfs. Yet before the emancipation laws were put through, an opposite "Slavophile" point of view made itself heard at court. As a result, instead of assigning the land to individual ownership, as liberals would have done, the law assigned ownership of the serfs' fields to the village community as a whole. Provisions were made for periodic reassignment of fields among the villagers. This arrangement was customary in most of central Russia. The reform of 1861 gave it full legal force and thus set off Russian ways

THE LADY WITH THE LAMP

When Florence Nightingale was seventeen years old, she heard a voice calling to her and believed that God had spoken. But for seven years she could not discover what she was called upon to do. Gradually, she decided that her mission in life was to nurse the sick; but her parents refused to permit her to do such a thing because at that time nursing was a very lowly occupation, and Florence Nightingale came from a wealthy English family.

But Miss Nightingale was nothing if not determined. She refused to marry and secretly read all she could about nursing and hospital administration. The more she read, the more she was sure that hospitals needed to be reformed, and that God had chosen her to accomplish the task. Eventually her parents gave way, and in 1851—when she was thirty-one years old—Florence Nightingale left home and went to Germany to get her first practical experience of nursing. The German hospital in which she worked was run by Protestant deaconesses, and it came nearer to her standards than any English hospital of the time.

On returning to England she began to set up a hospital, but she had scarcely started when the British government blundered into war against Russia, in the Crimea. Soon newspaper reports describing dreadful conditions in British military hospitals flooded into London. Officials of the government turned to Miss Nightingale and asked her to help. With thirty-eight nurses to assist her, in 1854 she sailed for the battle zone, and within a month had 5000 wounded and sick soldiers to look after.

more sharply than ever from the patterns of land ownership current at that time in western Europe.

Attempts at Social Reform   This result was what Slavophiles wanted. Their idea was to preserve everything distinctively Russian. Some believed that in this way Russia could bypass the capitalist, individualist stage of society characteristic of nineteenth-century western Europe and move directly into socialism—the social order of the future, according to their way of thinking. They argued that Russia might thus be able to leap ahead and, instead of being backward and despised, would find itself in the forefront of European social and historical development. Other Slavophiles feared and detested socialism and

revolution; they believed in the past for its own sake and resisted every change, including the abolition of serfdom.

Both liberals and Slavophiles tended to extremes. They agreed that something fundamental was wrong with Russia but disagreed on practically everything else. In between was a body of officials and piecemeal reformers—practical administrators who worked within the limits of the possible. Their trouble was that the limits of the possible seemed uncomfortably narrow. Russia's poverty made any large-scale program for industrial development, or even for constructing an adequate railway network, prohibitively expensive. Tax income was not large enough to finance the necessary undertakings, and private enterprise and capital were not available. Moreover, fear that reform, if pressed too vigorously,

To begin with, there were almost no medical supplies or facilities. But Florence Nightingale and her nurses set to work, cleaned things up, and did the best they could with what they had. They all put in long, hard hours; and Florence Nightingale worked harder than anyone else. Late at night, when her tasks for the day were done, she inspected each ward, carrying an oil lamp so as to be able to see. The sick and wounded soldiers soon nicknamed her "The Lady with the Lamp." She became a national heroine, universally admired and everywhere acclaimed.

Florence Nightingale used her position to demand, plead, and argue for a more adequate medical setup for the British army. Even after the close of the Crimean War, when she returned home and hid from her public admirers, Florence Nightingale continued to work from behind the scenes for much-needed reforms and improvements. Modern ideas about military hospitals and medical administration, as well as the modern profession of nursing, were created very largely through her work.

But after her hectic days in the Crimean War hospitals, she always remained out of the public eye—and most people assumed she had died. Actually, she worked at home with high officials of the British government until the 1870s. Thereafter she "retired" and spent much time in religious exercises. She lived until 1910, dying at the age of ninety. Having been idolized for two short years, during the Crimean War, Florence Nightingale remained mysterious, strong-willed, and independent all her life.

might awaken the sleeping giant of the Russian peasantry and provoke some vast outburst of peasant discontent soon hampered reform, even when changes did not cost much money.

Half measures and the endless delays of bureaucratic decision-making won no friends for the moderate middle road of gradual reform. Impatient young men, often priests' sons and students, began to gather in secret groups to talk of how Russia should be reborn. The spirit of revolution was fed by the fact that reform soon petered out. In 1864 the czar proclaimed a law setting up limited local self-government. Thereafter, the steam went out of the reform effort.

The basic fact was that the peasants were not satisfied with emancipation as handed down in 1861. They believed that the land was theirs by right. Some convinced themselves that wicked landlords had twisted the czar's intentions by keeping back part of the land. And while the peasant majority nursed its grievance, half in secret, the rest of the Russian society fell into hopeless disagreement. Fierce debate over whether Russia should imitate the Western nations or not, and how imitation should be carried through if it should be tried at all, continued to distract Russian public policy until 1917.

In central Asia and the Far East, Russian armies were still able to advance and, in fact, annexed important new territories in the years 1850–1865. But at home everything was in confusion. Straightforward programs of economic development, aimed at catching up with the West, seemed impossible. Where would the money come from that was needed to build railroads, factories, mines, and steel mills on the scale that would be required to come abreast of Great Britain or France? But without such a program, really adequate defense against the Western powers was impossible, as had been shown in the Crimean War. On the other hand, the only justification for the czar's autocratic government was that compulsion and authority were needed to protect Russia from her enemies. If the czar's government could no longer perform that function, what claim had it to the obedience and service of the Russian people? After the scoffing irreligion of Peter the Great and Catherine II, it was hard to revive the theory of divine right; but the only alternative theory was popular sovereignty, which was too risky. The people, if consulted, would want to overthrow the landlords; the czar's government was not ready, as it had been in the days of Ivan the Terrible and Peter the Great, to lead a revolution of that kind, with or without the support of the people.

The effect of the Crimean War on Russia, therefore, was to open up a series of painful riddles. Cooperation between monarch and nobles, operating mainly by means of the military-civil bureaucracy, in which nobles occupied all important posts, had made Russia great in the eighteenth century. After the death of Catherine the Great (1796), however, this cooperation slowly wore itself out. For a while, the conservative policy of Alexander I (reigned 1801–1825) and Nicholas I (reigned 1825–1855) hid Russia's inner strains. But the failure of Russian arms in 1853–1856 discredited the czarist regime at home as well as abroad—without, however, provoking thoroughgoing breakdown, thoroughgoing reform, or thoroughgoing reaction. Instead a patchwork of half measures disfigured the Russian ship of state. Meanwhile, the western nations of Europe built up their power through the Industrial and Democratic revolutions, leaving Russia to flounder, falling further and further behind.

The Consequences of Ottoman Victory

The Ottoman sultan, though among the victors of the Crimean War, was no better off. The war left a Turkish debt, owed mostly to French and British bondholders. For a few years, the sultan's government met interest payments on the bonds by floating new loans; but when investors became more cautious, the cycle broke—and indignant creditors, with the help of their home governments, fastened a foreign-managed "Ottoman Public Debt Administration" upon the helpless Turks (1881). This administrative corporation had the right to collect specified taxes, mainly customs dues, to pay off the bondholders. It operated on Turkish soil without being subject to Turkish control. The victor of 1856, in other words, emerged from the war with a "ball and chain" of debt, from which the Ottoman government was never afterward able to escape.

Special privileges for foreigners were nothing new in Turkey. Europeans resident in Turkey had enjoyed the right to be judged by their own law from 1569 when the Ottoman sultan first concluded treaties with Christian nations. The Turks took it for granted that foreigners, not being Moslems, could not be tried by Moslem courts. When the sultan was mighty and Christian traders existed on sufferance, the system worked well enough, from a Turkish point of view. When power relations were reversed, however, European consuls often gave protection to persons whose claim to be British or French subjects was very dubious. Shady characters sometimes escaped Turkish justice in this way. On the other hand, the unfairness of Turkish judges, especially when called upon to decide a quarrel between a Christian and a Moslem, gave European consuls grounds for extending their protection to persons who could not hope for a fair trial before a Turkish court.

Moslem Reform   The basic trouble with the Ottoman Empire was the lack of sympathy between Moslem rulers and Christian subjects. This, indeed, had been the real cause for the outbreak of the Crimean War. The Turks and their allies feared that if Russia were allowed to "protect" the interests of Orthodox Christians in the Ottoman Empire, before long the Russians would win over the loyalty of the Christians and be in a position to snuff out Turkish power in the Balkan peninsula whenever the czar wanted to do so.

The British ambassador to Turkey, Lord

Opening of the Suez Canal, 1869 The Suez Canal, built between 1859 and 1869, shortened the sea route from Europe to India by many thousands of miles and altered geopolitical relations by making the Middle East once again a crossroads for important traffic. This is an artist's drawing of the initial flotilla that started from the Mediterranean at Port Said in November 1869 and sailed southward to the Red Sea. The traditional appearance of the local inhabitants, who gathered on the bank to watch, contrasts with the new steam technology that propelled the larger ships shown here. To be sure, steamers were still in their infancy and needed sails as supplement since they could not carry enough coal for a long voyage. Hence tall masts still adorned these ships, though the plumes of smoke rising amidship attested the new power that had begun to transform sea transport, making it possible to carry larger cargoes more quickly, reliably, and cheaply than ever before. The Canal had a parallel impact, for it also made transport between Asia and Europe quicker, more reliable, and cheaper.

Stratford de Redcliffe, felt sure that energetic reform could cure this situation. If new laws were applied fairly to all the sultan's subjects—Moslem, Christian, or Jew—then the possibility of creating a stable, strong state would arise. Without reform, Lord Stratford felt, even the best efforts of the British government to prop up Turkish power would be in vain. The French and Austrian ambassadors agreed. Accordingly, just as the war was ending in 1856, the sultan proclaimed the equality of all his subjects before the law. Efforts to spell out this principle in detail continued for the next ten years. The European ambassadors and advisers wanted systematic codes of law. One

by one, such codes were drawn up, usually modeled on the French *Code Napoléon*.

But the reform program did not work. The sultan's Christian subjects did not trust their Turkish masters. Secret revolutionary movements soon sprang up, or took on new life. Prince Michael of Serbia (reigned 1860–1868), for example, plotted a general rising of all the Christian peoples against the Turks. The Turks, for their part, felt that the only people who benefited from the reform were Christians and Jews. They found it difficult to give up the Sacred Law. After all, if Islam were the true religion—and who could doubt that and remain a Turk?—then the Sacred

Law was in fact sacred, and no one had any right to annul its provisions. How, then, could the sultan take it upon himself to contradict the Koran and proclaim some newfangled nonsense about the equality of Jews and Christians? How indeed?

Nearly all Turks and other Moslems in the Ottoman Empire, therefore, tended to feel that the reform laws were mere window dressing. If the foreign ambassadors demanded such things, let them have them; but when it came to real, day-to-day personal relations, especially in the provinces, old habits persisted and the provisions of the new law codes were simply disregarded. This, of course, justified revolutionary conspiracy on the part of Christians; and the existence of such conspiracies, in turn, justified the Turks in disregarding the law.

Ottoman Sovereignty   Turkish efforts at reform were also damaged by the fact that the European

powers continued to chip away at Ottoman frontiers. Romania became independent as a result of the diplomatic settlement of 1856. This was no great loss, since the provinces had been effectively freed from Turkish rule since 1828; but the Turks did not like giving up their claim to these rich territories. Turkish troops were pulled back from Serbia in 1867, after troubles between the garrison of Belgrade and the Serbian populace provoked diplomatic intervention by the European powers. Turkish power over Lebanon was similarly hedged in with irritating restrictions after 1861.

On the other hand, the telegraph and, eventually, the railroad made it possible for the sultan to control what went on in remote provinces of his empire far more closely in the second half of the nineteenth century than had been possible before 1850. Hazy areas still existed in Albania, Armenia, Iraq, and Arabia, where tribal or other

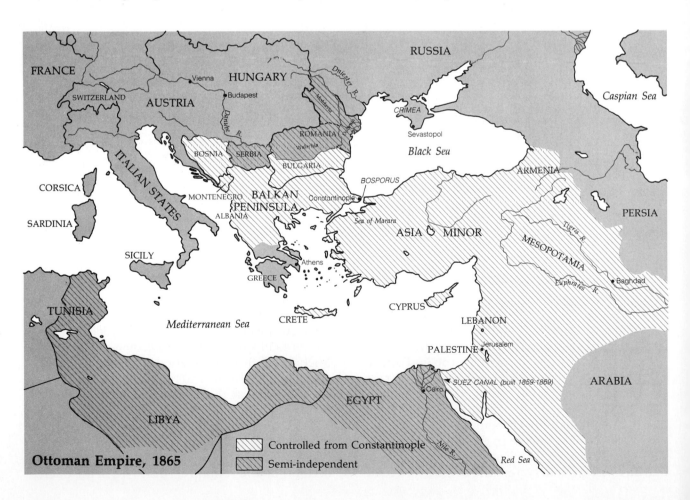

Ottoman Empire, 1865

Controlled from Constantinople
Semi-independent

forms of traditional local government competed with the authority of the sultan's governors. But even in the eastern portions of the empire—where tribalism was strongest—the authority of local chiefs tended to retreat into the desert regions, where nomadic life made any other kind of government impractical. This constituted a solid gain for the central government of the empire.

Some progress also was made toward modernization of the Ottoman army. Turkish troops, trained and equipped in the European fashion, had done well against the Russians in the Crimean War, and Turkish tradition made soldiering come easy. But the Ottoman government never even tried to build the industrial base needed to equip Turkish troops from home production. Instead, they relied on foreign-made equipment.

From 1839 on, the Ottoman government officially accepted the principles of free trade. This meant giving up any attempt to protect local artisans from the competition of European machine-made goods. As railroads were built inland, the disruption of artisan life, which resulted from this policy, moved inland too. But no one in authority cared very much, or even understood what was going on. Local resentments were fierce enough but usually found expression in rival nationalisms. Christian artisans, after all, suffered as well as Moslems. Each group blamed the other—and let it go at that.

In the aftermath of the Crimean War, therefore, the Ottoman Empire formally and publicly cut loose from the traditional Islamic ordering of society. Legal reform, along European lines, officially left the Sacred Law behind; but distrust among the different religious and national groups within the empire made the new laws unenforceable. The trouble was that laws imported wholesale from the West did not fit Ottoman society. Few Turks believed in the reform program, and Balkan Christians soon pinned their hopes on national independence.

The spread of nationalism was, of course, profoundly subversive of the Ottoman state, for the various nationalities that lived together under the sultan could not separate into independent nation-states without first destroying the empire. Yet this was what reform led to. How, then, could Turks and other Moslems support a program that asked them first to give up their relig-

ion and cultural identity, and then to watch their Christian subjects throw off Turkish control? But there seemed no alternative. The old traditions of Ottoman government were dead and gone, and the heirs of that tradition could not come up with any practical line of action.

Reforms in India

India, also, suffered drastic change between 1850 and 1865. The central event was what the British called the Sepoy Mutiny of 1857–1858. This was a rebellion of Indian soldiers, called sepoys, and it led to the suppression both of the Mogul Empire of Delhi and of the East India Company. The revolt, in turn, was touched off partly by news of Turkish (that is, Moslem) victories against Christians; but this was not the main cause.

The Indian soldiers, whom the East India Company hired to sustain its power in India, had many grievances. What started the mutiny was a rumor to the effect that a new drill routine would require the soldiers to violate religious taboos. To be exact, the British planned to pack powder charges for new muzzle-loading army muskets in little paper packets. In this way, an even amount of powder could be put in with each shot. To protect the powder from moisture, the paper was soaked with grease; and the Indian sepoys discovered—or assumed—that this was pig's fat, which was prohibited for Moslems, or else beef fat, which was prohibited for Hindus. The only way to open the packages was to bite off a corner, which, of course, meant ritual defilement.

This particular collision between new techniques and religious taboos was only one of many. British policy in India had changed. Before 1800 the East India Company went to great lengths to avoid offending local customs and respected all religious traditions. Christian missions, for example, had been forbidden, and the Mogul administrative language, Urdu, had been maintained even in provinces ruled directly by the Company. Once British power in India became clearly superior to any rival (1818), the original grounds for this policy disappeared. Moreover, the Company came under attack at home for not admitting missionaries and for allowing various "wicked customs and heathen habits" to go on unchecked.

In 1837 it was decided to shift the language of administration from Urdu to English; but the change came slowly, since it required the establishment of schools to teach English to clerks and other subordinate officials of the government. However, by the late 1840s British power really began to bite into traditional Indian life. James Andrew Ramsay, Lord Dalhousie, governor general of India from 1848–1856, put the whole force of the East India Company's administration behind such improvements as building a rail and postal system uniting all India, as well as the construction of telegraphic and road communications, irrigation projects, and similar public works. He also annexed important new territories, acting on the principle that when a ruling prince died without a direct heir, his territory ought to come under direct Company administration.

The Sepoy Mutiny of 1857 interrupted these enterprises, but only briefly. The soldiers acted in fear and anger. They knew vaguely what they were against: all the newfangled nonsense their British masters were bringing in so energetically. But they had no positive program, and the sharp differences between Moslems and Hindus failed to come into the open only because of their common enmity to the British.

For a few weeks the whole British position in India seemed threatened, for the Company kept very few white troops in India. Reinforcements soon arrived, however, and one by one the centers of resistance were reduced. Within two years, British power was fully restored. The British Parliament took the occasion to reorganize the government of India, bringing it under a cabinet minister in London.

The new regime plunged ahead with remodeling Indian government and law. The overriding idea was to unite the country by a system of communications and administration and to station enough English troops in the land to make sure that any local disturbances—such as those that started the mutiny—could be snuffed out before the flame of rebellion spread. In addition, the British hoped and believed that a just and fair administration, acting in accordance with published laws, would remove grievances and make the Indian people loyal and obedient subjects. In 1853, recruitment into the Indian Civil Service was put on the basis of competitive examination, with the result that graduates of Oxford and Cambridge, trained in the traditions of the English upper classes, began to govern India. Legal reforms, separating administrative from judicial functions, followed. In 1861 legislative and executive councils were established in which British administrators and Indian subjects sat

War in the Crimea and in India In the mid-nineteenth century, before photography had developed, artists recorded public events with drawings which were then reproduced in books and magazines that reached the interested public soon after the events had occurred. Here are two such works of art. On the left, is an episode in the battle of Balaklava in 1854—a bungled manoeuver made famous by Alfred Tennyson with his poem, "The Charge of the Light Brigade." On the right, a scene from India, showing the rebels scrambling for spoils while a battle against British is still in course. Neither of these representations is an accurate image of actual events. The artists were not eye witnesses and their purpose was to interpret what had happened for British readers safe at home. As a result, the image of war they conveyed was profoundly misleading. Old-fashioned cavalry dominate the pictures; but in fact it was rapid-firing hand guns, heavy artillery, and trench warfare that controlled the battlefields of the Crimea during the war of 1854–56. Sieges were also decisive in India, though the rebels' uncertain goals made their defeat comparatively easy once reinforcements from Great Britain arrived on the scene. Nevertheless, the survival of an outdated, heroic image of war among stay-at-homes was an important dimension of late nineteenth century Europe. Images, like these, showing victories over distant, alien foes, confirmed Europeans' sense of their superiority to everyone else and made it easy to mobilize support for continued imperial expansion in Asia, Africa and Oceania.

together to decide local problems of government.

In this way India came under the rule of a benevolent despotism, inspired by liberal principles. Those things that British custom assigned to the sphere of government were usually carried through with thoroughness, impartiality, and efficiency. Whatever belonged, by British practice, to the private sector was left strictly alone. The results were oddly lopsided. Efficient, limited government was superimposed upon age-old custom. Custom gave way where it had to, but elsewhere it remained little changed, since whatever was "private" in British eyes lay beyond the self-imposed limits of their jurisdiction. Private custom stood in the way of modern industrial development, for example. But because the government took British ideas of free trade and private business initiative for granted, public authorities did nothing to develop that sort of modernity.

Military security, however, was very much a part of the government's concern. In addition to making it routine to station significant numbers of British troops in the country, the government of India set out to erect a protective sphere of influence on every side of the subcontinent. The British occupied Aden, at the mouth of the Red Sea, in 1839; they intervened in Persia and Afghanistan to make sure that only rulers friendly to them should hold power there; they made similar arrangements in Zanzibar and Oman (1862). The situation in Egypt was more complicated, for there French influence competed, and sometimes cooperated, with the British. The great struggle was over whether or not to cut a canal through the Isthmus of Suez. In 1854 the ruler of Egypt agreed to let a French company build a canal, but the British opposed the scheme and managed to delay matters for several years. As a result, the Suez Canal was not opened for traffic until 1869. When the canal was completed, the British government bought the shares that had been assigned to the Egyptian government and thus secured an effective voice in the management of the canal company. With the opening of the Suez Canal the "life line of empire," connecting Great Britain with India, ran through the Mediterranean. In that sea, British naval power had to compete with French, Italian, and other navies; but further south, beyond Suez, the shores of the Arabian Sea, the Persian Gulf, and the whole of the Indian Ocean were firmly under British influence by 1865.

The new regime in India, together with British diplomatic activity in Arabia, Persia, and Afghanistan, reduced the eastern heartland of the Moslem world to nearly the same state of helpless dependency that afflicted the Ottoman Empire. By supplying a few guns, or refusing powder and shot to a stubborn sheik, the British could make and break dynasties and kingdoms along the shores of Arabia and the Persian Gulf. To the north lay Russia, whose appetite for Moslem territory was never in doubt. In 1849–1854, the czar's troops pushed back Persian frontiers, oc-cupying the Syr Darya Valley. Then the outbreak of the Crimean War interrupted their advance. After the war, the Russians resumed expansion at the expense of the Kirghiz people, who lived as nomads on part of the central Asian steppe.

In such a situation, most Moslems despaired of public life and military-political action. They concentrated instead on a more rigorous and exact performance of private religious observances. The central inspiration for this movement came from Arabia, where Abdul-Wahhab had founded a rigorist movement in the eighteenth century. At first, the Wahhabi reform was closely tied up with the military career of the Saud family; but when Egyptian armies defeated the Saudis in 1818, Wahhabism began to spread more widely among Arabs and Indian Moslems. Turks and Persians, on the other hand, were not much interested. The narrow emphasis upon Koranic lore could not appeal easily to these two peoples, whose native speech was not Arabic, and whose ancestors had brought the changes to Islam that the Wahhabi reformers set out to undo.

COLLAPSE OF THE FAR EASTERN CITADELS

Both the Manchu emperors of China and the Tokugawa shoguns of Japan found themselves in deep trouble in 1850. The key problems were internal. In China, the great mass of the peasantry had begun to stir. In Japan, it was the "outside lords" who were becoming restless. But in both cases, traditional methods of government seemed ineffective in meeting the new conditions. Dismay and uncertainty grew among the inner circle at court. No one knew what to do or how to do it.

China

China's case was by far the most critical. In 1842 the emperor had been forced to make terms with the British and to open key Chinese ports to European trade. Eight years later an obscure prophet, Hung Hsiu-ch'üan, announced the establishment of the "Heavenly Kingdom of Great

European Trade in Canton, China This is a view of Canton harbor about the beginning of the nineteenth century when it was the only Chinese port where European traders were allowed to come ashore. The artist was probably Chinese, but he suited his style to European taste, emphasizing the flags of six European nations and the separate shore establishments belonging to each, where exchanges actually occurred. The smaller boats in the harbor were designed for river and canal transport, which held the Chinese internal economy together. The three bigger vessels in the foreground may be intended to portray European sea-going ships but, if so, the artist did not know much about them, for no European ships ever had a double prow such as is pictured here. This amazing error illustrates the gap between Chinese and European knowledge and mutual understanding in the decades just before the Opium War (1839–41) humiliated the Chinese and opened the country to European penetration up and down the whole Pacific coast.

Peace" in Taiping. Hung Hsiu-ch'üan had spent a short time in a Protestant missionary school; later he began to see visions, mixing old Chinese ideas with Christian teachings about the end of the world and the Second Coming of Christ.

In ordinary times the words of such a man as Hung Hsiu-ch'üan would not have attracted much attention, but in 1850 he was able to arouse smoldering discontents that had been accumulating for years. The Taiping movement was mainly a peasant revolt. Millions upon millions of poverty-stricken Chinese peasants responded to the promise of a heavenly kingdom, interpreting it to mean the end of rents and taxes. But, of course, it was impossible to create or maintain an army without some kind of income. Hence, when an army became necessary to hold off and then drive back Manchu forces, the Taiping movement came face to face with the crisis that always besets a successful peasant rebellion: how to organize a new government that can be strong enough to survive when the rebelling peasants want only to be left alone and not have to pay anything to anybody.

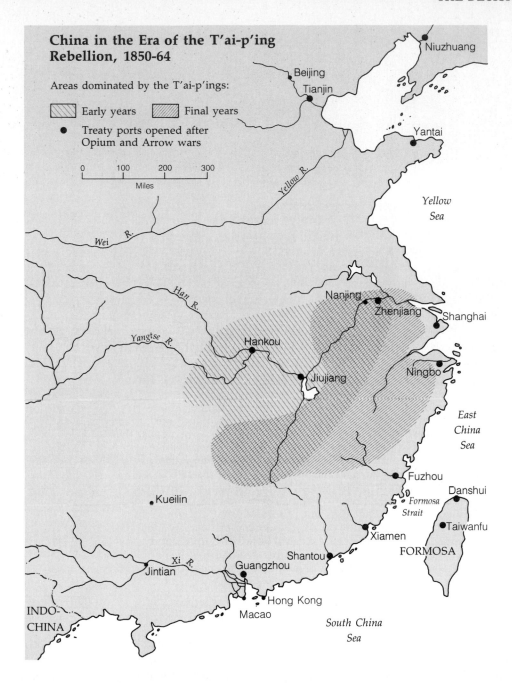

China in the Era of the T'ai-p'ing Rebellion, 1850-64

Areas dominated by the T'ai-p'ings:

☐ Early years   ☐ Final years

● Treaty ports opened after Opium and Arrow wars

0   100   200   300
Miles

The Taiping leaders never solved this problem. Hung Hsiu-ch'üan himself was a seer of visions, not an administrator. Some of his followers proved to be good generals, but they never had help from a regularly organized government supporting them in the rear. Consequently, the Taiping armies had to live by plunder. This hurt their popularity with the peasants and eventually allowed the forces of the imperial court to win. For several years, however, when the vision of the Heavenly Kingdom of Great Peace was still fresh and bright, the weakness at the heart of the Taiping movement was not apparent. From their point of origin in the southern part of China, the Taiping forces moved northward, reached the Yangtze River, and in 1854 captured Shanghai.

By then much of south China was in Taiping hands, and the peasants of the north were only waiting for the arrival of their liberators to join in the revolt.

Moslems in the western provinces of China organized a revolt of their own; so did other minority groups. Banditry broke out in other provinces. Then, on top of these disasters, new quarrels with the British and the French led, in 1857, to hostilities and fresh humiliation for the Chinese at European hands. The Treaties of Tientsin (1858) restored peace briefly. But when the Chinese delayed making some of the concessions promised by those treaties, the French and British organized a military raid on Peking and in 1860 burned down the emperor's summer palace. Such an act confirmed Chinese detestation of the "south sea barbarians," but for the time being the imperial government had to give in on all points of dispute. New treaties admitted British, French, American, and Russian diplomats, missionaries, traders, and adventurers to the capital and to any other part of China they cared to visit.

During these same disastrous years, the Yellow River changed its course. Instead of flowing to the sea south of the Shantung Peninsula, as it had done for centuries, the river broke its banks and found a new course to the sea far to the north of its former channel. But before the river settled into its new banks, vast and destructive floods spread over the lower plain of the Yellow River. Millions of Chinese died as a result. Yet the floods helped to save the Manchu government. When the Taiping soldiers started north for Peking, still in the first flush of their early successes, and when the peasants everywhere were still ready to welcome them as liberators, the floods stopped the advance.

Thereafter, the Taiping cause began to suffer defeats. The framework of Manchu administration had never broken down completely; so the emperor was able to keep soldiers in the field, even if they were dispirited and inefficient fighters. Soon quarrels broke out in the ranks of the Taiping army. Hung Hsiu-ch'üan expected miracles; none came. Instead, the imperial forces began to win victories until, by 1864, the Taiping Rebellion was crushed. Hung Hsiu-ch'üan poisoned himself.

Millions upon millions of people died as a result of the disorders and natural disasters that descended upon China in these years. This calamity, by itself, made life a little easier for those who survived. There was more land to go around and innumerable old debts washed away in the confusion. Thus the Chinese had a breathing space after 1865. Nevertheless, the government failed to use it effectively.

It is easy to understand why. The Taiping rebels had been put down by traditional measures. In the next few years, military operations against the Moslems and other unruly groups also proved successful. To be sure, the Westerners remained a thorn in China's side. Yet their impact was blunted by the poverty and disorder of the countryside, which interfered with trade and made missionaries' lives unsafe. Nearly all of China's rulers and learned men heartily disliked and despised the bad manners of the white barbarians from Europe and America. They hoped in time to be able to drive them away. In the meantime, the best thing to do was to neglect the intruders as much as possible.

This policy was foredoomed to failure, for China's weakness was too great. The traditional order that had achieved such brilliant heights a century before could not survive internal crisis and Western assault. The peasant crisis had not been solved, only postponed; still less had the Western challenge been met. The old order, as in Moslem lands and in India, was in hopeless disrepair. Yet no one knew what to do; agreement on new courses of action could not be achieved; confusion and bafflement reigned, as in the other lands that were feeling the effect of Western superiority.

Japan

Japan followed a very different course. A small, power-seeking clique of reformers set out to make Japan safe by making it strong. This required modern industry to supply an army and navy. But modern industry required new skills and knowledge, and these in turn required a new kind of school system and many other changes in traditional Japanese life. Yet, once launched on the path of radical readjustment, the Japanese leaders never flinched from undertaking the next necessary step.

Siam's Tribute to the West Like Japan, the Kingdom of Siam was never conquered by Europeans but in the 1860s, when Burma to the west had fallen to the British while on the east Cambodia and Laos were being subjugated by the French, the King of Siam appointed an Englishwoman as governess for his heir who all too obviously needed to become familiar with the ways of the West. While still a minor, the young prince succeeded his father, becoming King Rama V (1868–1910) and eventually built himself the palace shown here. The King chose to erect an architectural hybrid that combined east and west by putting Buddhist spires on top of a wholly European facade. This matched his government, which erected a European facade, featuring such novelties as a modern military establishment, telegraph, and railway, in order to defend his own sovereignty together with the other cultural traditions of the Thai people.

The first landmark of this extraordinary development came in 1854, when the shogun gave up the policy, in effect since 1638, of shutting Japan off from ordinary contact with the outside world. What triggered this decision was a U.S. naval mission sent to Japan under the command of Commodore Matthew C. Perry. When the American warships first appeared in 1853, they were rebuffed; but the next year, when Commodore Perry returned, the Japanese government meekly agreed to open two ports to foreign ships. In 1858 Japan agreed to a detailed commercial treaty with the United States, to which Holland, Russia, Britain, and France later adhered.

The shogun's weakness in knuckling under to the foreigners made a good rallying cry for patriotic warriors and clan leaders who were jealous of the position long held by the Tokugawa family. They focused their loyalty upon the person of the emperor. The ideas of Shinto, which had developed into an increasingly public religion, provided popular justification for the restoration of the emperor's powers. Behind the scenes, however, informal alliances and rivalries among the military clans stood at the center of politics.

The shogun's position was undermined by uncertainties about the right of succession, for

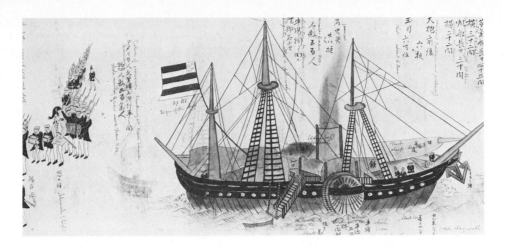

The Wonders of the West as Seen from Japan Above a Japanese woodcut records the features of the paddle wheel steamer that carried Commodore Perry into Tokyo bay in 1854, when he compelled the Shogun to sign a treaty opening Japan to foreign commerce. Inscriptions give further details: number of the crew, dimensions of the paddle wheel, information about the steam engine, and the like. (Later, someone provided English translations, so you can perhaps read what each inscription says.) Obviously the person who made this woodcut was fairly knowledgeable about the technology that supported American naval power and wished to communicate his information to others. A similar purpose pervades the woodcut below, which shows what the artist imagined things were like on the other side of the Pacific. He wanted his public to know that in America exotic architecture, exotic ladies, costumes, and a few other extraordinary things, like the American flag, provided a setting for such wonders as balloons that could carry people through the air and the great ships whose power had already impressed the Japanese so much.

direct heirs of the Tokugawa line had died out. The individuals who occupied the shogunate in its last years were weak and ineffective persons. In addition, they were by no means sure that the new policy of opening the country to foreign contacts was wise or safe. Consequently, they were divided and halfhearted; their rivals became more and more united around patriotic slogans— and the hidden figure of the emperor.

The upshot was a coup d'état in 1867. The shogun abdicated, and a new, young emperor officially took command of affairs. Members of the "outside clans" took over all the key positions around the emperor's person. Yet on their way to power, the new rulers of Japan had a sobering experience. In 1864 a combined British, French, Dutch, and American fleet bombarded and destroyed several Japanese coastal forts as a way of showing the displeasure of the Western powers at widespread antiforeign outbreaks in Japan. This demonstration of Western naval superiority convinced the men who took control in 1867 that anti-Western policies, without the power to defend the country, were not going to work. They therefore gave up their anti-Westernism, at least for the time being, in order to learn how to be strong.

Having once made this decision, there was no turning back and remarkably little hesitation. Whatever was needed for the creation of a strong, modern army and navy, Japan had to have. When it turned out that this meant an entirely new industrial technology with drastic educational, social, and political reforms, the Japanese leaders never faltered. Peasants and commoners obeyed; the leaders commanded; and modern Japan began to emerge with amazing rapidity, within a single generation.

The Japanese were, of course, aware of China's difficulties when they made their fateful decision to open their country to Western contacts. The news spread throughout southeast Asia, where the British pushed into Burma and the French went into Annam, Laos, and Cambodia in the 1860s. When China trembled, these satellite states shook. Their rulers made little effort to resist the force of European arms. Siam remained independent, more as a buffer between French and British imperial spheres than because of any inherent strength that the ruling dynasty

commanded. For another decade Korea, alone, remained an independent, hermit kingdom; but in 1876 that last, remote bastion of the Far Eastern circle of civilized communities also opened its ports to Western trade.

CIVIL WAR IN AMERICA

During the short period of time when these far-reaching changes were taking place in Asia, the United States of America came of age as a full-fledged participant in Western civilization. The national borders attained almost their present shape after a war with Mexico (1846) led to the annexation of California and Texas and territories in between. The Gadsden Purchase (1853–1854) added a strip of land in the extreme south of what is now New Mexico and Arizona, to facilitate construction of a transcontinental railroad. Then, in 1867 the federal government purchased Alaska from the Russians, thus attaining the country's present continental limits.

For a while it seemed uncertain whether a federal government would prove capable of holding such an enormous territory together. Loyalties to the separate states were strong; in the 1850s sectional loyalties began to create larger and scarcely less powerful political blocs. The issue that crystallized sectional feeling was slavery. In the southern states, preservation of the "peculiar institution" of Negro slavery attracted fanatical support, partly, at least, because the southerners were fearful of what would happen if the slaves were freed. Visions of economic disaster, if not of bloody revolution, haunted their dreams. In the northern states, meanwhile, dislike of slavery increased. It seemed uncivilized, inhumane, and a disgrace to America. Fanatical abolitionists matched southern fanaticism; compromise became more and more difficult.

In 1860 the Union fell apart. Abraham Lincoln was elected President, but without an absolute majority. Moreover, his support was wholly in the North and West; the South feared and distrusted him as spokesman and leader of the new Republican Party. Southern states decided to withdraw and form their own confederacy, appealing to the same principles that had

War in the United States By the 1860s, photography became a practicable way to record events. As a result, a realistic image of the American Civil War entered the record in striking contrast to what patriotic artists had provided just a decade earlier. Here is a photograph of a wall and trench as it looked a few hours after Union forces had swarmed over it during the battle of Chancellorsville in 1863. Discarded weapons and Confederate dead dominate the scene, not men on horseback swinging sabres as before. Nonetheless, the long, drawn-out struggle of the Civil War did not convince military observers from Europe that the character of war had changed. They preferred to believe that Americans were merely amateur soldiers, whose lack of professional skill prevented them from conducting quick, decisive campaigns like those which occurred four separate times in Europe during the wars of Italian and German unification between 1859 and 1871.

been used to justify the American Revolution. But Lincoln and the North refused to admit that withdrawal was permissible. War ensued: long, bloody, and desperate. The war was popular in the sense that both governments commanded strong emotional support from the rear. In the end the North won because of superior numbers and superior industrial output; but until almost the very end, the Southern will to resist was never in doubt. Such tenacity raised difficult problems for a national government that professed to derive its just powers from consent of the governed.

At first, slavery was not officially the issue, but in 1863 Lincoln decided to publish an Emancipation Proclamation. Thereafter the advance of Union armies into Southern territory meant liberation of the slaves. Full citizen rights were conferred upon the liberated slaves by the Thirteenth, Fourteenth, and Fifteenth Amendments to the United States Constitution. These were adopted between 1865 and 1870; but in practice, systematic discrimination against the new black citizens continued to be a marked feature of American life.

The long years of civil war created a great demand for everything needed to equip huge armies. Rapid expansion of railroads also opened a vast new market for iron and steel. The result was a tremendous boom in the North that quickly made the United States an important industrial producer. American factory technology came abreast of the latest English and European practices, and in some fields, such as the mechanization of agriculture, the United States took the lead over the rest of the world. As a result, dramatic increases in the export of wheat became possible, even during the war years when large numbers of farm boys fought in the armies and had to be fed, without themselves helping to produce the crop.

Victory for the North, therefore, meant victory also for an expanding industry and for mechanized agriculture. Hoe cultivation and hand-picking lasted in the cotton fields of the defeated South for another eighty years or so, but it was precisely this style of agriculture and the society built around it that had been defeated. America's future would not rest with a sharply divided society, in which the forced labor of slaves maintained a few plantation owners. A much more varied and complex society prevailed, in which market prices and individual shrewdness—at least in theory—regulated production and consumption.

This new and growing American society differed in some respects from the pattern familiar across the Atlantic in England and western Europe. Aristocratic elements were almost absent from the American scene, and barriers to the rise of individuals from one social class to another were weaker in the United States than in Europe. Despite such differences, Americans shared the skills and ideas of western Europe, and the eastern seaboard of the northern United States had almost caught up with England and France by 1865. Moreover, the United States had begun to fill in its political frontiers by planting technically skilled communities all across the continent. The energies of the American people were engaged in this task throughout the next generation, when, except in the defeated South, both the work and the means to perform it stood ready at hand; and no really important doubts troubled the public mind.

America's success contrasted sharply with the doubts and difficulties that afflicted Russia, China, India, and the Moslem world. Yet it would be wrong to forget that the nation's success simply side-stepped the problems created by the South's defeat. That region of the United States took little part in the industrial upsurge. The South remained backward, poor, and ignorant—only a marginal sharer in the busy, greedy, restless, and increasingly urban world of the North, which had come into its own so suddenly during the Civil War years.

THE REST OF THE WORLD

Improved communication and transportation, which brought Western power to bear upon the Asian civilizations so dramatically between 1850 and 1865, also had important consequences elsewhere. For one thing, European governments organized expeditions to explore the parts of the earth still uncharted by European map makers; and many of the obstacles that had previously prevented Europeans from traveling in unknown lands were overcome by these new, systematic efforts.

Three regions of the earth remained to be explored by Europeans. Two of them, the Arctic and Antarctic, were frozen wastes; the other, tropical Africa, had always been protected by the prevalence of lethal diseases. In the 1840s two English expeditions penetrated Arctic and Antarctic waters. Between 1840 and 1843, Captain James Clark Ross got closer to the South Pole than anyone before him. He skirted the shores of a considerable stretch of the Antarctic continent,

discovering a mountainous coast, an enormous ice shelf, and the sea that bears his name. Then in 1845, Sir John Franklin set out to discover a "Northwest Passage" from the Atlantic to the Pacific across the seas and straits to the north of Canada, but his ship got caught in the ice and all the members of the expedition died. In the ensuing decade a series of relief expeditions were mounted to find out what had happened. Traces of Franklin's disaster were eventually found, and in course of the search most of the islands of the Canadian north were mapped for the first time, and both the reality and the impracticality of the Northwest Passage, which English explorers had dreamed of since the time of Columbus, was finally established. The two poles remained out of reach until the twentieth century, when expeditions that traveled on foot reached first the North (1909) and then the South Pole (1911).

Learning how to travel safely in Africa was very different. There the problem was to escape malaria and other fevers that killed newcomers who lacked inherited and acquired immunities to the infections that caused the fevers. In the 1840s, when Europeans first began to secure a regular and dependable supply of quinine from Dutch plantations in Indonesia, it became possible for them to travel in the interior of Africa with far greater chance of staying alive, since malaria ceased to be a serious threat. As a result, a series of explorers penetrated regions previously unknown to European map makers. The most famous was David Livingstone, a Scottish missionary who crossed Africa between 1853 and 1856, walking from the east coast to the west coast and back again and discovering Victoria Falls on the Zambesi River. He subsequently explored some of Africa's great lakes and died encamped on the shores of Lake Tanganyika in 1873. But the relation between the lakes and the sources of the Nile and Congo rivers was not fully sorted out until an American, Henry Stanley, explored the upwaters of the Congo between 1873 and 1877.

Exploration was, of course, only part of European expansion. In Australia and New Zealand, for example, English settlement advanced rapidly in the years 1850–1865, stimulated by gold rushes following the discovery of placer gold in Australia in 1851 and in New Zealand in 1861.

In 1855, the British government abolished the last convict colony, setting up a series of self-governing provinces in Australia instead. (New Zealand became self-governing in 1846.) Sheep raising proved particularly successful in both lands; and when gold was exhausted, commercial farming became the backbone of both the Australian and New Zealand economies.

English settlement provoked violent collisions with the native inhabitants, since the newcomers needed land for their sheep. The Maori inhabitants of New Zealand were sufficiently warlike to fight back. Although twice defeated (1843–1848 and 1860–1870), they won the respect of the English settlers, and in subsequent decades the Maoris secured full rights of citizenship and established a comparatively easy relationship with the whites. In Australia, on the contrary, the natives were unable to organize any effective resistance, and the gap between Australian aborigines, living as Stone Age hunters and gatherers, and the English settlers proved to be quite unbridgeable. The fact that the Maoris were Polynesians, and impressed Europeans as being big handsome people, made the eventual reconciliation between the races easier, whereas the Australians were dark skinned, small of stature, and ugly as far as Europeans were concerned. Race prejudice therefore sharpened the collision of interests and led the settlers to drive the aborigines away from all the best land in Australia, banishing survivors to the desert wastes in the center and north of the continent.

In Africa, race feeling also disfigured whiteblack encounters. Europeans had known and exploited black Africans as slaves for centuries, and the abolition of slavery in the nineteenth century did not change European attitudes toward blacks very noticeably. Violent clashes concentrated in the south, where Boers, British, and black Africans fought one another in innumerable skirmishes and a few real battles. The upshot was the emergence of two Boer republics in the interior, and of two British self-governing colonies at the Cape and in Natal. The Boers made Africans work for them under conditions that approached old-fashioned slavery. In the English colonies a policy of protecting the blacks and (mostly mixed blood) descendants of the Khoikhoi (Hottentot) population prevailed, although full equality of legal rights was accorded only to a few of the mixed population known as "Cape Coloured."

Elsewhere in sub-Saharan Africa, local peoples and states continued much as before. The appearance of a handful of European explorers did not make any real difference at first, since it took a while before missionaries, traders and soldiers followed in their tracks. European political and economic control of the continent may have been foreshadowed by the way explorers crisscrossed the interior, but the reality was delayed until the 1870s and 1880s.

Latin America

In Latin America, the years 1850–1865 were not of especial significance except in Mexico. In 1861 the Mexican government stopped payment of interest on government bonds. France, Spain, and Great Britain decided to intervene. The French sent enough troops to install a Hapsburg archduke, Maximilian, as emperor of Mexico in 1864. Mexican "liberals" resisted the French. Their main enemy had been the Church, whose lands they wished to confiscate. French intervention widened and deepened the conflict. For the first time, peasants of Indian descent began to take part in the resistance to Maximilian.

When the American Civil War ended in 1865, the United States government made clear that it regarded French interference in Mexico (or anywhere else in the New World) as an unfriendly act. Napoleon III soon decided to withdraw his troops from Mexico. As a result, Maximilian was captured and killed (1867); and the liberals, led by Benito Juárez (d. 1872), himself a Zapotec Indian, came to power. The revolution did not go very far, although the Indian and mestizo majority asserted itself politically for the first time by challenging the dominance of a small upper class of purely Spanish descent.

CONCLUSION

Although Latin America was not particularly transformed between 1850 and 1865, and although these years were not particularly critical in western Europe, in most of the rest of the world the period was crucial. The Moslem and Far Eastern worlds were shaken up badly. Russia and the United States reacted to Europe's Industrial and Democratic revolutions in sharply different fashions. Everywhere barriers to the advance of Westerners came tumbling down. As never before, world-girdling communications bound all people together into a single interacting whole. A new age of global cosmopolitanism, centered upon western Europe, leaped into being—full-grown and formidably armed. Humankind could never be the same, nor could Europe. We shall devote the next chapter to a closer look at what was going on in Europe, before turning back to study the world's reactions to European expansion in the period before World War I.

Chapter 22

EUROPE
1850 to 1914

European political, economic, and cultural life in the second half of the nineteenth century and the first few years of the twentieth century was, for the most part, buoyantly self-confident. This was the great age of the European middle classes, who saw themselves and the rest of humankind becoming richer and wiser and, perhaps, even better as time went on. Not everyone believed in progress, but most Europeans who wrote and spoke about such matters took the idea pretty much for granted.

There were solid reasons for such confidence. New machines and new knowledge, especially in the physical sciences, came forward at an accelerating pace; and each new device or idea seemed clearly better than what it supplanted. Human life also became more comfortable, and health improved with the advance of medical skill. In politics, wider and wider circles of the population began to take part in elections and party organization. Education became more nearly universal. Riches increased, and even the poor and unskilled began to experience some benefits from Europe's advancing wealth.

To be sure, there was an underworld to all this progress. Women were legally subordinated to men in such matters as the right to hold property and to vote. Poor people were afraid of unemployment, and they suffered severely in time of illness. Labor in factories and mines was often dangerous and poorly paid. Strikes and the rise of socialist political parties expressed the discontent of industrial workers. Such problems were troublesome indeed for the European middle classes, but what toppled them from their privileged position as leaders of society was international instability. Each of the major European governments engaged in rivalries overseas, trying to build up its political and economic power in Asia, Africa, and other distant regions of the earth. Similar rivalries existed on European soil too, dividing France from Germany, Russia from Austria, and lining up each Balkan nation against others in a tangle that puzzled and dismayed the diplomats of western Europe.

The upshot in 1914 was the sudden outbreak of World War I, and through that war the breakup of much that had been characteristic of nineteenth-century Europe.

POLITICAL CHANGES

In the spring of 1848 a rash of revolutions spread across Europe, starting from Paris and reaching all the way to Berlin and Vienna. Before the end of 1849 the liberal hope of establishing free and constitutional governments in Europe had failed. In France, the Second Republic had come into existence when King Louis Philippe resigned; but in June 1848, bloody fighting broke out in the streets of Paris, between the poor, who wanted improvements in their economic lot, and the regular army. After the "June Days" the French middle classes, as well as the propertied peasants in the countryside, wanted a strong government. They therefore elected Louis Napoleon, the great Napoleon's nephew, first as president of the Republic (1848) and then in 1852 as emperor.

The failure of the 1848–1849 revolutions meant a split in the ranks of those who opposed the system of society and government that had emerged from the Congress of Vienna (1815). All over Europe, middle-class liberals lost confidence. Kings, officials, and landlords continued to run the government without paying much attention to liberal demands for a voice in public affairs. Worse than that, in central Europe elected representatives had been unable to agree among themselves as to where national boundaries ought to run. Nasty quarrels between Germans and Czechs, Germans and Hungarians, Hungarians and Croats—to mention only the most bitter—made it clear that these nationalities would not willingly agree to work together peaceably.

Who could really believe in the liberal ideal of popular self-government when representatives of the popular will had failed so miserably?

A second fear eroded the liberal faith. Could the lower classes be trusted? Could workers, whose numbers grew rapidly with the onset of the Industrial Revolution, really have an equal share in self-government? Would they not try to seize the property of others and vote for socialist or communist agitators? Many business leaders and professionals concluded that revolution was dangerous and futile. Cooperation with nobles and monarchs and with the army and police seemed necessary to keep the lower classes quiet and in their place.

Some radicals stuck to the older faith in popular self-government and even welcomed the idea of expanding the ideal of equality to include economic equality. The most important spokesmen for this position were two young writers, Karl Marx (1818–1883) and Friedrich Engels (1820–1895), who published a fiery little pamphlet in 1848–just before the revolutions began—entitled *Communist Manifesto*. It explained how all history had been a class struggle. First slaveholders, then feudal lords, and finally capitalists had dominated society by getting hold of the "means of production" (that is, first land and then, in more recent times, machinery and money). But, Marx declared, the capitalist system would bring its own destruction by concentrating wealth in fewer and fewer hands, while making more and more workers propertyless.

Marx had in mind, in making this prediction, the fact that machine-made goods had been driving small artisans out of business all over Europe and in other parts of the world. Such people often did lose their property, tools, and shops and had to start working for wages. Many artisans resisted the process, hanging on grimly to the bitter end, in hopeless competition with machines. By assuming that the destruction of independent artisans would go on unchecked until a tiny number of great manufacturers controlled the whole industrial process, Marx envisioned a time when the propertyless proletariat, millions strong, would find it easy to seize the means of production from the capitalists. Such a revolutionary act, he thought, would inaugurate the final communist stage of history, when universal brotherhood, freedom, and equality would prevail.

This vision of the future gave a more radical definition to the French revolutionary ideal of democratic equality. When political parties arose which accepted the Marxian program, they called themselves Social Democrats. Because of Marx and his followers, from 1848 onward the Democratic Revolution had a socialist as well as a liberal wing.

Unification of Germany and Italy

Middle-class liberals who feared socialism found an alternative in nationalism. Socialists emphasized the international brotherhood of the working class. But most persons, including members of the industrial working class, proved more interested in identifying themselves with a great and powerful nation than with internationalism of any kind. The problem was especially acute in central Europe, where the Germanies and Italy remained divided into numerous separate states.

The realignment of Europe brought about by the Crimean War (1853–1856) opened new possibilities. Moreover, leaders bold enough to take advantage of these possibilities arose in both Italy and Germany, so that by 1871 both these "geographical expressions" had become national states. Liberals supported the movement for the unification of Italy from the beginning. In Germany, they first opposed Otto von Bismarck's reliance upon "blood and iron" instead of elections as a way of settling matters. But when Bismarck turned out to be successful in defeating Austria (1866) and uniting north German states under Prussia, most of his liberal critics were silenced. He went on to pick a quarrel with France and defeated Louis Napoleon (1870), and then he persuaded the southern German states to join in a new German Empire (1871), with Prussia's king as emperor. In face of such a string of successes, liberal opposition to Bismarck's use of trickery and force evaporated. As "national liberals" they proved eager to cooperate with conservatives, such as Bismarck, to make a success of the new German Empire.

THE EMS TELEGRAM

In the summer of 1870, Count Otto von Bismarck, Prussian prime minister, wanted war with France. He figured that if the independent south German states could be made to fight alongside Prussia and the newly established North German Confederation, patriotic enthusiasm would make the final unification of Germany easy. So, indeed, matters turned out. But starting a war without seeming to be the aggressor took some doing.

Bismarck's chance came when Spaniards offered the vacant throne of their country to a prince of the house of Hohenzollern. The prince was a distant relative of King Wilhelm of Prussia. The French objected, and the prince promptly backed down. Everything seemed over. But the French wanted assurance from the king of Prussia, who was taking his ease at a holiday resort named Ems. What happened next is best told in the language of a telegram sent from Ems to Bismarck in Berlin by the king's aide:

> His Majesty the King [of Prussia] wrote me: "Count Benedetti [the French ambassador] approached me on the promenade and asked me—eventually in a very insistent manner—to authorize him to telegraph immediately saying that I promised for all time to come that I would never again give my consent if the Hohenzollern family should again become a candidate [for the Spanish throne]. I let him know, at the end a bit sternly, that no one could give such an assurance for all time. Naturally I said to him that I had received no new information, and since he was more currently informed from Paris and Madrid than I he very well knew that my government again was out of the running.
>
> His Majesty has, since then, received a message from the prince [that is, from the candidate for the Spanish throne]. Since His Majesty had said to Count Benedetti that he expected news from the prince, the king himself, thinking back to the aforesaid encounter, instructed Count Eulenberg and myself not to receive Count Benedetti again, but to inform him through an adjutant that His Majesty had just received from the prince the information that Benedetti had already had from Paris, and that the king had nothing more to say to the [French] ambassador.

Count Camillo Cavour (1810–1861) engineered the unification of Italy by using much the same methods that Bismarck used in Germany. The difference was that the kingdom of Sardinia, around which Italy united, was only a second-rate power and could not by itself hope to overthrow Austrian control over Italy. Cavour, therefore, reached an agreement with Louis Napoleon of France, according to which the French agreed to help the Sardinians in war against Austria. Louis Napoleon wanted glory such as his uncle had won in Italy. He also wanted to upset the Vienna settlement—and believed that it was good politics to be on the side of the people, when possible. He furthermore made Cavour promise to give France two small bits of territory, Nice and

His Majesty puts it to your Excellency [Bismarck] whether the new demand of Benedetti and its rejection should not be shared with the press and our ambassadors.*

When he got this telegram, Bismarck saw his chance. He edited the king's message and gave it to the press in the following form:

After the news of the renunciation of the Hohenzollern prince [of his candidacy from the Spanish throne] had been officially communicated to the imperial French government by the royal government of Spain, the French ambassador at Ems demanded additionally of His Majesty the King [of Prussia] that he authorized him [Benedetti] to telegraph Paris that His Majesty promised for all time to come never again to give his consent, if the Hohenzollern family should again return to candidacy.

His Majesty thereupon declined to see the French ambassador again and informed him, through an official adjutant, that His Majesty had nothing more to communicate to the ambassador.*

The result was all that Bismarck wished. Both sides felt insulted. The French rushed to declare war but Prussia and the other German states were far better prepared. Soon the Germans won great victories and started to besiege Paris. In a surge of patriotic feeling, the rulers of the separate German states gathered at Versailles in January 1871 to proclaim King Wilhelm of Prussia the emperor of Germany.

Thus a powerful, new, united Germany had its birth just outside Paris, in the palace which Louis XIV had built as a sign and symbol of the grandeur of France.

*The bracketed interpolations and translation are from *Bismarck, the Hohenzollern Candidacy and the Origins of the Franco-German War of 1870* by Lawrence D. Steefel, published by Harvard University Press.

Savoy, that would extend the French frontiers to the Alps.

Then Cavour picked a quarrel with Austria in 1859. The French came to his aid and defeated the Austrian armies in northern Italy but tried to make peace before Italy's unification was complete. That did not satisfy Italian nationalists, who provoked popular uprisings all through central Italy. A dramatic expedition of volunteers known as the "Redshirts," led by Giuseppe Garibaldi against the kingdom of Naples, brought the south into the new kingdom of Italy.

In the northeast, Venetia remained under Austrian control until 1866, and the pope continued to rule Rome until 1870. But the pope's power over Rome depended on the presence of

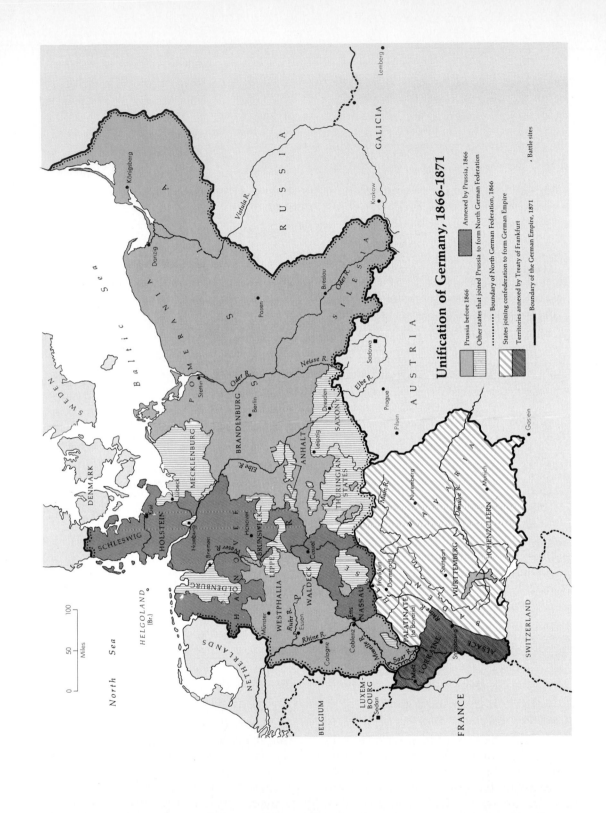

Unification of Germany, 1866–1871

Prussia before 1866

Annexed by Prussia, 1866

Other states that joined Prussia to form North German Federation

········· Boundary of North German Federation, 1866

States joining confederation to form German Empire

Territories annexed by Treaty of Frankfurt

──── Boundary of the German Empire, 1871

• Battle sites

North Sea

Baltic Sea

SWEDEN

DENMARK

HELGOLAND (Br.)

NETHERLANDS

BELGIUM

LUXEM-BOURG

FRANCE

SWITZERLAND

RUSSIA

AUSTRIA

GALICIA

SCHLESWIG

HOLSTEIN

MECKLENBURG

POMERANIA

PRUSSIA

BRANDENBURG

SILESIA

ANHALT

SAXONY

THURINGIAN STATES

HANOVER

OLDENBURG

WESTPHALIA

WALDECK

LIPPE

BRUNSWICK

NASSAU

HESSE

BADEN

WÜRTTEMBERG

BAVARIA

HOHENZOLLERN

PALATINATE (to Bavaria)

LORRAINE

ALSACE

Königsberg

Danzig

Stettin

Posen

Breslau

Berlin

Kiel

Lübeck

Hamburg

Bremen

Hanover

Münster

Essen

Cologne

Coblenz

Cassel

Leipzig

Dresden

Prague

Pilsen

Sadowa

Frankfurt

Darmstadt

Mainz

Metz

Strasbourg

Stuttgart

Nuremberg

Munich

Gastein

Krakow

Lemberg

Sedan

Vistula R.

Oder R.

Neisse R.

Elbe R.

Weser R.

Rhine R.

Ruhr R.

Moselle R.

Saar R.

Main R.

Danube R.

Miles

0   50   100

Unification of Italy, 1859-1870

Legend:

- Kingdom of Sardinia before 1859
- To Kingdom of Sardinia: 1859, 1860
- To Kingdom of Italy: 1866, 1870
- Italia Irredenta
- ■ Battle sites

FRANCE

SWITZERLAND

AUSTRIA

SAVOY

Trent

LOMBARDY

VENETIA

Trieste

Magenta
Novara

Milan

Custozza

Verona

Villafranca

Venice

Turin

Po R.

PARMA

PIEDMONT

MODENA

Po R.

Bologna

Genoa

ROMAGNA

"THE MARCHES"

NICE

Nice

"THE RIVIERA"

Leghorn

Florence

TUSCANY

PAPAL

To France, 1860

UMBRIA

CORSICA
(French)

KINGDOM

Rome

STATES

Adriatic Sea

DALMATIA

ALBANIA

KINGDOM

Bari

OF

Naples

APULIA

Taranto

SARDINIA

OF THE

TWO

SICILIES

CALABRIA

SARDINIA

Tyrrhenian Sea

Strait of Messina

Palermo

SICILY

Mediterranean Sea

AFRICA

Tunis

MALTA

(Br.)

Tripoli

0   100   200

Miles

French troops. These were withdrawn when Louis Napoleon blundered into war with Germany. The Italian government then moved in and made Rome the capital of united Italy. However, the pope refused to recognize their right to do so. Feuding between the papacy and the government of Italy continued until 1929, when a treaty gave full sovereign powers to the pope within the part of Rome where he lived (that is, the Vatican palace and some nearby areas). In return, the pope surrendered the papacy's historic rights to rule Rome and the papal states of central Italy.

New International Alignments

The loser in Italy and in Germany was Austria. And Austria lost largely because her old allies, Russia and Prussia, refused to continue to support the status quo in central Europe. Yet Bismarck was a thorough conservative in the sense that he believed in strong, authoritarian government, just as the Russian czar and the Hapsburg emperor did. As a result, when he had succeeded in creating the new German Empire around the Prussian kingdom, Bismarck was eager to restore the conservative alliance with Austria and Russia that had kept Europe's boundaries stable between 1815 and 1859.

For a short period, the Hapsburg emperor, Franz Josef I (reigned 1848–1916), dreamed of revenge; but after the defeat of France in 1870–1871, he gave this up and, in 1879, agreed to an alliance with Germany. The major reason behind this move was that Austria suffered from internal frictions among the many different nationalities that made up the empire. In 1867 a constitutional settlement between the Hungarians and the rest of the empire sharpened the political appetites of Czechs and other Slavs who wanted similar privileges for themselves. With such internal problems, the Hapsburg monarch badly needed all the outside support he could get, and the German alliance of 1879 served this purpose admirably.

In 1882 Bismarck also brought Italy into the alliance, making it a Triple Alliance; and in 1887 he succeeded in making a secret treaty with Russia. Behind all of Bismarck's diplomatic activity after 1871 was his wish to keep France from being able to start a war of revenge with any prospect of success. French pride had been deeply hurt by the German victory in 1870–1871. In addition, the Germans had taken the border provinces of Alsace and Lorraine from France and made them part of the new German Empire; but despite the fact that many inhabitants of these provinces spoke German, the majority considered themselves to be French. French patriots, therefore, refused to forget the lost provinces; however, as long as Bismarck was in charge of Germany's foreign policy, the French could find no allies and thus had to swallow their pride. Instead they concentrated on building an empire in Africa and southeast Asia, an enterprise that kept them constantly at odds with British empire-builders, who were trying to do the same thing.

Bismarck left office in 1890 after a new emperor, Kaiser Wilhelm II (reigned 1888–1918), came to the German throne. Wilhelm had great ambitions for his country. By 1890 enormous economic success in building the world's most efficient industrial system had created a public that wanted to see Germany, too, start establishing an empire overseas. Naval officers argued that a powerful fleet was needed to make Germany a really great power. Wilhelm agreed and thought that Germany should cut its ties with Russia and come to an understanding with the British instead. Accordingly, he dismissed Bismarck and set out to make Germany not just a European but a world power.

Wilhelm entirely failed to persuade the British to make a deal that would give Germany world power. Instead, everything that Bismarck had most feared started to happen. First the French and Russians made an alliance (1893); then the French and British settled their colonial disputes (1904); and eventually the British and Russians did the same (1907). The result, therefore, was to align three great powers—France, Britain, and Russia—in a ring around the Triple Alliance of Germany, Austria, and Italy. Moreover, Italy gave clear signs, even before 1914, of not being reliable from a German point of view. The more Germany built up its navy and claimed the right to an equal voice in European councils about colonial matters, the firmer grew the hostile ring. The result was a series of diplomatic crises beginning in 1905 (first Moroccan crisis) and ending in 1914

The Industrialization of War Above is a scene showing part of Alfred Krupp's gun-foundry in Essen, Germany. Big guns were made of bronze before 1850,
when Alfred Krupp displayed guns made out of steel
at the London Exhibition. Steel was stronger than
bronze but until Krupp discovered how to eliminate
casting flaws, it had been unsafe for use in artillery.
Thereafter, his firm grew great by selling his superior
new steel guns to the Germans and other governments.
To help with sales, he set up a firing range, shown
here, where he could show prospective buyers exactly
what his guns could do. This photograph dates from
about 1865 when enormous naval guns, like that trav-
elling behind the locomotive in the foreground, suddenly transformed battleship armament and design.
The result of a half century of technological competition among European navies is shown below: the
H.M.S. Dreadnought. When Dreadnought was
launched in 1906 it eclipsed all rivals, being both faster and more heavily gunned than any other battleship. This level of design was still dominant when
World War I broke out.

with the crisis that triggered World War I. The
alliance system worked in such a way that any
quarrel anywhere in the world tended to line up
the European great powers on opposite sides; and
each time one or the other side backed down, it
did so with the resolve not to do so next time. In
1914, therefore, the governments of Europe
moved toward war as though hypnotized. Doing
so, they plunged Europe and the world into a new
and violent era, in which many of the familiar
landmarks of Europe's past came tumbling down.

ECONOMY AND SOCIETY

The central fact of Europe's history between 1850
and 1914 was the rise and progress of industry.
Germany's great industrial boom left all other
European nations behind. Russia, too, from about
1890 began to see the rise of large-scale modern
industry, with consequences for the internal stability of the czar's government, which we will
study in Chapter 10. Everywhere cities grew in

size and rural life became less important; yet it is worth remembering that, in 1914, most Europeans still gained their living directly from farming. Only Great Britain had become a nation with more than half its population living in towns and cities away from the land.

Conservative Social Forces

The agricultural elements of European society were basically conservative. Patterns of command and deference, as between upper and lower classes in European society, survived as strongly as they did because so many people either still lived in villages or had left them recently. The authority of the father over his children and of men over women was also an inheritance from rural custom and continued to define the daily conduct of most Europeans, even those who lived in great cities.

Religion was another important conservative force. Early in the nineteenth century, many persons reacted against the religious skepticism

Bourgeois Europe at its High Noon This shows how prosperous Parisians took their ease on a Sunday afternoon in a park on an island in the Seine in the 1880s. The painting conveys the smug self assurance of the age, when prosperous Europeans felt that all was well with a world in which such elegance, comfort, and leisure were attainable, if not by everyone, at least by a favored few who knew how to take advantage of business and professional opportunities. The painting is interesting also for the way it exploited the latest scientific knowledge about light and visual perception for artistic purposes. The artist who made it, George Seurat, used tiny dots of contrasting colors throughout the painting, knowing what whoever looked at it would blend the separate dots into intelligible patterns, interpreting them as representations of human figures, trees, and all the rest. He believed that his painting would become more entrancing just because observers had to take an active part in making sense of what they saw. Scientific discovery and technological improvements were very much part of the age. This painting therefore reflects that aspect of Europe's nineteenth century achievement as well as portraying the serene self-confidence of the newly privileged bourgeoisie.

that had been so prominent among the leaders of the French Revolution. When liberal and nationalist movements came to the surface again, most churches opposed them. After some hesitation, Pope Pius IX (1846–1878) repudiated all the new movements he saw rising around him in Europe. To get support for his views, he summoned the first Vatican Council (1869–1870). The Council obediently proclaimed the infallibility of the pope, in matters of faith and morals, at the very time that the papal government of Rome was being overthrown.

Papal policy presented the governments of western Europe with awkward problems. Bismarck tried to compel German Catholics to obey the laws of the new German Empire instead of obeying the pope; this merely drove German Catholics into a single, opposition political party. Eventually Bismarck backed away from the fight because he felt that the socialist threat was even greater. In Britain, the Catholic issue took the form of the Irish question. Ireland was Catholic and oppressed, as well as poor; but Irish members of Parliament frequently held the balance of power between the liberal and conservative parties. In France the great issue was control of schools. This came to a crisis between 1901 and 1905 and ended in the legal separation of church and state and the suppression of most church-run schools.

Another problem that affected all European governments was created by the low cost of American grain. The price of grain became an acute issue after 1870 when railroad construction and the development of steamships made it possible for wheat from the American Middle West, or from the Argentine pampas, to be delivered to European ports at prices below European production costs. The British adhered to a free-trade policy and, as a result, nearly ruined British agriculture. Other European governments imposed special tariffs to protect peasants and landowners. This, of course, raised food prices for the cities and hurt the working class in the towns.

New Problems of Industrialism

Problems of this kind were long familiar to European political leaders. Church and state, tariffs and taxes, had been at the heart of European politics for centuries. Problems raised by the galloping growth of industrialism, however, were far more difficult because they were so new. Everywhere, even in Russia, governments tried to win the support of the working class. By 1914 the idea that all adult males ought to have the right to vote in elections for some sort of representative assembly was accepted by all European governments, although in Germany and in Austria, as well as in Russia, such representative assemblies had only limited powers. In eastern Europe, emperors, their ministers, and other high officials kept ultimate decisions in their own hands, and neither trusted nor were trusted by ordinary workers. In western Europe, the gap between rulers and workers was almost as great, but political parties supported by working men's votes were powerful enough to influence official policies.

Rise of Socialist Parties   Karl Marx and other revolutionaries advocated one extreme solution to Europe's social problems. In 1864 they organized the International Workingmen's Association in order to spread the doctrines of the *Communist Manifesto* and prepare the way for socialist revolution. But before Marx attracted many followers, the revolutionaries quarreled bitterly among themselves.

Moreover, in 1871, the city of Paris went through another crisis. Many Parisians felt that the government, which had made peace with the Germans and given up Alsace and Lorraine, was full of traitors. The city had been besieged for several months and suffered accordingly. A coup d'état, followed by municipal elections, brought a revolutionary Paris Commune to power. Its leaders remembered the heroic days of 1793 when Paris had rallied all of France against foreign tyrants. They were eager to do the same thing again, but they never had a chance. Instead, the French government sent in troops and suppressed the Commune, after bloody fighting. The end result was to discredit socialist plans for a popular rising to take power from the capitalists. The models offered by the French Revolution, when Paris crowds had been able to make and break governments, were becoming seriously out of date. As a result, the First International broke up in 1876.

Marx did not despair, however. Separate national parties, strongly under the influence of Marx's ideas, came into existence in most European countries during the 1860s and 1870s. The most important of these was the German Social Democratic party, organized in 1875. Bismarck responded by outlawing socialist agitation, and until 1890 the German party existed outside the law. In 1889 a Second International was founded to unite the socialists; but in spite of much talk about international solidarity, each national party went its own way in all essentials. By 1914, socialist parties had substantial representation in all of Europe's parliamentary assemblies. A French socialist had even cooperated with bourgeois politicians as a member of a short-lived government. A few socialists suggested that violent revolution might not be necessary. Reform might be able to win the rights workers were fighting for and introduce socialism gradually.

Nonsocialist Initiatives   From the other side of the political fence, conservatives, such as Bismarck, tried to blunt the effect of socialist propaganda by doing something about the grievances and hardships workers suffered. A series of social insurance laws resulted, whereby the state undertook to make payments to employees who fell ill or suffered disabling accidents. Such policies, combined with improvements in municipal services and the legalization of unions and of socialist parties, had the effect of reconciling many workers to their lot in life.

Great Britain followed a different path. Early experiments with socialist schemes for remaking the whole of society collapsed in the 1830s and left British workers deeply distrustful of what Karl Marx and his fellow revolutionaries were hoping to accomplish. Instead, beginning with the 1850s, labor unions arose, aimed only at improving working conditions through negotiation with employers or, if necessary, through strikes. The leaders of these unions, which to begin with were limited to skilled trades, avoided politics as a matter of principle. When the right to vote was extended to all adult males in 1884, miners and industrial workers supported Liberal party candidates for Parliament, as a rule. Between 1900 and 1906, however, the unions changed policy and began to support a new Labour party; but unlike socialist parties on the continent, the Labour party paid little attention to Marxist ideas and always expected to carry out its program through parliamentary legislation, not through violent revolution.

Tensions between industrial workers and the rest of society were thus eased, though not erased, between the 1870s and 1914. Like the middle class before them, the working class had secured legal ways to make their interests heard, even in the highest quarters of government. During these years, socialism seemed well on its way to making the kind of elaborate compromises with older vested interests that revolutionary liberalism had made in the decades 1850–1870.

New Forms of Industrial Organization

Adjustment to industrialism was not merely a matter of fitting the new working class into the preexisting structure of European society. New legal forms for business had to be invented. The limited liability company (or, as we call it in the United States, the corporation) met this need. Banking practices and the supply of capital were as critical as the supply of labor or of raw materials. Also, the boundaries separating private enterprise and profit from state operations and taxes had to be defined and constantly readjusted.

British Laissez Faire   In general, British practice stood at one extreme. Until late in the nineteenth century the British government was reluctant to intervene in economic and social questions, and it lacked a large, well-trained bureaucracy like that which most continental European governments had inherited from the eighteenth century. Having allowed workers to develop unions, pubs, and chapels and having seen business leaders develop the corporation, free trade, and the gold standard for currency, British politicians felt, for the most part, that the economic machine should be left to run itself with minimal interference or regulation by government. This policy is called "laissez faire"—a term borrowed from French economic theorists of the eighteenth century. The

British economy did, indeed, run itself; but British manufacturers tended to fall behind what the Germans were able to do, partly, at least, because the Germans took it for granted that the forms of industrial organization that had worked so well between 1775 and 1850–and had given Britain the lead over all the world—could be improved upon.

German Planning   The Germans came late to the industrial scene, for until railroads made low-cost overland haulage of heavy goods possible, German coal fields were of little value. But from about 1850, German industry grew rapidly, and by 1900 Germany had outstripped Great Britain in almost every branch of production. Three factors help to explain why Germany was so successful.

First, a few important German industrialists grasped the idea that theoretical science could help them in important ways. Beginning in the 1890s a few German corporations, mainly those working in chemicals and electricity, began to pay salaries to university-trained chemists and physicists whose only task was to discover new ways of doing things, or new products that could be manufactured and sold.

However familiar today, before 1914 this was a radical idea. Why pay good money to someone who, if successful, would outmode the machinery the company depended on for its profits? Why indeed? In earlier times, when an inventor hit upon some new method by tinkering in his attic or backyard, he secured a patent. This meant that no one else could use the invention without paying a fee. Then the inventor either sold the patent to someone else or went into business independently, hoping to make as much money as possible from the invention. A successful effort to find a still better device would simply spoil the patent. From this point of view, it was absurd to hurry on the day when the company's patents might become valueless because of some new invention!

Yet the absurdity was amply justified by results. Just because they made old methods and machinery obsolete faster than anyone else, German electrical and chemical industries outstripped those of other countries before 1914.

Their lead over other nations resulted directly from the use which German captains of industry made of the well-trained scientists and engineers produced by German schools and universities.

Secondly, German banks and businesses organized cartels on a scale unequaled elsewhere. A cartel is an agreement among producers of given commodities, coal for example, to divide the market among themselves and to sell at fixed prices. Such arrangements often led to increased profits; indeed, that was the aim. They also allowed managers to plan production schedules more exactly, and this sometimes evened out the "boom and bust" pattern that was so wasteful in British and American industry. Credit, also, was more highly centralized in Germany, so that financial as well as production planning operated with larger units and over longer time spans than was common in other countries. A firm could go deeper into debt and wait longer for returns on some new technique or product than was possible with the banking practices that prevailed in England. But, since some new technologies were very expensive and could not be tried except on a large scale, this meant that German financial arrangements and cartel organization could, if the managers so desired, take risks and introduce new things that small-scale businesses could not afford.

In the third place, the German government played a much more active role in economic policy than the British government did. Railroads were owned by the state, and freight rates could be adjusted to encourage or discourage any particular undertaking. The location of steel mills or of other important plants depended not only on geography but also on exactly how much it cost to haul a ton of ore or of coal from its place of origin to the place of manufacture. In setting up freight rates, military considerations were often taken into account. The German general staff cared where its ammunition came from and wanted to see a rail network that would permit troops to reach a threatened frontier faster than the enemy could bring up its forces. Thus the officials who managed the railroads and decided freight rates had a powerful tool at their command to affect the way German industry developed. They used this power to make Germany both prosperous and militarily strong.

Industrialism Elsewhere   Other European governments fell somewhere between the British and German extremes. No country relied as much on private initiative as did the British; none was nearly as successful as the Germans in manipulating and directing the growth of industry by governmental and semi-governmental (banks and cartels) action. Southern Europe fell behind. Coal fields were lacking there, and until 1914 industry was based overwhelmingly on energy derived from coal. Water power and petroleum were only beginning to offer alternatives, and southern Europe was not particularly well endowed with either oil fields or waterfalls. Eastern Europe, being poorer agriculturally, had always lagged behind the western nations and continued to do so, despite the opening up of a few large mines and factories in Russia.

Underlying everything was a rapid expansion of population. During the nineteenth century, some 60 million people left Europe for America and elsewhere. In spite of this exodus, the population of the continent rose from about 187 million in 1800 to about 401 million in 1900. Factors that affect population are not fully understood, but it seems clear that one important cause for this extraordinary growth in numbers was the progress of medicine, which allowed doctors and public officials to take effective steps against diseases spread by contaminated drinking water. This check on the spread of disease allowed more babies to survive infancy; they grew up to have children of their own, thus setting off a population explosion of the sort that has become familiar, all around the globe, in our own time.

THOUGHT AND SCIENCE

Europe's continued self-transformation under the twin impulses of the Industrial and Democratic revolutions in the years 1850–1914 must be counted as extraordinary. All the internal strains and struggles, one piled on top of the other, added up to progress in the eyes of nearly everyone who lived at the time. A similar extraordinary achievement transformed science and the arts. There too, vigor and variety, in a reckless effort to expand the limits of the possible, were evident at every turn.

It seems useful in the period 1850–1914 to

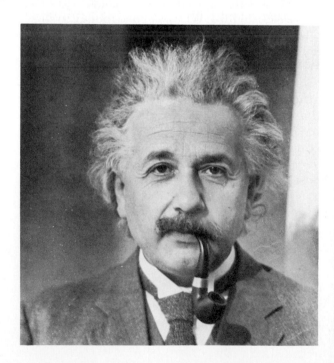

Four Shapers of Modern Thought The four men shown here changed prevailing ideas about the world and human life in different but complementary ways between 1859, when Charles Darwin (opposite page left) revolutionized biology with his theory of evolution and 1916, when Albert Einstein (opposite page right) revolutionized physics with his general theory of relativity. Between these two dates, Karl Marx (above left) published *Capital* in 1867, arguing the inevitability of proletarian revolution that would restore long lost equality and freedom to human societies and, beginning in 1895, Sigmund Freud (above right) probed the sub-conscious levels of human minds and made older confidence in the power of reason seem naive. What emerged from the writings of these four men (supplemented by the work of innumerable others) was an evolving universe, in which physical and biological as well as social and psychological realities change with time and place.

divide European thought and science into three schools: the "hard," the "soft," and the "crazy," or, in more formal language, the systematic, the evolutionary, and the irrational. The hard sciences were mathematics, physics, chemistry, astronomy, and economics. In each of these fields, the goal was to discover laws or patterns of behavior that were true everywhere and at all times.

The fundamental point of view behind these efforts had been worked out in the 1600s by the great pioneers of modern science: Galileo, Descartes, Newton. What scientists in the later nineteenth century did was to generalize the scientific laws they had inherited from their predecessors and find innumerable practical applications in industrial technology.

The Systematic Sciences

On the theoretical side, mathematicians were able to do such surprising things as work out several non-Euclidean geometries and rules for converting one mathematical system into another. Chemists worked with matter and discovered how its building blocks could be combined and recombined according to more or less predictable patterns. Physicists were able to discern how mechanical motion, heat, light, and the entire spectrum of electromagnetic radiation were all forms of energy, and they worked out rules for converting one into the other. The key figure in this development was a Scotsman, James Clerk Maxwell (1831–1879), who first realized that light belonged in a much wider spectrum of electromagnetic radiation. No single chemist had quite the status of Maxwell among the physicists; but a Russian, Dmitri Mendeleev (1834–1907), first arranged the elements into a "periodic" table. This table showed gaps where hitherto unknown elements were needed to fill out Mendeleev's overall pattern. Later research discovered all of these missing elements. This confirmed in striking fashion the correctness of the pattern Mendeleev had first perceived.

Toward the end of the nineteenth century, both physicists and chemists had begun to zero in on the electron. At one and the same time, the electron was the smallest building block of matter (in which chemists were interested) and a particle that radiated energy (which physicists found so fascinating). Puzzling problems multiplied. Electrons sometimes seemed to act like waves rather than like tiny billiard balls. Matter sometimes spontaneously sent off radiation. And radiation itself seemed sometimes to come in quanta, or bundles.

The Theory of Relativity From a quite different angle of approach, astronomers also had turned up unexpected data. The planet Mercury seemed not to obey Newton's laws of motion perfectly. Most puzzling of all, light sent out from the moving platform of the earth seemed to travel at exactly the same speed, no matter what direction it followed. This contradicted common sense, as well as Newton's laws of motion, since in some directions the earth's motion should have added to the speed of light launched from its surface, and in other directions should have reduced the speed with which the same light traveled through space. Yet nothing of the sort could be detected, even with extremely sensitive instruments.

In 1905 a German Swiss, Albert Einstein, (1879–1955), proposed a special theory of relativity to explain some of these puzzles. Ten years later he followed his first suggestion with a more general theory, and gave the fullest explanation of his ideas in a book published in 1929. Einstein took the four basic terms of Newtonian physics—space, time, matter, and energy—and suggested that they were not fixed, firm, and separate frames within which all natural objects existed, but were, instead, all mixed up with each other. It followed that measurements of space, time, and motion were relative to one another and that matter might be converted into energy, and vice versa, according to a simple mathematical formula, $E = mc^2$; that is, energy equals mass times the speed of light squared. Thus, at the very end of the period with which we are here concerned, Einstein arrived at the greatest generalization of all by giving a new definition to the basic terms of the physical sciences.

Economic Theory Economics rates as a hard science, despite having to do with unpredictable human beings, because economists kept on trying to find universal laws that would explain, impersonally, how markets worked. They even hoped to learn how to predict what would happen, in the way that physicists, chemists, and astronomers were able to do. In this they were faithful to Adam Smith's habit of mind. In limited degree, they were successful in much the same way that the other hard sciences were successful. This is to say, succeeding theorists were able to bring more and more kinds of data into their system. A grand synthesis was achieved in the 1880s by an Englishman, Alfred Marshall (1842–1924), who introduced the concept of marginal utility as a master key to analyze fluctuations in prices, interest rates, wages, and rents. But Marshall's system, impressive and closely reasoned though it was, never explained adequately the boom and bust pattern of the business cycle.

The prestige of the hard sciences was reinforced by their practical applications. Chemistry, in particular, allowed the creation of new industries and new products, such as dyes, drugs, electroplated metal, and many more. Incandescent electric lights, invented in 1879 by the American Thomas A. Edison (1847–1931) began to replace gaslights in homes and offices; other electrical inventions, such as the phonograph and the telephone, followed one after the other. Yet, as we have already seen, it was not until the end of the period, and then only in a limited way—mainly in Germany—that scientific theory and technical processes of manufacturing were systematically brought together. The potentialities of this combination had not really been grasped by anyone before 1914.

The Soft Sciences

By comparison, the soft sciences seemed impractical, since they had no distinct applications in industry, even though new ideas about the human past, present, and future certainly did change behavior and in this way altered the conditions of European life almost as much as the technical changes for which the hard sciences were responsible.

The basic philosophical approach common to the soft sciences was newer than the effort to discover mathematical, timeless, and universal laws that characterized the hard sciences. The soft sciences all emphasized change through time, but not until after 1800 did anyone try to work out the full implications of a world of ceaseless and universal change. More than any other single man, the German philosopher Georg Wilhelm Friedrich Hegel (1770–1831) was responsible for developing such a vision of reality. According to Hegel, everything changes always, doing so by a series of reversals or movements from one extreme to another. To use his own terms—a thesis confronts its antithesis and in time both are absorbed into a synthesis, which in turn becomes a thesis for the continuing unfolding of reality.

The Theory of Evolution   The concept of development through time particularly fitted biological and human affairs. Early in the nineteenth

century, geologists discovered numerous fossils of plants and animals different from living forms. Studies of the distribution of different species of plants and animals also showed a pattern of resemblances and differences that made traditional ideas of the separate creation of each species difficult to believe. Charles Darwin (1809–1882) put these observations together to develop the idea of organic evolution. In his great book *On the Origin of Species* (1859), he argued that since many more living creatures are launched upon life than ever survive to adulthood, there is a struggle for survival that goes on constantly. In such a struggle, some variations help the organism to survive. These survivors tend to spread because more such individuals grow up to reproduce their kind. In different environments different features help survival, so that in time such differences may become great enough to make what had been a single species separate into two or more different species.

Darwin's theory aroused angry debate because of its implications for religion. Some Protestants argued that belief in the literal truth of the account of creation in the Book of Genesis was fundamental to Christianity, since if the Bible could err in one passage, how could one believe it at all? The debate was complicated by the fact that scholars in Germany had already begun to subject the text of the Bible to critical methods that had been developed, ever since the Renaissance, for the study of ancient manuscripts. By treating the Bible as the work of human beings, such scholars had begun to unravel the various strands from which the biblical text had been put together long ago. But that sort of study, too, seemed to call the truth of Christian doctrine into question.

Some persons responded by arguing that religious truth, like everything else, develops and changes through time. Truths and insights valuable for one generation might cease to have the same meaning or importance for later generations. God's revelation, according to such ideas, could be a progressive and gradual process, even including the most recent and shocking discoveries of a scientist such as Darwin, or a philosopher such as Hegel. "Modernist" doctrines of this sort were emphatically repudiated by the Roman Catholic church at the first Vatican Council of 1870. Protestant churches divided, some pinning their faith on the literal truth of the Bible, others admitting, in varying measure, the idea that religious truth and knowledge changed and developed through time.

The Study of Human Society   The social sciences, with the exception of economics, emphasized the idea of development. History achieved a new accuracy in detail as a result of seminar training in German universities, pioneered by Leopold von Ranke (1795–1886). The mass of facts that rapidly accumulated was kept in a sort of loose order by the idea of progress—in particular, the progress of limited constitutional government, of equality before the laws, and of personal, individual freedom. The historian who, more than any other, put this vision of the European past into focus was Lord Acton (1834–1902). Sociology was developed by a Frenchman, Auguste Comte (1798–1857), who also believed in progress. Anthropology, likewise, when it emerged from the study of primitive customs and religions, was organized by such pioneers as Lewis Henry Morgan (1818–1881) in terms of a supposed development from savagery through barbarism to civilization. Behind and beneath these sciences lay the study of early civilizations, revealed with greater and greater detail by archaeologists. And geologists probed still deeper into time through their study of sedimentary rock layers.

The result of the combined efforts of so many specialists was to create a panoramic vision of the nature of things in which change was universal. The whole human adventure on earth shrank to the proportions of a last-minute flourish, when measured by the geologic time scale or by the scale of organic evolution. But in a world in which everything changed—even the established truths of religion—what was there left to believe in, except the fact of change itself?

Irrationalism

This chilling conclusion troubled many people even before 1914, when the violence and destruction wrought by the First World War shocked millions more. There had been a small number of thinkers throughout the nineteenth century who emphasized the weakness of reason, the emptiness of progress, the folly of the age. Apostles of despair were listened to mainly by literary people and artists, who responded more to their feelings than to abstract thought. But the handful of philosophers who used their power of reasoning to argue how weak or useless reason really was, hardly mattered to scientists and professional specialists.

Yet, in Vienna, shortly before World War I the psychologist, Sigmund Freud (1856–1939), began to explore subconscious levels of the human mind. He found sexual drives and jealousies at the bottom of many kinds of behavior and concluded that human conduct was, for the most part, controlled by dark, elemental impulses over which we have only very limited conscious control. Freud's ideas won little attention before World War I, beyond the circle of his personal followers. The widespread impact of his ideas came later. Other thinkers, the Italian Vilfredo Pareto (1848–1923), for example, emphasized the irrational aspects of social behavior and argued that myths and exaggerated slogans were the only means political leaders could use to mobilize their followers to action. Another school of thought tried to apply Darwinism to human affairs and interpreted history as a struggle in which only the fittest could expect to survive. Often this theory was thought of in racial terms, with the comforting (for Europeans) conclusion that the white race must be superior because it was at that time able to conquer everybody else. Others applied the idea of struggle for survival to conflicts between rich and poor; they concluded that any sort of political intervention to help the poor or weak members of society was dangerous in the long run because it would allow the unfit to survive.

Such ideas, together with those of Freud and others who emphasized the irrational side of human life, directly challenged the theory of democratic government. In the eighteenth century, when democratic political ideals were first clearly set forth, everyone assumed that all persons were fundamentally rational and could judge in a reasonable way the alternatives their political leaders set before them. If this was not, in fact, the case, then the original justification for

Where Are We Going and Why? Artists on the eve of World War I occasionally gave expression to urgent fears that lurked beneath the surface of everyday life even at the peak of Europe's dominion over the rest of the earth. On the left, "The Scream" by Edvard Munch, a Norwegian, dates from 1895; on the right, "Unique Forms of Continuity in Space," by Umberto Boccioni, an Italian, dates from 1913. The one conveys a sense of nightmare fear; the other a mechanized rush into an unknown, dehumanizing future. Such anxieties became more prominent among Europe's intellectual and cultural leaders in the decade before 1914 as faith in progress, which peaked sometime in the 1870s and 1880s, began to wane. (*Left*: National Gallery of Art, Washington, Rosenwald Collection./*Right*: Collection, The Museum of Modern Art, New York. Acquired through the Lillie P. Bliss Bequest.)

democratic self-government would have to be abandoned.

Answers to this and other ultimate questions were not found; but European thinkers never drew back from any line of inquiry because it was too dangerous or too shocking to those in authority. A tremendous range of attitudes and ideas churned through questioning minds. New perspectives, new theories, new information competed for attention as never before in human history. In this, as in other respects, the years between 1850 and 1914 were something of a golden age for Europe's prosperous middle class.

ART AND LITERATURE

Artists and writers valued originality above all else in the nineteenth century. Nearly all of them felt that superior craftsmanship within an established style was unworthy of true artistic genius.

The result, of course, was that as time passed it became harder and harder to rebel because there was no established standard of taste against which to measure the personal originality of the artist.

From a historian's point of view, this characteristic of nineteenth-century artistic life makes it particularly difficult to say anything that is the least bit meaningful about countries, periods of time, or groups of artists. And outstanding individuals in the arts were so numerous it is hard to know whom to mention. There is some justification for making a distinction between the first half of the nineteenth century, when "romantic" art flourished, and the second half, when "realism" dominated the scene. But romantic attitudes lasted throughout the century, if by "romantic" we mean the effort to express inward personal feelings through art and an urge to explore remote times and places, fantasy, folklore, and things strange, new, and mysterious. Realists may have paid more attention to the lives of poor and humble people and dealt more frankly with ugly and brutal sides of human life than their predecessors usually cared to do. But this was a matter of degree. Moreover, realists who seized upon ugly and disgusting matter for their art were, in their own way, romantics. They too projected inward feelings upon the world. They too sought out strange and mysterious themes by exploring the slums of Europe's new industrial cities.

Impact of New Techniques

One general factor that altered many forms of art during the century was the development of new techniques and materials. In architecture, for example, steel and concrete allowed buildings to rise much higher than before. The Eiffel Tower, 984 feet tall, erected in Paris for a world's fair in 1889, was a particularly dramatic example of what could be done with steel. Skyscrapers, first developed as office buildings in Chicago in the 1880s, gave practical use to the new techniques of construction. Musicians exploited a series of new instruments, and painters acquired innumerable new tints as a result of chemical discoveries. Some of them also tried to apply sci-

entific theories of light and vision to their work by using tiny specks of different colors which, when seen from a distance, blended into a livelier, more interesting surface than could be attained by painting with solid colors. Literature, of course, was limited to words that could be understood, and language changed slowly even in the nineteenth century. In this sense it was the most conservative of the arts.

Painting and Music.   Painting, on the contrary, was the most radical. Until about 1875, the basic idea of how to paint a picture, which had been first defined in Italy in the 1400s, continued to be taken for granted. A picture, according to this tradition, ought to look like "real life," and rules for giving an illusion of three dimensions on a flat two-dimensional surface had been carefully worked out. In the latter part of the nineteenth century, however, a cluster of great artists, who worked mostly in France, began to reject this idea. They wished to make their paintings not a "pretend window" to be looked through, but a thing to be looked at for its own sake. Violent colors, quite unlike those of nature, and distorted patterns vaguely resembling familiar objects were perfectly all right when the point of the picture was to be looked at for itself. Accordingly, such painters as Paul Cézanne (1839–1906), Vincent van Gogh (1853–1890), and Paul Gauguin (1848–1903) cut loose from older rules and restrictions and began to explore the possibilities of two-dimensional patternmaking by putting paint on canvas.

In the decade immediately before the outbreak of World War I, a new generation of artists began to abandon familiar shapes and to twist fragments of visual experience in playful and novel fashions. Henri Matisse (1869–1954) and Pablo Picasso (1881–1973) were among the most effective of these innovators. Strangely, the way they filled their paintings with twisted bits of familiar shapes and forms, seen from different angles or, as it were, at different times, seemed like a prophecy of the way in which traditional European culture was about to break up under the shock of World Wars I and II. Art often seems to hold a mirror to society. Europe's painters did so in the prewar years with unusual sensitivity and power. In this case, at least, the restless striving for new, original, and personal styles of expression achieved singular success.

Musicians made attempts to experiment with such novelties as the twelve-tone scale, but with rather less success. The hold of the classics, from Johann Sebastian Bach (1685–1750) to Ludwig van Beethoven (1770–1827), was never shaken. Richard Wagner (1813–1883) tried to create a supreme art that would combine music, poetry, and dramatic spectacle. He found subject matter for his operas in Germanic folklore and pagan myth, believing that here could be glimpsed and expressed the innermost spirit of his own nation. Wagner gathered a circle of admirers around himself, but his notion of the priestlike role his art ought to play offended as many people as it attracted. Older, more classical ideas were upheld by Johannes Brahms (1833–1897) and, in some degree, also by Gustav Mahler (1860–1911).

Literature   Literature was divided into separate compartments by language differences. This makes generalization difficult. No great and commanding figures arose in Germany after the death of Johann Wolfgang von Goethe (1749–1832). His masterpiece, *Faust*, retold the story of how the devil tempted Dr. Faustus with unlimited knowledge and power if he would sell his soul; but in Goethe's version, Faust escaped damnation because of his true love for a simple girl, Marguerite. This long poem, the second part of which was published only after Goethe's death, was soon recognized as a world masterpiece.

In English, the novels of Charles Dickens (1812–1870) were immensely popular in his own time but seem long-winded today. A cluster of great "romantic" poets flourished in the first half of the century: William Wordsworth (1770–1850), Samuel Taylor Coleridge (1772–1834), George Gordon, Lord Byron (1788–1824), John Keats (1795–1821), and Percy Bysshe Shelley (1792–1822). Robert Browning (1812–1889) and Alfred, Lord Tennyson (1809–1892) scarcely achieved the same heights in the latter part of the century.

French literature was abundant as always. Major novelists included Victor Hugo (1802–1885), Stendhal, pen name for Marie Henri Beyle (1783–1842), and Honoré de Balzac (1799–1850) in the first part of the century; and Gustave Flaubert (1821–1880), Emile Zola (1840–1902), and Anatole France (1844–1924) in the second half. French poetry took a new turn with the work of Charles Baudelaire (1821–1867), who was an admirer of the American Edgar Allan Poe. Both men were misfits who tried to find escape in the beauty of words and the images they could arouse in imagination. The next generation of French poets are commonly called symbolists because their poems conveyed meaning indirectly and by symbolic suggestion—if, indeed, they conveyed any distinct meaning at all. The famous symbolists are Stéphane Mallarmé (1842–1898), Paul Verlaine (1844–1896), and Arthur Rimbaud (1854–1891). French experimentation with sentences that were not quite sentences and with words whose meaning rested on the associations the reader brought to them was influential upon English and American writers after World War I. In this sense, as in art, France led the way and the rest of Europe followed.

In the nineteenth century, literary figures of world reputation were absent from Italy and Spain; but in Norway, Henrik Ibsen (1828–1906) shocked and fascinated European audiences with plays that were written in prose and dealt in a realistic manner with such topics as women's rights. European drama from Renaissance times had been poetic, full of high-flown language and heroic posturing. Ibsen's effort to capture ordinary, everyday speech and to deal with everyday situations thus represented a rather sharp break with tradition—in its way, almost as great a break as the changes painters were making in art.

In Russia, a cluster of famous novelists burst upon the scene in the mid-nineteenth century. Ivan Turgenev (1818–1883), Feodor Dostoevski (1821–1881), and Count Leo Tolstoi (1828–1910) were the greatest. Turgenev's realistic sketches of Russian country life brought that strange, rude society alive for a Western reader as nothing else did. Dostoevski explored the feelings of his characters in extraordinary detail. He illuminated Russian society from within, as Turgenev did from without. Tolstoi, in later life, founded a cult around himself that glorified the simple life. His greatest work, *War and Peace*, dealt with Russia's struggle against Napoleon in the "Fatherland War" of 1812.

The United States also entered the international "republic of letters" in the nineteenth century. Among the more distinctive American voices, those of Ralph Waldo Emerson (1803–1882), Henry David Thoreau (1817–1862), Walt Whitman (1819–1892), and Mark Twain, pen name for Samuel Langhorne Clemens (1835–1910), deserve mention along with Edgar Allan Poe (1809–1849).

CONCLUSION

The overwhelming impression that this hasty survey should leave is one of richness, variety, and confusion. European artists and thinkers reached for the sky. They did not quite make it; but, in failing, they expanded enormously the range of human achievement and knowledge. Their successes, however, created the problem with which we still struggle, for the great ideals of truth, beauty, and goodness tend to get lost amid so many truths, so many beauties, and so many private, personal, or partial kinds of good and evil. The historian's problem of what to choose for attention becomes everyone's problem. Amid so many competing voices and ideals, where should one turn? How does it all fit together? Does anything make sense? Answers were not forthcoming before 1914—and what has happened since that date has only added to the confusion in which Westerners, and humankind, find themselves.

Yet, for most of those who lived at the time and for us looking back the gains in knowledge, power, and sensitivity were probably worthwhile. The nineteenth century, of all centuries, was an age of progress. Where it will lead remains to be seen; but, in and of itself, European civilization attained a final flowering between 1850 and 1914, before submerging itself, like the other civilizations of the world, into the still-emerging cosmopolitanism of the twentieth century.

Europe kept its traditions and its sublime self-confidence longer than other civilizations were able to do. In a paradoxical way, Europe was, therefore, both ahead and behind the rest of the world. Ahead, because what the rest of the world had to become accustomed to and adjust to was what the Europeans were doing and thinking. Behind, because until after 1914 Europeans remained smug and self-contained within the broad limits of their inherited tradition of civilization and had not yet come to realize, as other peoples had been compelled to do, that their way of doing things was only one of many ways and not always or necessarily the best.

Chapter 23

WORLD REACTIONS TO EUROPE'S ACHIEVEMENTS
1850 to 1914

Three developments changed the lives of nearly all humanity between 1850 and 1914. These were, first, the very much improved forms of transportation and communication; second, rapid population growth; and third, the imbalance arising from Europe's superiority to the rest of the world in a wide range of critical skills.

TRANSPORTATION AND COMMUNICATION

Before 1850, in nearly all parts of the world, human beings lived in almost self-sufficient communities. News from outside a radius of twenty to fifty miles arrived only occasionally. Since it was difficult to carry goods for long distances, nearly all the basic requirements of life had to be found approximately within the same radius. Most people were farmers and raised nearly everything they consumed in their own fields. Usually the surplus produce which they sold did not travel far, but was used in local towns. Because transportation was slow and expensive, people lived where there was food, rather than trying to bring food to where they lived.

Rural localism was modified by the fact that water transportation was comparatively cheap. This allowed the maintenance of large imperial states, such as China, Russia, and the Ottoman Empire. Canals, rivers, and seas made it possible to feed large populations in the Chinese capital at Peking, Russia's capital at Moscow (later at St. Petersburg), and the Ottoman capital at Constantinople by transporting food and other supplies by water across hundreds of miles. A state that depended largely on land transportation, such as the Mogul Empire of India, had to be weak, since wagons and animal packtrains simply could not bring enough supplies to a central point to make the emperor definitely stronger than local governors.

When railroads began to spread from Britain (1840s) to the European and North American continents (1850–1870) and then to other continents (1870–1910), the age-old limits upon the movement of goods and people disappeared. Cities, hundreds of miles away, became easy to get to. And when the growing railroad systems were connected with ocean-going steamships, the lands and seas of all the world were caught up, by degrees, in a single transportation network.

The effect upon human society was similar to the evolutionary emergence of animals with a central nervous system. Human communities had sprawled over the earth's surface throughout historic time, like a loosely coordinated assemblage of cells. Stimuli passed from one segment to another, but in a slow, haphazard fashion; and because conductivity was low, many stimuli failed to pass from one part of the world to another for long periods of time. The advent of railroads, steamships, and telegraph wires, and the appearance of newspapers with a mass circulation and of telephones meant that stimuli began to travel enormously faster and more purposefully.

Experts could communicate with experts all around the globe. The price of wheat in Chicago, of jute in Calcutta, of coffee in São Paulo, and of money in London governed decisions made halfway across the world. Technical skills, political ideas, and artistic styles moved as quickly as they attracted experts' attention. Sudden change could reach out to extremely remote regions of the earth. In the 1880s, for example, the Japanese deliberately went shopping for a constitution and, after careful study of European and American models, decided that the constitutional arrangements of Bismarck's Germany were best for them. Sometimes stimuli went the other way. Thus, Parisian artists in the 1890s borrowed motifs from African ceremonial masks, plundered from West Africa by French soldiers and sold in the Paris "flea market" at prices that even a poor artist could afford.

When it began, the new communications and transportation network was mostly controlled by Europeans. And as railroads were built inland, the effect was to extend the reach of European goods and of Europeans' political, military, and financial advantages. Nevertheless, the opening of the Suez Canal in 1869 and of the Panama Canal in 1914 changed the world's strategic patterns in a way that foreshadowed the weakening of Europe's dominance. The Suez Canal put the Middle East back into the center of Old World communications, where it had been before Europe's sailors had opened up the oceans; and the Panama Canal strengthened America's position in the world by improving the flexibility of the naval and military power of the United States. However, neither of these changes did much to undermine the reality of Europe's dominant position before 1914.

POPULATION GROWTH

Population growth acted in most parts of the world to check and limit the impact of the new communications and transportation. Poor peasants, on the edge of starvation, took little advantage of the possibilities opened to them by railroads and telegraphs. They continued to live much as their ancestors had done. This constituted a massive conservative force in world society. Yet the peasantries of the earth also nursed a potential for revolt. Inert and helpless they were, but hungry and resentful, too; and as their numbers increased, the old ways of life became more and more impossible to maintain, since tiny holdings had to be divided and divided again among the members of each new generation.

Why world population spurted upward so dramatically is not clear. Medical measures to check disease were important in some parts of the world, but they scarcely affected the immense numbers of rural Chinese and Indians before 1914. Increased food supplies due to better seeds, better methods of cultivation, or, in some parts, better fertilizers, irrigation, new crops, and pest control had some bearing on population growth. The pacification of great regions of the earth, brought about by improved communications,

also allowed many persons to survive who in an earlier age would have perished through local violence. Famine relief was also important, especially in India where railroads made it possible to transport large amounts of food to regions where crops had failed. Lessening of epidemic diseases, through a more or less continual exposure to small doses of all sorts of infections, was another factor behind the world's population explosion. This resulted from improved transport, which circulated disease germs as well as goods and ideas throughout the world.

Traditional authorities could not cope with rising population pressures in Asia, but neither could European administrators in India or missionaries in China. Only Japan was able to absorb its rapidly rising population by finding new industrial occupations for the rural surplus. But in the Americas, Africa, and parts of southeast Asia, there was still room for expansion. Between 1850 and 1914, in all of these regions, uncultivated land could be brought under cultivation without much trouble and without any basic change in familiar farming methods.

For this reason, African and American societies did not undergo any very acute upheaval before World War I. The establishment of European political administration in Africa made only minor differences to most Africans. Old ways, minus the slave trade, local wars, and some customs of which Europeans disapproved, went on much as before. The same was true in the New World, both for newcomers of European or African descent and for the Amerindian peasantry of central America and northern South America.

IMPACT OF EUROPEAN SKILLS

The impact of improved communications and of population growth was largely unconscious, in the sense that no one decided in advance what to do about them. The third worldwide phenomenon, the impact of superior European skills upon other peoples, was very much a matter of conscious decision-making. People living outside of western Europe had to come to terms, in some fashion or other, with the facts of European superiority over local society and civilization. Although peasants could and did neglect the question, their cultural and political leaders could not afford to do so.

It is useful, perhaps, to distinguish between the attitudes of an "inner ring" of peoples who shared the European inheritance in greater or less degree and an "outer ring" of peoples who did not. Russians and Balkan Christians to the east were partially in and partially out of the circle of European civilization and felt both ashamed and proud of this fact. Overseas, the United States and the British Commonwealth countries, together with those parts of Latin America where Spanish and Portuguese settlers did not depend on Amerindians and Negroes to do the manual labor, also belonged to the "inner ring." Their problem was to catch up with Europe by settling the empty lands around them, after which the refinements of civilized life—which were still only poorly developed in these regions—could (they hoped) be expected to grow automatically.

The "outer ring" faced a much more difficult decision. Chinese, Hindus, and Moslems had to weigh the costs of giving up essential parts of their own treasured past in order to try to catch up with Europe's power. Japan chose to borrow from the west and soon forged ahead. No other proud and old civilized people was able or willing to make the hard decisions such a policy required. Instead, these communities hesitated, worried, floundered, and endured.

Africans south of the Sahara, and Amerindians in the middle regions of the New World, were subjected to European rule during the period with which we are now concerned. This was nothing new for the Amerindians. In their most developed centers, Amerindians had seen the Spaniards destroy their political leadership and higher culture before 1600. African kingdoms and tribes, however, were only brought under the control of European administrators during the later years of the nineteenth century. The degree to which African cultures and political organizations were altered by the arrival of Europeans differed a good deal from case to case. In general, the British tried to keep as much of the preexisting political and social system as possible; whereas the French, like the Spaniards in the days of the conquistadors, were more inclined to impose their own patterns of government and education upon their African subjects.

Weaker peoples found the conditions created by improved world communications all but impossible to survive. In Australia, for example, the aborigines, who had inhabited the continent for many thousands of years, could not adjust their ways to those of the intrusive whites. The same was true of Tasmanians and of some of the Pacific islanders; of Eskimos; and of Amerindian tribes who inhabited most of North America and the more southerly parts of South America. In these regions, contact with the outside world resulted in destructive epidemics of disease and paralyzing breakdowns of custom. In most cases these populations did not die out utterly, but their customary framework of life fell apart drastically and dreadfully.

HOW THE "INNER RING" GOT ALONG

The United States of America was by far the most important overseas member of the "inner ring," corresponding, in many ways, with the vast overland semi-European power, Russia. Russia's relations with the Balkan Christians and with the western Slavs (Poles, Czechs, Slovaks) were similar to the relations of the United States with Canada and Latin America. Interesting parallels as well as important differences may be detected in the internal development of Russia and the United States.

U.S. Domestic and Imperial Growth

Both the Democratic and Industrial revolutions had already gone a long way in the United States by 1850. Americans could proudly claim to be the earliest pioneers of rational self-government, and "Yankee ingenuity" in matters industrial was as great as any in the world. What was lacking in the United States was capital, population, and

New York and Brooklyn in 1894 New York became the principal commercial and financial center for the United States in the nineteenth century. Millions of immigrants from Europe, most of them fresh from peasant villages, arrived in New York between 1845 and 1914, and their labor helped to build the city seen here. The photograph features approaches to the Brooklyn bridge, which connected Brooklyn with Manhattan. Started in 1869, its builders ran into a series of technical problems, so that fourteen years elapsed before it opened for traffic in 1883. At the time, it was an engineering marvel, featuring the longest span (1595 feet) in the world. The use of steel wires to suspend the bridge from mighty pylons, rising from the bottom of the East river, was also a first. Such an achievement showed that Americans were not only catching up with European technological skills but actually surpassing them by increasing the scale with which new materials and methods were applied to engineering and industrial undertakings.

cultural refinement. With the end of the Civil War (1865), Americans set out to remedy all three deficiencies as fast as they could.

Capital came from Europe, especially England, in the form of short-term and long-term credit. In addition, shrewd industrialists like Cornelius Vanderbilt (1794–1877), Andrew Carnegie (1835–1919), John D. Rockefeller (1839–1937), and Henry Ford (1863–1947) quickly learned how to accumulate capital by plowing profits back into their businesses. They were free to set prices at what the market would bear. When very expensive plants became necessary to produce steel or oil or motor cars, competition (which in theory was supposed to keep prices close to the cost of production) worked imperfectly. Large profits reinvested in new enterprises thus created vast fortunes very rapidly. By 1914 the United States, although still a "debtor nation" in international money markets, had already begun to export large amounts of capital to the Caribbean, Mexico, Hawaii, and other foreign parts.

Population growth came from European immigration, as well as from the natural increase of people already living in the United States. As the decades passed, the flow of immigrants to North America from the British Isles and from Germany and Scandinavia slackened. Other nationalities from southern and eastern Europe became more numerous. Italians, Poles, Czechs, Croats, Jews, Greeks, Ukrainians, and many other ethnic groups swarmed across the ocean into the growing cities of the United States. There they provided labor for new factories, construction work, and the more menial services which city life required.

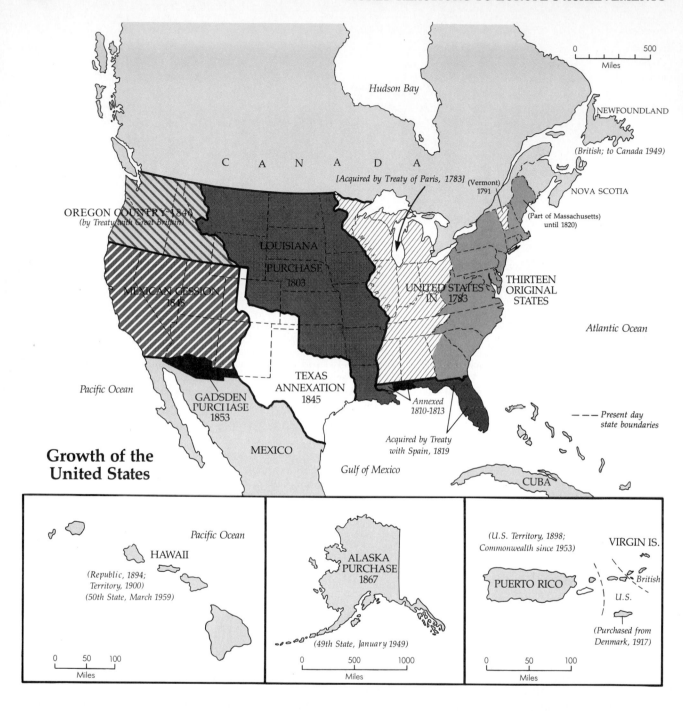

Growth of the United States

Political Problems at Home   Both the growth of capital and the flood of immigration created problems for a democratic political system. Farmers and small businesses often felt that the railroads and other big moneyed interests were squeezing them unfairly. Public regulation of railroad rates (1887) did something to remove the grievance, but a long agitation for cheaper money and credit failed to take the United States dollar off the gold standard. Similarly, popular movements aimed against immigrants succeeded only in closing the doors against Chinese and Japanese "cheap labor." Labor unions achieved a stable national existence after 1886, when the American

Federation of Labor was founded. At first only a few skilled trades were organized. In these occupations immigrant labor, lacking the necessary skills, was not much of a factor.

Political collisions between old and new immigrants and between workers and capitalists were cushioned by the fact that, until 1890 or so, the United States still had an agricultural frontier where public land could be acquired easily and quite cheaply by anyone willing to cultivate it. Hardships and grievances could never be very bitter when such a resource permitted the discontented to start afresh. Settlement of the western parts of the country tended to bypass the arid regions of the southwest, at first. As a result, Arizona and New Mexico were not organized as states until 1912, at a time when American expansion had already been carried overseas to the Philippine Islands and Puerto Rico, which were acquired from Spain after a brief and victorious war (1898) against that decaying empire.

U.S. Expansion Abroad   With the Spanish-American war and with American diplomatic and military interventions in Panama, Nicaragua, Haiti, Mexico, and other Latin American states that swiftly followed, the United States joined the circle of imperialist powers. Germany, too, entered the field at about the same time, demanding its "place in the sun." Great Britain, in effect, made room for Americans and for the Japanese as well, who also built up a navy and began to create an empire for themselves in the Far East after a victorious war against China (1894–1895). The British simply gave up any pretense of controlling the seas in the Japanese and American parts of the globe. German rivalry close at home was too dangerous for any other policy to seem practical. The result was to keep British and American policies harmonious, even in the absence of any formal treaty of alliance. This was a fact of the greatest importance for the lineup of powers in World War I.

Culture and Society in the United States   On all these fronts, the United States met with solid success. In the material sense, there was no doubt that the nation was catching up fast with the most advanced European countries. But cultural equality was harder to attain. Captains of industry, such as Vanderbilt, Carnegie, Rockefeller, and Ford, all arranged that a large part of their personal fortunes should be used to support institutions intended to improve the quality of American cultural life. As a result, universities, libraries, symphony orchestras, opera companies, and similar organizations sprang up like mushrooms in every large American city after about 1890. But real cultural creativity lagged behind the physical and financial support Americans provided so eagerly.

Before 1914, few artists or thinkers of the first rank lived in the United States. As a matter of fact, quite a few highly cultivated Americans, such as the novelist Henry James (1843–1916), preferred to live in Europe because they found their compatriots crude and unsympathetic. American culture had not really escaped from provincialism in 1914, in spite of all the money and conscious effort devoted to its cultivation.

One of the backward aspects of American life was concentrated in the Old South. After the Civil War, halfhearted efforts to bring blacks into full participation in public life failed. By the late 1870s, relations between whites and blacks settled down to patterns not so very different from those that had prevailed in the days of slavery—patterns which enjoyed the legal sanction of so-called Jim Crow laws. Black sharecroppers, therefore, hoed cotton and tobacco in nearly the same way that slaves had done before 1863; and their education, skill, voting rights, and familiarity with newer aspects of modern life were not much greater than what had existed under slavery. In search of greater opportunities, some blacks did move into cities, mainly in the South. In fact, it was black musicians in New Orleans who invented jazz, the first truly original and compelling cultural innovation that bears the stamp *Made in America*. But in 1914 jazz remained hidden in the back streets of New Orleans, Memphis, and Chicago; the majority of people in the United States, along with the rest of the world, discovered it only after World War I.

Canada and Australia

In almost all respects, Canada lagged behind the United States by a generation or so but followed much the same curve of development. Australia

Saving Labor on American Farms The United States led the world in developing labor-saving farm machinery from the 1830s, when mechanical reapers were first introduced. These photographs show the McCormick reaper as it existed between 1852 and 1865 (above) and an improved model of about 1890 (below). The older machine needed two men to make it work: a driver and a man who raked the stalks of grain off the mower, forming clumps like those seen in the foreground. Others then had to pick the loose bunches of grain from the ground and tie them into bundles (called sheaves), like the one standing in the foreground of the second photograph. The grain then had to dry for a few days before being carried to the barn and thrashed. The early McCormick reaper thus left a lot to be done by hand. Nevertheless, it allowed the northern states to fight the Civil war without suffering food shortages, even though hundreds of thousands of young men left the farms to join the army. The second photograph shows how the reaper's design was improved. In particular, only one man was now needed to drive it because the grain was bundled automatically and ejected onto the ground. Someone still had to stand the sheaves up to dry, as you see in the foreground, but the saving of labor at harvest time was still enormous.

and New Zealand differed in one important respect. From the 1880s both countries passed laws that made it difficult for anyone not of British origin to immigrate. This slowed population growth. In addition, elaborate laws for the protection of workers slowed down the development of industry in comparison to what was happening in the United States in the same period. When the separate Australian colonies united to form the Commonwealth of Australia (1901) and New Zealand also became a fully self-governing dominion (1907), both countries were almost entirely agricultural. They were divided between vast stretches of nearly empty sheep pasture and an extraordinary concentration of population at two or three port cities, where import-export businesses and the processing of raw materials for export were concentrated.

Clearly, such societies had a long way to go before they could hope to equal European complexity and sophistication. But, as in the case of the United States and Canada, the people from "down under" often asserted the superiority of their way of life to that of the Old World, where—they quite correctly pointed out—high civilization had been built partly upon the exploitation of the poor by the rich.

South Africa

A different situation prevailed in South Africa. The Boer descendants of Dutch settlers kept their own language and, until 1901, defended their rural way of life, with guns in hand, against British intrusion. First the Boers withdrew inland; then when diamonds (1867) and gold (1886) were discovered on Boer soil, they tried to disfranchise the English-speaking miners who swarmed to the scene. Meanwhile, British empire-builders decided that all of eastern Africa, from Capetown to Cairo in Egypt, ought to come into British possession. The most active advocate of such an expansion was Cecil Rhodes (1853–1902). After making a fortune in gold mining, Rhodes turned to politics. His schemes led to a hard-fought war between Boers and British (1899–1902). In the end, the British won, but only after cutting off supplies for the Boer fighters by putting their women and children into specially guarded "con-

centration camps" and by burning the farmhouses and buildings.

Another feature of South African life was the presence of large numbers of Bantu-speaking Africans, as well as the "Cape coloureds" whose ancestry mingled European, Indonesian, and Khoikhoi strains. When the Union of South Africa was established (1910), Boers, British, and "Cape coloured" populations all secured voting rights; but the Bantus were excluded. Boers regarded the Bantus as servants and inferiors; the British, when they did not share Boer attitudes, thought that tribal government should be maintained to make the transition into modern life easier and smoother.

South America

The situation in South America was again different. Argentina, southern Brazil, and Chile all remained hospitable to immigrants from Europe. But the distances involved made passage more expensive than to the United States, so fewer people made the ocean passage to those countries. Agricultural expansion inland, largely dependent on railroad construction, was rapid; and foreign capital, much of it British, was important. But the absence of coal fields severely handicapped the development of industry.

The miners, coffee growers, and entrepreneurs of the southernmost provinces of Brazil treated the rest of that enormous country, where black and Indian populations were numerous, as a sort of colonial domain. In addition, Brazilians, in alliance with Argentina, overthrew a remarkable regime in Paraguay, where, after the destruction of the Jesuit missions, three military dictators in succession organized the Guarani Indians into a tightly disciplined army. The war was bitterly fought (1865–1870), and it ended only when the Paraguayans had suffered enormous loss of life.

Somewhat later Chileans again proved that a population of European descent, and therefore possessing European skills, could exert superior military power, when they defeated Bolivia and Peru (where most of the population was Indian) in a war (1879–1884) aimed at seizing undisputed

REPUBLIC

OF

MEXICO

CUBA
(Sp.)

REPUBLIC OF
HAITI

PUERTO RICO
(Sp.)

BELIZE (Br.)

JAMAICA
(Br.)

Atlantic Ocean

UNITED PROVINCES
OF
CENTRAL AMERICA

Caracas
VENEZUELA

GREAT
COLOMBIA

Bogota

GUIANA

Pacific Ocean

Quito
ECUADOR

Amazon R.

Lima

PERU

EMPIRE OF BRAZIL

BOLIVIA
La Paz

CHACO
(claimed by Bolivia and Paraguay)

**Latin America, 1828
(after the Wars for Independence)**

PARAGUAY

Rio de Janeiro

Asuncion

0   500   1000

Miles

PROVINCES
OF
LA PLATA
(Argentine
Confederation)
Buenos Aires

URUGUAY

Montevideo

Santiago

CHILE

PATAGONIA

(conquered by Argentina, 1878-1879)

control of the valuable guano deposits of the coastal desert. These deposits, made from bird droppings, were rich in nitrogen, and before 1914 constituted the world's cheapest and best source of artificial fertilizers.

Russia

Overseas countries inhabited mainly by people of European descent enjoyed the advantage of having weak neighbors. In trying to catch up with

Europe, they could, therefore, afford to pay little attention to building up military power. This was not true of Russia, whose landward frontier against western Europe had always been difficult to defend. Throughout the nineteenth century, Russia was a great power and wished to remain so. But this required heavy expenditure for the army and navy, and such expenditures left little to spare for building up industry. Yet modern industrial plants were vitally needed to equip the army and navy with efficient weapons. Financing railroad construction on the scale required by Russia's vastness also strained the resources of the country, though it was obvious that without railroads Russia could not remain a truly great power.

Failure of Autocratic Government   This difficulty was tied in with more strictly political problems. Ever since their defeat in the Crimean War (1856), many Russians had wanted to see changes in their government. But a Polish revolt (1863–1864) stopped the movement toward creating some sort of representative system of government in Russia. Czar Alexander II (reigned 1855–1881) had tried to win the Poles over by allowing partial self-government. Instead, the Poles revolted and fought a bitter guerilla war before being put down. The rulers of Russia drew the conclusion that it was dangerous to dabble with representative institutions. Absolute Russian dominance over all the subject nationalities of the empire seemed the only way of strengthening the state. Unbending autocracy, supported by the secret police and a strong army, looked like the only kind of government that could prevent open revolt.

Reaction fed revolution. Students plotted to overthrow the czar and his government but efforts to rouse the peasants failed. As a result, in 1879 a small circle turned to terrorism and embarked on a plan to assassinate leading officials. In 1881 the czar himself was killed by one such terrorist.

This confirmed the worst fears of Russian reactionaries. In the next years, energetic police measures broke up most of the revolutionary circles. But the government could not rely only on repression. To keep strong, an active policy of building railroads and industry seemed abso-

lutely vital. But Russia, like the United States, was short of capital. The people were already severely taxed to maintain the army and bureaucracy at existing levels.

A solution was found through the diplomatic alliance with France, concluded in 1891. The French government allowed the Russians to float large loans in Paris. These loans enabled the Russian government to start a crash program of railroad building and industrial development. The Trans-Siberian Railroad, built between 1891 and 1903, was the greatest single achievement; in addition, many new armaments and textile plants came into existence in Moscow and St. Petersburg; and in the Ukraine, coal and iron mines provided the basis for a new and modern steel industry.

The difficulty with this policy was that it increased the danger of revolution. Factory workers, often miserably treated and badly housed, responded readily to preachers of revolution. A tiny Marxist party, the Social Democrats, founded in 1898, vigorously exploited this fact. Soon after, in 1901, a new terrorist group, the Socialist Revolutionaries, organized themselves, intending to appeal primarily to the peasants by advocating abolition of landlord rights.

As long as the Russian government remained successful abroad and the czarist police and army functioned with reasonable efficiency at home, the plans and hopes of Marxists and other revolutionaries were not important. And Russia was, on the whole, successful abroad. New stretches of central Asia were annexed to the czar's empire between 1865 and 1876. A victorious war against the Turks in 1876–1877 had a less satisfactory outcome because the European powers whittled away the "Big Bulgaria" the Russians had created in the Balkans. Even so, the czar annexed Bessarabia (1878). In the following years he added Merv (1884) in central Asia and acquired extensive rights in Manchuria and Outer Mongolia, in the Far East.

In 1903 the Marxists quarreled among themselves. A fiery and stubborn young leader, Vladimir Ilich Ulyanov (1870–1924), who went by the revolutionary alias Lenin, insisted that the party must become a secret group of professional revolutionaries who would obey without question whatever instructions the elected leaders of

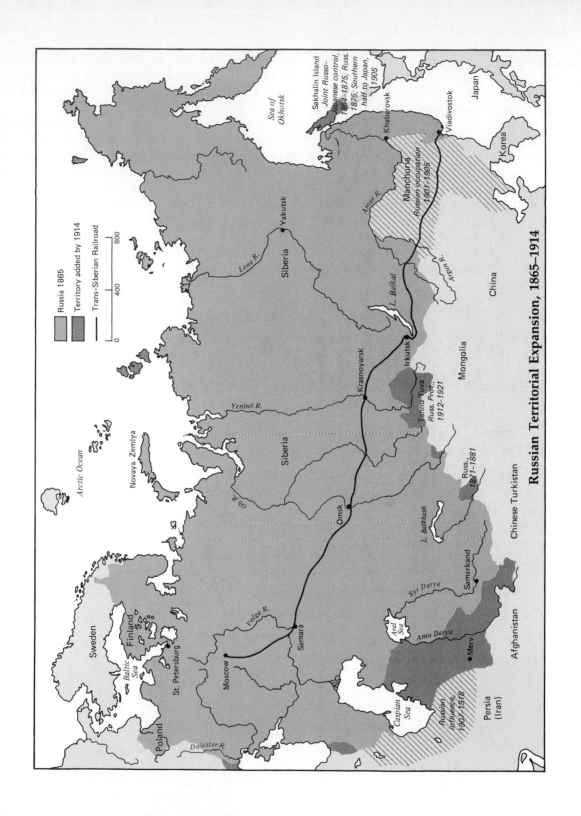

Russian Territorial Expansion, 1865–1914

Legend:
- Russia 1865
- Territory added by 1914
- Trans-Siberian Railroad

Scale: 0 — 400 — 800

Map labels:

Arctic Ocean

Novaya Zemlya

Sea of Okhotsk

Sakhalin Island – Joint Russo-Japanese control, 1864–1875; Russ. 1875; Southern half to Japan, 1905

Yakutsk

Lena R.

Siberia

Siberia

Yenisei R.

Ob R.

Krasnoyarsk

Irkutsk

L. Baikal

Amur R.

Argun R.

Khabarovsk

Vladivostok

Japan

Korea

Manchuria Russian occupation 1901–1905

Tannu-Tuva Russ. Prot., 1912–1921

Mongolia

China

Chinese Turkistan

L. Balkhash

Omsk

Russ., 1871–1881

Syr Darya

Samarkand

Aral Sea

Amu Darya

Merv

Afghanistan

Persia (Iran)

Russian influence, 1907–1918

Caspian Sea

Volga R.

Samara

Moscow

St. Petersburg

Finland

Sweden

Baltic Sea

Poland

Dniester R.

the party judged to be advantageous at the moment. Some of the delegates at the Party Congress refused to agree; but a majority, the Bolsheviks, accepted Lenin's doctrine. Most of the rank and file of the party, however, followed the anti-Leninist, or Menshevik, group.

Russia's internal situation changed suddenly in 1904–1905, when the czar's armies and navy met unexpected defeat at the hands of the Japanese in the Far East. Failure in war provoked revolution at home. The czar soon yielded, declaring that he would govern henceforth with the advice and consent of an elected duma (parliament). However, when the crisis had passed and the army came back to European Russia, reaction set in. The powers of the duma were reduced, and the government set out to improve the equipment of the Russian armies by getting armaments from France and retooling factories at home. The Russian rulers badly wanted a breathing space, such as that which had followed the Crimean War. Instead, a series of crises in the Balkans (1908, 1912–1913) led the Russian and Austrian governments to such a pitch of rivalry that when still another crisis arose in the summer of 1914, neither would yield. The result was World War I and the downfall of both empires.

Art and Intellectual Life   Yet, while Russia's public life was thus heading toward a fateful explosion, Russian writers, musicians, and scientists moved as equals in the world of Paris or Berlin. Their numbers were fewer, perhaps, than those of the West, but the genius of the novelist Feodor Dostoevski (1821–1881), of the musician Piotr Ilich Tchaikovsky (1840–1893), and of the chemist Dmitri Mendeleev (1834–1907) equaled anything their Western contemporaries achieved. This did not erase Russia's deep-seated love-hate feeling toward Germany, France, and England. Inner uncertainties expressed themselves either in extravagant praise for Russia's own peculiar past or in equally sharp rejection of that past in order to erase the remaining differences that separated Russia from the West.

Many Russian writers had a guilty feeling about the peasantry, whose harsh, poverty-stricken lives cut them off from sharing in the polite culture, as well as in the political life, of the country. Yet efforts to reach the peasants merely roused their suspicion. The famous novelist Count Leo Tolstoi (1828–1910) in his old age pretended to live like a peasant, but Tolstoi's playacting was no more effective in communicating with the mass of Russian society than earlier revolutionary preaching had been.

THE ASIAN "OUTSIDE RING"

The gap between the Russian upper classes and the Russian peasantry was like the gap that opened between those Chinese, Japanese, Hindus, and Moslem individuals who mastered aspects of European civilization and the majority of their compatriots. In this, as in many other respects, Russia stood halfway between Europe and the societies of Asia.

China

In China old ways of thought survived almost unshaken among the ruling class until 1895. After the severe crisis of the Taiping Rebellion (1850–1864), China enjoyed a kind of respite. But the respite was squandered; inactivity prevailed.

The trouble was that no educated Chinese who had spent his formative years studying the Confucian classics could really believe that fundamental changes should be made in the way China was governed. Nevertheless, some reforms were undertaken, often entrusted to foreigners. Thus, for example, a customs service was organized in 1863 by an Englishman, Robert Hart, who made it the most efficient branch of Chinese government. Other new enterprises, such as a nationwide postal system (introduced 1896), began as branches within the customs service, which, in fact, served as a training school in the methods of a modern bureaucracy.

Gestures were made toward creating a modern army and navy, but they remained half-hearted. Between 1875 and 1878, Chinese armies were able to reconquer Moslem and Turkish areas of central Asia, thus restoring China's boundaries to their former limits. Chinese control over Tibet and Mongolia was infirm, but never formally sur-

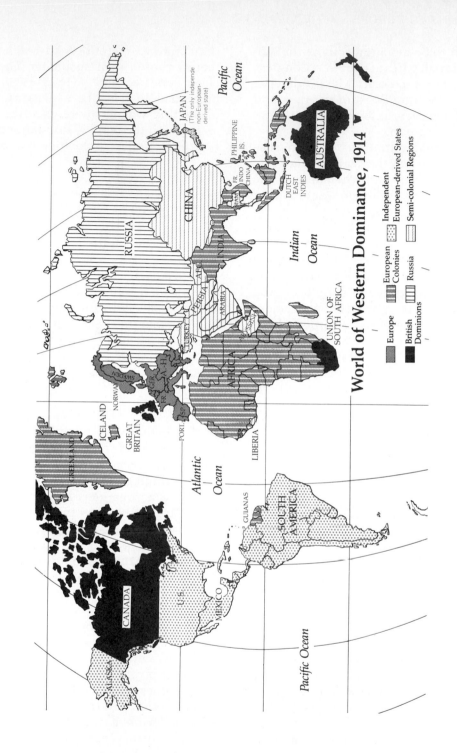

World of Western Dominance, 1914

Legend:
- Europe
- British Dominions
- European Colonies
- Russia
- Independent European-derived States
- Semi-colonial Regions

How Westerners Penetrated China The drawing above portrays China's first railroad in action. It opened in 1876 but this drawing appeared about ten years later in a popular magazine, published for Chinese readers in Shanghai. The dragon, breathing fire and smoke, had been the symbol of imperial power in China for centuries; but this kind of mechanical dragon proved far more powerful than anything the will of the emperor could summon to repel the foreigners, as the painting below illustrates. It was made by an American artist to record fighting in 1900 between a detachment of U.S. marines, armed with rifles and bayonets, and the Boxers, whose weapons were swords and spears. Superior technology, both military and industrial, made the Westerners literally irresistable, even though millions of Chinese wished to have nothing to do with them.

rendered. On the other hand, the Russians advanced into Manchuria, the French took over Annam (1883), and the British conquered Burma (1886), thus shearing off outlying territories which had previously recognized Chinese suzerainty.

Missionaries from Europe and the United States penetrated considerable distances into inland China, and in the 1880s railroads began to open up the Chinese interior to Western goods. In the north, some coal and iron mines, equipped along Western lines, also started operation. But none of these things altered the fundamental Chinese conviction that their own ways were superior.

Then Japan and China quarreled over Korea. War broke out in 1894, and the Japanese won a series of rapid victories. This was a crushing blow to Chinese pride. For half a century, the Chinese had been forced to live with the fact that Western barbarians possessed the secret of winning wars. The Chinese had not really tried very hard to find out what that secret was. But now it was all too evident that the Japanese, who had started at no better technological level than the Chinese, had somehow learned that secret. Inaction could no longer be justified; something drastic had to be done.

Reaction to Foreign Powers   The urgency of action was all the greater because Europeans began to make plans for dividing China into spheres of influence. Germany appeared on the scene and in 1897–1898 secured concessions from the Chinese government in the Shantung Peninsula. This set off a frantic scramble on the part of other imperial powers, each eager to pin down its rights to local concessions. Control of railroad rights-of-way into the interior was the prize immediately at stake. Russia gained control of the railroads in Manchuria; Britain planned to open up the Yangtze with steamboats and railroads; the French concentrated in the south, driving a railroad northward from Hanoi to Yünnan. The Germans, as latecomers, concentrated in the region nearest Peking, where foreigners had hitherto been kept at bay. As for the United States, it advocated an "Open Door," meaning the right of every foreign power to enjoy equal access to all parts of China.

China's first reaction was a desperate effort to throw out the foreigners. A secret society, the so-called Boxers, preached hatred of all outsiders but made the mistake of relying on magical protection against European bullets. In 1990 when the Boxers attacked the European legations in Peking, tiny staffs fought them off until a relief expedition could be sent in from the coast. The Boxers were then shot down ruthlessly. The Chinese government was required to pay an indemnity for the losses suffered by the Westerners.

Failure of the Boxer Rebellion forced the reluctant Chinese to face the necessity of change. In 1905, accordingly, the imperial government abolished the ancient system of recruitment to the ranks of officialdom. Examinations testing mastery of the Confucian classics were abandoned. The effect upon Chinese life was profound. Young men who formerly had pored over the pages of the ancient sages now swarmed into missionary schools and colleges, hoping to prepare themselves for government jobs by finding the secret of Western greatness. Many young Chinese went to Japan, and the United States decided to use its share of the Boxer indemnity payments to bring Chinese students to study at American universities.

Obviously, it took time for Western-style education to take effect, since the language barriers to be crossed were unusually difficult. But the impatient Chinese could not wait for a new generation to arise, trained in Western-type schools. Revolutionary secret societies had long been a feature of Chinese life; and after the war with Japan (1894–1895), they took on new life. Sun Yat-sen (1866–1925) was the leader of one such group. He searched the political writings of Western and Japanese authors—hunting for ideas that might work in China—and came up with a hodgepodge of nationalist and socialist ideas.

In 1911 revolution broke out in China. The next year the emperor (a six-year-old boy) abdicated, and the Manchu Dynasty came to an end. Confusion only increased. Sun Yat-sen, now leader of the Kuomintang party, challenged more old-fashioned war lords who, for their part, probably dreamed of establishing a new imperial dynasty rather than carrying through a thorough-going revolution. Foreign diplomats and business interests added to China's troubled times; and the Japanese, who had meanwhile annexed Korea (1910), showed signs of wishing to put a puppet of their choosing on the Chinese throne. The outbreak of World War I, in 1914, freed the Japanese from having to take European diplomatic objections to their further advance until after the end of the war in 1918.

Japan

Japan's history contrasted in every respect with China's unhappy experience. In 1867 the die had been cast for radical reform with the "restoration" of the emperor. By good luck, the young man who took the title *Meiji* for his reign (1867–1912) proved to be unusually wise, judicious, and strong-willed. Over and over again, in time of crisis, his decisions as to which advisers to appoint to office were of critical importance. Under the Meiji emperor, Japan was therefore able to pursue a consistent policy. It did so with a truly amazing success.

Reforms in Government   The first and central aim of the whole undertaking was to make Japan strong, so that the nation would no longer have to fear foreign gunboats. Very quickly the clique of warriors who engineered the overthrow of the shogun recognized that this required far-reaching changes in the Japanese social scene. Thus they "abolished feudalism" between 1869 and 1871. This meant destroying the rights of the warrior class to collect rice rents from the peasants. The dispossessed warriors received handsomely engraved government bonds instead.

A postal service, a daily newspaper, and a ministry of education, whose job it was to set up schools that could train the Japanese in what they needed to know about the West, quickly followed. In 1872, universal military service was decreed. It takes a moment to realize how radical this was in Japanese society, where the right to bear arms had always been a jealously guarded privilege of the warrior class. Now peasants and merchants,

even the despised outcasts who had traditionally been charged with menial tasks, were admitted to the ranks of the army. Appointment and promotion within the officer ranks were made to depend not on birth or traditional status but on competence and seniority. This established a career open to talent, appealing especially to poor peasant sons. It also provoked an armed rebellion on the part of disgruntled warriors of the old school (1877), but the new army stood the test by defeating the rebels. After the victory, the old order of things disappeared beyond all hope of recall.

The Japanese never looked back. In 1889, the emperor proclaimed a new constitution designed to resemble Bismarck's imperial system in Germany. Voting rights were limited to the richer classes. The elected diet (parliament) had only modest powers. The diet did, however, give the Japanese who mattered politically a way of making their will known to the highest circles of government. This was exactly what it was intended to do. Next came revision of the laws according to European patterns of justice. And in 1897, Japan attained respectability by putting its currency on the gold standard.

All the while, energetic efforts to introduce modern industry continued, so as to be able to supply and maintain a modern army and navy. Usually the government tried new things first. Then, when a factory had begun to turn out the desired product, the government sold it, sometimes at very low prices, to private capitalists. This meant, in effect, that the costs of starting up enterprises were carried by the government, which, with its tax income, was able to bear initial losses. But once private owners took over, more or less free market prices came into play. This required considerable efficiency on the part of the Japanese firms, for European and American factory-made goods were only lightly taxed on entry into the country. As a result, by 1914 some Japanese products, particularly textiles, were beginning to compete quite successfully with European and American products in the export markets of the Far East.

The Western powers recognized Japan's success by giving up extraterritorial rights (1899) which had been secured by the first treaties after

Modernizing Industry and Agriculture in Japan The Japanese worked hard
to catch up with Western technology, not only in industry, as the woodcut
above indicates, but also in agriculture, as you can see below. The woodcut
was made about 1880 when electrical generators were still very new in the
western world, yet here we see how the Shibura Engineering Works put them
into service in Japan. The man examining the generator coil in the foreground is wearing European clothes and may represent a foreign expert,
brought in to get the new machines started. What look like military costumes
on the other workmen were equally exotic of course but those wearing them
were Japanese and may well have been soldiers in their new, western-style
uniforms who were assigned the task of serving the national interest by learning how to start up this new and important technology. For a long time,
peasant life remained little changed; but eventually labor saving machinery
reached the paddy fields of Japan too, as can be seen in the photograph
below.

the opening of Japan. Two years later, Great Britain concluded a military alliance with Japan; and in 1904–1905, the Japanese amazed all Asia and most of Europe by defeating the Russians. They annexed Formosa in 1895 after defeating the Chinese and took over control of Korea in 1910 by suppressing a Korean revolt aimed at driving them out of the country.

Throughout, the Japanese peasantry remained obedient, hard-working, poor to the edge of hunger, but energetic and ambitious all the same. At first, capital for industrial development came mainly from the peasants in the form of heavy taxes. Later, industry financed itself from profits, which came from the Japanese consumers. Later still, when Japan was able to build up a substantial export trade, the burden shifted, in part, to Koreans, Chinese, and others.

This success story was made possible by the unwavering social discipline of the Japanese. The imperial authority, exercised by a changing circle of ministers and informal advisers, operated upon a society in which the habit of command and obedience had been cultivated for centuries. Military clans had formerly been in control; now it was shifting cliques of advisers to the emperor, eventually diluted by a sprinkling of ordinary commoners, who gave commands. The aim was much the same, that is, military strength and greatness, not any longer for a single clan, but rather for Japan as a whole.

Universal elementary education opened Japanese minds to many aspects of Western civilization beyond the merely technical. But the idea of equality or of liberty, as developed in the West in the nineteenth century, made little impression. The Democratic Revolution, in other words, did not come to Japan with the Industrial Revolution. Instead, the speed and smoothness with which the Japanese adopted Western industrial and military technology depended on the survival of old-fashioned inequality.

India

Hindu India was like Japan in one respect. A considerable number of Indians went to European-type schools and acquired some familiarity with European civilization. Yet the differences between Japan and Hindu India were far greater than the likenesses. The liberal principles of British administration in India required the government to keep its hands off most economic matters. These were thought to belong, as in England, to the sphere of private enterprise. But, except for a small number of Parsis (believers in Zoroastrianism) and other foreigners, no one in India was ready or able to start up modern industry or bring in new techniques, as the Japanese government did so successfully.

Consequently, despite a fine railroad network, a remarkably honest government, and legal freedom to act, industrial development came very slowly to India. The government's policy of allowing free trade meant that Indian manufacturers were exposed to competition from British factories. The Japanese labored under the same handicap at the beginning, when their tariffs were fixed at a very low rate by treaty agreement with the Western powers. Free trade alone was not to blame, as Indian nationalists have often claimed. It was, basically, the lack of will on the part of any significant group of people to do anything about the down-to-earth business of factory production. To British-educated Indians, the prestige of work in a government office was so great that other careers seemed unattractive.

Population growth made famines serious. Systematic countermeasures, begun in 1883, had the effect of keeping more people alive in time of crop failure. But this failed to solve the problem and, indeed, only made it worse. Too many persons remained alive to be fed properly from the available land, given the existing level of agricultural skills.

In the sphere of politics, Hindu India was more active. In 1885, the Indian National Congress met for the first time. Delegates discussed political questions and petitioned for a larger share in government policy-making. The Congress leaders took the ideals of the British liberal parliamentary tradition seriously. And although they did not get all they asked for, little by little the British did bring Indian representatives into the higher councils of government.

In 1905, political agitation showed a different face. The British decided to divide the large and wealthy province of Bengal into two. This roused suspicion that the British were really try-

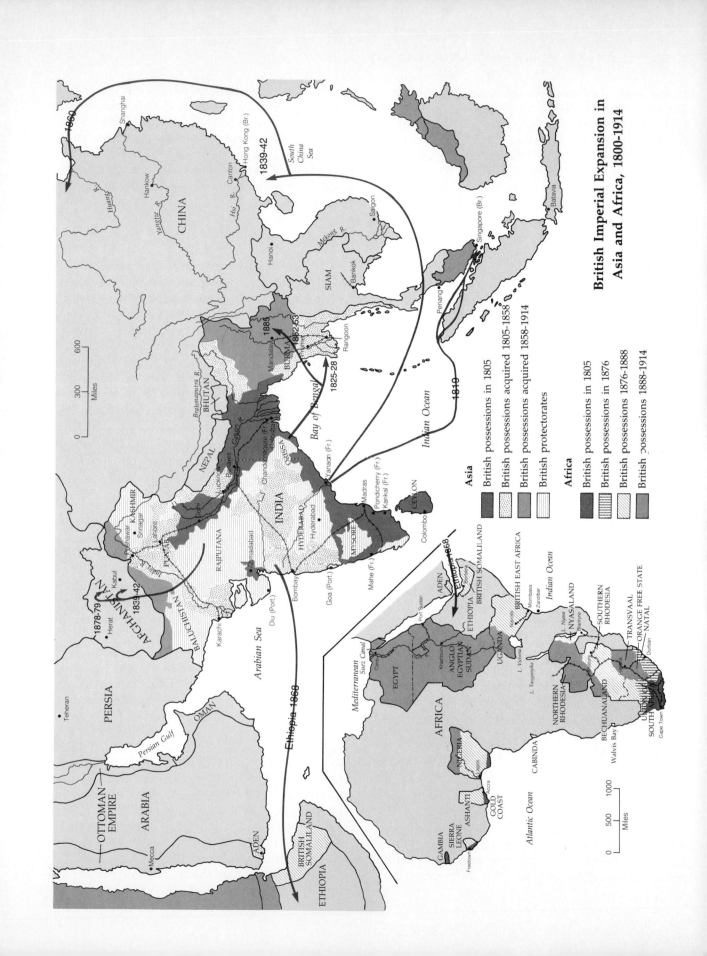

British Imperial Expansion in Asia and Africa, 1800–1914

Asia

- British possessions in 1805
- British possessions acquired 1805–1858
- British possessions acquired 1858–1914
- British protectorates

Africa

- British possessions in 1805
- British possessions in 1876
- British possessions 1876–1888
- British possessions 1888–1914

ing to create a predominantly Moslem state in one half of Bengal (what is now Bangladesh) and a Hindu state in the other half, in accordance with the ancient precept of divide and rule. Protests were organized, not only among the educated upper class but also among the rank and file of Calcutta and other cities. A handful of terrorists tried to use assassination as a way to register their opposition to British rule. The British responded with repression but, in 1911, decided that the wiser course was to unite the two halves of Bengal once more.

Except for this flare-up of popular agitation in Bengal, most Indians remained untouched by political debates. When the capital was moved to Delhi in 1911, the new king of England, George V, came to India to be crowned Emperor of India. A splendid gathering of Indian princes seemed to prove the loyalty and contentment of the Indian peoples under British rule.

Islam

Indian Moslems seldom attended British schools, and few of them entered the Indian administration. They played larger roles in the army, but, by and large, the Moslems of India found it difficult to accustom themselves to Christian rule. This was also true of other Moslems, even though by 1914 a very large part of the Islamic world was under the political control of Europeans. The French began to move into North Africa in 1830, capturing Algiers in that year. In 1881 they took over Tunis to the east. In 1912 the French protectorate over Morocco, to the west, received international recognition, although only after German opposition had twice triggered international crises. French power also reached southward across the Sahara and overran most of the Moslem kingdoms of West Africa, and Moslem areas of Africa which escaped the French were conquered by the British.

Italy took Tripoli in 1911 after a war with the Turks, and Egypt fell under British control in 1882. When a sectarian leader proclaimed himself the Mahdi (that is, divinely appointed leader of all true Moslems) and drove Egyptian administrators out of the Sudan, British arms were summoned to impose Anglo-Egyptian control throughout the region. The Red Sea and Persian Gulf shorelines were also under British influence; so was the southern portion of Persia and Afghanistan. Most of these lands retained nominal independence, but by giving and withholding subsidies and supplies, the British were able to put their friends in power and keep their enemies on the run.

From the landward side, Moslem states fared no better. The Russians and Chinese, between them, squeezed out the last independent khanates of central Asia by 1884. Russia controlled the northern third of Persia as a result of a general agreement reached with Britain in 1907. In the Balkans, the Ottoman Turks lost ground to Bulgars and Albanians, as well as to the Serbs and Greeks who had won their independence in the first half of the century. No ray of hope relieved this dismal record of defeat and retreat. Everywhere Moslems continued to suffer defeat in war. Military failure was all the harder to endure because from the days of the Prophet Mohammed, success on the battlefield and the blessing of Allah had been closely linked in Moslem minds.

Internal Problems   Turks, Persians, and Afghans still ruled nominally independent states. Each had all the makings of a nation, with a history, language, and military tradition of its own. But the two strongest of these nations, the Turks and the Persians, faced a dilemma; for if they became out-and-out nationalists, they stood to lose an empire over other peoples.

In 1908, for example, a secret society of army officers and reformers, who went by the name "Young Turks," started a revolution in the Ottoman Empire. They wished to make the empire over into a secular state. In this fashion they hoped that the age-old conflict between Moslems and Christians would disappear. Everyone, it was hoped, could learn to be a good "Ottoman," whatever his religion might be. The Young Turks took it for granted that Turks would continue to rule the state. When elections resulted in a parliament in which Bulgars, Greeks, Armenians, Albanians, and other nationalities all stubbornly defended their own self-interests, the Young Turks resorted in disgust to a coup d'état. They then established an authoritarian regime whose leading figures turned more and more to Pan-Turkism as a substitute for Ottomanism. The idea was to arouse the Turkish-speaking subjects of the Russian and Chinese empires to a sense of their common destiny with the Ottoman Turks. The leaders of the Young Turks began to dream of a vast Asian empire, in which Turks would be a majority of the population and rule the state. This brought the Turkish government into World War I on the German side, since Pan-Turkism could only become a political fact after the dismemberment of the Russian Empire.

As for the Persians, their subject nationalities were mostly of Turkish speech. What made such Turks "Persian" was the Shia form of Islam they had inherited from the Safavid period. Any shift from the traditional religious basis of the Persian state therefore threatened an immediate breakup, which no Persian welcomed.

The Arabs and the Indian Moslems were, of all Moslems, the most confused. Arabs found it difficult to choose between the ideal of a local nation-state—Egypt, Syria, and so forth—and the ideal of a Pan-Arab empire. More important, they could not decide between trying to build a strong secular state and remaining faithful to the Sacred Law of Islam. Yet the fact remained that one interfered with the other; and, wanting both, the Arabs got neither. Up to 1914, they remained sullen and angry, almost untouched by either the Industrial or the Democratic Revolution. As for the Moslems of India, they had only a choice of evils. Having no country of their own, they feared the Hindu majority around them as much as, or more than, they disliked being subjected to British rule.

There were parts of the world where Islam continued to prosper. In much of Africa and in southeast Asia, the faith of Mohammed continued to make converts, despite the competition of Christian missionaries. Islam offered peoples emerging from isolation all the benefits of a civilized faith: literacy, a world view that answered all fundamental questions, and a code of conduct that could be used to guide everyday behavior. It had the further advantages of allowing a man to marry more than one wife (an important consideration among polygamous peoples) and of not being associated with the politically dominant whites from Europe. But continued Moslem missionary success in these regions of the world offered small comfort to the Moslems of the heartlands. They scarcely knew what was happening in such distant parts, and even if they had known, it would not have helped them to solve their own pressing problems.

AFRICANS AND AMERINDIANS

The men who explored the interior of sub-Saharan Africa between 1850 and 1880 were only the advance guard for other Europeans who followed hard on their heels, eager to bring the blessing of Christian civilization to the "Dark Continent." These blessings took different forms, and the motives of the men who brought them were no less varied. Some devoutly and devotedly sought to save souls, and Christian missionaries helped many thousands of Africans to live better in this world too by founding schools and hospitals. Others wished only to get rich, and they tried to do so by making Africans work for them, either on plantations or in mines. After the 1880s, gold and diamond mines in South Africa and copper mines in the Congo combined African labor with the most up-to-date European technology.

Sometimes wages could not persuade Africans, accustomed to subsistence farming, to give up their traditional ways and work for the European newcomers. In such cases, impatient entrepreneurs resorted to forced labor, which differed only in legal form from old-fashioned slavery. Nevertheless, when news leaked out about the way a company organized by King Leopold of Belgium was using forced labor in the Congo, widespread protests in Europe persuaded the king to abandon the practice, and his company, unable to make a profit, was taken over by the Belgian government.

The decision by the Belgians to take formal control over the Congo was an instance of another very powerful motive operating among European imperialists in Africa. By annexing new lands European adventurers felt that the greatness and prestige of their nation was enhanced. New col-

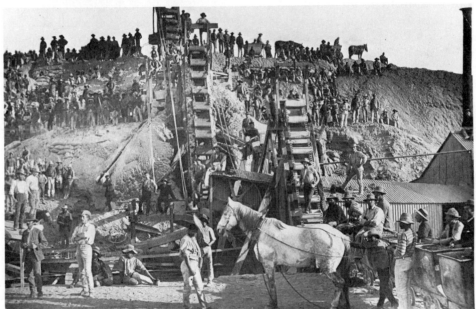

Opening Africa: The European Viewpoint Above an artist's imagined portrayal of how the American reporter, Henry Stanley, encountered the missionary-explorer David Livingstone on the shores of Lake Tanganyika in 1871. Livingstone had been reported dead and Stanley set off to find him amidst a blaze of publicity. Subsequently, he informed an excited English-speaking world about the heroic explorer who had refused to leave Africa, even though he was ill. In fact, Livingstone died just two years later, still looking for the sources of the Nile and hoping by his example to inspire his fellow countrymen to promote Christianity, commerce, and civilization in Africa and suppress the slave trade. Below, is a photograph that reveals a part of what European commerce meant for Africa. It shows the surface machinery needed by a mine at Bultfontein, South Africa to wash diamonds out of the hard clay that enveloped them. By the 1880s, when this photograph was taken, Africans had been set to work in the mines under conditions approaching slavery. They found themselves under the supervision of rough and ready white miners, some of whom are visible here in the foreground.

onies under the British, French, Belgian, German, Italian, Portuguese, or Spanish flag—as the case might be—offered the colonizing power a chance at new wealth. Above all it meant that rival European powers were excluded from the area being taken over. Competition at first lay mainly between the French and the British. Not infrequently, ambitious officers, bored with garrison duty, set out to pacify some neighboring region, and having defeated local forces they took the initiative in annexing the new territory on behalf of their home governments. Newspapers made much of victorious colonial campaigns, and politicians at home went along when they did not actively encourage military adventures.

By the 1880s, Germany and Italy joined the scramble for colonies. This only made the French and British more anxious to get there first. When resulting competition in central Africa threatened to get out of hand, Bismarck called a conference that met in Berlin in 1885. There the European powers drew more or less arbitrary boundaries on the map to delineate their respective colonial possessions. Frictions did not cease after the Berlin conference, however. France and Britain clashed again in 1898 over the upwaters of the Nile, for example. Troubles began in 1882 when the British occupied Egypt, excluding the French, who had previously been the most influential European power in that country. Beginning in the next year, fanatical Moslem dervishes, seeking to restore the purity of the faith, seized power in the regions of the upper Nile, throwing out Egyptians and their new British advisers. But the insurgent Moslem regime on the upper Nile got into difficulties after the death of the prophet who had founded the movement in 1885. The French saw a chance to gain control of the Nile's flow and embarrass the British in Egypt by sending an expedition into the region. They arrived at Fashoda on the banks of the Nile in 1898, a few weeks before a much larger British expedition, having defeated the dervishes, arrived to claim possession of the river banks. A brief but intense diplomatic crisis led to a French retreat. Yet a short five years later the two governments chose to bury their differences overseas by entering upon an informal alliance against the rising power of Germany.

Even so, Africa remained a bone of contention for the European powers. The main clash came in Morocco, where the Germans opposed French ambitions to control the sultan and his government. Two intense diplomatic storms resulted (1905, 1911). This time it was the Germans who backed down, but not before hard feelings had been stirred on both sides of the European alliance system. In this way, colonial rivalries in Africa contributed a good deal to the psychological and diplomatic climate that triggered World War I.

Imperial rivalries and ambitions among the European powers met with only ineffective resistance. African states were in disarray; and the rapid development of new weapons—repeating rifles and machine guns became normal equipment for European armies between 1870 and 1890—meant that even small detachments of European soldiers could defeat African forces with ease. In addition, European military and political organization allowed their troops to move across previously insuperable obstacles. In 1868, for example, when the British invaded Ethiopia, they built a railroad to deliver supplies from the coast. Even after they withdrew, the railroad remained to connect a hitherto almost inaccessible kingdom with the outer world. Other railroads in other parts of Africa had similar effect, opening up the interior to European access as never before. River steamers and telegraph wires were also important in allowing Europeans to exercise political control over territory in a way that local kings and tribal chieftains could not match.

Yet even when resistance was hopeless, African warriors and rulers found it difficult to submit. Thus, the Ashanti federation in West Africa clashed repeatedly with the British before 1900, when it was finally broken up. The French similarly destroyed the kingdom of Dahomey in 1892 after two wars. Other armed clashes occurred throughout East and South Africa; and sometimes desperate African resistance led to mass killings, or death through starvation and disease.

The disbalance of force was so great that by 1914 only two African states remained genuinely independent. One was Ethiopia, where King Menelik defeated an Italian effort to conquer his country in 1896. The other was Liberia in West Africa, set up as a home for liberated American slaves

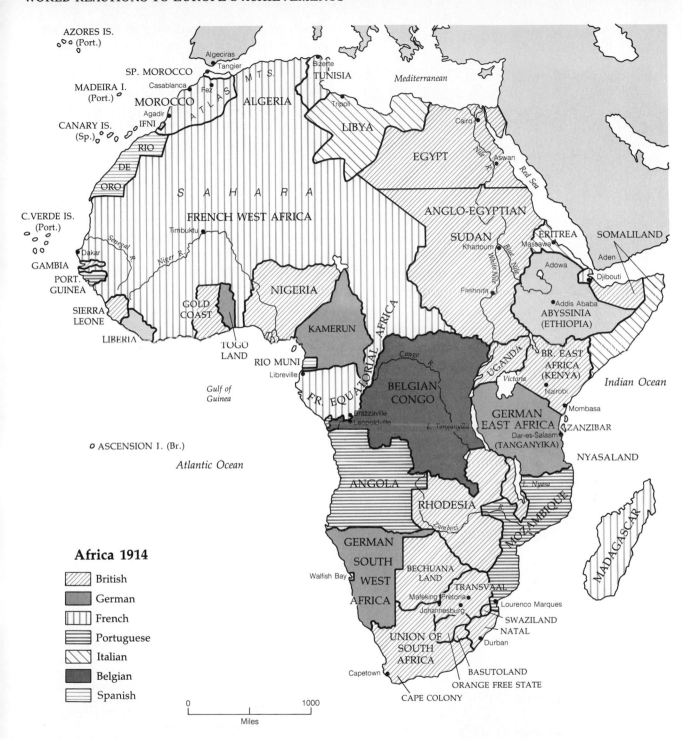

Africa 1914

- ▨ British
- ▓ German
- ▥ French
- ▤ Portuguese
- ▨ Italian
- █ Belgian
- ▦ Spanish

0 — 1000
Miles

in 1822. In many parts of Africa, to be sure, old kingdoms and tribal communities retained a shadowy sort of existence. The British liked to govern their colonies indirectly, depending on native leaders to carry out whatever new policies the British felt might be necessary, but in other respects leaving customs and traditional practices alone. In theory, the French aimed at making their African subjects into Frenchmen with black skins; in practice, they usually left the existing

structure of African society and administration more or less in place simply because there was nothing else a handful of French imperial administrators could do. German, Belgian, and Portuguese administrators were in the same position, even when backed up by private businessmen and missionaries from the colonial power.

Indeed, the most marked feature of Africa in its colonial years was the discrepancy between the framework of European imperial administration and the human reality that continued to exist on the ground. The boundaries drawn across the face of Africa seldom corresponded to geographical or social frontiers. Often very different peoples were grouped together in a single colony. Occasionally, kindred peoples found themselves split up between rival European administrations.

Africa as a whole remained extremely varied. The continent exhibited greater racial variety than existed elsewhere. Pygmies of the Congo rain forest and such extremely tall people as the Tutsi represent extremes of human stature, for example; and other differences divided the inhabitants into numerous physically distinct groups. Hundreds of African languages also existed, some of them spoken only locally, while others, like Arabic and Swahili, served as languages of trade and culture among many different peoples. The Bantu family of languages can claim a certain

African Rulers, Old and New Above is a King of Benin, cast in bronze with his attendants about 1600; below is a portrait of Queen Victoria carved out of wood by one of her African subjects in Sierra Leone about 1880. Neither sculptor was much interested in accurately reproducing the individual appearance of the two rulers, although Queen Victoria's thin lips and sharp nose were probably intended to underline the way white features departed from African norms. But the real message of both of these works of art is to show how far above ordinary folk the two rulers were. Thus in both cases, elaborate headdresses and a haughty, half-threatening stare, convey a lively sense of the power and dignity of royalty. It seems safe to say that the artist who carved this bust of the English Queen held fast to established African ideas of what kingship meant and knew very little about the realities of Queen Victoria's Britain.

preeminence in Africa, however, being spoken very widely in both western and southern Africa.

European administration constituted a thin veneer, half hiding for a while the ancient human variability of Africa. New schools and laws and military service in European-style armed forces did make a difference, of course. So did the new modes of transport, new circulation of diseases, new taxes, and new economic activities. But most Africans remained in their villages and lived much as they had before Europeans appeared on the scene. Except in the extreme north (where French and Italian settlers became numerous in Algeria and Tunis) and in the south (where Boers and English occupied a good deal of the landscape), Europeans always remained very few. Consequently, until after 1914, the European impact on Africa was drastic yet superficial. Old ways were in retreat, and old forms of political organization had been discredited or destroyed; but very few Africans had yet had time or opportunity to think of how to regain the initiative in their encounters with white men. Only after World War II did that possibility arise; and when it did, European empires crumbled even faster than they had arisen.

Amerindian Peoples

The other large human population existing on the fringes of civilization between 1850 and 1914 lived in the central portion of the Americas, between Peru and Boliva on the south and Mexico on the north. They were the descendants of Amerindians, who had inhabited these regions before the Spaniards came, with some admixture of Spanish blood. When Spain fell under French control in 1808 as an incident in the Napoleonic wars, "loyal" Spaniards in the Americas refused to recognize the authority of Napoleon's puppet government in Madrid. Even when the French were driven out of Spain (1814), the Spanish colonies in America remained in turmoil. Fighting between liberals and conservatives led to a liberal victory and the establishment of republican governments. By 1824, the success of the Latin American revolutions was established. More stable governments gradually emerged.

In the parts of the Spanish Empire inhabited chiefly by people of European descent, the liberal ideals that had come to the front during the revolutionary years offered no special difficulties. The church was the main target of the liberals; control over church lands was a principal bone of contention among military and party leaders. In the regions where Amerindian populations were a majority, however, the liberals faced a special problem. Should the ideals of self-government extend also to the Amerindians? In South America, the white ruling classes answered this question in the negative. In Mexico, on the contrary, the answer was in the affirmative. Benito Juárez—the liberal champion against Emperor Maximilian and the French from 1860 to 1872—was of Indian parentage and got much of his support from the Indians and men of mixed blood. Later, to be sure, Mexico came under the control of Porfirio Díaz (1876–1911), who favored foreign investment and the landowning class more than the poor. In 1911 he was overthrown by a revolutionary movement aimed against United States capital as well as against the rich at home. Resulting diplomatic disputes between the United States and Mexico led in 1916 to minor military skirmishes along the border between the two countries.

Meanwhile, the ruling cliques of Peru, Ecuador, Bolivia, Colombia, and Venezuela quarreled vigorously among themselves for control of the government. But they always stopped short of appealing to the Amerindian villagers—partly, perhaps, because the peasants would not listen and partly because the whites feared for their position in society if ever the Amerindian majority should enter actively into politics. Therefore, being unable to mobilize wide support in their countries, all such regimes remained comparatively weak and were often unstable.

CONCLUSION

In spite of the survival of remote Andean villages almost untouched by world events and the existence of similar village communities in some other parts of the globe, it still remained true that the world had become united as never before. Between 1850 andf 1914, Europe, like a great spider, had spun a web of rails and telegraph lines around the globe. All humankind was caught in it. Struggles to escape, to withdraw, to get back to the good old times when strangers and outsiders didn't matter, were in vain. In the next chapters we will survey the whole globe, decade by decade, to see what people have, to date, done with the unparalleled opportunities and difficulties this new state of affairs created for humanity and for each segment, class, group, and individual that, taken together, make up humankind.

Transportation and Communication

To those who lack long-range means of travel and communication, walking is the only way to go and talking face to face the only way to communicate.

Through most of history this was the case, although from the beginning of civilization, ships and pack animals gave some people a longer reach. Using relays of horses or simple sailing vessels, a person could travel up to 100 miles a day, whether by land or by sea.

BREAKING DESERT BARRIERS

Between A.D. 200 and 600 caravans acquired a new efficiency thanks to the domestication of camels. Thereafter, deserts became passable as never before. And since camels could live on wild herbage growing along the way, they cost very little. Cheap long-distance caravan transport gave Moslems an advantage over everyone else before about A.D. 1000, allowing Moslem traders to cross the Sahara to West Africa and penetrate all the deserts of Central Asia.

Highlights

Overland transport by caravan could carry only small loads. Trade was therefore restricted mainly to luxuries.

Camels broke through desert barriers after A.D. 600, opening new frontiers to Islamic trade and civilization in Africa and Asia.

BREAKING THE OCEAN BARRIERS

Between 1400 and 1500, Europeans learned how to make ships that could travel safely across stormy seas and in waters where tides ran swift and high. Strongly built hulls, a big rudder, and multiple masts with sails that could be put up or down, according to the strength of the wind, all played their part in making ships safer and more maneuverable.

With such vessels, long voyages across the oceans became easy. But how to get back? This required new methods of navigation, which would allow a ship to find its position by observing the sun or the stars. European sailors—especially the Portuguese—worked out this problem, too, by 1500.

Finally, how to protect oneself against strangers, whether on sea or land? The answer was to put cannon on board ship. Strong hulls, built to hold up against heavy waves, could also withstand the recoil of heavy guns.

Highlights

Within less than thirty years (1492–1521), European seafarers broke through the vast ocean barriers that had previously divided humanity into separate continental blocks.

The opening of the oceans by European ships started new kinds of interaction among the peoples of the world. Trade, migration, and exchange both of diseases and of new food crops all took new paths.

PRINTING

Printing from wooden blocks was invented by the Chinese before A.D. 800. Since Chinese writing uses thousands of different signs or characters, it was easier to carve a whole page at a time than to assemble separate bits of type made in advance.

In Korea and in Europe, however, alphabetic writing required only a small number of different signs. Therefore it made sense to cast type for each letter in multiple copies ahead of time and then to assemble the movable type into words.

In Europe the first book printed in this manner was made in Germany by Johann Gutenberg in 1454.

Highlights

Printing made it possible to produce large numbers of copies of a text cheaply and accurately. This had revolutionary effects in Europe but a conservative effect in China. In China, printing was used to reproduce the Confucian classics and commentaries upon them. Wider familiarity with these texts simply strengthened Confucian ideas and attitudes.

Among Europeans, an intensified interaction of old and new ideas and information shook established beliefs.

INLAND TRANSPORT

Since the invention of ships, water transportation had always been much cheaper than land transport. Canals could extend the advantages of water transportation inland, even where natural riverways were absent. Locks allowed barges to travel up over a watershed, crossing from one river basin to another. The first country to take advantage of this possibility on a big scale was China, where the Grand Canal linked the Yangtse Valley with the Yellow River Valley after A.D. 605. By building feeder canals upstream (initially to irrigate rice paddies) a new, cheap transport system came into existence. Cheap transport, in turn, allowed trade to flourish, and China became the richest and most skilled country in the world for about five hundred years (1000–1500), thanks to its superior internal transport system.

In Europe, canal building became important for inland transportation between 1750 and 1850. Canals could carry heavy loads cheaply once they were built, but in many cases construction and maintenance were costly.

Roads used by wheeled vehicles must have some kind of drainage; otherwise, the rain softens the surface, mudholes develop, and the road soon turns into a quagmire. The Romans built narrow roads of paving stones. After 1700, Europeans discovered a much cheaper way of making durable roads by scattering gravel on the roadbed so that rain could drain away without leaving mudholes behind. Smooth roads allowed higher speed, so stagecoaches carried goods and passengers as much as 100

An Illustration of a Viking Ship.

miles a day, reaching the old limit civilized peoples had known ever since they tamed the horse.

Highlights

Cheaper movement of heavy goods by water and faster movement of goods and passengers by land intensified interaction across longer distances.

Rapid economic development resulted, with remarkable growth of both industry and agriculture.

POPULAR PRESS

Early presses were worked by men using their own muscles to press a sheet of paper against a bed of ink-covered type. Even with the help of carefully designed levers this went rather slowly.

Faster printing came by making the type fit onto a curved, cylindrical surface. Such a cylinder could print by spinning around while a long sheet of paper rolled past. Cylinder presses made on this principle could print many thousands of sheets in an hour.

A Chinese War Junk, ca. 19th Century.

GLOBAL COMMUNICATION

Smoke signals and fire beacons spread alarms in very ancient times. Semaphore flag stations carried more complicated messages during the Napoleonic wars. But from the 1830s the electric telegraph offered a far superior way of sending messages over long distances.

Waterproof cables, laid across the ocean beds, soon linked continent with continent. Key points in the world came into instantaneous contact with one another.

After 1876, telephone communication speeded up the process, since words can be spoken faster than a telegraph operator can send letters by code. Over long distances, however, background noise often made spoken words unclear when telegraph signals could get through.

Highlights

Telegraph and telephone extended the range of human communication enormously, by linking up the globe into a single communications network.

Orders for purchase and sale could reach around the world. This created a world

Highlights

High-speed printing gave birth to mass circulation newspapers and magazines.

Newspapers and magazines read by millions created a new kind of interaction between the government and the public.

Government action supported by the aroused will of a whole people attained much greater force than had been possible before mobilizing greater resources, both human and material, to carry through common purposes.

STEAM RAILROAD

Railroads reduce friction between wheels and the ground by concentrating comparatively large weights on very narrow, hard rails. This principle was first used mainly in hauling coal, both inside the mines and on the surface.

The railroad came into its own when steam power was set to work moving whole trains of cars along metal rails. More powerful locomotives and carefully prepared roadbeds allowed the trains to reach speeds up to 100 miles per hour.

A 19th Century Printing Press.

Passenger Train about 1950.

market for standard bulk commodities like wheat.

Central command and precise control, both in peacetime diplomacy and in war, became possible for the first time.

MASS COMMUNICATION

Wireless communication uses electromagnetic waves to transmit messages at the speed of light. Complicated transmitters and simpler radio and television receivers allow massive communication at low cost. The only important limitation is that electromagnetic waves travel in straight lines and, unless bounced off reflecting layers of the atmosphere, soon leave the earth.

Highlights

Radio and television stations create a new form of mass communication, since the same messages can be sent into millions of homes at small cost to the sender.

Political propaganda by radio and television exercise a strong influence, especially in countries where the government maintains control of sending stations.

Radio and television tend to reduce class and regional differences within the radius of the broadcast.

AIR AND SPACE TRAVEL

Flying changed patterns of long-distance travel fundamentally. Old barriers fell. Mountains, deserts, and valleys ceased to matter much for overland travel; harbors, tides, and shoals ceased to affect travel overseas. For long flights earth became a sphere, making the Arctic a particularly strategic region. This is because major population concentrations are in the Northern Hemisphere, and the shortest air routes between distant population centers always follow the bulge of the earth northward toward the Arctic. The earth became still smaller when rocket propulsion opened the possibility of escape from earth's gravity and exploration of the solar system.

Highlights

Air and space travel changed transport routes and shortened time of travel between distant portions of the globe.

In case of a war, air and space travel mean that every state's borders are in danger.

Humanity's exploration of the earth and space beyond the earth continues with consequences—psychological, political, economic, and ecological—still unknown and unknowable.

An Illustration of the Westar IV Communication Satellite.

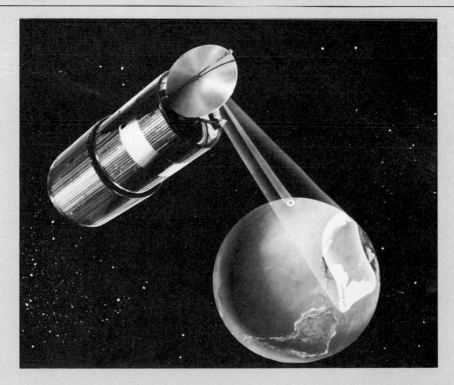

Chapter 24

WORLD WARS OF THE TWENTIETH CENTURY

1914 to 1945

The two world wars of the twentieth century, World War I, 1914–1918, and World War II, 1939–1945, were similar in many ways and should be discussed together. Both began in Europe and pitted Germany against a coalition of allies, and in both wars Germany was eventually defeated. But Germany's defeat came only after American resources and manpower were brought into action on European soil; and by 1945 the national power of the United States had clearly outstripped all other nations, not just in Europe but all round the globe. American predominance was temporary, to be sure. But the rise of the United States, together with that of the Union of Soviet Socialist Republics (USSR) and of Japan, marked the end of the era of world leadership by nations of western Europe—an era that dated back to the sixteenth century.

The wars marked the end of an era in another sense as well. Before 1914, democratic and parliamentary government, together with the private pursuit of profit in the marketplace, seemed the wave of the future—the path of progress along which all peoples might be expected eventually to travel on the way to a peaceful and prosperous future. However, the wars showed that things were not that simple. The brutality and bloodshed of warfare itself—an experience more shocking in 1914 than in 1939—was obviously incompatible with the old confidence in civilized progress. In addition, it became clear that politically organized effort, overriding the rules of private profit, could increase production and magnify national power far more efficiently than anyone had previously imagined. Managed economies worked wonders, more spectacularly in World War II than in World War I, making a return to unregulated private pursuit of profit impossible.

Democratic and parliamentary government also met with new challenges. The communist regime of Russia after 1917 and the Fascist regime of Italy after 1922 both emphasized an ideal of *solidarity*—class solidarity for Lenin and his fol-lowers in Russia, and national solidarity for Mussolini and his followers in Italy. Communists and Fascists agreed that democratic parties and elections simply allowed selfish pursuit of private interests. This, they claimed, was both wicked and inefficient. Instead, some sort of socialist management or corporate organization of human effort would get more done and leave the old liberal, bourgeois selfishness of prewar society behind. Fascism was discredited by the defeat of Germany and Italy in World War II; and after World War II, Russian communism began to look more and more inefficient. But the pre-1914 assurance that the democratic, liberal, and parliamentary recipe for good government was universally applicable and adequate for all situations could never be recovered.

Finally, the experience of World Wars I and II altered popular attitudes toward war. In 1914, the prospect of a short, victorious campaign was welcomed by millions of civilians who were called up to serve in the national army in accordance with mobilization plans laid down long in advance. War seemed a test of fitness, a way of asserting and preserving national greatness, and a useful instrument of statecraft. Years later, after two global wars, and after millions of people had been slaughtered, the glory and heroism of war diminished almost to the vanishing point. Yet fear of war did not prevent continued preparation for war. Instead, an ever more costly arms race broke out after 1945 even more vigorously than before 1914. And today, though nuclear weapons have made World War III plainly suicidal, that arms race continues.

In all these respects, the two great wars of the twentieth century constitute a turning point in world affairs, whose full implications and long-range consequences we do not yet know. But it looks as though they will mark the end of what used to be called the modern era of world history—an era that began about 1450 and ended, perhaps, in 1945. We have no name for the new era, if indeed the course of future events will make it seem proper to call the period since 1945 a new era. We who live through it can only wonder and wait to see how things turn out.

OUTBREAK OF WORLD WAR I

In Sarajevo, the capital of Bosnia, on June 28, 1914, an angry young man named Gavrilo Princip shot and killed Archduke Francis Ferdinand, heir to the throne of Austria-Hungary. Princip was a Serb, and the Austrians held the Serbian government responsible for the assassination. Friction between Serbia and the Austro-Hungarian monarchy was already acute. Serbs lived on both sides of the border between the two countries, and Serbian nationalists wanted to unite their people into a single sovereign state. So when Princip resorted to murder, the Austrian government decided to teach the Serbs a lesson. They believed, mistakenly, that other European governments would not support assassins; and, indeed, if Austrian demands on the Serbian government had been more moderate, or if the Serbian government had not gone very far toward meeting Austrian demands, it is likely that the crisis would

have remained limited to the Balkan cockpit where it started.

But the rival alliances into which the European great powers had divided since 1907 came immediately into play, making a diplomatic crisis into a catastrophe. Russia backed the Serbs; Germany backed the Austrians; France rallied to the Russian side against Germany; and Great Britain after hesitating and trying to find a peaceful solution through negotiation, finally came in on the side of France and Russia. Only Italy, which had been formally allied with Germany and Austria, held back. Thus the crisis escalated into full-scale war, breaking out between July 28, when Austria declared war on Serbia, and August 3, 1914, when Great Britain declared war against Germany and Austria.

One reason for the way things turned out was that the great powers of the European continent all had carefully worked out mobilization plans. These could be put into effect by a simple order, but once started, could not be altered without the risk of paralyzing confusion. Each plan was designed to bring a maximal number of soldiers into action in the shortest possible time, using railroads to deliver soldiers and supplies to strategic locations in accordance with very pre-

Triggering World War I This photograph shows the arrest of Gavrilo Princip (right) moments after he had fired the shots that killed the Archduke Franz Ferdinand, heir to the Hapsburg throne, in Sarajevo on June 28, 1914. Princip swallowed a poison capsule after firing his pistol but it only made him sick. He was therefore brought to trial by the Austrian authorities and being a minor (he was eighteen years of age), received the maximum penalty of twenty years imprisonment. He died in the hospital, of tuberculosis, in April 1918, six months before the Hapsburg empire collapsed as a result of the war his act triggered. The diverse styles of dress seen in the photograph reflect the clash of cultures that was then taking place in Bosnia, where western styles—both military and civilian—mingled with traditional local costume; and where Moslems wore the fez to permit them to put their foreheads to the ground when praying (as their faith required), Christians advertised their different identity by wearing caps and hats with brims.

cisely calculated timetables. Whichever army got going soonest with the largest forces would be able to impose its strategic plan on the enemy, and, according to plan, could then expect to win a decisive victory in a matter of a few weeks. Everything depended on speed, numbers, and the quality of troops and material brought to the field of battle. Delay or hesitation, once the first mobilization order had been given, was too risky to contemplate. As a result, the Austrian decision to attack the Serbs provoked Russian mobilization, quickly followed by German and French mobilization; and once rival mobilization plans went into action, there was no turning back.

As events showed, the German war plan was the most effective. A vast German army began to march across Belgium, intending to cross into northern France, surround Paris, and then take the French army, deployed along the German frontier, in the rear. The plan worked for the first few weeks, but as the Germans approached Paris, early in September, a gap opened between two of the advancing columns, and the French were able to attack through the hole that had opened up in the German front. Fearing that their vanguard might be cut off, the Germans decided to withdraw behind the Marne River on September 9, 1914.

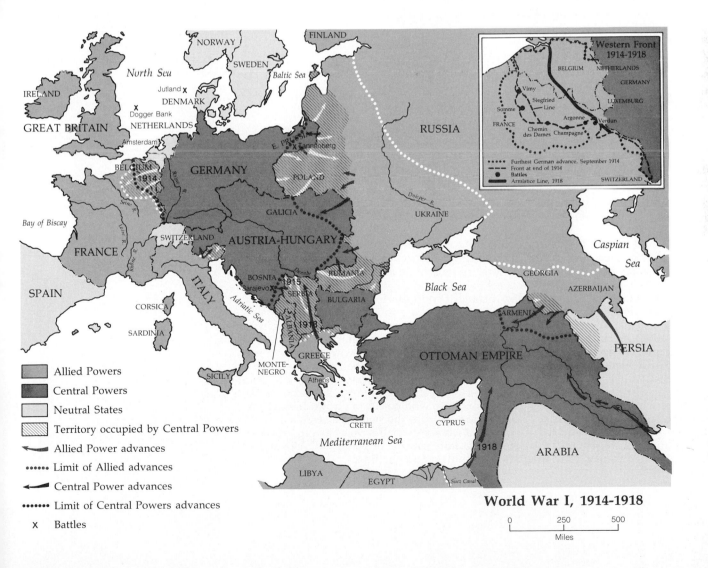

World War I, 1914-1918

Allied Powers
Central Powers
Neutral States
Territory occupied by Central Powers
Allied Power advances
Limit of Allied advances
Central Power advances
Limit of Central Powers advances
x   Battles

World War I: The Glory and the Pain War became unpopular in Europe and America during World War I in a new way because of the enormous discrepancy between what everyone had expected and what actually happened in the trenches of the Western Front. On the left is a photograph of parading American soldiers, marching through London in 1917. Marching to music with plaudits from the crowd was exhilerating in itself; and bringing victory to the Allied side, as the Americans eventually were able to do, made war seem glorious again. Such enthusiasm echoed the far more frantic enthusiasm that had greeted the outbreak of fighting in 1914, when people in England, France, and Germany welcomed release from the frictions and boredom of everyday, confidently expecting glorious victory, according to plan, by or before Christmas, 1914. On the right, you may glimpse the painful reality of what the war actually meant for those who got to the front. It shows a wounded soldier about to be carried off from the rear on a stretcher. The narrow confines of the hastily built trench are clear but you have to imagine the mud and blood, and the depressing daily routine of perpetual alert and ever present danger from machine gun bullets and shelling.

Stalemate and Intensified War Effort

This meant that the German plan had failed; but the French plan for attacking Germany directly across the frontier had also failed disastrously, and Russian armies, advancing into East Prussia, were turned back by September 15 as well. Even the Austrian forces assigned to conquer the little state of Serbia were unsuccessful. Machine guns and rifle fire proved far more lethal against attacking infantry than anyone had expected. The only thing to do was to dig in furiously, for even hastily built trenches could protect soldiers from rifle and machine gun bullets.

In France, accordingly, a system of trenches came into existence by the end of 1914 that ran unbrokenly from the Swiss frontier in the south to the shores of the English Channel in the north. Efforts to break through proved futile throughout the ensuing four years, though both sides tried, over and over again, to win decisive victory on this, the western, front. In the east, geographic distances were such that trench systems never ran continuously along the entire front. Armies were therefore able to take the offensive and move scores or even hundreds of miles at a time, forward and back. But until 1917 stalemate also prevailed on the eastern front. Even the most smashing victory soon petered out because an advancing army inevitably ran out of supplies, while the defeated forces recovered their fighting capacity by getting closer to their own sources of food and ammunition.

In this unexpected situation, European governments saw two ways of winning. One was to find new allies, thus extending the front, and strengthening one side at the expense of the other. By 1916, diplomatic pressure, promises of territorial gains, and a coup d'état in Greece divided most of Europe between the two sides. Italy, Romania, and Greece joined France, England and Russia (The Allies); Bulgaria and Turkey joined Germany and Austria (The Central Powers). Even after Serbia was overrun by a combined German, Austrian, and Bulgarian offensive in 1915, the Serbian army fought on, based on Greek soil; and the Central Powers, despite their initial victories in Belgium and northern France, and subsequent advances into Polish territory in the east, remained almost completely surrounded by hostile forces. Until 1917, when the United States entered the war, the policy of finding new allies therefore proved ineffective in tipping the balance one way or the other in any decisive fashion. It simply engaged more countries and peoples in the struggle and made the eventual peace settlement more complicated.

The second way to win the war was to intensify mobilization, bringing more men into combat and equipping them with more and more artillery and other heavy weapons. Military experts agreed that a really massive preliminary bombardment by thousands of guns could smash the enemy's trenches and permit a decisive breakthrough. The flaw in this plan was that surprise became impossible as the open trenches of 1914 were turned into ever more elaborate underground fortifications and became able to withstand even a prolonged bombardment.

Consequently, an energetic British effort to win the war by building a new mass army equipped with hitherto unheard of quantities of artillery turned out to be in vain. A long and bloody Battle of the Somme in 1916 only sufficed to relieve pressure on the French, who were barely able to withstand an intense German assault aimed at the fortress of Verdun. But as before, the end result was stalemate.

Despite these failures, mobilization of the rear to provide more and more shells and other supplies for the front had important consequences for European countries. In effect, the principal combatant governments learned to make their nations over into a single war-making firm, maximizing output of goods and soldiers needed for the war effort by subordinating everything else to a national plan. Rationing of scarce goods, allocating critical materials, and keying industrial production to the needs of the armed forces all came into being. The effect was to raise war-making capacity to unimagined heights, but all for naught, as one attack after another failed to achieve expected results.

1917–1918: The Years of Decision

Some governments were, nonetheless, better equipped than others to mobilize resources efficiently. The Austro-Hungarian monarchy, for ex-

THE SEALED TRAIN

Vladimir Ilich Ulyanov took the name "Lenin" when he became a revolutionary. The czarist government arrested him; later he fled from Russia and lived in Switzerland. He was there when World War I broke out. Switzerland remained neutral, completely surrounded by warring nations.

News of the March 1917 uprisings in Petrograd, the Russian capital, made Lenin desperate to get back. He wanted to take command of the Bolshevik party he had founded and carry the revolution onward to more and more radical stages. He wanted to end the war by overthrowing the landlords and capitalists, first in Russia and then in all the world. But how could he hope to escape from his Swiss refuge?

German agents in Switzerland knew a lot about Lenin and his plan for "turning imperialist war into class war." They thought, "Why not help Lenin to get back home and let him stir up the Russians to fight one another instead of fighting us?" The German Supreme Command had no objection. When the kaiser heard of the plan, he suggested that Lenin should be sent copies of all his latest speeches!

But Lenin was afraid. Perhaps the Germans only wanted to capture him by offering to let him ride a train through Germany to neutral Sweden. And his enemies might discredit him as a German agent if he took advantage of such an offer. All the same, he simply had to get back if all his dreams and life's work were not to fail.

ample, had to depend on help from Germany to make up for gaps in home production of artillery and other war goods. Internal frictions among the different nationalities of the empire became more intense as the war went on and paralyzed the state by 1918. Turkey, too, depended on Germany for war supplies; and frictions between the Turkish government and some of its Arab subjects turned into a critical weakness by the last months of the war.

But the most important country that got into serious trouble on the home front was Russia. The czarist government achieved remarkable results in increasing its armament production, but by 1917 food and other essential civilian commodities began to disappear from the cities where all the guns and ammunition were manufactured. Total food production declined because so many

men were taken from their villages to serve in the army. Those who remained on the land began to consume more of what they raised because there was nothing for them to buy in town.

Economic hardship fostered political discontent. Revolutionary parties had long existed in Russia, and the handful of Marxists who followed Lenin (original name, Vladimir Ilich Ulyanov, 1870–1924) soon began to win mass support in the hungry cities. Distrust and demoralization weakened the czar's government, and in March 1917 strikes by armament and other industrial workers in the capital, together with mounting criticism from the upper classes, persuaded the czar to abdicate. A provisional government then proposed to hold elections for a Constituent Assembly that would draft a new constitution for Russia; in the meanwhile the war had to go on.

On April 9, 1917, Lenin settled the issue. He would accept the German offer, provided the Germans would seal off the train so that no one could get on or off while passing through German territory. In this way, Lenin hoped that he could escape the charge of cooperating with the Germans. A train was made ready at once, and about twenty Russian revolutionaries, chosen by Lenin, got on board.

The trip lasted several days, with long delays in various switching yards. Each time the train stopped, the little group of Russians wondered whether they would all be arrested or perhaps killed. But the delays were caused by the fact that the German authorities had to clear the plan for sending Lenin and his friends to Russia through Sweden with officials of the Swedish government. By April 13, all was ready. Lenin crossed the Baltic to Sweden by ferryboat. The travelers continued by rail to Stockholm and then to Finland and so at last to Petrograd, Russia's capital. They arrived there on April 16, exactly a week after leaving Switzerland.

Both Lenin and the Germans got what they wanted from this deal. Lenin not only got back to Russia; within seven months he won supreme power and a chance to put his ideas into practice. From the start, his propaganda against the war proved very effective. Many Russian soldiers listened to Lenin and stopped fighting the Germans. As a result, the Russian army melted away and Germany was able to concentrate its remaining strength on the western front.

Shortages simply got worse; and when Lenin proclaimed the slogan "Peace, Land, Bread," more and more Russians agreed "Peace" was obviously needed to set things right. "Land" invited peasants on landlords' estates to seize control of the fields they cultivated. "Bread" meant life itself to hungry city dwellers, though how anyone would be able to deliver it to them was never made clear. Given the situation in Russia, Lenin's slogans were irresistible. In particular, peasants drafted into the army decided that they had to get back to their villages in a hurry so as to be sure of getting their share of the land. Desertions therefore multiplied, and the discipline of the army wavered. Continuation of the war became impossible.

On the night of November 6–7, 1917, Lenin seized power in the capital city of Petrograd (formerly St. Petersburg, later renamed Leningrad). Red Guards, organized by workers in the factories of the city, were the instrument he used; but the real basis of Lenin's power was the appeal of his propaganda and the small corps of dedicated revolutionaries he had shaped into the Bolshevik faction of the Russian Social Democratic (that is, Marxist) party before the war. Marxist doctrine held that proletarian, socialist revolution was destined to occur first in the most industrialized countries, not in a predominantly peasant land like Russia. And so when Lenin took power, he confidently expected revolution to break out at any moment in Germany, France, and England. To hurry socialist revolution along, he declared peace unilaterally, denounced capitalist governments for continuing the war, and published secret treaties according to which the czar's gov-

ernment had agreed to share the spoils from the Austrian and Ottoman empires with France, Britain, and Italy.

Disintegration of the Russian army became almost complete after Lenin took power, and the Germans were therefore able to advance eastward more or less at will. But they did not want to go too far; instead, they wished to profit from Russia's collapse by concentrating their forces on the western front, where decisive victory remained to be won. Small bodies of German troops remained in the east, and in 1918 the Germans signed a peace treaty with the Bolsheviks at Brest Litovsk that separated Poland, the Ukraine, Transcaucasia, and the Baltic provinces from Russia.

Success in the east was meaningless, however, unless the Germans could also defeat the French and British in the west. That became far more difficult after April 6, 1917, when the United States became a belligerent. Throughout the war, Americans had prospered by supplying food and munitions to the Allies. When the Germans responded by declaring unrestricted submarine warfare in the Atlantic and began to sink American ships, President Woodrow Wilson asked Congress to declare war. It took time to train American soldiers and send them to France; but as the

Political Prophets of the Twentieth Century Two visions of how international society ought to be ordered emerged from the confusion of World War I. One was based in Russia and proclaimed the onset of world Communism; the other, based in the United States, advocated a scarcely less revolutionary ideal of international cooperation based on popular sovereignty. The preeminent spokesmen for these rival ideals are shown here. Above, Nicolai Lenin's bald head and piercing glance suggests his fiercely domineering, charismatic personality. Lenin was a Marxist but refused to wait for spontaneous, mass revolution as predicted by Karl Marx. Instead, he organized a tightly disciplined following, the Bolsheviks, and succeeded in seizing power in Russia, where wartime hardships and failures had discredited the old regime. But until the day of his death in 1924, Lenin expected proletarian revolution to break out in the more developed capitalist countries of Western Europe and did all he could to hasten world revolution, using the secret, conspiratorial methods that had been so successful in Russia. Below, is a photograph of Lenin's principal rival, Woodrow Wilson, President of the United Sates. Wilson's hope for a League of Nations to adjust international disputes peaceably assumed that popularly elected governments, genuinely reflecting the will of the people, would never again want to make war. He, too, did all he could to make his vision come true; but, like Lenin, he failed.

Russian army disintegrated, a new American army was coming into being, thus counterbalancing Russia's collapse.

Moreover, American military power was matched by a powerful propaganda, designed in part to counteract Lenin's appeals for socialist revolution. In January 1918, President Wilson summed up American war aims in fourteen points, including the "right of national self-determination" and the establishment of a League of Nations that would settle future international quarrels peaceably. America, Wilson declared, was fighting a war to end war and make the world safe for democracy. It was a program quite as revolutionary in central and eastern Europe as Lenin's Marxism, and it appealed powerfully to war-weary people everywhere.

Early in 1918, German troops began their final offensive on the western front. For a while it looked as though a decisive breakthrough might be possible, but the weary French and British held, and fresh American units hurried into battle. Soon the balance tipped in the Allies' favor, and the Germans started retreating. Before the battle line reached the German border, however, revolution broke out in the rear of the German army, and a new, socialist German government signed an armistice on November 11, 1918. The war was over at last, for Turkey, Bulgaria, and Austria had also admitted defeat in the preceding weeks.

THE PEACE SETTLEMENT: 1918–1923

The armistice ended the fighting but said nothing about the terms of peace. Peacemaking was complicated by the fact that both Russia and the United States rejected treaties defining postwar territorial arrangements that the Allies had made during the war. President Wilson advocated "open covenants, openly arrived at" and wanted to draw national boundaries anew on the basis of majority preferences among the local populations. Lenin continued to denounce the whole capitalist system and expected further revolutions to bring fellow Marxists to power in other European countries. The communist government of Russia simply refused to have any dealings with the "Allied and Associated Powers," to give the victors the name they officially assumed at the peace conference. This meant that peace could not come to eastern Europe until 1921, when civil wars in the Ukraine and elsewhere had been fought to a finish. It took even longer for peace to come to the Near East, where a Greek-Turkish war lasted until 1923.

In the Far East, upheaval continued in China throughout the interwar period, though Japanese expansion was temporarily checked in 1922. During the war, Japan had conquered German colonial holdings in the Far East, then demanded special privileges in China, and when the Russian empire seemed about to break up also sent an army into Russia's Far Eastern provinces.

The victorious allies entered the peace-making process with differing aims. The United States wished to check the Japanese and establish democratic governments in Europe so as to be able to get back to what soon came to be called "normalcy." The British government had similar goals and also wished to get control of Palestine and Iraq so as to safeguard the route to India. The French wanted the return of Alsace and Lorraine, provinces taken from them in 1871; but more important, they wished to make sure that Germany could never again become so powerful as to threaten French security. The Italians wanted territories along the Adriatic and in the eastern Mediterranean that they had been promised in 1916 in return for their entry into the war.

But the victors were only partly in control of the situation. Throughout eastern Europe, where the Austrian, Ottoman, and Russian governments had ruled before the war, confusion reigned. Socialists and nationalists collided, and rival nationalities disputed rights to nearly every territory and province. Germany, too, was in turmoil. Everywhere socialists split between those who supported Lenin's recipe for the future and moderates who preferred to cooperate with the Western powers. The choice for central and eastern Europe rested, in a sense, between Wilson's ideal of democratic, national self-determination and Lenin's ideal of proletarian revolution. But French and British wishes also mattered; and they, burdened with war debts owed to the United

Peacemaking in 1919: Warmaking in 1939 On the left, the "Big Three" of the Paris Peace Conference, 1919–20, are seen walking along a street between sessions. David Lloyd-George, Prime Minister of Great Britain, is on the left; George Clemenceau, Premier of France, is in the middle; and President Woodrow Wilson of the United States is on the right. The three leaders differed about how to make a just and enduring peace; and their eventual compromises, embodied in the Treaty of Versailles, were imposed on Germany in 1920. Nearly all Germans felt that the Treaty was unjust; and in the 1930s, after Adolf Hitler had come to power, Germany shattered the Treaty of Versailles bit by bit. Hitler first rearmed and reoccupied the Rhineland; then he demanded the right to bring Germans living in other lands into the Third Reich. He succeeded in extending German borders to embrace Austria and German-populated parts of Czechoslovakia, but when he also demanded parts of Poland, where Germans lived scattered among Polish populations, France and Britain reluctantly went to war. The photograph on the right shows the scene in the Reichstag on September 1, 1939, when Hitler announced that German soldiers had begun to march into Poland to liberate their fellow nationals, thus inaugurating World War II. Hitler stands in the exact center of this photograph, a small and almost inconspicuous figure, amidst a forest of arms raised in the Nazi salute.

States, hoped to punish the Germans and make them pay for the costs of the war by imposing heavy reparations payments.

When the Peace Conference met at Paris in 1919, therefore, the problem was how to combine Wilson's principles of democratic self-determination with punishment for Germany, while hoping that Lenin's challenge to the existing social order would soon disappear. It made for an unsatisfactory peace. The Treaty of Versailles, presented to the Germans for their signature in 1919, imposed unilateral disarmament and sliced off bits of German territory to allow Poland access to the sea, while prohibiting German Austria from ever uniting with Germany. Nearly all Germans felt that such provisions violated Wilson's promises. Even more deeply resented was the "war guilt clause" which declared that Germany had been responsible for starting the war and therefore had to pay reparations for all the war's costs. This provision was unenforceable in practice and threw a monkey wrench into the new League of Nations, upon which President Wilson pinned his hopes for future peace.

Further east in Europe, events on the ground mattered more than decisions at Paris. The collapse of German power in 1918 provoked complicated civil wars in ex-czarist lands among communists, "White" Russians, and various kinds of nationalists. France and Britain sent expeditionary forces to Russian ports and gave some help to the "Whites." The United States likewise sent a few soldiers into the Far Eastern provinces, as much to watch the Japanese as to oppose the communists. But war weariness was almost as intense in the West as in eastern Europe itself, and by 1920 the contestants were ready to make peace. Resulting treaties set up independent states throughout the western borderlands of the old Russian Empire. Russia's frontiers with the newly independent states of Finland, Estonia, Latvia, Lithuania, and Poland conformed pretty closely to the existing military lines of demarcation. But the Ukraine, Transcaucasia, and the Far Eastern provinces all returned to Russia within a very few years.

Hunger and disease were rampant, and in 1921 Lenin announced a "New Economic Policy" whereby private trading was allowed. It looked as though the communist principle of public ownership of the means of production had proved unworkable, just as critics in the West had always said. Lenin's ideals, as much as Wilson's, had indeed been compromised. Europe seemed about to settle into a new mold, giving France primacy on the continent, thanks to German disarmament and to alliances the French concluded with most of the new states of eastern Europe.

To the south, the treaty prepared at Paris for the Ottoman Empire proved unenforceable. Turkish national feeling rebelled against the provisions of the treaty that assigned territory on the eastern shore of the Aegean to Greece; and when the Greeks tried to enforce the treaty, Kemal Mustapha organized a makeshift Turkish army, which defeated them and proceeded to drive all Christians from the Asian side of the Aegean. A million and a half refugees fled to Greece. In return, Turks and Bulgarians were expelled from Greek soil to make room for the newcomers. The Treaty of Lausanne ratified and regulated the mass exchange of populations in 1923.

The Arab lands of the Ottoman Empire were assigned as "mandates" to France (Syria and Lebanon) and Britain (Palestine and Iraq). A mandate was a new legal invention, requiring the administering power to treat the territory in question as a temporary trust under the supervision of the League of Nations. Eventually, it was assumed, mandated lands would become capable of democratic self-government. Former German colonies in Africa and the Far East were also made into mandates and assigned to one or another of the victors, including Japan. Local populations sometimes resisted, as happened in Syria, but not for long.

Palestine presented a more complicated problem. During the war, the British government had endorsed the idea of establishing a national home for Jews in Palestine. This Zionist ideal had begun to gain momentum among European Jews from the 1890s, but Arabs in Palestine opposed the idea vigorously. The new British administrators antagonized both parties by vainly trying to find a compromise.

In the Far East, Japan's wartime activities in China and the Russian Far Eastern provinces had aroused intense American suspicion. Britain, allied with Japan since 1903, felt compelled to cooperate with the United States. When the Japanese faced up to this fact, they decided to draw back. The decisive negotiations took place in 1922 in Washington, where a naval limitations treaty defined the number of warships the principal naval powers of the world could have. Britain, the United States, and Japan agreed upon a 5:5:3 ratio for capital ships. Japan's overall inferiority nevertheless assured the Japanese navy of the preponderance in Far Eastern waters it already enjoyed, since neither the British nor the Americans could ever expect to concentrate their whole fleet so far away from home bases. But the Washington treaties of 1922 did nothing to stabilize conditions in China, where local disorders dating back to the overthrow of the Manchu Dynasty in 1911 continued to distract the country.

THE LONE EAGLE

Charles Augustus Lindbergh, born in Detroit (1902) and raised in Minnesota, was too young to take part in World War I, but he learned to admire the aviators who dueled in flimsy airplanes high above the trenches in France. As soon as he could, he enlisted as a flying cadet in the United States Army Air Corps. When he graduated, the Air Corps put him on reserve status, and he got a job flying the mail between St. Louis and Chicago.

After doing this for two years, learning a lot about wind and weather and the ways of airplanes, he decided to compete for a prize offered for the first nonstop flight between New York and Paris. Backers in St. Louis paid for a plane built to his specifications. They named it *Spirit of St. Louis*.

On May 20, 1927, all was ready. A few minutes before 8:00 A.M., Lindbergh lifted the overloaded plane off the grass of Roosevelt Airfield at Garden City, Long Island, New York, and headed for Paris. Flying in those days was rather hit-or-miss. For long hours Lindbergh could not be sure where he was, for everywhere the ocean looked the same. He could figure out how far he had gone through the air, but had to guess how much the winds were blowing his plane from its compass course.

A second problem was sleepiness. He took off early in the morning and landed in Paris late in the evening of the following day, after more than thirty-three hours in the air. The noise of the engine and the whistle of the wind sounded monotonously; yet Lindbergh had to stay awake and keep the plane headed on a steady course. Otherwise he might waste precious gas by swerving to and fro across the ocean, or he might even plummet into the sea and drown.

The peace settlements, 1918–1923, were therefore imperfect and partial. Seeds of future troubles were all too apparent, especially in Europe, where a disappointed Italy became the seat of an ambitious Fascist government in 1922, and where German resentment against the Treaty of Versailles was deep and abiding.

STABILIZATION AND RENEWED CRISIS: 1923–1933

Russian economic recovery came slowly under the New Economic Policy. The communist regime was weakened first by Lenin's incapacity (an assassin's bullet followed by a stroke) and then by his death in 1924. The United States, too, withdrew from European affairs in 1920 when the Senate refused to ratify the Versailles treaty. Relations between the two remaining victors, France and Britain, also unraveled, when the French attempted to enforce their rights under the Versailles treaty by occupying part of Germany in 1923 in order to compel the delivery of reparations. Economic collapse then threatened to provoke either a communist or a fascist revolution in Germany, and this prospect brought the United States back into action. An economic settlement of sorts was agreed upon (the Dawes Plan), whereby American bankers lent money to Germany, thus allowing the Germans to pay rep-

The struggle to stay awake was his most difficult task, for the plane functioned perfectly and his guesswork about the winds turned out to be very nearly right. He sighted Ireland on the second day and could then fly on to Paris by following the map from point to point across southern England and northern France.

As he approached Paris a new problem arose. A vast crowd streamed out to greet him as news of his approach spread through the city. (His plane had been recognized over Ireland, and newspapers had followed its progress hour by hour thereafter.) And it was getting dark. How could the weary aviator see the landing place? Cars with their headlights gleaming were hastily arranged to show Lindbergh where to land, and the police kept the runway clear until the plane touched down safely.

Then the crowd broke through police lines. Excited people even started to tear the canvas skin off the *Spirit of St. Louis* for souvenirs. Lindbergh was completely taken aback. He struggled to get his plane safely locked in a hangar. Then he collapsed from fatigue. He awoke to worldwide renown.

Lindbergh's later life was anticlimactic. He soon came to hate the publicity and hero worship that surrounded him. In 1932 his eldest son was kidnapped. This caused a second wave of intense public excitement and ended in tragedy, for the kidnapper killed the child. Lindbergh was later accused of being too much impressed by Hitler's achievements, and President Roosevelt refused to allow him to fight in World War II. Thus politics clipped the "Lone Eagle's" wings; Lindbergh became an inconspicuous civilian consultant to airplane manufacturers.

arations to France and Britain, who, in turn, paid installments on their war debts to the United States. This arrangement worked for a while and even provoked a burst of industrial prosperity in Germany. The United States, too, enjoyed a tremendous postwar boom as new mass-produced consumer goods—automobiles, radios, washing machines, and so forth—came into more and more American homes and profoundly changed old patterns of living.

In 1929 boom turned into bust, following a rhythm that had existed for centuries but which no one really understood. Bank failures in Austria triggered panic in the United States. Suddenly the loans that had sustained the German recovery were no longer available. The same financial panic closed off credit for factories in the United States, so manufacturers had to shut down or cut back production drastically. In earlier times, crises of this kind had been endurable because most economic activity was agricultural and many of the people thrown out of work when factories shut down could go back to relatives on the farm and wait until new jobs opened up again. In the 1930s this was no longer possible in countries like Germany and the United States. Too many people lived in cities, without relatives in the country they could turn to.

Private charity and public relief were the alternatives if unemployed workers were not to starve. But why were idle factories unable to produce goods, and why were idle workers unable

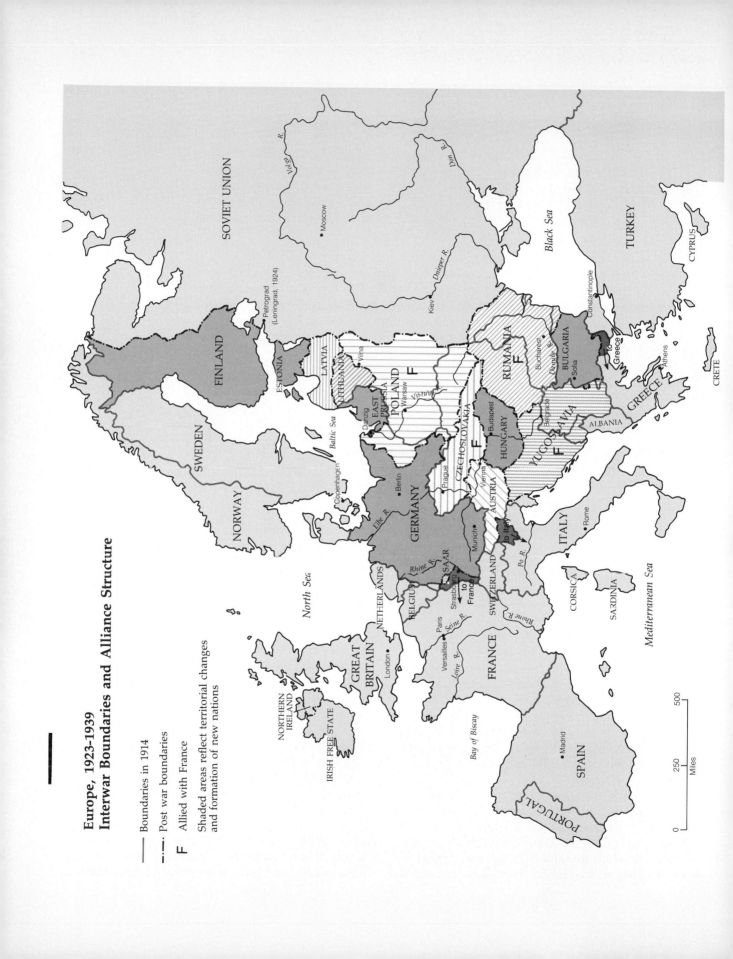

Europe, 1923-1939
Interwar Boundaries and Alliance Structure

—— Boundaries in 1914

—·—·— Post war boundaries

F Allied with France

Shaded areas reflect territorial changes and formation of new nations

SOVIET UNION

• Moscow

Volga R.

Don R.

Dnieper R.

• Kiev

Black Sea

TURKEY

• Constantinople

CYPRUS

Athens •

CRETE

GREECE

to Greece

FINLAND

Petrograd (Leningrad, 1924) •

ESTONIA

LATVIA

Vilna

LITHUANIA

Danzig

EAST PRUSSIA

POLAND

Warsaw •

Vistula

F

RUMANIA

F

Bucharest •

Danube R.

BULGARIA

Sofia •

YUGOSLAVIA

F

Belgrade •

ALBANIA

SWEDEN

Baltic Sea

Copenhagen •

CZECHOSLOVAKIA

F

Prague •

• Berlin

GERMANY

Elbe R.

Budapest •

HUNGARY

Vienna •

AUSTRIA

• Munich

to Italy

ITALY

• Rome

Po R.

NORWAY

North Sea

NETHERLANDS

BELGIUM

Rhine R.

SAAR

Strasbourg to France

SWITZERLAND

Rhone R.

CORSICA

SARDINIA

Mediterranean Sea

GREAT BRITAIN

London •

Paris •

Seine R.

Versailles •

Loire R.

FRANCE

NORTHERN IRELAND

IRISH FREE STATE

Bay of Biscay

Madrid •

SPAIN

PORTUGAL

0   250   500

Miles

Boom and Bust between the Wars The Empire State building, shown here, aptly symbolizes the business and engineering accomplishments of the inter-war years in the United States and the disappointments that followed the stock market crash of 1929. Planners undertook to construct the tallest building in the world at a time when the boom of the 1920s made profits from erecting a new office building in New York look like a sure thing; but by 1931, when the building was finished, the Great Depression had set in. Just as had been planned, the hundred and two storied structure rose 1250 feet above the sidewalk and remained the tallest building in the world for the next twenty three years. But it also became something of a white elephant for its owners since rents fell and tenants were hard to find in the depression years and when prosperity returned, the mid-town location of the Empire State building in Manhattan lost some of its prestige when new sites, both uptown and downtown, overtook the older business center of the city.

to buy what they needed to live? No one had a good explanation at the time. Marxist prophecies about the crisis of capitalism seemed to be coming true. The situation was made more acute by the fact that beginning in 1928 the Russian government, now controlled by Josef Stalin (1879–

1953), had launched a vast Five Year Plan of industrial development and continued to announce new victories in the struggle to build modern power plants and factories at a time when economic depression made life miserable for millions in the West. Russian peasants paid the cost of Stalin's forced pace of industrialization by providing both labor and food for the industrial effort without getting anything back in return; but this was not clear at the time.

DRIFT TOWARD WAR: 1933–1939

Economic suffering and discontent in Germany and the United States triggered drastic political departures. In Germany, Adolf Hitler (1889–1945) and the National Socialist German Workers' Party (Nazis, for short) came to power in January 1933. In March of the same year, Franklin D. Roosevelt (1882–1945) became president and launched what he called the New Deal to cope with the Great Depression. Hitler and Roosevelt, despite the many contradictory currents that flowed among their supporters, had this in common: they both fell back on World War I methods of national mobilization to meet the crisis of the depression and were fairly successful in doing so. On other matters, the two regimes differed profoundly, for Hitler was a fanatic nationalist, intent on undoing the Versailles settlement, while Roosevelt was a democrat and an optimist, with no very deep convictions about international affairs.

Hitler set out to establish a fascist dictatorship, far more efficient and powerful than the original fascist regime in Italy. Between 1922 and 1927, Benito Mussolini (1883–1945) had fastened the dictatorship of his Fascist party on Italy; but Mussolini's praise of national solidarity at home and imperial expansion abroad met with a mixed reception among Italians. Old patterns of peasant life still prevailed in the south, and the Roman Catholic church together with other conservatives acted as a second restraining force. Mussolini's efforts to build a Mediterranean empire at the expense of Yugoslavia and Greece were successfully checked by France and Britain, acting through the League of Nations. But in 1933, when Mussolini attacked Ethiopia to revenge the defeat Italian soldiers had suffered in 1896, the League huffed and puffed but failed to prevent the Italians from conquering the whole of Ethiopia by 1936.

Before coming to power, Hitler partly modeled his Nazi party on Mussolini's Fascists; but national socialism, as defined by Hitler, differed from Italian fascism in being racist. Hitler proclaimed the superiority of the so-called Aryan race and asserted that German Aryans had been corrupted by Jews and other inferior races. One of his goals on coming to power in 1933 was to drive Jews from all walks of German life. He also wanted to restore German military power and had to cope with all the millions of unemployed whose votes had helped him come to power. Vast public works, especially road building, reduced unemployment; and after 1935, when Hitler felt it safe to denounce the Versailles treaty and begin rearmament openly, the unemployment problem disappeared.

By 1936, French and British opposition to Italy's invasion of Ethiopia made Mussolini into Hitler's ally; and between 1936 and 1939 Italy and Germany helped a fascist government, headed by Francisco Franco (1892–1975), come to power in Spain after a bitter civil war. The demoralization of the French, torn by domestic strife and unwilling to accept a wartime style of national mobilization, had become plain. Hitler therefore turned attention to building up the German armed forces so as to be able to undo the territorial settlement of 1919 on Germany's eastern border. Appealing to the right of national self-determination, Hitler annexed Austria and then dismembered Czechoslovakia in 1938; in 1939, he turned on Poland. This time resistance was better organized, and when Hitler persisted, World War II broke out.

In the United States recovery from the depression remained precarious until late in the 1930s, when armament programs designed to face up to German and Japanese threats had the effect of mopping up remaining pockets of unemployment. The Americans began rearmament reluctantly, but events in Europe together with a resumption of Japanese expansion on the main-

land of Asia tipped the balance of opinion within the United States.

Japan's aggression against China began in 1931. It was triggered, at least in part, by the fact that after years of disorder and sharp division among local war lords, China seemed about to unite under the leadership of Chiang Kai-shek (1887–1975). Chiang became leader of the Kuomintang Party with Communist support. But in 1927 he quarreled with them, expelling all of the Communist faction from the Kuomintang Party and killing all he could lay hands on. Survivors fled to the countryside. Under the leadership of Mao Tse-tung (1893–1976), the Chinese Communists eventually made their way to the province of Yenan, on the Russian border, where a trickle of supplies from the Soviet Union helped them keep going. In the rest of China, however, old war lords were compelled, one by one, to come to terms with Chiang's forces or face defeat.

Before China's unification could be completed, however, the Japanese intervened in Manchuria. Swiftly they occupied the entire province and proclaimed a descendant of the Manchu Dynasty as Emperor of Manchukuo. The League of Nations denounced but failed to check Japan's aggression, and neither the Chinese nor the Americans were willing to recognize the new state of affairs in the Far East. Instead, animosity increased and in 1936 the Japanese invaded north China, pushing southward along the coast and trying vainly to subdue the vast bulk of China completely. Rapid build up of heavy industry in Manchuria helped to support the Japanese armed forces, which began to play a more and more independent role, not only on the mainland of Asia but within Japan itself. The so-called China incident, committing the Japanese army to operations on the mainland, merged into World War II after 1941. Indeed, the conventional date for the beginning of the war, September 1, 1939, is arbitrary. Active operations in Asia dated back to 1932, when, from a Far Eastern point of view, the war really started.

Before describing World War II, a few words should be said about other parts of the world and how they fared during the interwar years. Africa remained politically quiet under colonial rulers. Even Italy's conquest of Ethiopia had little obvious effect on the rest of the continent. India, on

Two Men Who Shook the British Empire This photograph shows Mohandas Gandhi and Jawaharlal Nehru conferring in 1942. At that time, the Congress Party they headed was debating what to do about Britain's war with Japan that had just begun. The two leaders decided to demand that the British grant India independence at once and proposed to resist all efforts at mobilizing their country against the Japanese. The British promptly jailed them for the duration of the war but mass protests that had stirred all India in the 1920s and 1930s, when Gandhi first organized civil disobedience against British rule, were muted by the fact that most Indians did not want to be overrun by Japan. That risk seemed very real when the Japanese occupied India's neighbor, Burma, in 1942, and in fact the British were able to use Indian manpower and resources in their struggle against the Japanese quite effectively. Yet when the war ended, India's independence followed swiftly in 1947, accompanied by bloody riots between Moslems and Hindus. Gandhi's efforts to halt the violence led to his assassination in 1948. Nehru on the other hand became the first prime minister of India and retained that office until his death in 1964.

the other hand, became the scene of a struggle between the British rulers and the Congress party, whose leader, Mohandas Gandhi (1869–1948), demanded independence and national self-determination. He preached passive resistance, relying on "soul force" to overcome opposition. The British found Gandhi's campaigns very embarrassing, for how could they support democracy and self-determination in Europe and deny it in India? Several times Gandhi went to jail after defying British regulations; but this only increased his following in India. On the other hand, Indian Moslems were uncomfortable with Gandhi's movement, fearing that an independent India would become a Hindu India in which their religious identity and social status might be undermined. By the late 1930s some Indian Moslems had begun to demand an independent state of their own, separate from India. This may have strengthened the British position in India in the short run, but in another sense it simply consolidated opposition among another segment of the Indian population against continuation of British imperial rule.

In Latin America, the interwar years brought no very conspicuous changes. A bitter war between Paraguay and Bolivia ended in 1935 when mediators arranged a new boundary between the two nations. Further north, relations between Mexico and the United States entered upon a comparatively friendly era after 1933, when President Roosevelt proclaimed a Good Neighbor policy, which meant, in effect, that old U.S. claims to compensation for properties confiscated by the Mexican government during and after the revolution of 1911 would not be pursued any further.

Elsewhere, in the islands of the Pacific and in the British Dominions of Canada, Australia, and New Zealand, for example, life went on quietly for the most part. World affairs were dominated by the drama of European politics where Hitler's challenge to existing international relationships had become obvious and urgent by the mid-1930s. When war began in Europe in September 1939, the struggle soon spread round the globe, making it a world war, more truly than in 1914–1918.

WORLD WAR II: INITIAL AXIS VICTORIES, 1939–1941

France and Britain reluctantly came to Poland's aid in September 1939 when the German army launched its attack. Memories of World War I weighed on everyone's mind, in Germany as well as elsewhere. No rejoicings like those of 1914 took place. But Hitler had prepared the ground for victory this time rather more skillfully than the German government of 1914 had done. First of all, he signed a non-aggression treaty with Russia on August 23, 1939, just a week before the war began. Secret clauses partitioned Poland between the two powers and provided that Russia would supply Germany with food and other raw materials needed for the war effort. Stalin, who had previously been among the most vehement of Hitler's enemies, had changed sides and by doing so prevented a repetition of the World War I blockade, which had done a good deal to weaken the German war economy.

Blitzkrieg

Hitler had also prepared his armies for what the Germans called "Blitzkrieg"—lightning war. This referred to the use of tanks, trucks, and airplanes to speed up the pace of military action. Columns of tanks, supported by motorized infantry and low-flying airplanes, could break

through on a narrow front, penetrate many miles into the rear, and, by attacking headquarters, disrupt the enemy command and control system. In such a situation, it was always unclear just who had surrounded whom, for tanks needed fuel and ammunition in enormous quantity and without it were helpless. But troops cut off from headquarters, with an enemy in the rear, and with hostile airplanes overhead, were likely to panic; and an armored column, probing the enemy rear, could often capture the gasoline it needed to keep on advancing. Blitzkrieg tactics had been dreamed up by British officers at the very end of World War I, but it was the Germans who developed the idea and the machinery needed to restore mobility to warfare and overcome the long standstill in the trenches that had prevailed during World War I.

Hitler hoped and believed that blitzkrieg would bring quick victory and make war profitable once again. His long-range goal was to seize territory in eastern Europe to assure the German "race" of a sufficiently large geographic space to become a world power. This meant displacing Slavs, of course; but in 1939 he also had to cope with the French and British, who, to his surprise, had not backed away from war when news of the non-aggression pact with Russia reached them. Nevertheless, the Allies were unready to attack; instead they manned prepared fortifications along the French border and waited for something to happen.

Happen it did. First of all, the Russians set out to improve their position by recovering control of lands lost after World War I. Stalin sent soldiers into Estonia, Latvia, and Lithuania and tried to do the same to the Finns, but they resisted and even drove back an invading Russian army in the winter of 1939–1940. The French and British saw an opportunity in this situation to end the cooperation between Russia and Germany by sending an expeditionary force across Norway into Finland while simultaneously attacking oil fields in the Transcaucasus, thus cutting off oil supplies for both Russia and Germany.

But before the Allies were ready to act, Hitler seized the initiative by first sending troops into Norway and Denmark and then, in May, attacking France, Belgium, and Holland. It was 1914 all over again with the difference that tanks

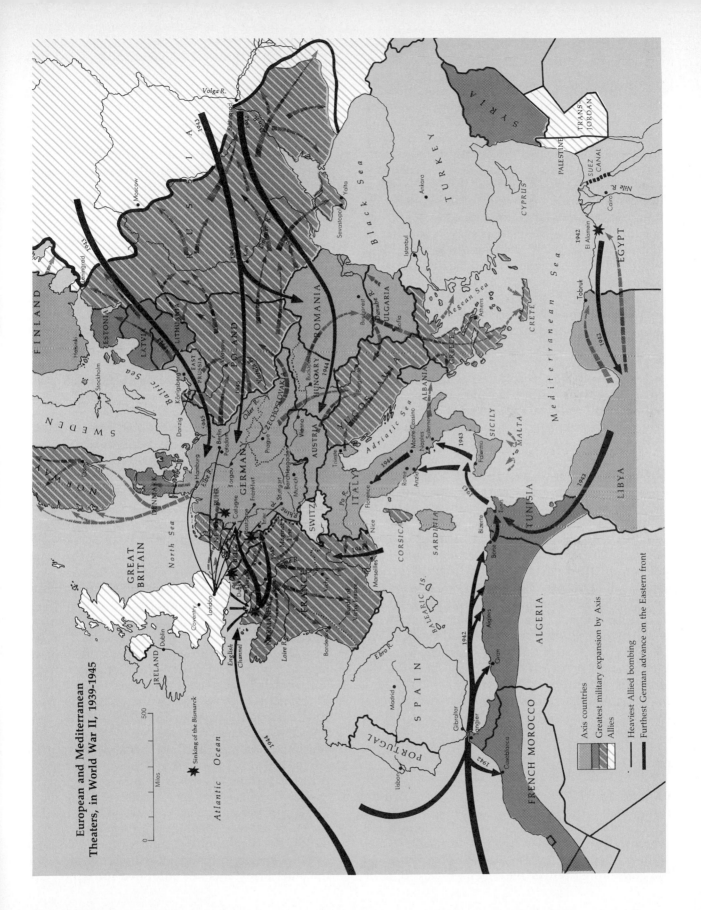

European and Mediterranean Theaters, in World War II, 1939–1945

Atlantic Ocean

Miles
0   500

★ Sinking of the Bismarck

IRELAND   Dublin •

GREAT BRITAIN
London •   Coventry •

North Sea

English Channel

NORWAY   Oslo

SWEDEN   Stockholm •

FINLAND   Helsinki •   Leningrad 1943

Moscow •

Volga R.
Stalingrad 1942

R U S S I A

Baltic Sea   ESTONIA
LATVIA
LITHUANIA
Königsberg
E. PRUSSIA

Danzig
Hamburg   POLAND
Berlin
Potsdam   Oder R.   Vistula R.
Cologne   RUHR   CZECHOSLOVAKIA
Frankfurt
Prague •   Vienna •
Stuttgart   Munich •   Berchtesgaden
G E R M A N Y   AUSTRIA
SWITZ.   HUNGARY

ROMANIA   Bucharest •
Danube R.
BULGARIA   Sofia •

Black Sea   Sevastopol
Yalta

TURKEY   Ankara •

Istanbul

Aegean Sea   CYPRUS

SYRIA   TRANS-JORDAN

PALESTINE   SUEZ CANAL
Nile R.   Cairo •

EGYPT
El Alamein   1942
Tobruk   1942

LIBYA

Mediterranean Sea

CRETE

GREECE   Athens •

ALBANIA   Adriatic Sea

YUGOSLAVIA

Trieste   ITALY
Florence   Po R.
Rome   Anzio
Monte Cassino   Naples
Salerno   1943
Palermo   SICILY
MALTA
Bizerte
Bône   TUNISIA
Algiers   Oran
Bougie

Nice   Marseilles
FRANCE
Bordeaux •
Loire R.
Bourg   Rhône R.
Lyon
Vichy France
Toulon

CORSICA
SARDINIA

BALEARIC IS.

S P A I N
Madrid •
Ebro R.
Gibraltar
Tangier   ALGERIA

PORTUGAL
Lisbon •

FRENCH MOROCCO
Casablanca •   1942

1942

1943

1944

Legend:
- Axis countries
- Greatest military expansion by Axis
- Allies
- Heaviest Allied bombing
- Furthest German advance on the Eastern front

and airplanes moved much faster than men and horses, and this time there was no eastern front for the Germans to worry about. French morale soon cracked, and in a mere six weeks the campaign was over. Most of the British expeditionary force escaped from the beaches of Dunkirk in small boats. After this surprising turn of events, the British public reacted to the disaster as though it had been a victory. But for the French there was no escape. Instead they concluded an armistice on June 22, 1940, in the same railway car in which the armistice of 1918 had been signed. To all appearance, Hitler had won.

But Britain refused to admit defeat. The Norwegian campaign, and British failures to stop the Germans from seizing control of that country, had provoked a change of government. Winston Churchill (1874–1965) became prime minister and brought a new resolution and recklessness to the British war effort. He embarked on all-out mobilization and mortgaged the future by buying what Britain could not produce for itself in the United States and elsewhere. Most of all, his speeches rallied the British people against the Nazis, even when German success seemed assured by the fact that the resources of most of the European continent lay at Hitler's beck and call.

Hitler was not prepared to mount an invasion of Great Britain. The German navy could not control the English Channel, and that meant that landing barges were vulnerable to naval attack. Hitler, nevertheless, ordered preparations for an invasion and launched heavy air attacks on British airfields. When that failed to drive British planes from the skies, the Germans attacked London and other cities, without changing the strategic situation. In September 1940, Hitler's invasion plan had to be postponed—as it proved, forever.

Invasion of Russia

Prolonging the struggle with Great Britain threatened to distract Hitler from his main goal— seizure of territory in the east on which to build a great Germany. He therefore decided in November 1940 to attack Russia, thinking that when the communist power had been destroyed, Brit-

ain would have to make peace. This decision proved fatal to the Nazis, and in retrospect it seems amazingly reckless. Why invite a war on two fronts when Stalin was doing everything he could to cooperate? But at the time, almost every military expert believed that the Russian army was poorly led and lacked the will to fight. The Red Army's poor performance against the Finns seemed to prove what prewar treason trials, followed by massive purges of disloyal officers in the late 1930s, had led outsiders to suspect. Hitler therefore counted on a swift and easy victory against Russia, like the easy victories he had already won against Poland and France. And by attacking communist Russia, he could again live up to his principles, for one of the main themes of Nazi propaganda had been denunciation of communism.

Before beginning the invasion of Russia, however, Hitler was distracted by a brief Balkan campaign. This was because shortly before the end of the campaign in France, Mussolini declared war against France and Britain. Fighting in North Africa between British forces stationed in Egypt and Italian troops in adjacent Cyrenaica (Libya) followed, and the Italians suffered some embarrassing defeats. Then in October 1940 Mussolini attacked Greece, hoping to restore his damaged prestige. Once more the Italians were defeated, and in the spring of 1941 British troops arrived from Egypt to help the Greeks. This threatened the German flank, so Hitler ordered an attack on Yugoslavia and Greece in April 1941. As before, victory came quickly and the British were driven back to Egypt.

On June 22, 1941, a few weeks later than first planned, the German war machine was finally ready for the assault on Russia. As before, blitzkrieg tactics worked wonders at first. Vast Russian armies surrendered without much of a fight. But the Russian spaces were immense, and German columns could not advance more than about 100 miles at a time without pausing to bring up supplies. Roads were miserable, and the deeper the Germans got into Russia, the more difficult it became to deliver everything needed to renew the offensive. Russian morale wavered but did not crack, and eventually the onset of cold weather began to hamper German mobility, for the Nazi army was not equipped for winter operations, lacking even the proper clothing for sub-zero temperatures. By December 6, 1941, although the Nazis were within a few miles of Moscow and had almost surrounded Leningrad, Hitler had to call off the offensive, ordering the German armies to hold fast everywhere they had conquered.

Easy victories had stopped. Instead, the Germans faced a two-front war once again, and their situation was worsened by the actions of the United States, where sympathy for Britain and hostility to the Nazis led President Roosevelt to offer Hitler's enemies all help short of war. Americans started by selling armaments and other strategic goods to France and Britain. Then, when the British began to run out of funds, Congress passed the Lend Lease Act (March 1941), whereby the United States offered to supply what Britain and Hitler's other enemies needed without charge, on the theory that they were contributing to the security of the United States by opposing Hitler and should not be required to pay back the costs of things actually used up in the course of the struggle. Then, when the war ended, whatever was left over could be returned or paid for at some agreed price. In this way, war debts, like those that had plagued international relations between the wars, would not accumulate, and by becoming "the arsenal of democracy" the United States might not have to send its own soldiers into battle.

Pearl Harbor and Initial Japanese Victories, 1941–1942

Affairs took a new turn on December 7, 1941, only a day after the German offensive in Russia halted, when the Japanese attacked the American naval base at Pearl Harbor. All the anchored U.S. battleships were sunk, but U.S. aircraft carriers were at sea and remained unscathed. The attack was a profound surprise. It had been decided upon as a sort of desperation measure, in response to the U.S. decision to embargo the export of oil and scrap iron to Japan. The Japanese armed services then foresaw a time when shortages of oil would prevent them from continuing their operations in China and Vietnam. The American embargo

had, indeed, been designed to compel the Japanese to draw back from China; instead it caused them to risk everything on the Pearl Harbor attack.

Japanese strategists thought that if they could paralyze the U.S. Pacific fleet, then it would become possible for them to capture oil fields in the Dutch East Indies (Indonesia) and thus assure themselves of sufficient oil to maintain the army and navy indefinitely. By creating a vast "Co-Prosperity Sphere" throughout Southeast Asia, China, and islands of the Pacific, the Japanese hoped that they would be able to hold off counterattack indefinitely. Given existing methods of warfare, and the difficulties of landing on a defended beach, this hope was not unreasonable.

For six months after Pearl Harbor, everything the Japanese military had counted on seemed to be coming true. A series of brilliantly successful campaigns brought the Philippines, Malaya, Burma, and the Dutch East Indies under Japanese control, and the Japanese also garrisoned a number of smaller islands of the Southwest Pacific. "Asia for the Asians" was a slogan that appealed to the inhabitants of former British, French, and Dutch colonies; but the Japanese had difficulty in converting hostility to European colonialism into active support for what amounted to an empire of their own. Moreover, Chinese resistance continued, and the population of India, after hesitating, settled down under British management to create a vast new army to protect its exposed frontier in Burma from any further Japanese advance.

TURNING THE TIDE: AMERICAN MOBILIZATION AND ALLIED OFFENSIVES, 1942–1945

Despite these initial successes, the Japanese were no match for American power, once the resources of the United States were fully geared for war. And the American response to Pearl Harbor was all-out mobilization, harnessing all available manpower and know-how to the task of creating

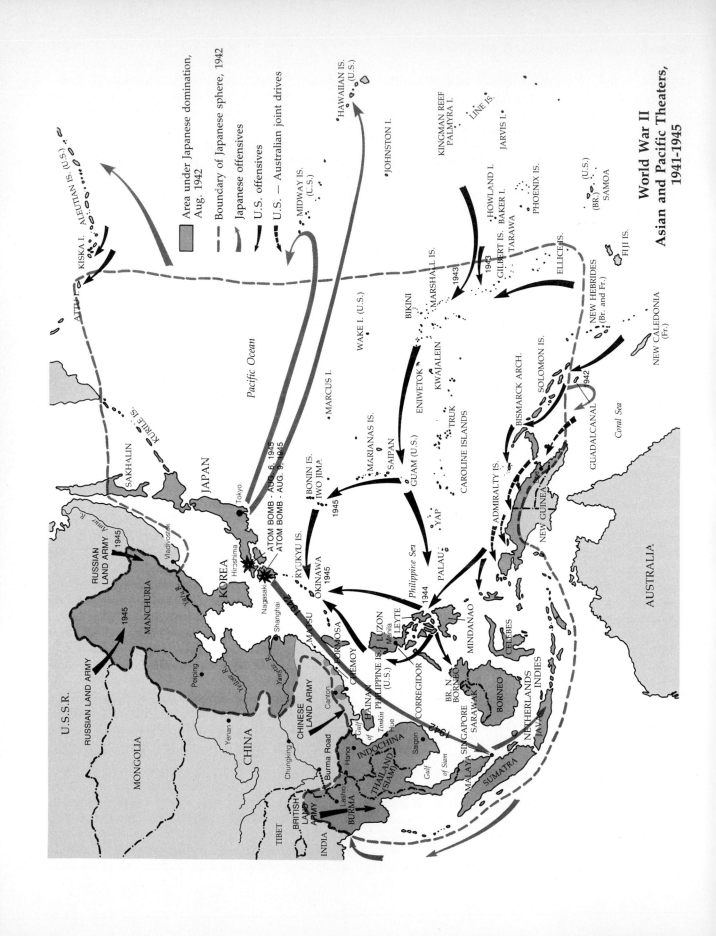

**World War II
Asian and Pacific Theaters,
1941–1945**

Area under Japanese domination, Aug. 1942
Boundary of Japanese sphere, 1942
Japanese offensives
U.S. offensives
U.S. – Australian joint drives

THE SECOND BEST IS NOT THE PACIFIC

In July 1942, the war was going badly for the Allies. Japan controlled a vast region of the Pacific. The Germans' second summer offensive in Russia was thrusting toward the Volga. In the North African desert, other German soldiers were at Egypt's doorstep.

Earlier in the year, America, Britain, and Russia had agreed upon their strategy for 1942. Anglo-American forces were to land in northern France and open a second front to relieve the Russians. Everything else was to be subordinated to that effort. But by July, the British decided that the plan would not work. Landing craft and other supplies were lacking. Reinforcing the defenses of Egypt and of India seemed even more important than landing in France, for it took only a little imagination to believe that the Axis' next move would be for Japanese forces to move into India while the Germans drove past Egypt to meet them somewhere in the Indian Ocean.

The Americans were very reluctant to change the agreed-on plan. What if Russia should collapse or make a separate peace? But without the British, a landing in France was clearly impossible. What to do? On July 10, the Joint Chiefs of Staff recommended that in such a case major effort should be shifted to the Pacific against the Japanese.

This brought President Franklin D. Roosevelt up against the most important strategic decision of the war. If he accepted the advice of his chiefs of staff, the British and Russians would be left to fight the war against Germany on their own. Each of the great Allied nations would in effect be conducting its own war, with little real cooperation. This seemed unwise. It seemed even more unwise to concentrate on Japan when everyone agreed that the Germans were a more serious threat to the long-range security of the United States.

On July 15, 1942, President Roosevelt talked the problem over with his friend, Harry Hopkins. The two men sat in the White House on a summer's evening, wondering what to do. In the end, Roosevelt decided to try once again to work out a plan for joint action with the British. He sent Harry Hopkins and General George C. Marshall to London to make the attempt. Ten days later, they agreed on a landing in North Africa. In greatest haste, a vast expedition was made ready under the supreme command of a young American general, Dwight D. Eisenhower. As a result, on November 8, 1942, less than four months after the decision had been made, American and British troops went ashore in French North Africa.

The Russians were not fully satisfied with this second front. But British and American cooperation became closer and more intimate than ever before. Soon afterward, the turning point of the war came: at Stalingrad in Russia, at Guadalcanal in the Pacific, and in North Africa. And as the Allies took the strategic initiative, they made it a genuinely cooperative effort—all because President Roosevelt had decided on July 15, 1942, that even if a landing in France was not possible in 1942, "the second best is not the Pacific."

a truly formidable army and navy as quickly as possible. How to manage an all-out war effort had already been worked out by the British, building on World War I precedents. The American government was therefore able to achieve a remarkably efficient system for channeling resources into the war effort, all in conformity with strategic plans devised by the Joint Chiefs of Staff. Production goals, once seemingly impossible, were soon achieved and surpassed. American industrial and agricultural productivity was so great that the flow of Lend Lease goods to Britain, Russia, and other Allied powers actually increased while the American armed forces were being built up and then sent into action overseas.

Hitler declared war on the United States just after the Pearl Harbor attack, even though the Japanese had not informed him of their plans and refused to attack the Soviet Union in the Far East, despite German requests that they do so. Hitler's declaration of war made it easy for the United States to confirm and strengthen cooperation with Britain and with the Soviet Union by deciding, in spite of the Japanese attack at Pearl Harbor, to concentrate first against Germany, on the ground that if Hitler were left alone to defeat Russia in a second campaign, he would become difficult or impossible to overthrow. As a result, Allied military campaigns were far better coordinated than anything the Germans, Italians, and Japanese were able to achieve.

Results of American mobilization and Allied planning began to show towards the end of 1942. By far the biggest action came in Russia, where a second German advance was turned back at Stalingrad on the Volga, beginning in late August. The Russians had to rely almost entirely on their own resources, for Lend Lease shipments were still small owing to shortages of shipping. But they were able to produce tanks and guns, thanks to factories in the Urals and still further east that had been built just before the war; and once the harshness of Nazi rule became clear, the Russian population rallied behind the communist regime.

On the other fronts, too, the balance began to favor the Allies in the second half of 1942. Japan's victories ended in June, when the Americans won a sea battle off Midway Island; and later in the year, hard fighting on Guadalcanal, in the Southwest Pacific, led to a second American vic-

tory, this time on land. Against Germany, the first important Anglo-American success came in the Atlantic, where German submarines threatened for a while to sink so many ships as to prevent the successful deployment of American forces overseas. By midsummer 1942, that danger had been largely overcome; and in November the Americans and British were able to combine forces for a large-scale landing in North Africa. A few weeks earlier, British troops had won a decisive victory in Egypt over a combined German and Italian army; and by May 1943 the whole southern shore of the Mediterranean was in Allied hands. From there, the Anglo-American forces invaded first Sicily (August) and then the Italian mainland (September). By this time, most Italians were anxious to make peace, and a coup d'état in Rome overthrew Mussolini. Prompt German reaction, however, meant that northern Italy remained under their control. A German taskforce even freed Mussolini from prison, but he was no more than a hollow puppet from then on.

On the Russian front, a third German offensive, launched in July 1943, was quickly turned back; and from that time onward, it was the Russian army that advanced, while the Germans fought desperately to hold them back. Lend Lease deliveries began to supplement Russian home production significantly by 1943; in particular, American trucks, shoes, and food kept the Red Army mobile.

Problems of the Peace

Russia's growing military success meant that concerting plans with American and British leaders became necessary. A conference at Tehran (November 1943) brought Stalin, Roosevelt, and Churchill together for the first time, and they were able to agree on future strategy. In particular, the United States and Britain promised to attack across the Channel in 1944, in spite of the very great technical difficulties of landing on the French coast. Everyone expected that a successful landing would lead to Germany's defeat, since the Russians promised a massive offensive in the east to coincide with the landings in France.

On June 6, 1944, Allied landings on the Normandy beaches proved successful, and within a

The Big Three of World War II This photograph, taken during the Yalta Conference in February 1945, shows Winston Churchill, Prime Minister of Great Britain, Franklin D. Roosevelt, President of the United States, and Josef Stalin, Generalissimo of the Soviet Union, seated with some senior staff advisors standing in the rear. This was the second time the three heads of government came together to concert plans and policies. At Tehran in 1943 strategic decisions about a second front in France were agreed upon; at Yalta political questions about the future of Europe were more urgent than military planning. Even in the Far East, where Stalin did commit himself at Yalta to entering the war against Japan within three months of the end of the hostilities in Europe, military cooperation soon seemed less important than political agreement about what sort of post-war governments were to exist in liberated and conquered lands. On this issue, real cooperation proved impossible; and polite fictions accepted at Yalta soon proved unworkable in practice. The Great Alliance of World War II was already wearing thin when this photograph was taken. It evaporated entirely two years later.

few weeks German armies were driven from France. But the Allies barely got across the German border before bad weather set in, and in December Hitler was even able to launch a counteroffensive. Russian armies in the east got into Poland but had to stop short of Berlin, the German capital. Victory in Europe was thus delayed until May 1945, when Russian and American forces finally met at the Elbe River. Hitler had killed himself a few days previously. With his death, the Nazi movement collapsed utterly, though only after murdering millions of Jews and others in special extermination camps and bringing massive destruction on most of Europe.

How to arrange the postwar map of Europe was more than the Allies could agree on. Until Hitler had been destroyed, differences could always be papered over, as happened at Yalta in February 1945, when Roosevelt, Churchill, and Stalin met for a second time; but when German resistance finally collapsed, hard decisions had to be made, and it soon became obvious that the sort of "friendly" governments the Russians wanted in eastern Europe were undemocratic and unacceptable by British and American standards. For a while, the United States continued

to hope that such differences could be amicably settled, especially since they wanted Russian help against Japan.

Toward the end of 1944, however, the limitations of Japanese war-making ability became clearer and the American wish for Russian help in the Far East diminished accordingly. United States submarines succeeded in sinking so many ships that the Japanese became unable to tap the resources of their "Co-Prosperity sphere." Moreover, beginning in November 1943, the Americans learned how to send taskforces thousands of miles from base with everything needed for a successful assault on a defended beach. This meant that the Japanese defense perimeter in the Pacific became vulnerable, since even the bravest garrisons, cut off from home, could not survive very long without food and ammunition. With giant steps the Americans were therefore able to advance first toward the Philippines, then toward the Japanese home islands.

The final blows came swiftly. On August 6 and 9, 1945, American airplanes dropped newly invented nuclear bombs on Hiroshima and Nagasaki. Then, on August 9, the Russians began marching into Manchuria. These disasters per-

Horrors of World War II Between 1914 and 1918, the long stalemate in the trenches took the romance out of war. The revival of mobile warfare in 1939, thanks to the tactics of Blitzkrieg, might have restored the glamor of successful combat if World War II had not also turned into a prolonged and bloody struggle that was eventually decided by the Allies' superior industrial production. As victory drew near, two new horrors of war profoundly affected public opinion. On top is a photograph taken in May 1945 of the Nazi concentration camp at Buchenwald. It shows Jews and other enemies of the Nazi regime on the verge of starvation by the time the American army reached them. Many others had already died and their bodies lay exposed in open mass graves. Photographs like these shocked American public opinion profoundly. Earlier reports of Nazi death camps had often been discounted as mere war propaganda. But here were certain proofs of unprecedented brutality and bureaucratic mass murder: a new horror indeed. On the bottom is a photograph of the mushroom cloud that rose above Nagasaki, Japan on August 9, 1945. It signaled a new kind of horror: the mass destruction wrought by nuclear weapons.

suaded the Japanese government to sue for peace on August 15. Formal surrender was arranged on September 2, 1945, just five years and a day after the war in Europe had begun.

CONCLUSION

World War II was over, at least officially. Urgent unsolved questions remained; and in the hurly-burly of everyday decision-making, no one really took time to wonder whether the two world wars of the twentieth century, and the changes they had brought about, marked the end of an era. But with nearly half a century's perspective, it now seems probable that historians will need a new label for the period since World War II.

The modern era that began with the great European voyages of discovery in the latter part of the fifteenth century was marked by the rise of western Europe to world predominance. But European world power came to an end with the breakup of colonial empires in the aftermath of the war, and with the rise of new superpowers, east and west of the old center of world leadership. To be sure, both the USSR and the USA inherited or borrowed a great deal from western Europe; but neither Americans nor Russians were quite the same as the peoples of the west European nations who had lorded it over the rest of the earth before the wars.

The era of the two world wars also marked an end to the delicate balance between public and private enterprise that had characterized bourgeois Europe. That balance had initially been struck in a few city-states of Italy and the Rhinelands in the fourteenth century; it had spread to the Netherlands, England, and France during the sixteenth and seventeenth centuries, and had then been imperfectly imitated in central and eastern Europe in the eighteenth and nineteenth centuries. It gave wide scope to private accumulation of capital and pursuit of gain by buying and selling at prices negotiated anew for each deal in accordance with the best estimate of personal advantage each party could make at the time. Intervention in the market by political and military authorities was always important. Taxes and tariffs affected market prices, often in

very important respects; and fixed "fair" prices for food and other necessities were often enforced as well, especially in times of crisis. But as compared to other times and places, bourgeois Europe gave the market far freer scope than usual.

The two world wars reversed this trend, sharply. Rationing, price control, direction of labor, compulsory military service, planned industrial production, all took over. In each of the principal belligerent countries, military and civilian planners set out to make economic production fit strategic war plans. Careful calculation and management proved able to achieve wonders. Goals that seemed impossible were in fact achieved, over and over. As long as everyone agreed that the effort was worth while, and millions of common folk willingly put up with all the discomfort and deprivation that wartime conditions involved, the efficiency of what we may call "command" economy as against the traditional "market" economy was undeniable.

Bourgeois society could never be the same after such a demonstration of what state intervention in the market was able to achieve, although the problem of maintaining general agreement on the political goals to be pursued in peacetime turned out to be far more difficult than it was to agree that wartime enemies must be defeated. After 1917, the Soviet Union defiantly rejected bourgeois free-market rules and set out to build a new socialist society. The nations that remained "capitalist" and democratic compromised between free-market and command principles for the management of their economies. But everywhere the role of the state and of deliberate public planning was much increased as compared to conditions before 1914, while the scope for strictly private pursuit of profit was correspondingly reduced by all sorts of new regulations and controls aimed at narrowing gaps between rich and poor, or in other ways advancing political goals. In this respect, as much as in the displacement of world leadership from western Europe to the United States and the Union of Soviet Socialist Republics, the world wars of the twentieth century seem likely to mark a new era in world history.

We will discuss some of its characteristics in the remaining chapters of this book.

Chapter 25

THE WORLD SINCE 1945

In coming close to our own time, problems of historical perspective become acute. We are creatures of place and time, inevitably, and can only look about us and try to pick out what matters most, or seems likely to matter most, in the rush of recent events.

Overall, rivalry between the United States and the Soviet Union seems one obvious, dominating feature of the post–World War II world. Diplomatic rivalry spilled over into an arms race of enormous technical complexity—a race that threatens the very survival of humanity if nuclear warheads should ever be used on anything like the scale that is now possible. World politics and international relations have been fundamentally altered by this new reality and by the fear it creates.

Another obvious feature of the post–World War II world is massive population growth, more rapid in poor and predominantly agricultural lands than in the industrially developed, richer countries. This was accompanied, at least until the 1970s, by sustained economic expansion that brought rising standards of living to many millions of persons, so that, even in the poorest countries, growing numbers of human beings were at least able to find enough food to remain alive. Economic growth rested partly on the diffusion of new skills, especially agricultural skills, and partly on the diffusion of improved forms of economic management, both national and transnational in scale.

A third obvious feature of our time is the growth of cities with all the changes in daily experience that city living brings. It is worth reminding ourselves that until about 1950 most human beings still lived in villages and worked in the fields. After that date, city dwellers, depending on food raised by others, became more numerous than rural folk, though in some poor countries city living still remains a minority way of life. Many changes go along with this shift from rural to urban existence. Weakening of family ties is perhaps the most important. New, individual lifestyles, much influenced by TV and movies, also find greater scope in cities than in villages. Sports, sex, and crime achieve new visibility and, perhaps, new importance. But contrary currents also arise. Religious revivalism, seeking to get back to a true, pure way of life is one expression of the revulsion against the urban breakdown of traditional values. Efforts to maintain and strengthen ethnic and other local identities run in a parallel direction. Which current predominates varies from time to time and from one part of the world to another.

Finally, it is worth remembering that any effort to understand what goes on around us is likely to overlook something that will seem critically important in time to come when its consequences and implications become apparent, while some of the things that seem most important to us may shrink to triviality in the light of subsequent events. The rivalry between Americans and Russians, for example, may prove to be less important for the history of the world than something happening in Africa or China—or in space. Everything depends on how things turn out, and this we cannot know. We need to realize, always, how surprising human affairs are likely to be, as much in the future as in the past. Who, for example, could have anticipated the consequences of Columbus' voyages? Or of Christ's teaching? Who could imagine the role of gunpowder when it was new? Or of agriculture when it began? Discoveries, inventions, and the teaching of new doctrines continue among us and are likely to transform human life in the future at least as surprisingly as ever happened in the past. Consequently, modest, tentative judgments about what really matters is all we can hope for.

WORLD POLITICS SINCE 1945

Even before hostilities ceased in World War II, quarrels among the victors had broken out. The conference at Yalta (February 1945), where Roosevelt, Churchill, and Stalin met for a second time, made vague promises on paper without solving the differences between Russia and the Anglo-American powers over the postwar settlement in Europe. By July 1945, when the Allied heads of government met at Potsdam, just outside Berlin, frictions were sharper, but the need to end the war with Japan, arrange for peace treaties, and settle the military administration of defeated Germany kept the alliance from breaking apart. At a conference that met in San Francisco in 1945 the Allies agreed to establish a new international body, the United Nations. Long term peace keeping and all other international problems were to be entrusted to the UN, but it got off to a rocky start in 1946 because the Great Powers could no longer even pretend to cooperate.

Instead, open quarrels, openly arrived at, prevailed. Stalin carved out a sphere of influence in eastern Europe wherever the Russian army was in possession of the ground. A matching Anglo-American sphere of influence formed in the rest of Europe, though by the end of 1946 it was clear that Great Britain could no longer afford to play the role of a great power. The result was that by 1947 the Americans confronted the Russians across what Churchill aptly termed an iron curtain, splitting Europe into communist and non-

Occupation Zones of Germany and Austria, 1945

communist parts. Europe's most powerful nation, Germany, was divided between the two blocs.

In Asia a similar division took place. Japan fell within the American sphere of influence, whereas China, thanks to the victory of Mao Tse-tung's Red Army over Chiang Kai-shek's forces, became communist in 1949. Korea and Southeast Asia, like Germany, were divided between communist and noncommunist regimes, depending on how lines of demarcation between rival occupying forces had been drawn at the end of the war.

In China and adjacent lands the new communist rulers were fervent nationalists, although that fact was partly hidden at the time by their use of Marxist revolutionary phrases. In India and Africa, however, nationalism remained separate from communism; so when these lands became independent after World War II, they and some other poor and ambitious countries began to constitute a "third world" that belonged neither to the Russian nor to the American side in what came to be called the Cold War.

But third world peoples remained poor and weak compared to Japan and Europe. In the rich countries, where administrative and industrial skills had attained high development, the ravages of war were swiftly repaired by applying to the tasks of reconstruction the same sorts of management that had worked so well in war. In western Europe, reconstruction was facilitated by generous grants from the United States—the so-called Marshall Plan, 1948–1952. American officials required Europeans to plan recovery from war damages on a continent-wide basis, and the habit proved catching so that European managers developed forms of international cooperation that evolved into the European Economic Community by 1957. This rather clumsy association, uniting France, West Germany, Italy, Belgium, Holland, and Luxemburg, nevertheless managed to agree on important economic policies that sustained a prolonged surge of prosperity in western Europe; and it even accepted Great Britain, Ireland, Denmark, Greece, Portugal, and Spain as members when those countries applied for admission between 1973 and 1984.

Recovery in eastern Europe involved greater hardships, since outside assistance was not forthcoming. Nevertheless, the planned economies of the Soviet Union and of its new satellite countries, Poland, Romania, Hungary, Czechoslovakia, and East Germany, made a remarkably rapid recovery too, even though living standards remained far lower than in western Europe.

Japan's Economic Boom

Japan's economic revival began as a by-product of a war in Korea, 1950–1953. The communist rulers of North Korea invaded the southern part of that country in 1950, apparently under the impression that no one would really try to oppose this expansion of their power. But American commitment to legal settlement of international issues through the United Nations was still lively, and American distaste for any further spread of communism, after Mao Tse-tung's success in China, was intense. As it happened, the Russians had walked out of the United Nations in protest over another issue and so were unable to veto the decision to oppose North Korea's attack on the south. The United States then took the lead in organizing a U.N. army to defeat the communists. When victory seemed almost complete, the Chinese Red Army intervened and drove the U.N. forces back to something close to the original dividing line between North and South Korea. Then, after lengthy negotiations, a truce was agreed upon in 1953, perpetuating Korea's division into two rival halves.

During this war, U.N. forces found it convenient to order all sorts of supplies from Japan. The resulting demand for goods set Japan's economy off on a postwar boom that eventually left all the rest of the world behind. Japan's phenomenal success in building ships, cars, electronic devices, and other high-tech goods depended on old patterns of life and work, dating back to the feudal past, combined with a modern educational system and national management of key aspects of the economy. As a result, the Japanese began to produce better goods at lower prices than anyone else. In many branches of light industry, their principal rivals were other Far Eastern lands—South Korea, Taiwan (where Chiang Kai-shek's Chinese nationalists found refuge after

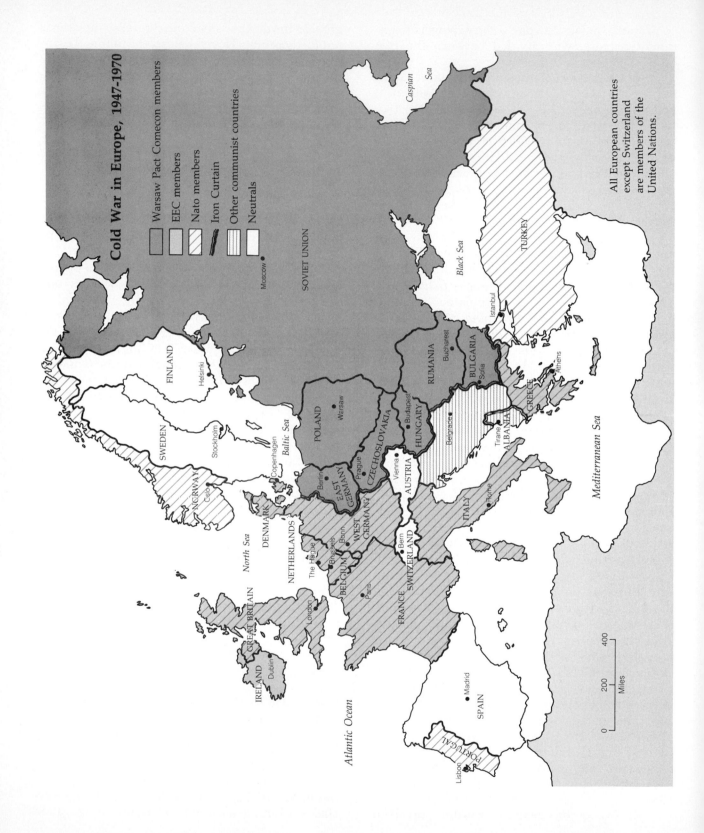

Cold War in Europe, 1947-1970

Warsaw Pact Comecon members

EEC members

Nato members

Iron Curtain

Other communist countries

Neutrals

● Moscow

SOVIET UNION

FINLAND
● Helsinki

SWEDEN
● Stockholm

NORWAY
● Oslo

Baltic Sea

DENMARK
● Copenhagen

North Sea

GREAT BRITAIN
● London

IRELAND
● Dublin

Atlantic Ocean

NETHERLANDS
The Hague ●

BELGIUM
Brussels ●

● Paris

FRANCE

SWITZERLAND
● Bern

WEST GERMANY
● Bonn

EAST GERMANY
● Berlin

POLAND
● Warsaw

CZECHOSLOVAKIA
● Prague

AUSTRIA
● Vienna

HUNGARY
● Budapest

ITALY
● Rome

YUGOSLAVIA
● Belgrade

RUMANIA
● Bucharest

BULGARIA
● Sofia

ALBANIA
● Tirane

GREECE
● Athens

Black Sea

TURKEY
● Istanbul

Caspian Sea

Mediterranean Sea

SPAIN
● Madrid

PORTUGAL
● Lisbon

All European countries except Switzerland are members of the United Nations.

0 200 400

Miles

Super Modern Japan Japan's economic success since World War II arose in large part from the readiness of government and industry to introduce the newest technology with the least delay. When transport between Tokyo and Kyoto began to clog seriously, the Japanese government decided to build a completely new high speed railway running for over 300 miles between the two cities. Heavy, wide-gauge tracks that avoided sharp curves and steep grades were designed to allow the trains to travel at speeds above 120 miles an hour; and double tracks permitted trains to shuttle back and forth along this heavily travelled route at frequent intervals. From its opening in 1961, Japan thus achieved the swiftest and most efficient train service in the world, as the photograph on the top suggests. On the bottom is a scene from a Japanese automobile factory where robots are seen welding a car body automatically and without human intervention. Labor-saving machinery like this helped to make Japanese cars cheaper and more reliable than cars built elsewhere.

1949), Hong Kong, and Singapore. Beginning in the late 1950s, European and American factories proved unable to match the quality and price of many different kinds of goods produced by these new Far Eastern competitors. If this situation persists, it will mark a fundamental change in world balances, ending an era, at least 200 years old, in which European and then American factories drove artisans of other lands out of the market by offering cheaper and sometimes better goods for sale than could be produced locally even by the most highly skilled workers.

A factor in Japan's extraordinary economic success in the postwar period was that the peace treaty concluded in 1947 prohibited armaments. Japan, like western Europe, found shelter under the umbrella of the American armed forces and became free to concentrate on producing civilian rather than military goods. This may be an advantage. On the other hand, recent military research and development has led to important new industrial products and processes in such fields as communications, computers, airplane manufacturing, and atomic reactors. But most of the new weapons have no civilian use, and resources devoted to their production in the Soviet Union and in the United States have therefore been subtracted from the civilian economy.

The real issue, probably, is organizational: how efficiently different firms and nations are able to combine the efforts of large numbers of persons to get things done cheaply and well. By that measure, Americans and Europeans are not far behind the Japanese, and all of them are far ahead of third world peoples. Wealth and power have therefore remained concentrated in American, European, and Japanese hands; and world politics has turned largely on their decisions, and especially on the decisions of the American and Soviet governments, whose armed forces, population, and organizational skills left everyone else behind.

News reporting focuses on quarrels and confrontation: the more violent, the more interesting. This is liable to distort our judgment. The fact is that since 1945 the world has not suffered any really major war, and most of the wars that have been fought have not lasted long nor killed very many people. Compared with past human behavior, this is unusual. Twenty-one years separated World War I from World War II; the post–World War II period of approximate peace has already lasted more than twice that long.

The Arms Race

One reason for this record is that all concerned are profoundly afraid of all-out war. The atomic bombs dropped on Hiroshima and Nagasaki in the last days of World War II announced a new level of destructive power, and those formidable weapons were far surpassed when the Americans and Russians both discovered how to build vastly more powerful H-bombs after 1950. War took on a completely new guise when, after 1957, the great powers also acquired rockets capable of carrying city-destroying nuclear missiles to any part of the earth's surface. No effective means to intercept intercontinental rockets existed; hence outbreak of war between the two great powers threatened the sudden destruction of most of the population of the two combatants, all within a few minutes of the start of hostilities. Recent calculations even suggest that a few hundred nuclear explosions might alter the atmosphere and disturb the conditions for life on earth so radically that human and all other higher forms of life would perish utterly. No one wants that sort of disaster; and so far the two governments have managed to back away from situations in which resort to ultimate force seemed likely, such as the confrontations over Berlin (1948–1949) and Cuban missile crisis (1962).

Efforts to control the arms race have not been very successful. In 1972 the two great powers signed a Strategic Arms Limitation Treaty (SALT) that prohibited research and development of some new forms of weaponry, but negotiations to reduce the total number of nuclear weapons failed when the United States refused to ratify a second treaty in 1980. In 1988, however, the two great powers did agree to dismantle short-range nuclear missiles that had been poised against one another in Europe. Efforts to prevent the spread of nuclear weapons to other countries have not prevented Britain, France, China, and probably Israel and India from developing nuclear arsenals of their own; and several other countries—Pakistan, Libya, Iraq, South Africa, Argentina, and Brazil, for example—may have secret nuclear arms programs as well. How the balance of war and peace will tilt if these and perhaps still other countries acquire nuclear weapons is difficult to foresee. But no one doubts that world politics will be altered, perhaps disastrously, if almost unimaginably powerful means of destruction come within the control of fanatical and insecure governments.

One of the ironies of the situation is that the overwhelming destructive power of existing nuclear weapons does not give Russians and Americans the ability to control other governments, even those close by and partly dependent on aid or trade with them. Yugoslavia actually succeeded in breaking away from the Russian orbit after 1946, before the nuclear stalemate had set in. When the stalemate became clear to all concerned, China broke openly with the Russians in 1960, while Poland and Romania exhibited various degrees of independence without directly defying the Russians or overthrowing their local Communist party dictatorships. The American alliance system, NATO (North Atlantic Treaty Organization), also showed signs of weakening, and France withdrew from full membership in 1966.

Nevertheless, NATO and the Russians' military alliance system, the Warsaw Pact, maintained a balance of armed forces in Europe that neither side was eager to test. On both sides of the iron curtain, combined, multinational military commands, modeled on those that had proved so effective in World War II, remained in place, prepared to spring into action if war should break out on European soil.

Within Europe national sovereignty was seriously compromised by these new forms of military organization, as well as by the European Economic Community that regulated the internal economic policies of west European nations. Clearly, Europe's rival nationalisms, which had been so prominent during the nineteenth century and sustained World Wars I and II in the twentieth, were weakening. But in other parts of the world, nationalism boiled to the surface, sometimes assuming religious, or quasi-religious forms, and sometimes hiding behind Marxist revolutionary phrases.

Independence in the Third World

Asian and African nationalisms were directed, initially, against European colonial government. In some parts of Asia and Africa, agitation for political independence had developed before World War II. This was particularly true of India, where Mohandas Gandhi had mobilized millions in his campaigns of nonviolent resistance to British rule. A fundamental turning point came in 1946, when a newly elected Labour government in Great Britain decided to give up the empire and encourage local peoples to set up governments of their own. In India, political parties and leaders already existed who were ready to take on the tasks of government. Independence therefore came quickly (1947), although not without provoking mass riots between Hindus and Moslems. A new state, Pakistan, was carved out of British India to accommodate the millions of Moslems who preferred a state of their own to citizenship in a predominantly Hindu India.

In Africa, too, the old basis of European colonial rule collapsed abruptly after World War II. Graduates of mission schools led the way in demanding independence and were soon joined by soldiers who had been trained by colonial authorities who needed African manpower for their armies. The British government did not resist the new movement for political independence very strenuously, though it did make some halfhearted efforts to defend the interests of European settlers in Kenya and Rhodesia. But when African demands for political independence became unmistakeable, the British handed over sovereignty rather quickly. As a result, all the British colonies in Africa attained independence between 1956, when Sudan led the way, and 1963, when Kenya became independent. The French first hoped that some sort of new, more or less voluntary association between France and its African colonies could be maintained; but a nasty war in Algeria

Old and New in the Third World Extraordinary discrepancies result from the importation of high technology into countries where older ways of living continue unchanged, at least for a while. These photographs illustrate how old and new co-exist. Above, women and children in India gather on a river bank to wash clothes and fill their water jugs, while across on the other side a new electric generating station, built with World Bank funds, stands stark and square. But since ordinary households still lack electric washing machines and pumps to make what the women are doing unnecessary, age-old household routines persist indefinitely into the future, creating scenes like this. Below, is a similar juxtaposition of old and new from Kuwait, where oil wealth allowed a good many residents to acquire such new gadgets as TV sets and automobiles. Even the porter, carrying the TV set across the square, though dressed in traditional garb and carrying his exotic load in a thoroughly traditional fashion, is wearing tennis shoes!

CONQUEST OF MOUNT EVEREST

Mount Everest rises 29,028 feet above sea level, higher than any other mountain on earth. Icy winds blow fiercely around the high slopes of the mountain; temperatures of 30 or 40 degrees below zero are common near the top. Not only that, the air gets thinner with every increase in altitude. Men whose bodies are built to breathe at or near sea level cannot get enough oxygen into their bloodstream to keep their muscles strong at altitudes as high as Everest's peak. For many years, this seemed to make it impossible to climb to the earth's highest point.

But the word "impossible" was a challenge. Improved equipment for dealing with rock, ice, and snow at high altitudes allowed skilled mountain climbers to get higher and higher. In 1921 the first effort was made to use these skills on Everest. The expedition did not get anywhere near the top, but it proved one very important thing: tanks of oxygen, strapped to a climber's back, allowed oxygen-starved muscles to revive their strength in spite of the thin air. So the extra weight was worthwhile; and with this discovery, the conquest of Mount Everest became a real possibility.

But difficulties were immense. Between World Wars I and II, five Everest expeditions set out, each better equipped than the previous one had been; and five times they failed. Then World War II interrupted mountaineering in the Himalayas until the 1950s. All the early expeditions had approached Mount Everest from the north, only to reach an impassable face near the very top. In 1951 a new route, approaching from the south, was reconnoitered. A Swiss expedition tried this approach in 1952 and almost reached the top before bad weather interfered. The next spring a British party, helped by Sherpa tribesmen who were accustomed to living at very high altitudes, renewed the assault.

Day after day the climbers leapfrogged higher. Toward the top, the party divided up into smaller groups of two or three men. One such group went on ahead to explore the best line of ascent and set up a camp, from which the next group could take off and do the same thing over again. On May 28, a camp only 1,100 feet below Mount Everest's crest was set up. The honor of making the final climb fell upon two men: Edmund Hillary, a New Zealander, and Tenzing Norgay, a Sherpa. Starting from the advance camp in the early morning, the two men reached the highest point on the surface of the earth before noon, May 29, 1953. Unlike many of those who had tried before, they got back down safely.

Thus another landmark in the restless effort to test strength and skill by doing what has never been done before entered the record of human achievement.

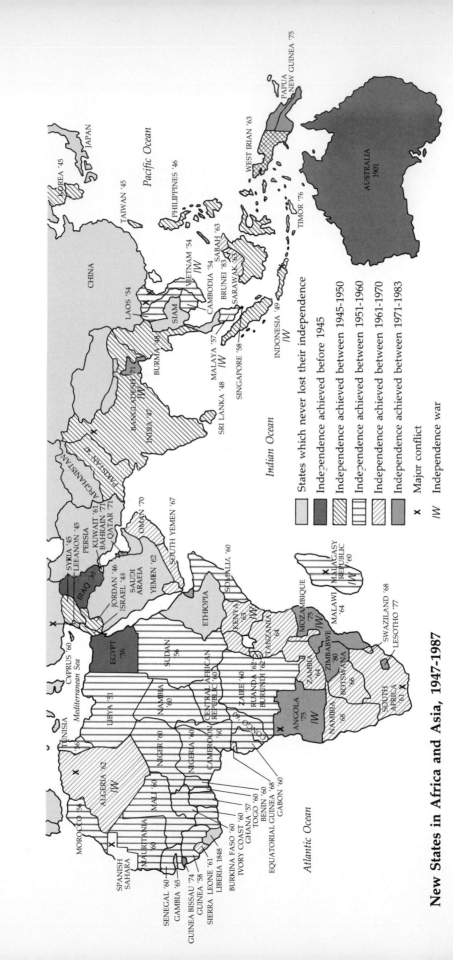

New States in Africa and Asia, 1947-1987

States which never lost their independence

Independence achieved before 1945

Independence achieved between 1945-1950

Independence achieved between 1951-1960

Independence achieved between 1961-1970

Independence achieved between 1971-1983

X   Major conflict

IW   Independence war

(1954–1962) convinced the French government that it was best to allow full independence to all the colonial governments that wanted it. The French Empire therefore dissolved very quickly after 1960. Belgium pulled out of the Congo in 1960 and the Portuguese, who held out longest, withdrew from Angola and Mozambique in 1975. By that date, politically at least, Africa was once again in African hands, even though economic dependence continued, while rising populations put heavy pressure on local living standards.

Partly for that reason, the end of European colonial administration did not end conflict, since local rivalries, sometimes supported from outside, often led to violence and coups d'état. This was true of Africa's most populous country, Nigeria, where a civil war (1967–1970) ended in reassertion of the integrity of the country, despite on-going Moslem-Christian friction among the different peoples living there. Zaire (formerly the Belgian Congo) also experienced a bout of civil war, but U.N. intervention helped to keep that country united, in spite of its internal diversity.

Indeed, the really surprising fact about the new African countries was that with the sole exception of Somalia the old colonial boundaries, however arbitrary they had been, were everywhere upheld by the new African governments, even when it meant keeping very different peoples together under the same political roof. But in most of the new countries of Africa, just because the populations were so diverse, government fell into the hands of relatively small cliques, often originating among army officers who had been trained in European ways and could count on obedience from their soldiers. Civilians and political parties found it difficult to create any effective alternative base for government.

Withdrawal of European colonial rule in Africa prepared the way for a harsh collision in South Africa between whites and blacks. In line with the general establishment of local sovereignties, the Boers revenged themselves for their defeat in 1899–1902 by setting up their own South African Republic in 1961 and withdrawing from the British Commonwealth (an informal association of nations that had once been part of the British Empire). The new government proceeded to segregate blacks from whites by law, establishing a regime of apartheid that cooped black Africans up in special reserves and subjected them to harsh police control. Demands for equal rights of citizenship were flatly rejected, even though the general climate of world opinion became extremely hostile to the racial policies of the South African government.

In Southeast Asia and the islands of the Pacific, European empires proved no less fragile. At first, efforts were made to keep control over lands that had been far more profitable to the colonial powers than Africa had ever been; but when armed resistance developed, the Europeans decided that restoring their rule was not worth the cost. Consequently, Burma, Indonesia, Malaya, and Vietnam, along with several smaller countries, all became independent soon after the end of World War II, although Vietnam was divided between a communist north and a noncommunist south. When guerrillas from the north threatened to overthrow the government in the south, the United States decided on armed intervention to stop this new advance of communism. The result was a long and frustrating war, 1964–1973, in which the Americans were never successful in winning heartfelt support from the Vietnamese people—or even from all Americans at home. The North Vietnamese, in contrast, appealed to deep-seated national and revolutionary feelings and in the end compelled the Americans to withdraw, despite the enormous technological superiority that American troops enjoyed over their enemy.

Complexities in the Middle East

By far the most complicated political situation, however, developed in the Middle East. European imperial control of Arab lands, extended after World War I by the system of mandates, had already worn thin before World War II broke out; and countries like Iraq and Egypt won at least formal independence in the late 1930s. During the war, Palestine and Syria remained under British and French administration respectively, at least in theory. But Jewish settlers in Palestine wanted full sovereignty for themselves, particularly after news of the wholesale destruction of Jews in the Nazi death camps reached them. A national homeland, where Jews could enjoy the protection of an armed state of their own, had always been part of the Zionist ideal. Now it seemed urgent to achieve that goal, since the wartime fate of Jewish minorities in Europe showed how vulnerable they were, not just to discrimination, but to genocide as well. The Jews therefore organized for seizure of power, by force if necessary, while the Palestinian Arabs tried to oppose them with an armed force of their own.

The British could not control the situation and decided to withdraw, calling on the new United Nations to decide what should happen in Palestine. In fact, action on the ground proved decisive. Jewish armed groups seized control of part of the country; other parts remained in Arab hands; and in 1948 the United Nations ratified what had happened by recognizing the territory the Jews controlled as a new sovereign state of Israel. Arabs in Egypt, Syria, and other neighboring lands had tried, vainly, to prevent the Jews from achieving independence. They all refused to recognize the new state of Israel until 1979, when Egypt did so. The issue was further embittered by Arab refugees from the part of Palestine which the Jews had conquered who organized the Palestine Liberation Organization (PLO) to fan Arab resentment and seek revenge. Israelis, for their part, wanted to expand the territory under their control so as to secure more nearly defensible frontiers and come nearer to reconstituting the biblical Kingdom of David.

Arabs were far more numerous, but the Israelis, reinforced by Jews who streamed into the country from all parts of the Moslem world and from much of Europe, were better organized and had the advantage of financial support and a supply of arms from the United States and elsewhere. As a result, renewed warfare in 1956, 1967, and 1973 led to further Israeli victories. The Israelis took possession of Jerusalem and all the Palestinian territory west of the Jordan River, though other governments, even those most sympathetic to Israel, did not recognize the annexation of this additional territory. In 1982 the Israeli army invaded Lebanon to disperse PLO encampments near the border and strengthen the political position of the Christian minority in that country. This time, however, success eluded them. The PLO was badly damaged, but radical Moslem groups among Lebanon's population gained new

scope and power in an on-going civil war by opposing the Israelis. American efforts to mediate failed; and in 1985 the Israelis withdrew.

Moslem anger at what happened in Palestine after World War II was only part of the dismay that pious followers of Mohammed felt at the course of public events. Ever since the 1920s, the governments of Iran and of Turkey had tried to modernize by abandoning the traditions of Islam in order to import skills and ideas from the European world. Ironically, success—even partial success—in modernizing provoked a powerful popular reaction against godlessness and the repudiation of Islam. Preachers of traditional religion easily convinced ex-peasants, concentrated in vast city slums, that return to Islam was the only way to salvation. In Iran, where oil wealth allowed the government to modernize very rapidly, popular revolution broke out in 1979. A new pious regime came to power, inspired by the teaching and preaching of Ayatollah Khomeini (1901–1989), who sought to impose the Sacred Law of the Shia version of Islam in every detail. In Turkey, however, modernization had started sooner and came more slowly, so the shock was smaller. Moreover, Turkish Moslems were divided among many different sects. Disagreeing with one another, they could not carry through a popular revolution as the Iranians, who were almost all Shiites, had done.

Nevertheless, the Iranian revolution sent a quiver of excitement throughout the Moslem world. For the first time in two centuries, Moslems could argue convincingly that the wave of the future did not require abandonment of the faith and customs of their forefathers after all. Khomeini's example showed how to act on the belief that Allah still ruled the world and would reward his faithful servants as in former ages. Buoyed by such hope, Shiite Moslems in Syria and Lebanon became more assertive. Similar responses occurred in Afghanistan and throughout the Arab lands. The failure of Israel and the United States in Lebanon in the 1980s was connected with this resurgence of Moslem and specifically of Shiite piety. The Soviet Union, for its part, invaded Afghanistan in 1979 to prevent Moslem revolutionaries from overthrowing a communist puppet government there. Guerrilla resistance to the Russian invaders proved as

Arab-Israeli Wars and Boundaries 1946-1989

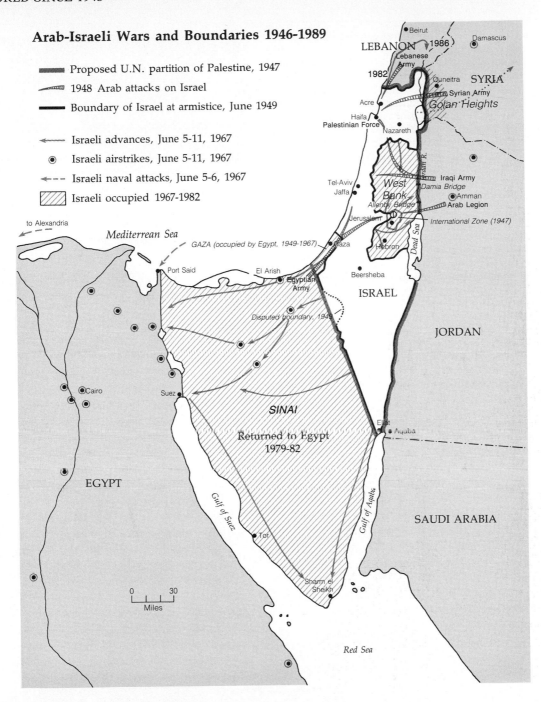

Proposed U.N. partition of Palestine, 1947

1948 Arab attacks on Israel

Boundary of Israel at armistice, June 1949

Israeli advances, June 5-11, 1967

Israeli airstrikes, June 5-11, 1967

Israeli naval attacks, June 5-6, 1967

Israeli occupied 1967-1982

stubborn as anything the Vietnamese had offered to the Americans in the decade before, and the Russians decided to withdraw their troops from the strife-torn land in 1989 without being sure whether their communist puppet regime could survive or not.

To cap the complexity of Middle Eastern affairs, the revolutionary Iranian government started out with a lively hope of freeing fellow Shia believers from the secularizing rule of the government of Iraq. Iraq attacked in 1980, provoking eight years of bitterly fought war. But by

Recent Revolutionaries These photographs record the most important successful revolutions of the post-World War II era. Above, Mao Tse-tung, Chairman of the Chinese Communist Party, makes a public appearance in 1959 at a time when the "Great Leap Forward" was in mid-course. In 1959 Mao was near the peak of his influence and prestige as a revolutionary leader. He had brought the Chinese Communists to power in 1949 and then defeated United Nations troops in Korea in 1952–53. In 1958 he undertook the Great Leap Forward to show Marxists everywhere (and especially the Russians) how to achieve the goals of real Communism without suffering from the bureaucratic socialism that, Mao claimed, had diverted the Soviet Union from the true path of revolutionary Marxism. Subsequently, the failure of the Great Leap Forward dimmed Mao's reputation at home and abroad; and the increasingly obvious failures of Marxist regimes made religiously inspired revolution of the sort that came to Iran in 1979 far more attractive. Below is a photograph of an Iranian crowd, demonstrating in front of the American Embassy in Tehran in 1979. Placards bearing the visage of Ayatollah Khomeini and a crude caricature of U.S. President Jimmy Carter show the two poles of the movement: revulsion against the influence of the United States, on the one hand, and an effort to return to old fashioned Moslem righteousness, as defined by the Ayatollah, on the other. Yet for all their desire to get back to a religiously defined way of life, the revolutionaries in Iran consciously used TV to influence opinion in the United States, as the symbols and writing on the Carter caricature plainly show.

1988 mutual exhaustion persuaded the combatants to try to make peace under U.N. auspices. In the meanwhile, American and European navies had begun to patrol the Persian Gulf to make sure that oil deliveries were not interrupted. No one could be sure whether peace would hold, or whether fighting would flare up again in a part of the world where religious and ethnic antagonisms remained at white heat.

Other quarrels, based partly on ancient religious differences, divided Libya from Egypt almost as bitterly as Iran opposed Iraq. Lebanon was also distracted by feuds among its Moslem sects as well as by Moslem-Christian frictions. Ironically, the more Islamic peoples and governments tried to make political action conform to their faith, the bitterer their divisions became.

Other parts of the world lagged behind the Middle East in mingling religion with politics. Nonetheless, renewed commitments to traditional religious identities made themselves felt elsewhere. The clash between India and Pakistan was heavily colored by religious differences, for example; and some guerrilla movements in Africa and Latin America assumed a religious or at least partly religious overtone—sometimes Christian, sometimes Moslem, and sometimes mixing in Marxist ideas as well. In other places, more traditional, secular forms of Marxism roused warmer response; but in spite of their theoretical internationalism, Marxists, too, could quarrel as short-lived wars between Vietnam and China and between Vietnam and Cambodia showed.

Despite these and other local wars and guerrilla actions, the overall pattern of world politics since 1945 was more peaceful than in most past ages. Fear of atomic annihilation was a powerful restraint, but the remarkable economic expansion that took place after World War II also had much to do with the general climate of politics.

POPULATION GROWTH AND ECONOMIC EXPANSION

The modern worldwide population expansion dates back to about 1750, but after World War II its pace accelerated so much that experts began to speak of a population explosion. The main reason for the sudden surge in human numbers was that death rates in poor countries dropped very suddenly when the World Health Organization (WHO), set up in 1948, helped local governments to apply scientific public health measures on a worldwide scale. Diseases like malaria, cholera, tuberculosis, and many others that had traditionally snuffed out a great many lives were sharply reduced, thanks to new antibiotic drugs and other treatments. The greatest triumph came in 1980, when the WHO was able to proclaim that smallpox, one of the most lethal of all human diseases, had been entirely eliminated.

Worldwide application of scientific medicine to human health problems, beginning in the late 1940s and 1950s, allowed far more infants to survive than before; and they, in turn, began to have children by the 1970s and 1980s. The result was indeed extraordinary. World population had reached about 2.5 billion in 1950; by 1985 the total had almost doubled to just under 5 billion. Such figures stagger the imagination and make the decades after World War II unique in world history. By the mid-1980s statistics seemed to show that dropping birth rates had begun to reduce the global pace of population growth; if that trend continues, the population history of the three postwar decades will stand out as unprecedented and unparalleled. But, short of war or some other global catastrophe, even if future birth rates continue to decline, population will increase for a long time to come simply because so many millions of children are still coming of age in the poor countries of the earth and will themselves begin to have children in the years ahead.

The rapidity with which human numbers increased, especially in the poorer, mainly agricultural countries of the world, created difficult problems. Whenever increasing numbers of young villagers could not find enough land to cultivate in the way their parents had done, they faced awkward choices. Some remained at home, cultivating smaller plots of land more intensively than before. Other millions sought escape from creeping impoverishment by migrating to towns and cities. But with so many rural youths coming in from the countryside, jobs became hard to find. Nearly always, conditions of life for newcomers to the cities were bleak and unsatisfactory. Inevitably, millions of such people felt that something was fundamentally wrong with the world, and competing remedies—religious, revolutionary, or a combination of the two—found ready response. Political upheavals and guerrilla movements of the most diverse kind fed on such discontents; and, of course, wherever prolonged violence broke out—in Vietnam, Ethiopia, El Salvador, Afghanistan, and Lebanon, for exam-

Poverty, Rural and Urban Rapidly growing populations put enormous strain on Asian, African, and Latin American societies. When so many young people come of age in the villages, new land to cultivate as their ancestors have done before them is often hard to find; but migration into town does not solve the problem if urban employment is not available in sufficient amount. These two photographs suggest the rural and urban sides of this dilemma. On the top, Indonesian peasants are busily transplanting rice plants; on the bottom, a street scene from Calcutta in India shows people sitting idly on the sidewalk. The back-breaking work of the paddy fields is age old; but in Indonesia, as population has grown, there is less and less rice land to go round. In India, massive emigration from an overcrowded countryside into Calcutta has helped to create a concentrated mass of poor and discontented people. The Communist party of India tries to win their support, as the slogans and symbols painted on the walls in this photograph show. Nevertheless, religious and other conservative influences have preserved both India and Indonesia from large scale civil violence and revolution since their liberation from European imperial control in the aftermath of World War II.

ple—economic disruption intensified the crisis and hardened opposition among rival groups.

The surprising thing, really, is that nearly doubling the world's population since 1950 provoked so little violence. One reason was that the improvements in public health, which allowed more people to survive, were matched by improvements in agricultural methods, which expanded the total food supply and thus allowed more people to get enough to eat—somehow. In effect, scientific agriculture ran a race with scientific medicine, allowing increasing food production to keep up with increased human numbers on the global scale, even though local supplies did not always match local needs. Agricultural scientists developed genetically redesigned seeds that gave larger yields, especially when used with chemical fertilizers. Sometimes irrigation was possible, or improved implements gave better results. The spread of more efficient agriculture to much of Asia and through parts of Latin America and Africa constituted what has been called the "Green Revolution." It allowed growing populations to survive, however precariously. Nevertheless, vulnerability to drought, flood, and other natural stresses increased as agricultural production intensified. The race between population growth and increased food production continued to skirt disaster.

Migration of Populations

A second aspect of postwar population history introduced another kind of strain on world relationships. After a decade-long "baby boom" in the late 1940s and early 1950s, birth control checked population growth in all the developed countries of the earth. As a result, the demographic gap between poor and rich tended to increase. In some places, Hungary, for example, replacement of existing population became problematic; in all the rich countries—European, American, and Japanese alike—as children became fewer, the elderly became more numerous, making relations among age groups different from before. In addition, fewer young people seeking work meant that the nasty jobs were hard to fill, and this opened an opportunity for migrants from the populous poor countries, especially

those located nearby. In Europe, such immigrants were often Moslem: Turks in Germany, Algerians in France, Pakistanis in Britain. In the Soviet Union, too, Moslems from central Asia grew in numbers while Russians and other peoples of European origin saw birth rates plummet. The United States, for its part, attracted growing numbers of immigrants from Latin America and the Caribbean Islands, who played a parallel role in American society.

Assimilation of these immigrants was unlikely, at least in the short run; and just how relations between old inhabitants and newcomers will work out in future is an unsolved question for everyone concerned. The fate of immigrant communities in rich countries affects the countries of emigration too, sometimes emptying out poor villages and destroying traditional ways of life, sometimes allowing old ways to continue in seriously overcrowded circumstances, thanks to money sent back home by the emigrants. Improved transport and communication means that migrants do not need to break off contact with their places of origin. Instead, they can return frequently, thus creating a new sort of link between rich and poor lands. Intensified frictions compete with better understanding across ethnic and cultural barriers in these circumstances. As usual in human affairs, the upshot remains problematical.

Changes in Subsistence Agriculture

Another postwar change of far-reaching importance was the awakening of the peasant mass of humanity to new possibilites of political and economic action. As population grew and as new methods of cultivation spread, traditional patterns of subsistence agriculture retreated. Even poor peasants had to try to find something to sell so as to be able to buy what they needed for the new kinds of farming. For the first time in history, agriculture was fully, or almost fully, incorporated into the exchange economy that dominated the globe. This was true in communist as much as in noncommunist lands. Instead of depending mainly or entirely on what each family could produce for itself, as most peasants had always done before, rural as well as urban dwellers began to produce goods or supply services for others, getting what was needed for his or her own life in exchange.

From the very beginning, the power and wealth of civilized society had depended on occupational specialization; but for thousands of years, specialization affected only a few. A minority of rulers, priests, artisans, soldiers, and other city folk consumed food that others had raised, while the rural majority supplied that food by paying rents and taxes in kind. They seldom had much left over after attending to their families' needs. Thus, until the last few centuries, most human beings worked in the fields and consumed only a part of what they produced, while supporting the few who engaged in other occupations. They did so without getting much of anything in return except the (often undependable) benefits of peace and order.

Nevertheless, as discussed in earlier chapters, slowly and gradually improved transportation allowed human beings to exchange goods over longer and longer distances. As a result, market relations gradually began to affect the lives of more and more persons. The process accelerated after A.D. 1000 with improvements in shipping and got into high gear in the eighteenth century with the Industrial Revolution. But even after the Industrial Revolution it took a long time for the vast rural mass of humanity to enter actively into the network of economic exchange. The process is not complete even today; but the tiny communities of hunters and gatherers who still survive in the Amazon basin, the Kalahari desert, or on the Arctic sea ice, and the larger numbers of herders and subsistence cultivators who continue to exist in remote regions, have become a small minority in the world as a whole. The vast majority of human beings, urban and rural alike, depended instead on a flow-through economy, exchanging goods and services with strangers, sometimes across thousands of miles and across political boundaries.

Advantages were real but risks were great. In particular, any interruption in the smooth exchange of goods and services became potentially devastating to hundreds of millions of persons. The depression of the 1930s showed how paralyzing bad times could be in countries where sub-sistence agriculture had almost disappeared. In the postwar decades, this kind of vulnerability spread from the highly industrialized countries to the whole world.

New Techniques of Economic Management

In partial compensation, techniques of economic management improved so that the old pattern of alternating boom and bust was damped back to minor proportions throughout the first thirty years of the postwar era. This was achieved, in large part, by using in peacetime methods of management and control that had been developed to fight the two world wars of the twentieth century. New kinds of statistics and new modes of data processing, made easy by computers, allowed managers to adjust the flow of goods and services, both on the level of great private corporations— sometimes operating across national boundaries—and on the national, governmental level as well. Goals varied. But whether it was full employment, maximal profit, or fulfillment of production quotas assigned by a Five Year Plan, managers could come considerably closer to achieving their purposes than before. In the rich and powerful noncommunist countries, official manipulation of indirect economic regulators, like interest and tax rates, sustained a boom from the mid-1950s to the mid-1970s. In communist countries, official plans for economic development achieved parallel results by assigning resources to particular projects in accord with a system of priorities.

Communist and Capitalist Patterns

The communist pattern of economic change got results by relying mainly on official rules and commands; the capitalist pattern mixed governmental commands and rules with private pursuit of gain as affected by changing market prices. Communist command economy worked best when an underemployed rural population could be set to work in mines and factories to exploit new resources. But when careful rationing of labor, raw materials, and machinery became critical, as happened in the Soviet Union from about the 1970s onward, the system of command began to look clumsy, since there was no measure of efficiency that could be easily brought to bear as long as prices were set at arbitrary and often unrealistic levels.

The managed economies of the capitalist nations had their own weaknesses. In particular, unequal rewards among individuals and firms—and among different nations and regions of the globe—put great strain on the system. Even when economic expansion made most people at least a little better off, those who found themselves at the bottom of the income scale were liable to feel jealous of the rich. Poor countries were especially sensitive to the difference between their own level of life and that of richer lands. Theories of underdevelopment that blamed the gap on continuing capitalist exploitation or on past political colonialism were attractive to peoples and governments that could not manage their economies very well at home. Their difficulties were only partly due to low levels of skill and to local social traditions that ran against the grain of market behavior. They also had to face the crushing disadvantage that changing prices for their exports could reward or hurt them in ways completely beyond local control. Efforts to escape dependence on the export of a few commodities by developing industries and other new forms of economic activity required the borrowing of large sums of money. Such loans were difficult to repay, even when the borrowed money was sensibly invested, and when, as often happened, it was ill spent, repayment became all but impossible.

Problems of a Global Economy

A second difficulty in the economic system that arose after World War II affected communist and capitalist methods of management alike. On both sides of the iron curtain, national governments were the main units of economic management. But economic relationships were worldwide, and insofar as what happened depended on international exchanges, no one government—not even the government of the Soviet Union or of the United States—was able to manage affairs at home very effectively.

This became evident in the 1970s when both the superpowers discovered that they needed to import critically important goods at prices they could not control. As oil fields at home ran dry, the United States, along with most other countries of the noncommunist world, began to import more and more oil from abroad. Then, in 1974, a new association of oil-producing countries (OPEC) suddenly raised the price of oil by about four times. The resulting shock to the world economic system was considerable. Poor countries had difficulty paying for more expensive oil and had to cut back on activities that used the precious fuel. A few oil-rich governments, located mainly in the Middle East, found themselves with more money than they could use at home. And the industrially developed countries of western Europe, Japan, and the United States had to adjust to the new level of fuel prices by changing the way they used oil and other resources.

The long postwar boom faltered under the strain. All the governments concerned preferred inflation to taxation, with the result that rising prices changed the rules of economic behavior in ways many people found confusing and unjust. Even when OPEC nations ceased to cooperate with each other, and the price of oil dropped, the international economic system did not recover its former expansiveness. Inflation continued, rapidly in some countries, more slowly in others, while a heavy debt burden weighed down the poorer countries of the world. The discrepancy between national economic management and a growing dependency on goods and services coming from outside national boundaries was not overcome. In effect, the rich and powerful countries of the world were given a small taste of the weakness and dependency that poorer countries had always known. International agencies, like the World Bank, and regional international unions, like the European Economic Community, were too weak and too local to manage the world economy effectively. No one was in charge; no single policy could prevail. Thus the limitations of economic management on the national scale, as developed during and after World War II, became increasingly apparent; but no one knew what to do about it.

Limitations of the Soviet System   The Russians, too, ran into increasing difficulty in the 1960s and 1970s. Their dependency on foreign supplies was even more vital than that of the United States, for the collective farms of the Soviet Union failed to produce enough grain to feed their people comfortably. In 1963, after a bad harvest, the USSR had to buy millions of tons of grain from the United States; and Soviet grain shortages had to be made good by massive foreign purchases in other years as well, whenever bad weather hurt the crops. The weakness of Soviet agriculture was due less to geography than to their policy-makers' long-standing preference for industry, especially heavy industry and arms production. Indeed, the strength and weakness of the Soviet system rested on the fact that communist managers could and regularly did disregard market prices and real costs of production by giving special importance to a particular goal, and then assigning to it all the labor and resources needed for its accomplishment—regardless of what happened to other, competing activities and needs.

Yet the necessity to import food was even more embarrassing than the Americans' need to import oil. It advertised shortages and put Russian economic planning at the mercy of the weather and fluctuating grain prices that were set partly by other governments and partly by supply and demand on the world market. The limitations of communist-style economic management, even on the territorially vast scale of the Soviet Union, thus became glaringly apparent shortly before the American-style of nationally managed capitalist economy began to show its no less real limitations in the 1970s.

The Russians also found it difficult to cooperate smoothly with their neighbors, despite the fact that communist parties, all theoretically committed to the international solidarity of the working class, came to power in eastern Europe and China after the end of World War II. But in practice each new communist government wished to develop its own national economic system, minimizing dependency on outsiders, including the Soviet Union. Advantages of specialization were thereby reduced, and since prices were arbitrary in each communist country, trade agreements became occasions for political haggling. Sometimes the Soviet Union drove a hard bargain, offending neighbors who felt exploited. Sometimes advantages ran the other way, when the USSR granted generous terms to a communist regime in need of aid. Poland benefited in this way in the 1980s; Cuba did the same because of its geographical location at America's doorstep. But economic subsidies, however helpful to unpopular governments, could not buy loyalty to the Soviet Union, as the Poles' simmering discontent showed.

Problems in the Chinese Economy   The most important neighboring country with which the Soviet Union had to deal was China. Until about 1960, efforts at cooperation continued, but the Chinese communists wanted aid for economic and military purposes which the Russians were unwilling or unable to give. Friction between the two governments became open in the 1960s, when Mao Tse-tung accused the Russians of not being true Marxist revolutionaries any longer. Russian aid was withdrawn, and border quarrels actually led to a brief armed encounter in 1969. Meanwhile China attempted to exemplify Mao's revolutionary ideals by making a "Great Leap Forward" on the strength of its own resources. Backyard furnaces to smelt iron and organized assault on class enemies disturbed Chinese society and wrought economic havoc. After Mao Tse-tung died (1976), a reaction brought new men to power who sought support from the United States to counterbalance the threat they felt from the Soviet Union. Greater reliance on market prices at home provoked a rapid increase in China's agricultural production, but efforts to check population growth by imposing penalties on those with too many children showed that the government was by no means liberal or prepared to rely on the market to adjust population to available resources.

The Third World   China's enormous population—a quarter of the human race—makes its future important to every other nation. India, Africa, and Latin America are the other poor and populous lands where more than half the world's population struggles to survive. Here, as much as in the rich and powerful countries of Europe and America, the future of humanity will be decided in time to come. Increased production, intensified exchanges, more skillful management, may suffice to accommodate the increasing population of these lands, or even raise local living standards slightly, as has been the case since World War II. On the other hand, vulnerability to major disaster increases with economic development that depends on continuous circulation of goods and services among millions of persons and across long distances. If disaster does strike, in time to come the economic expansion of the decades since 1950 will seem as exceptional as the population history of those same decades. So far at least, and compared to any earlier age, the economic history of the post–World War II world looks like a triumph of management and luck in the face of rapid technological change and the enormous pressure of a doubling of the world's population.

THE IMPACT OF COMMUNICATIONS

Despite the importance of economics, human lives depend only partly on material goods. Wealth and poverty, contentment and distress, arise from what people expect for themselves and others; and that, in turn, depends on communications. In villages where traditional subsistence agriculture prevailed, food might become scarce each year in the weeks before the harvest, while in bad years everyone starved. But as long as economic differences between families remained slight and reflected how hard each family worked, no one was likely to feel poor. Hardships were part of life: normal, natural, and expected. Custom and habit sustained individual lives and defined what to expect, individually and collectively.

Buying and selling introduced new complications and new possibilities of economic differentiation. Contact with townspeople who never worked in the fields and yet often lived far more comfortably than villagers often made rural life seem harsh and unattractive. Landlords and moneylenders, where they existed, led an even easier life without working at all. Civilized societies lived with these contrasts for many centuries, and village custom somehow accommodated the inequity, usually by treating urban folk and landlords as a different, alien sort of being. By refusing to compare themselves with such outsiders, villagers could retain their own community values and way of life, regardless, or almost regardless, of what happened outside the village itself.

This sort of psychological insulation of rural from urban standards of living arose and flourished when communications were slender, so that the great majority of individuals lived out their lives in a village context and encountered outsiders only a few times a year and in more or less standard ways—raiding, paying rents and taxes, or buying and selling as the case might be. Until quite recently, therefore, expansion of market relations among villagers did not necessarily disrupt local patterns of life, even if more buying and selling did introduce new material goods and technical possibilities into rural society.

As long as villagers' communication with outsiders continued to be mainly oral and face to face, this ancient accommodation between the rural majority of humankind and the urban minority survived. Printing, although extremely important for urban specialists, was slow to affect rural communities. After all, peasants could not read until someone decided that schooling was useful, even for poor and humble countryfolk. In European lands, rural schooling was seldom available before 1850, and in other parts of the world, school systems that reached into the villages came a good deal later, and, indeed, have not become universal yet.

In the twentieth century, however, new and powerful communications shortcuts arose in the form of movies, radio, and TV. Movies existed before World War I but came into their own during the 1920s as a new form of popular entertainment. Radio networks began to attract large audiences during the 1930s in Europe and America and became important in poor countries after World War II. TV broadcasting started in the 1940s but soon caught up with radio in the sense that broadcast stations became nearly universal, even though receiving sets, since they cost more, remained far fewer. But display in public places made TV broadcasts available to hundreds of millions, both in city streets and buildings and in innumerable village squares. The same was also true for movies and for radio broadcasts, although cheap receiving sets made it far easier to own a radio privately and use it in the home. From the 1970s, recorded tapes added still another dimension to the new forms of communication and made smuggling prohibited messages across political frontiers comparatively easy.

An important feature of all these means of communication was that they did not depend on literacy and schooling. As long as the movie or broadcaster used a language familiar to listeners, messages came across very much in the way face-to-face encounters had always brought messages to the attention of ordinary people in everyday life. TV's visual images reinforced spoken words with a different sort of communication, comparable to the effect that travel to new lands and experience of strange societies might otherwise have on those watching the screen.

The full force of these new modes of mass communication has yet to be felt. Their political impact was sufficiently obvious that nearly all governments monopolized the control of broadcasting within national boundaries and sometimes used jamming stations to interfere with messages coming from abroad. In west European and some other democratic lands, laws prescribed more or less equal access to radio and TV for rival parties during election campaigns. But decisions about how to present the news, made on a daily basis by some sort of official or quasi-official authority, had enormous power over public opinion and gave those in control of the media a systematic advantage against all rivals.

In communist countries and in lands where a single party or military faction ran the government, access to radio and TV was tightly controlled to prevent dissenters from broadcasting criticism of official policies and points of view. In such circumstances, tapes sometimes played an important role in spreading a rival version of the truth. Ayatollah Khomeini's leadership of the Moslem revolution in Iran, for example, rested very largely on taped sermons in which he denounced the shah's godlessness from the security of a French villa. These were then smuggled into the country and played on tape recorders to secret gatherings and in private homes, convincing

most Iranians of the righteousness of the revolutionary cause.

The United States was unusual in consigning control of radio and TV to private companies whose main concern was making money from paid advertising. The political or social impact of their programming took second place to the aim of appealing to the largest possible audience, so as to increase advertising income. Even political campaigns began to be conducted with the powerful aid of paid advertisements. Equal access rules for formal political speechmaking by the major candidates and parties modified without cancelling the commercialization of American elections imposed by the way the country's radio and TV networks were managed.

Sports, criminal violence, and sex proved powerfully attractive in the competition for mass attention that American broadcasting companies engaged in. Programs often set out to shock viewers by pressing against the conventional and legal limits on what could be broadcast. Movies went even further, and a new market for pornographic films arose when legal rules against them were voided by American courts.

What the effect of such programming may be on actual conduct and attitudes is a matter of considerable debate in the United States and elsewhere. No one knows for sure, but it is hard to doubt that family relations and religious attitudes have been changed by movies, radio, and TV, working alongside other aspects of contemporary life. The cult of physical fitness as much as the prevalence of crime in the streets of American cities probably reflects the power of the media to affect popular patterns of behavior.

In the world's rich countries, modern communications fostered the emergence of a distinct youth culture, expressed and propagated primarily by musical recordings and performances celebrating sexual and other forms of sensory indulgence. In the 1960s, when those born during the postwar baby boom came of age, the gap between youths and older age groups widened. This was especially true in the United States, where the Vietnam War heightened the collision between the ideal of sensual self-expression, on the one hand, and the values of military discipline and self-sacrifice on the other.

Poor countries, in general, could not even afford blue jeans—the uniform of America's youth culture; and in communist countries, official censorship screened out most of the message, though official exhortations to work hard so as to achieve the goals of the current economic plan did not find ready acceptance among young people either. But dissent, where it existed, found almost no public expression, so differences among age groups, that figured so prominently in Japan, western Europe, and the United States, were pretty well hidden from view.

Another important feature of modern communications is that they readily cross political boundaries, whether or not governments approve. Agitation via the media which led to the Iranian revolution of 1979 offered by far the most spectacular example of successful defiance of a government. News and information services directed to foreign listeners are broadcast by the world's leading governments with the aim of affecting public opinion in foreign countries in ways favorable to the sending nation. What effect such broadcasts have is difficult to measure; but it means that no government, not even the most tyrannical, can be completely sure of controlling public opinion among its own people by censoring the news disseminated through its own broadcasts and newspapers, since messages from other sources can be received via the airwaves.

Propaganda from governmental sources soon breeds skepticism among a population subjected to it. This blunts the effect of official efforts to control public opinion without making such efforts entirely futile.

Effects of American Media

A more subtle yet perhaps more powerful effect on human consciousness arises unintentionally from entertainment programs whose messages, political or otherwise, are only implied. This side effect makes the widespread showing of American movies and TV programs in foreign lands one of the most significant cultural phenomena of our time. Mass media exports are not an American monopoly. Other countries have some success in exporting entertainment as well. Great Britain

produces several programs shown in the United States, for example; and there are some other established exchanges, for example, the circulation of Egyptian films to other Arab lands, and of Russian films within the communist bloc. But these are all dwarfed by the sale of suitably dubbed American films and tapes to the TV stations and movie houses of other countries. Since costs had been met already by their showing within the United States, the producers of these programs can afford to offer them abroad at com-

Schooling in Nigeria The poor countries of the world are poor because their people lack skills and habits of cooperation that are necessary for efficient use of modern machinery and for the effective coordination of human effort. The most obvious way to escape the trap of poverty is to set up schools in which the young may learn needed new skills, beginning with the simple ability to read and write and do arithmetic. Accordingly, since World War II much effort has gone into schooling in the newly independent countries of Africa and Asia. Here we see a school in Nigeria, housed in a rather makeshift fashion, and with minimal furniture. But the presence of the two TV screens attest the impact of new technology and the way the children are dressed shows the impact of western and specifically American styles on the young. Clearly, at the moment this photograph was taken, the TV sets have taken over the classroom. What message they communicate we can only guess.

paratively cheap prices. American films and tapes have held popular attention by appealing to elemental human emotions, by having no overt political message, and, above all, by being available in abundance, whereas in smaller countries locally produced programs simply cannot fill all the broadcast time.

The effect of such broadcasting in poor and backward countries is even more uncertain than the effects within the United States itself. Many foreign viewers perhaps react to screen portraits of the streets of Los Angeles and other American cities as a sort of never-never-land and treat the whole thing as a fairy story. But patterns of personal behavior, exemplified in westerns, soap operas, and other staples of the American entertainment business, are likely to suggest new possibilities to viewers in distant lands where family traditions and expectations are profoundly different from those prevailing in the United States. How the old and new will combine remains to be seen. Change in patterns of personal behavior, rapid and unpredictable in its results, seems sure to follow from the mingling of such discrepant elements. It is still too soon to tell.

Countercurrents to the mass culture of the broadcast media as commercialized in the United States are powerful and obvious. Most of the world's governments produce at least a few radio and TV programs of their own, intended to assert and maintain local traditions and values. Some countries prohibit American entertainment entirely, so its circulation becomes clandestine. This is true of the Soviet Union and of most other communist countries. Many Moslem lands also prohibit or censor American programs.

Even within American society itself, and in other countries where the mass media are not strictly controlled by official authority, private persons and organizations deliberately reject some or all of the values implied by commercialized mass entertainment. Religious groups, seeking to uphold old certainties, are by far the most important of these counterweights in American society. Some of them use radio and TV to propagate their teachings in direct competition with secular entertainment. Ethnic groups also sometimes seek to maintain their unique heritage despite the attractions of the American melting pot and rely on radio as well as ethnic newspapers to do so.

All this is a counterpart, within American society, of similar movements in the world at large among peoples who wish to be modern, rich, and powerful all right, but who also wish to maintain their customs, their language, their religion, and their uniqueness against all the temptations and corruptions of the outside world. Since nearly everyone feels pulled in both directions—toward the new and toward the old—how any particular group or country will choose between alternatives in time to come remains very uncertain. It is silly to suppose that American mass culture will prevail everywhere; it is equally foolish to deny that those who reject it most strenuously, like the Iranian revolutionaries, will nevertheless be influenced in reaffirming their own tradition by what they oppose.

CONCLUSION

The one thing certain in our world is the rapidity and irresistibility of change in almost every aspect of human affairs. Thus, for example, the political rivalry between Russia and the United States suddenly took a new turn when Mikhail Gorbachev came to power in the Soviet Union in 1985 and began a program of reform at home and withdrawal from military adventures abroad. Instead of trying to build more weapons, Gorbachev proposed arms reductions and the American government went along, a little reluctantly at first, by making arms reduction proposals of its own. If this new sort of competition lasts and real reductions in military expenditure take place, other political alignments of the post-World War II world will shift as well. The partitioning of Germany (and of Korea?) might end; and a new balance in Europe, perhaps dominated by Germany, might emerge as suddenly as the Cold War alignment of the late 1940s arose out of the ruin of Hitler's Germany.

This sort of political change is matched in economics. Indeed, economic difficulties clearly underlie Gorbachev's political program. The United States, too, has had serious economic problems in trying to keep up with Japan and other Asian countries. Rapid transfer of skills and capital to new lands and resulting changes in the market have made all the world far more interdependent than ever before; and while national governments can affect what happens, none of them can hope to control the ever-changing flow of goods and services that keeps the economic system going.

As far as society is concerned, the same sort of changeability prevails. In particular, the surge of population and intensification of communications is altering ideas about how we ought to behave. Old routines, habits, and customs are challenged almost everywhere; but how to replace them is yet to be determined.

Living in such a world is sure to bring surprises. Risks and opportunities abound. How they will balance out, time alone will decide.

Chapter 26

THOUGHT AND CULTURE SINCE 1914

Since 1914 deep and far-reaching changes have come very quickly in the way people think and act. From country to country, great differences appear; and even within a single country, different age groups and different economic classes, different races and different religious bodies, sometimes disagree with one another about nearly everything. Or so it seems to anyone who reads the newspaper headlines and listens to all the quarreling voices that compete for public attention all round the world.

General trends are difficult to detect. Certainly, communication has increased. We know far more about events in distant parts of the earth than our grandparents or great-grandparents did, and far more people travel than ever before. This may tend to even out differences—but only in the long run. In the short run, as people become more aware of their many differences, more frequent contacts often merely underline the things that split humankind into quarrelsome parts.

Since World War I, scientists have mastered new secrets at a great rate; atomic physics, genetic codes, psychological motivation, humanity's evolutionary past—these and many other fields have opened important new vistas since 1914. Yet we have also learned how much human action depends on irrational and unconscious impulses. Artists have tried to express and explore the subconscious levels of life, both in words and through the visual arts.

Some people feel that the result of so much change amounts to a breakdown of all civilized traditions. Others argue that the Western world is undergoing one more internal transformation, like the shift from medieval to early modern or from the Old Regime to nineteenth-century industrial and liberal society. At the moment, no one knows which of these judgments will stand up in time to come. Caught as we are in the midst of it all, no one is wise enough to foresee the outcome or understand everything that is happening. In this chapter, therefore, we can only make an attempt to point out some things that seem important, and may turn out to be so—or may not.

THOUGHT AND CULTURE

From close up, at any rate, it looks as though specialization and professionalization of art and thought had run riot since 1914. Artists who are so original that no one understands them are easy to discover in any art colony. Scholars whose interests are so specialized that only a few others in the entire world can understand what the argument is about also exist on many university campuses. On the other hand, the gap that used to exist between local folk cultures and the concerns of the upper classes was probably no greater than the gap between experts and the masses in our own day. What has happened is that the popular level of culture has achieved visibility through the mass media of communication, whereas before, popular culture passed from generation to generation invisibly, by word of mouth and by example.

Taking the world as a whole, the dominating fact about popular culture is the break it represents with folk traditions of every kind. Wherever economic conditions allowed, peasants and ex-peasants left traditional local styles of living behind them as fast as they could. New city-made clothes and gadgets of all kinds tend to be the first things that matter. People emerging from traditional peasants ways of life may find their most fascinating introduction to civilization in studying an illustrated mail order catalogue or the advertisements in a glossy magazine. This allows them to learn about what can be wished for. The next thing is actually to possess a bicycle, then household appliances; and the climax is a car. But to have a car in such societies is still reserved for a tiny few who have made it all the way to the top.

Mass Media and Popular Culture

Somewhere about midway in this curve of rising expectations, people start to pay serious attention to the mass media. To begin with, it was nearly always government initiative that brought the radio and roads to the countryside and to urban slums. During World War II, for example, the United States Information Service distributed thousands upon thousands of cheap radio speakers to villages in many different parts of the world. These radios were tuned to a central radio station and were usually planted in a public place near the center of the community. In many regions of the world where official propaganda and news had never penetrated on a regular basis, it now became possible to speak daily to the villagers. An entirely new kind of political life thus became possible.

Even the busiest politicians have to stop talking sometimes. This means that national radio and television hookups must fill the time with other sorts of material, exposing hundreds of millions of human beings to new forms of cultural expression. Popular music, and popular TV programs, differing from country to country, did something to close the gap between city and village populations. Performers attracted a following among the vast numbers of persons who became able to listen to them or see them on the screen. And new art forms arose as well: westerns, crime shows, soap operas, quiz shows, jazz, rock music, and the like.

The most original creation of American popular culture was jazz. This originated in the black ghettos of New Orleans, Memphis, and Chicago. It came to the attention of whites in the 1920s and spread widely through Europe and round the world. After years of resistance, even the Russians have begun to let jazz be heard in public. Popular music in the jazz tradition soon cut loose from its folk roots and became big business. One style succeeded another as popular performers vied for attention.

In the 1950s a countercurrent manifested itself. Students and other Americans became interested in folk music found mainly in the South and picked up old songs or invented new ones. Thus, while most of the world was trying to leave oral folk traditions behind, in the United States,

at least, an influential group tried to recover something of the old simplicities of folk culture.

Standardization of Language   An important by-product of mass media culture is standardization of language.

A few "world languages" attained greater importance with the rise of mass communications. English has profited most, for United States and British radio programs, movies, and phonograph records have spread literally around the world. Russian has met with great success inside the borders of the Soviet Union, where all the other nationalities have learned Russian and use it increasingly in daily encounters. In other parts of the world, the pattern is unclear. In India, for example, government effort to make Hindi a national language has met with organized local resistance, and English still retains some importance for the well-educated. The future of European languages in Africa remains completely uncertain; but in Latin America, Spanish and Portuguese seem to be encroaching on the Indian languages that still survive. In China and Moslem lands, however, the old classical languages, enriched by new coinages to fit new conditions, have had their power reinforced by the advent of mass media. The end result, in all probability, will be to reduce quite sharply the number of living languages. Speech patterns familiar to only a few people will have trouble resisting the new means of communication.

Links between popular mass culture and highbrow thought and art seem unimportant. Artists sometimes have tried to find roots for their work in the folkways of their nation. Thus, for example, a Mexican school of painters, of whom Diego Rivera (1886–1957) was the most famous, sought to arouse popular response by reviving pre-Columbian styles of art. In the 1930s, Parisian artists experimented with creating visual surprises by cutting out parts of magazine advertisements and pasting them together in absurd or shocking patterns. In the 1960s "pop" art tried similar techniques with paint and canvas, and in a different way the revival of folk music in the United States tried to accomplish the same thing.

In times past, when schoolteachers were the most important link between popular and highbrow culture, upper-class tastes tended to seep downward with the passage of time. Perhaps a similar process will continue if the persons who manage the mass media, searching for something new to put before the public, find use for what began as inaccessible highbrow stuff. But it is certainly not clear that seepage downward will be the prevailing movement. Popular mass culture may instead crowd out at least some aspects of upper-class culture, or transform it. So far, neither process seems very important. Instead, highbrows go one way and the mass media go another. At any given moment in time there seems to be little in common between the two levels of thought and feeling.

THE SCIENCES

Although enormous amounts of new data have been gathered since 1914, the hard sciences that allow prediction have not achieved any radically new breakthrough since Albert Einstein proposed his theories of relativity in 1905 and worked them out in 1915. All the same, it took physicists some time to get used to the sort of universe that Einstein's formulas implied; and ordinary people found it still more puzzling to be told that space and time were not clearly separate, and that waves and particles, as well as matter and energy, were somehow the same thing.

Advances in Physics

In the 1930s, new machines were invented for accelerating electrons and other charged particles to great speeds. With these instruments, exploration of atomic nuclei became possible. High-speed particles could be made to hit an atom nucleus, and special instruments could then record information about the fragments that resulted from the collision. By measuring sizes and speeds, scientists could figure out what had been in the nucleus before the collision took place. As time went on, more and more powerful accelerators were constructed, and the number of particles that could be detected and measured increased.

For a while, it seemed possible to explain all observations by making a geometrical model of atomic structure. A Danish physicist, Niels Bohr (1885–1962), developed the idea that the nucleus was surrounded by revolving electrons, moving in more or less fixed orbits at different distances from the nucleus. Bohr's atom was a little like a miniature solar system, with the nucleus as sun and the electrons as planets. But during the 1930s, various new observations could not be fitted into this geometrical model. Physicists gave up the whole effort, preferring mathematical and statistical expressions to describe subatomic relationships. To ordinary people who habitually think of physical matter in spatial, geometrical terms, this breakdown of visual models was very puzzling. Fanciful names for subatomic particles made advanced physics into a sort of Alice-in-Wonderland world, where quarks come in flavors and leptons spin and collide with dozens of other odd entities.

Even though the language of physics, as it became more mathematical, became more unintelligible to everyone but experts, practical applications did not cease to arise. During World War II, for example, Einstein's formula for the equivalence of matter and energy was translated into the controlled release of nuclear energy. The atom bombs dropped on Japan in 1945 were the first and most dramatic result of this application of theory. Atomic reactors that energize electrical generators and drive submarines are among the more important later applications of the nuclear techniques that physicists and engineers began to explore during World War II.

The potential importance of these inventions staggers the imagination. Total destruction of human life is one possibility. An almost unlimited supply of energy, if the costs of disposing of atomic wastes can be met, might be another. In either case, old limits on human powers have been broken through; whether for good or ill remains to be seen.

Earth Sciences

A second area in which scientists have been unusually active since 1914 is exploration of the earth and space. New ways to explore the at-

Exploration of Space Powerful rockets, designed to be capable of delivering atomic warheads to any part of the earth's surface, could also be used to explore space. Artifical satellites, like the one pictured on the left, could circle the earth, or alternatively, could rotate with the earth and thus always appear in the same location. This opened enormous new possibilities for collecting information about the earth below and the skies above. Reflectors, like those seen here, collected energy from the sun and converted it into radio and other electromagnetic waves. Connected with cameras and scanners sensitive to different wave lengths and pointed in different directions, these waves could then carry detailed information to receivers on the earth. Both weather patterns and military movements became visible as never before with such devices hovering overhead; and when pointed towards the depths of space, artifical satellites also discovered new objects in the heavens. The most spectacular feat of space exploration, however, was sending men to the moon and bringing them back again safely. On the right is a photograph of an American astronaut walking on the surface of the moon in 1969, just twelve years after the Russians had launched the first artificial satellite into orbit.

mosphere and the regions of space close to the earth were introduced, mainly after World War II. As a result, new data have come in much faster than anyone has been able to put them together into a tidy theory.

The first rocket to put an artificial earth satellite into space went up from Russia in 1957. Since then, hundreds of rockets have thrust their payloads into orbit around the earth, where they perform many new tasks: photographing the surface of the earth; relaying radio and TV waves around the earth; measuring gravity, magnetic fields, and other variables with a new precision; and observing the heavens without the fuzziness created by the atmosphere. Other rockets escaped earth's gravity entirely, extending probes toward Venus, Mars, and more distant orbiting bodies. These probes sent back limited information about earth's fellow planets. Far more spectacular, however, was the assault upon earth's nearest neighbor in space, which saw the United States reach the moon with a series of manned flights, beginning in 1969. The Russians, for their part, landed an unmanned vehicle on the moon in 1970, which traveled short distances across the surface and sent back information about what it encountered. American moon flights not only put in position various "sensors" (devices which respond to physical stimuli) to detect moonquakes and other changes on the moon but were also able to bring back samples from different regions of the moon's surface.

Spectacular photographs and a lot of detailed information about the moon resulted from these efforts. In addition, space explorers wrote a new chapter in the record of human venturesomeness and technical achievement. But so far, theoretical understanding of earth and sky has not been much affected by these first efforts to extend humanity's dominion into the fringes of earth-space. Perhaps there has not yet been enough time for the new data to challenge old theories; even when existing theory cannot explain observed phenomena—for instance, the discovery that sources of radio waves in stellar space are not the same as sources of visible light—no new general interpretation has yet emerged.

Exploration of the world's oceans also achieved a new thoroughness and scope after World War II. Accurate plotting of ocean bottoms revealed a complicated pattern of ridges and deeps, together with differences in the underlying rocks. These new observations prove that North and South America are slowly drifting away from Europe and Africa, making the Atlantic wider and the Pacific narrower, inch by inch. Earthquakes and mountain-building can be related in important ways to this newly discovered pattern of continental drift, and the possibility of understanding and perhaps some day predicting movements deep within the bowels of the earth now seems open.

But this is still in the future. So far, the principal practical application of the new data which earth scientists have gathered so successfully is better weather prediction. Satellites are capable of photographing wide areas of the earth continuously and can transmit the picture to the ground. This technique allows the paths of storms to be plotted and their course predicted with much greater precision than before. In addition, the military significance of photographic reconnaissance from space is obvious. Orbiting cameras make military secrets much harder to keep than they used to be.

Molecular Biology

In biology, a dramatic new idea was broached in 1953 when Francis H. C. Crick and James D. Watson proposed that biological inheritance was carried from one generation to the next by large molecules that took the form of spiral chains. Even though these chains could be very long, they had a relatively simple repetitive structure. Small changes in the exact order in which sets of atoms appeared in such a molecule made all the difference between the genetic inheritance of human beings and even the simplest of living forms, such as bacteria and algae.

Many other, less spectacular discoveries extended detailed understanding of biological processes. More and more of what happened in living

The Decipherment of DNA This photograph shows James Watson and Francis Crick with a model of a DNA molecule that they constructed in 1953. Their model proved accurate, despite the complexity of the structure they were analyzing. It provided a new understanding of the chemical basis of life on earth and won the two young men world fame and a Nobel prize.

THE DOUBLE HELIX

As a senior in college, James Dewey Watson decided he would try to discover the chemistry of genes. Genes were what carried biological inheritance from one generation to the next; but though biologists had been talking about them for a long time, no one knew exactly what genes were. From the University of Chicago, Watson went to Indiana for a Ph.D. in genetics; then he was awarded a postdoctoral fellowship for study in Europe. He resolved to use it to get started on his dream project: unraveling the chemical structure of genes.

At Cambridge, England, he found a colleague in Francis H. C. Crick. Crick was thirty-five years old, brilliant, and brash. Watson was also brilliant and brash—and eleven years younger. The two men hit it off from the start; and they agreed that to get at the secret chemistry of heredity, the thing to do was to construct a model of a molecule known as DNA. DNA is short for deoxyribonucleic acid—a material found in the nucleus of all living cells.

But DNA molecules are among the biggest known to exist. These enormous molecules were made up of hundreds of thousands of atoms, grouped in thousands upon thousands of subassembly blocks. How could anyone hope to discover how such a thing was put together? It was like trying to assemble the millions of parts of a big computer while blindfolded, for even the giant DNA molecules were far too small to be seen. Other research biologists thought that the staggering complexity of DNA would have to wait until the structure of smaller molecules—like the proteins that also exist in all living cells—had been worked out.

But Watson wanted to find out about genes, and he believed that DNA, not proteins, held the secret. So he plunged stubbornly ahead. When Crick and Watson started on the project, they had the advantage of others' work. The separate building blocks out of which DNA was made were already known. The proportions of each kind of material in DNA had been measured quite accurately. Most important of all, a way to fix DNA molecules into crystal form had been invented. This allowed x-ray photographs to be taken of the

tissues could be explained in chemical terms. Numerous applications of this knowledge came in medicine, as doctors invented chemical treatments for conditions that previously had been incurable. Some breakthroughs came by accident. In 1928, for example, Alexander Fleming noticed in some "spoiled" experiments that the growth of certain kinds of mold destroyed germs. This led to the discovery of penicillin (1929), the

first of numerous antibiotic drugs that have since save innumerable lives.

Computers and Their Applications

The development of workable electronic computers was another important breakthrough that came at the close of World War II. Designs for molecules. The difficulty was that what showed on such photographs was not a shape or even a shadow of the molecule itself, but patterns of x-ray reflections as they bounced off the various atoms that made up a DNA molecule.

Such bits of information added up to a vast puzzle. What could be done with it? What Watson and Crick did was to make guesses, and then try to build a model—out of wire and bits of metal—that would have a place for everything that had to fit into the giant DNA molecule. They made several false starts: leaving not enough space for all the necessary building blocks, or attempting a chemical bond between next-door neighbors that would not work. But in less than two years, they hit upon what turned out to be the right form—a double helix—after seeing some new x-ray photographs of DNA that had been made in London.

By the beginning of April 1953, the model had withstood all tests. The two young men were ready to announce their discovery. They did so by publishing a short article—only slightly over 900 words long. It began thus:

> We wish to suggest a structure for the salt of deoxyribose nucleic acid (DNA). This structure has novel features which are of considerable biological interests.[*]

This was grandiose understatement. Biologists everywhere soon realized that the double helix form allowed reproduction of similar molecules. By splitting the two strands of the double helix apart, a new strand could form to fit the old half. Thus the structure of the DNA unraveled part of the mystery James Dewey Watson had set out to solve. He had in truth learned something about the chemistry of genes—the innermost machinery of life itself.

---

[*]J. D. Watson and F. H. C. Crick, "Molecular Structure of Nucleic Acids," *Nature* 171 (1953): 737.

---

computers were fairly familiar from the work of nineteenth-century mathematicians, and the principle of storage and retrieval of information was well understood before transistors made it possible to make a machine that would really work. In the years since 1945, several different generations of computers have come into existence, each more flexible and with greater storage capacity than its predecessors.

The uses of computers are many. Banks, libraries, and income tax collectors can use them to keep track of individual accounts. In science, much more complicated uses arise, for computers can make calculations and pick out answers that fit given conditions much faster than human minds, unaided, can. This, in turn, makes various kinds of mathematical information available to scientists and engineers that simply could not be

The Wonders of Computers Computers can store and rearrange words and numbers with speed and accuracy that far surpass anything human beings can do without their assistance. This permits new forms of communication, new forms of science, and new forms of business and government administration. In addition, computers can create diagrams, such as the one shown in the screen in this photograph, so that engineers can try out plans for the design of a new machine by seeing how it will look ahead of time. They can also improve their design whenever a careful look shows up flaws in what had first been intended. In these and still other ways, computers have extended human powers of control and management far beyond older limits. So powerful are these new devices that one may ask whether human beings really control computers, or do they control us instead?

had if they were forced, as before, to sit down and figure out each step with pencil and paper.

Another frontier of inquiry opened by computers is investigation of how the human brain handles its input and output of data. There are some resemblances between the way a computer works and the activity of the brain. As computers become more flexible, they resemble brains more closely, so that theoretical insight into the one seems likely to rub off upon investigation of the other.

Understanding of the structural limits of languages and of logic is also likely to be affected by computers. Sociology and history may be transformed in the future as data describing in-

dividual human lives are put on tapes and become available for analysis by computers. At least in principle, this ought to make possible statistically precise generalizations about different aspects of social behavior among a population whose individual life histories have been recorded in detail.

Advances in the Social Sciences

Computers thus span the gap between the hard and soft sciences. They may in the future make some of the soft sciences a good deal less soft, that is, make possible more nearly accurate prediction of human behavior. Predicting election

Civil Rights in the United States Segregation of Blacks on buses and in other public places became law in most southern cities in the 1870s and private agreements prohibiting Blacks from owning or renting houses in a white neighborhood were common in the north. Pictured here is the man who first challenged these and similar forms of discrimination effectively. Martin Luther King, Jr. was a Baptist minister who borrowed Mohandas Gandhi's idea of attacking unjust laws by organizing non-violent disobedience on a mass scale. He began in 1955 with a boycott of the bus system in Montgomery, Alabama, and after about a year succeeded in abolishing segregated seating there. Soon he was leading a nation-wide movement for civil rights. This photograph was taken in 1963 at the height of King's career as a political activist, as he addressed a vast crowd of sympathizers from the steps of the Lincoln Memorial in Washington, proclaiming his dream of achieving racial equality and brotherhood. As a result of his agitation, in 1964 Congress passed a Civil Rights Act prohibiting racial segregation and King won the Nobel Peace Prize. Four years later, aged 39, he died of an assassin's bullet, after having compared himself with Moses in his last public speech, saying: "I may not get to the promised land with you, but I want you to know tonight that we as a people will."

results has already become almost a science, thanks to computers. Other similar changes may follow, particularly in economics, since fuller data on exchanges of money and of materials ought, again in principle, to permit far more accurate forecasting of future economic conditions than has yet been achieved.

Marxian Straitjacket in Communist Lands In the hard sciences, little difference exists between the communist and noncommunist worlds. Stalin did, for a while, try to impose Marxian linguistics and Marxian biology upon Russian scientists; but the effort was given up after Stalin's death. Physicists, chemists, mathematicians, and earth scientists have little trouble understanding one another or agreeing upon new discoveries as they are made, no matter on which side of the political fence.

The soft sciences are different, for Marxist doctrine limits and directs communist research. The fact is that many of the predictions Marx and Lenin made have not come true. Workers in capitalist countries have not become poorer and poorer, for example; and communist revolution has come not to the highly industrialized lands but to peasant countries, or countries just beginning to emerge from peasant status. Yet communists treat the writings of Marx and Lenin as though they were sacred scripture. Efforts to apply the doctrine to particular circumstances left plenty of room for invention and differences of opinion. But the basic truths, communists claimed, had been laid down forever and ever, and if the facts failed to conform to the doctrine, it was too bad for the facts. The "real" revolution and the "real" impoverishment of the workers would show up sooner or later.

New Perspectives in Economics, History, and Anthropology This attitude made honest thought about society impossible. In the Western world, however, the half century following World War I gave birth to at least three far-reaching new ideas. The first was the "new economics," developed since 1936 by John Maynard Keynes (1883–1946) together with his critics and followers. Keynes set out to explain what went wrong during the Great Depression of the 1930s, when unemployed workers and unemployed machinery in Britain and elsewhere existed side by side

671

with unsatisfied human wants. Keynes argued that governmental intervention could counteract the boom and bust pattern that had proved so harmful. During World War II his ideas gained new scope and precision in actual practice, when the British and American governments did intervene and directed economic activity into new channels with great success. After the war, economic management, using indirect methods favored by Keynes, became normal in the entire noncommunist world, though practice often departed from anything Keynes and his fellow economists ever dreamed of.

A second new concept of general importance was the widened historical vision that archaeology, anthropology, and exploration of the history of the non-Western world made possible. In 1914 most Westerners still knew little and cared less about other civilizations. Indeed, many Europeans and Americans believed that the Asian peoples had no history. They thought that after a first spurt of change, nothing new had happened in Asia. Progress, they believed, was limited to the West. But as changes came to all the world, this naive misunderstanding of the facts lost any shred of plausibility. Many careful scholars, both Westerners and Asians, set out to discover and write histories of all parts of the non-Western world.

At the same time, archaeologists discovered evidences of the beginnings of civilization in Sumer (1920s), China (1930s), and India (1920s). In 1914 Egypt had seemed the oldest civilization. By the 1940s it was known that this was not true, because the ancient Egyptians had borrowed some important ideas from the Sumerians. In the 1950s archaeological discoveries in Africa began to reveal new details of prehuman and human evolution.

The result of these lines of inquiry was to make it possible to see all the separate histories of nations, civilizations, barbarian peoples, and savages as part of the larger adventure of humanity. Much disagreement over details and even over the pattern as a whole remained. Oswald Spengler (1880–1936) and Arnold J. Toynbee (1889–1975) suggested that civilizations rose and fell according to a standard pattern, each remaining distinct from the others. This book, on the contrary, has tried to portray different civilizations and other less complex societies all at once, in the belief that they acted and reacted upon each other from the beginning. Still other patterns have their supporters; for instance, the Marxian view that all societies pass through slave, serf, and wage stages of development. Whatever room for argument remains—and it is very wide—it still holds true that a far more spacious and inclusive vision of the human past has become available as a result of progress in historical study in the past half century.

Freudian Psychology   A third important change in Western thought about humanity and society is connected with the name of Sigmund Freud (1856–1939). His most important books were written before 1914, but his ideas attained wide circulation only after World War I. The details of Freud's effort to describe the unconscious levels of human minds are not likely to last because the structure and function of the brain seem not to match the different levels of mental activity that Freud tried to distinguish. But the significant thing was this: Freud showed in thoroughly convincing ways that people often act under impulses that come from below the threshold of consciousness. Language sometimes simply disguises real motives. Freud's second lasting discovery was that one of our deep urges is sexual, and that this drive spills over into many other kinds of behavior and relationships.

In the 1920s, such ideas were new and shocking to many people. The implications of Freud's insights for politics and economics even yet have not been fully taken into account. Democratic theory, after all, assumes voters to be rational and able to choose rationally. Economists expect the same. But if unconscious levels of human motivation are in fact important on a private and personal level, then unconscious drives must also affect public behavior in ways we do not really understand.

ART AND LITERATURE

Although social scientists were, and still are, slow to react to the new ideas that Freud brought before the public, writers and artists in Western lands reacted at once and with considerable enthusiasm.

The communists, once again, stood aside. In Russia and other communist states, art was supposed to serve political purposes by helping to shape the new consciousness that communism required. It was a branch of propaganda, a kind of engineering of the soul. In the first years of the Russian Revolution, wild experimentation had been allowed, even encouraged. But from the 1920s, official directives instructed writers and artists what to do. Uplifting, inspirational subjects were prescribed; what was produced was often dull and trite.

Dullness and triteness were exactly what Western artists and writers were most anxious to avoid. Novelty, experiment, adventure to the limits of intelligibility, attracted them. To do what others had done seemed a confession of failure, of lack of genius. Self-expression on the part of the artist and remorseless analysis of his or her subject were characteristic of the most famous writers and artists of the age.

Old Genres in New Forms

In the 1920s both artists and writers experimented with new forms. Painters had only to carry on with the effort begun before World War I. Bits and pieces of ordinary visual experience were jerked out of context or distorted to the point where recognition by the viewer became hit-or-miss. Symbols aimed at affecting the subconscious mind were deliberately sought after. A desire to surprise and shock was a second goal pursued by many artists. The greatest names had already emerged to fame before World War I: Pablo Picasso (1881–1973), Georges Braque (1882–1963), and Henri Matisse (1869–1954) among them.

Non-objective paintings that made no effort whatever to look like anything else carried the breakaway from the Renaissance ideal to its logical conclusion. Piet Mondrian (1872–1944) and Vasili Kandinski (1866–1944) were among the pioneers of this kind of painting. The ideal of non-objective painting was "pure design," mathematical, geometrical, like music in its underlying principles.

In Germany an influential group of architects and industrial designers, the Bauhaus School, arose in the 1920s, inspired by the same ideas. The so-called international style of architecture resulted. It was characterized by the free use of new materials such as concrete, steel, and glass for walls, and by spare, rectangular, functional shapes. One great advantage of the new style was the lower costs of construction. Walls of glass were lighter, less expensive, and resulted in bright, open interiors. The Bauhaus style spread round the world within a couple of decades. Nearly all of the world's airports, for example, are in this general style, as well as thousands of new buildings in every important city of the world outside of the communist countries, where brick and mortar (more recently, concrete) continued to be preferred to glass.

Writers such as the novelist James Joyce (1882–1941) or the poet Thomas Stearns Eliot (1888–1965) experimented with words. By inventing new words, using fragmentary sentences, and stretching grammar, they and other writers tried to affect subconscious levels of their readers' minds in much the same way that artists were trying to do. But even in the hands of a master, tinkering with language quickly degenerated into mere unintelligibility; so this was not a very promising field to explore—nothing to compare with what painters were able to do. Accordingly, in the period after World War II, this line of literary development almost stopped. Writers, instead, concentrated on other ways of breaking with the past. One technique was the shock value of exploring previously forbidden themes, such as sex. Another was to celebrate the antihero, that is, to create a fictional character who did not impose his will on people and things around him in the way heroes had done since the time of Homer but became instead the helpless victim of circumstances.

Amidst all this striving for novelty, there were some writers who clung closer to old themes and conventions; among them were the playwright George Bernard Shaw (1856–1950), the poet Dylan Thomas (1914–1953), and the novelists Thomas Mann (1875–1955) and William Faulkner (1897–1962). It is impossible to tell which of these artists will turn out to be the more important authors of the age.

Modern Sculpture: Brand New and Age Old "Bird in Space" by the Rumanian sculptor, Constantin Brancusi (left) and "King and Queen" by the English sculptor, Henry Moore (right) both depart from older notions of artistic excellence by not trying exactly to resemble anything seen in nature. This makes them modern. But these two works are opposites too. Despite its title, Brancusi's slender, geometric shape soars from its base like a rocket more than like a bird, aptly expressing the extraordinary technological mastery over nature that science and technology have achieved in the twentieth century. The haunting, only half-human faces of Moore's gaunt figures, on the contrary, hark back to myth and subconscious memory, expressing a different side of twentieth century scientific accomplishment—the exploration of the irrational levels of human consciousness. (*Left*: Philadelphia Museum of Art: Louise and Walter Arensberg Collection./*Right*: Hirschhorn Museum and Sculpture Garden, Smithsonian Institution.)

New Genres in Old Forms

If popularity is any standard to depend upon, the really outstanding authors of the post–World War I period were the writers of murder mysteries. This branch of literature became popular before World War I with the tales by Arthur Conan Doyle (1859–1930), which told how a gentlemanly detective, Sherlock Holmes, used his powers of observation and deduction to solve mysteries. Hundreds of authors followed in Sherlock Holmes's footsteps, and millions of people read their works.

Still another new form of writing that came to the fore after 1914 was children's literature. Better understanding of how children grow from year to year made it possible to write more effectively for different age levels. Some stories became so well known as to populate the English-speaking world with a host of new characters: Pooh, Dr. Doolittle, Charlie Brown, and many more. Talking animals and clever children, generally speaking, took the place of the witches and fairies of older nursery tales.

Comic books, too, first gathered together from already published newspaper strips and then printed as an independent form of literature, also became very popular, appealing mainly to young and not fully literate readers.

Perhaps the most influential form of writing in the last fifty years has been manuals on how to raise infants and small children. Once upon a time, knowledge concerning the care and feeding of infants was handed down from generation to generation without being written down. In the 1920s, however, the movement of people from country to city meant that millions of young women married later in life after forgetting how their own mothers had looked after them as children, and they had no close relative nearby to pass on traditional lore. In addition, new information about vitamins and infant health gave doctors something new to say to mothers. The result was a rash of "How to" books. Millions of middle-class American mothers raised their babies according to instructions laid down in such books. Since then, "How to" books have covered a vast range of other subjects, replacing or supplementing older "hands-on" ways of transmitting practical skills from one generation to the next. The impact upon the national life was tremendous. In other countries, such manuals had less importance, perhaps; but everywhere the breakdown of oral tradition, linking the generations, required books of this kind.

RELIGION AND PHILOSOPHY

Most of the recent developments in science and thought have paid little attention to traditional religion. Yet Christianity, Judaism, Islam, Hinduism, and Buddhism remain. They are massive facts of the human scene. Their power over human minds is probably as great as ever. After all, religious groups also can use the mass media to spread their doctrines.

Among Christians, the most striking development of the years since World War I was the growing willingness of different sects and denominations to seek common ground. For a long time, this ecumenical movement was the work of Protestant groups, especially in the English-speaking world. Pope John XXIII (1958–1963) brought the Roman Catholic church into much more sympathetic relationship with this movement. He summoned the Second Vatican Council (1962, 1963), which defined Roman Catholic relationships with Jews and with other Christian sects in a conciliatory way.

Although mainline Christian churches began to emphasize the points that they have in common, new sects—with strong and uncompromising views—continued to arise and flourish, especially among poor and disadvantaged people. Jehovah's Witnesses is an example of one of these sects in the United States. This sect has also won converts in Africa and Latin America among peoples emerging from traditional peasant life, who felt the need of new, clearly defined guidelines for conduct and belief.

Perhaps, therefore, the movement toward reconciliation and unity is about evenly balanced by the rise and spread of new uncompromising sects. Even if this is true (and statistics seem unavailable to prove one thing or another), the existence of these two contradictory Christian movements is evidence of the vitality churches continue to enjoy.

Church and Society

A second important, new emphasis within Christianity was the result of efforts to apply Christian principles to changing social, political, and economic conditions. Missionaries in Asia and Africa tended to shift away from emphasis on simple religious conversion and instead put medical and educational service in the forefront. In the English-speaking world, members of the clergy took leading parts in movements for social reform. The Labour party in England, for instance, was deeply colored by Methodism; and the civil rights movement in the United States, whose most famous leader, Martin Luther King, Jr. (1929–1968), was himself a Baptist minister, attracted much Church support.

All round the world, Marxism rivaled Chris-

The International Style of Architecture
A new ideal of architecture arose in Germany in the 1920s. It centered in Marburg at the Bauhaus, seen above. Use of cheap, new materials like concrete and glass, was one departure from older practices: simplicity of form and a distaste for mere ornament, was equally important to the Bauhaus pioneers. The idea was catching, largely because it made buildings cheap and useful, as well as handsome in a spare, rectangular way. An example of how the style spread and evolved may be seen in the photograph below, which shows the Brazilian parliament buildings under construction in the brand new capital city of Brasilia in 1959.

tianity (and other religions) by offering an atheistic explanation of the human condition. Marxist parties were nearly always anticlerical; and where they came to power, they tried to undermine Christian faith by propaganda and sometimes by active persecution as well. Nevertheless, in Russia and in other east European lands where communist governments came to power, Christianity retained considerable influence among the people.

The Nazi movement in Germany also challenged Christian principles by glorifying teutonic paganism and rejecting Christian morality. A few Germans, inspired by Christian ideals, plotted actively against Hitler; indeed, Christian faith proved the most effective rallying ground for the German opposition to Nazism. In other European countries, too, Christian belief played an important role in inspiring resistance movements against the Nazis during World War II. As a result, after the war, powerful new Christian-Democratic parties emerged in all the important coun-

How to be Architecturally Different The International style of architecture
soon generated an opposite tendency emphasizing what made each particular
place different from everywhere else. Here are two spectacularly successful
examples of how to be different. On top, is the opera house in Sydney, Australia, with the bridge connecting the two sides of Sydney harbor in the background. The concrete arches of the opera house roof mimic the sails of the
ships that brought the first English settlers to Australia. Perched on the water's edge with the bridge behind it, this spectacular building erected in the
1960s, aptly symbolizes the way European settlers and civilization were suddenly implanted in a strange new environment. The spare, rectilinearity of
the Central Library of the University of Mexico, seen on the bottom, is countered by the brilliant mosaic decoration of its surface. Juan O'Gorman, who
designed this mosaic in 1950, set out to portray the history of Mexico all the
way back to Aztec times in order to celebrate the uniqueness of his country
and its blending of Indian and European heritages.

tries of western Europe. These parties have, in fact, dominated the post–World War II governments of Italy and West Germany.

On the other hand, in Spain and some of the Spanish-speaking countries of South America, the Church pursued a conservative if not downright reactionary policy. In these lands the Church remained a target for liberal and anticlerical reformers.

A third issue for Christians was how to react to secular thought and science. Many Protestants rejected Darwinian evolution and put their faith in the literal accuracy of the Bible. This was challenged by "Modernists" who believed that religious truth (like other kinds of truth) evolved over time, so that Bible writers were mistaken on some points and headed in the right direction on others.

Among Roman Catholics, modernism had been prohibited by the Vatican Council of 1869–1870. Yet a Jesuit philosopher and archaeologist, Teilhard de Chardin (1881–1955), developed an evolutionary philosophy which included religion. In this, as in other ways, the gap between Protestant and Roman Catholic thought seemed to be narrowing, as both found it possible to adjust to the progress of science without giving up continuity with older tradition and doctrine.

Judaism

Among Jews, the Nazi persecution in Germany, climaxing in the death camps of World War II, had tremendous impact. Nearly all European Jews were uprooted. Of those who survived, many went to Israel after the war or followed earlier emigrants to the United States, South Africa, Argentina, and elsewhere. The Israeli War of Independence in 1947 provoked another wave of persecution that ran through the entire Moslem world. As a result, nearly all "oriental" Jews were forced to flee to Israel.

Within Israel, opinions differed widely as to how a Jewish state ought to handle religion. Secular-minded Jews, who want a modern, industrial, and socialist society, predominated; but there were also Orthodox Jews who regarded any departure from rabbinical rules as religious heresy.

The outbreak of vicious anti-Semitism in Nazi Germany and the rise of Israel as a Jewish state persuaded many Jews in other lands that it was neither possible nor desirable to try to merge into the general population by giving up all ties with traditional Judaism. This "assimilationist" idea had flourished in Germany ever since the later 1700s, when special laws against Jews began to be repealed. Intermarriages between Christians and Jews had become quite common, and differences between Jews and other Germans were less than in almost any other land. If Hitlerism could break out in Germany, therefore, the whole ideal of assimilation into secular society and of ceasing to be a separate social group seemed to be proved dangerous and false.

At the same time, in the United States and England, widespread reaction against the Nazi barbarism discouraged open expression of anti-Semitic feelings; and various social barriers against Jews tended to fall, one by one, without the public outcry and legislation that was needed to batter down discrimination against American blacks. In Russia, however, traces of old anti-Semitic feelings, which had been strong before World War I, survived in spite of official communist disapproval.

Islam

The ecumenical movement among Christians tried also to reach out toward Jews in order to soften the historic clash between the two faiths. This was not true of Islam. Few Christians knew much about the faith of Mohammed, and the Moslems had no interest whatever in associating with Christian clerics, whom they regarded, as they did the Jews, as hereditary enemies and preachers of false doctrine.

Yet Islam found itself in an embarrassing position. The Moslem Sacred Law, like the Jewish law, was at the heart of traditional religion. Its rules were plainly incompatible with Western thought and made it next to impossible to build up a strong Moslem state. Still, to reject the Sacred Law meant losing the past. The Turks tried to do so in the 1920s. But in the 1950s Islam began to come back and even won official recognition in Turkey because voters remained Moslem despite the efforts of the revolutionary government to discredit the faith. On the other hand, in Arabia, where red-hot Wahhabi reformers had come to power in the 1920s, the discovery of vast oil reserves brought huge sums of money into the country. With this new wealth some of the warmth of the Wahhabi faith vanished, at least in court circles. Pakistan was a religious state, carved out of British India in 1947, because its citizens were Moslems. But when it came to deciding what a Moslem state ought to be like, the old dilemma of how to treat the Sacred Law proved insoluble. A military coup d'état brought westernized army officers to power who systematically sidestepped the issue by concentrating on inherited quarrels with Hindu India.

Throughout the Moslem world, communist doctrine collided with traditional religion. Marxist atheism and materialism contradicted Mohammed's revelation, and neither side tried to disguise the fact. As a result, there were few communists in Moslem lands. Only people who were willing to throw away their cultural heritage could become communists, and this was always a small minority. The mass slaughter of the Indonesian communist party in 1966 was a bloodthirsty demonstration of how Moslems feel about Marxists.

The collision between Islam and the modern secular outlook achieved new intensity in Iran in 1979 with the victory of Shia fundamentalists over the shah's government. But how to apply the Sacred Law under contemporary conditions remains problematic, and how to combine the pursuit of holiness with other goals has not been resolved. For the Iranian revolutionaries, like other people, want wealth and power as well as wishing to obey Allah; and the two are difficult to combine.

This is the crucial dilemma of the world of Islam. No resolution of the problem seems in sight.

Hinduism, Buddhism, Confucianism, and Shinto

Hindus and Buddhists, on the contrary, saw no vital contradiction between Western secular ideas and their traditional religions. Long ago, both these faiths made room for an infinite variety of doctrines. Atheism was nothing new or shocking to Hindus and Buddhists. Buddha was an atheist, and many Hindu philosophers were, too. Marxism thus was able to fit in as another partial truth—mistaken, of course, inasmuch as Marxism taught that the material world was real—yet, perhaps, useful in its own limited way if it helped social reform or forwarded national independence.

As a result, Indians living in the southern part of India, where various local languages survived, often became Marxists as a way of protesting against domination from the north, where Hindi was the common speech. Similarly, in Vietnam and other parts of Southeast Asia, all kinds of halfway-houses between Buddhism and communism existed, without any particular sense of strain being felt on either side.

Confucianism in China and Shinto in Japan, however, appear to be dying faiths. The schools that once trained generations of Chinese in the Confucian Classics were abandoned after 1905, and a new generation grew up with little acquaintance with that past. Since 1949 the communists have done all they could to discredit old ways of thought. Maoism was deliberately invented to replace Confucianism, but in many ways it resembled what it displaced. Anything else would be strange, for Mao was educated in a traditional way until his twenties, when as a young college student he first met Lenin's ideas and began his career as a Marxist. Other Chinese communist leaders, as well as many in the rank and file, have a similar personal history. Massive carryover from the Confucian past is, therefore, inescapable, even if the old doctrines have been officially repudiated.

As for the worship of the sun goddess and of her divine descendant, the emperor of Japan, the events of World War II thoroughly discredited that form of Shinto. After the war, the emperor publicly denied his divinity, and the crown prince of Japan married a commoner before succeeding to the throne in 1989. Nothing much remained of the old Shinto beliefs, though temples and rituals from the Shinto past remained attractive to many Japanese. Traditional religion was represented in Japan mainly by remodeled forms of Buddhism. Buddhism's main rival was Marxism; but Japanese Marxists do not yet seem to have

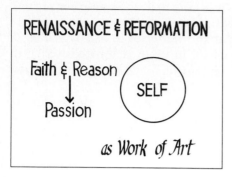

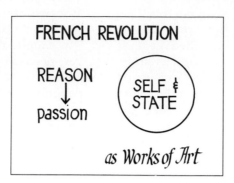

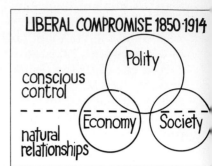

Two Ways to Think about Modern Times These diagrams summarize long-term changes in the way people think and act. In the first three diagrams, the expanding scope of conscious, deliberate management—from self, to state, economy and society—is represented along with schematic suggestion of changing relationships among the guides to human action as they were understood at the time. The diagrams below describe the same historic process over a shorter period of time, emphasizing the growth of governmental activity since the French Revolution. Such diagrams simplify historic processes, leaving out local differences and much else. But simplification may also make the main lines clearer, as long as you remember to take account of specific differences when thinking of any particular event, time, or place.

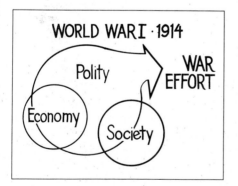

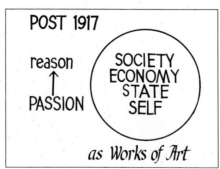

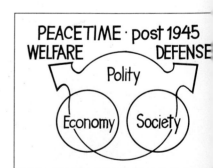

invented their own national brand of the faith, as have the Russians and Chinese, not to mention the Yugoslavs and other East Europeans.

CONCLUSION

Human societies, thought, and culture have changed very fast and fundamentally since 1914. No end is in sight, although past ages of really rapid and far-reaching change have all been relatively brief—a matter of two or three generations, usually. But this time, older limits have been left behind. The majority of human beings no longer must work in the fields to feed a privileged few who are doing other things. For the first time in history, modern machines and methods allow a few to feed everyone else. Cultural consequences of this fundamental change remain unclear. All we think and do reflects and contributes to this basic departure from life patterns that prevailed throughout previous civilized history. It makes our age a time of adventure into the unknown on a greater scale than before—perhaps more than ever before.

How future generations will evaluate the time in which we live is impossible to know but interesting to wonder about. If the pace of change levels off eventually, as seems inevitable in the long run, it is possible that our remote descendants will regard this as a great, heroic time in which the ground rules of their own societies were laid down by us—stumbling, uncertain, and anxious though we be. Confusion, which seems to dominate every aspect of our age, even its science, can be immensely fertile. It offers future generations a multitude of models from which to pick and choose. Such, perhaps, may be the long-range historical importance of the twentieth century.

Breakthroughs in the Use of Energy and Fuel

Muscles came first: arm, leg, and tongue. Then were tamed a few big animals strong enough to carry heavy loads or pull great weights. The horse, ox, camel, and water buffalo were the most important of these sources of power; and until 200 years ago they remained, with human muscles, the principle sources of power humans knew.

Yet from very early times people also tapped inanimate forms of power. Fire, for example, unlocked chemical energy—and from Paleolithic times, hunters used fire to warm themselves and to cook. Later civilized peoples made fire to bake pottery and smelt metals as well.

This was only the beginning. Wind, water, coal, electricity, and most recently nuclear energy have all been put to work for human purposes with consequences—good and bad, foreseen and unforeseen—that have entirely transformed our natural environment.

NATURAL POWER OF WATER AND WIND

The Romans made the swift-flowing river Tiber grind grain into flour to feed the swollen populace of their city in the first century B.C. The principle was simple A paddle wheel half in and half out of the river revolved as the flowing water pressed against each paddle.

Windmills worked on a similar principle but were invented later. The earliest known came from central Asia, where Buddhists used them to launch prayers to heaven. Later, windmills were put to more practical uses—for grinding grain, pumping water, and driving other machines.

Highlights

Wind and watermills provided a new source of mechanical power that could be put to many uses.

The great advantage was that, once a mill had been built, the power cost nothing and it could be put to work whenever the water flowed or the wind blew.

The main disadvantage was that, for many centuries, no one had a steady flow of grain to be ground or wood to be sawed. The superior work capacity of water and wind was wasted.

Since it was expensive to build mills initially, they were not much used until the sixteenth and seventeenth centuries in Europe, when improvements in transportation did make it possible to keep water and windmills steadily at work.

EXPLOSIVE POWER OF GUNPOWDER

Gunpowder is a chemical mixture that does not need to take oxygen from the air in order to "burn." When ignited almost all of it turns into gas. The effect, in an enclosed chamber, is explosive.

The Chinese discovered gunpowder about A.D. 1000. They used it first to blow up fortified gates by filling hollow chambers of bamboo

Water Mill for Grinding Grain.

with the explosive mixture and pushing them under the closed gates. Soon afterward the Chinese began experimenting with hollow metal pots, filled with gunpowder and open at one end, which they used as primitive guns.

Europeans started similar experiments in the fourteenth century, having learned about gunpowder probably from China via the Mongol Empire. By 1500, Europeans excelled in the manufacture of big guns, perhaps because they already had a highly developed metallurgy. Peaceful uses for explosives, as in mining, for instance, came later, mainly in the nineteenth and twentieth centuries.

Highlights

Gunpowder altered warfare and government in far-reaching ways all over the world.

Big guns were expensive, and only a few rulers could pay for them. Those who did could knock down their rivals' castle walls. Large territorial states could be built with the help of big guns.

Handguns became important in warfare only in the seventeenth century. Infantry armed with guns overcame the age-old superiority of steppe cavalry. This allowed the Russian and Chinese empires, in the eighteenth century, to divide the steppelands of Eurasia between them.

EXPANSIVE POWER OF STEAM

Modern steam engines let steam under pressure flow into a cylinder, closed at one end by a close-fitting piston. Steam pressure then makes the piston move. There were different ways of bringing the piston back again. The earliest type of engine in common use allowed the steam to condense, so that atmospheric pressure pushed the piston back. James Watt in 1776 improved upon this method by using valves to let the steam both into and out of the cylinder. A heavy balance wheel carried the piston back, expelling the old steam and

readying the cylinder for the next rush of high-pressure steam.

The steam engine was soon put to work at many different tasks, like pumping, driving trains, and activating machinery in factories.

Highlights

Steam engines could be set up where fuel was easily found.

Since coal fires were the easiest way to produce steam, available coal beds became the prime factor controlling the location of heavy industry after 1850, when the steam engine came into its own.

Because the steam engine was invented in Great Britain, the British achieved a head start over all other peoples in exploiting the potential of the new, cheap, and flexible source of power.

The many possibilities opened by the use of steam power between 1776 and 1850 made this the era of the Industrial Revolution in Britain and western Europe.

Dutch Musketeer about 1600.

Steam Turbine.

INSTANTANEOUS POWER OF ELECTRICITY

Lightning and static electricity awed and puzzled humankind from earliest times, but not until the nineteenth century did anyone begin to learn how to control the power of electrical currents. Electric motors on a toy scale were known as early as 1831, but it was the 1880s when engineers began to conceive of building large-scale dynamos to supply electric current to large numbers of customers.

Electric power was first used for interior lighting. But in the twentieth century innumerable uses for electricity in industry have been found, with the result that heavy cables have largely replaced steam engines as energy sources in modern factories.

Highlights

Electricity as a source of power is clean, and it can be precisely controlled.

In time, electricity opens the possibility of modulating power at short intervals. This allows refinements in manufacture otherwise unattainable.

In space, electrical power can reach down to the level of individual molecules and atoms by ionizing them. This opens the possibility for new kinds of processes, like silver-plating.

Electrical power also allows worldwide instantaneous communication, making precise information readily available to government, business, and other decision-makers.

ENORMOUS POWER OF THE ATOM

All humanity's earlier adventures in harnessing diverse forms of energy have been dwarfed by the most recent breakthrough: the controlled release of nuclear energy. The first successful experiment took place in Chicago in 1942, and atomic energy was initially used for making the bombs dropped on Nagasaki and Hiroshima at the close of World War II. Peaceful uses of atomic energy include the generation of electricity and underground blasting.

Atomic energy was developed by highly trained scientists acting on extremely abstract mathematical theory. Theory and practice had been closely linked in the development of electrical power too, but not as deliberately and consciously or on such a scale as in this case.

Highlights

By converting matter itself into energy, atomic power offers an almost limitless supply of energy.

Such a storehouse of potential energy can be used for any and all of the peaceful purposes to which electrical and other forms of power have been put.

At the same time, atomic energy has the potential for destroying all higher forms of life.

Systematic application of scientific theory to the improvement of techniques was car-

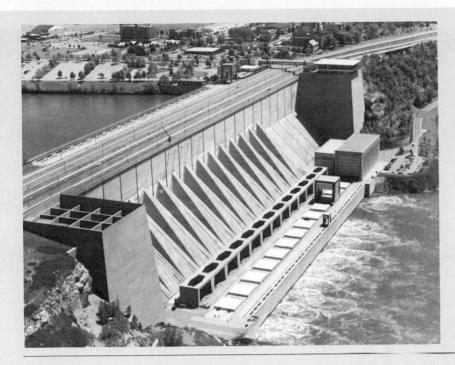

Water Power for Electricity.

ried through successfully in unlocking atomic energy. The development of new products and manufacturing processes is faster than ever.

COSTS OF POWER OVER NATURE

Humanity's enormous triumphs in using power for its own purposes involve unexpected and unwished-for costs. Too rapid changes in machinery strained modern society by asking people to alter their habits too fast; too reckless a use of power in manufacturing products has upset the natural environment in ways we do not fully understand.

Still, some of the risks are clear. Carbon dioxide added to the atmosphere by burning coal and other fuels alters the way sunlight reaches the earth. A "greenhouse effect" may melt glaciers, raise sea levels, and alter climates.

The risks of nuclear radiation are more obvious and sure. Disposal of radioactive wastes from nuclear power plants is difficult, and the risks of accidental disaster are immensely dangerous, as the Russians found out in 1986 at Chernobyl.

Control Panel for a Nuclear Power Plant.

THE STATE OF THE WORLD TODAY

At the close of this sort of survey of recent events, it is well to remind ourselves of how blind we are likely to be to new things that will attain great importance in years to come. Perhaps some obscure groups of men hold the future in their hands, as followers of Buddha, Christ, and Mohammed once did. Or some scientific discovery may give people undreamed-of power to influence the way others behave; and by using that power, they may then alter themselves and their fellows in ways we cannot imagine.

No one knows what the future will bring; until it comes, the meaning and shape of the past remain unclear. Each generation must reshape its past to fit its present and assist transition to the future. New nations have to discover, or invent, a history; and in the same way, as humanity changes, its past as well as its future alters shape, values, and meaning.

If this book helps its readers to shape their understanding of the past in a way that seems reasonable and convincing, it will have succeeded in its purpose. Other histories have been written and will be written from other points of view. People living today in other parts of the world will not share the ideas that underlie this book. Yet even when one knows this, and knows that future generations will disagree in still other ways, the effort to see the human past whole and complete, as it *really* was and according to the best and fullest evidence we can discover, is not absurd. Accuracy and scope do improve as time passes. Errors and naive exaggeration can be reduced. And by recognizing how partial and imperfect our own best efforts to understand the past (or the present, for that matter) must be, we can deal more intelligently, with less surprise or anger, with other people from other parts of the world, who think and act differently from ourselves.

Relativity in physics has improved human knowledge and power; relativism in social judgments can paralyze society if everyone simply says, "Everything goes; it makes no difference." A wise and true vision of human affairs will show, however, that it does matter how people behave.

People have quarreled endlessly and differed deeply on matters of faith and morals. Nevertheless, across generations and centuries, a rough but effective process of selection has taken place, resulting in better tools, better ideas, and better attitudes. Certainly, unless people are willing and able to work together in groups, they cannot long survive as individuals. Conformity to local habit and custom is, therefore, absolutely necessary. Individuals who refuse to conform become criminals or madmen.

The real pinch comes when conformity to one group creates conflict with another group. Gang fights, race riots, international wars, and all other kinds of organized violence arise from collision between group loyalties. Every individual in a modern society belongs to many different classes and groups, each claiming loyalty and demanding conformity to its own standards of conduct.

There are no rules as to how to thread one's way among these competing demands—none, at least, that the study of history provides. What that study can make clear is that communities have lived with this dilemma for a very long time and have tended to build for themselves larger and larger political units within which some sort of peace could be maintained. The process goes on. Your lives will be part of it; so, in all probability, will your children's lives and your children's children's.

Thus we end where we began: unsure of where the world is going. Rapid change is sure to continue, at least for a while. Human consciousness is in flux as never before, thanks to new patterns of communication that have risen within the past generation. Human numbers increase and press on the means of subsistence more acutely than in any former age. Ecological disaster on the one hand and atomic annihilation on the other may upset or destroy the world as we know it. But human intelligence and adaptability allowed our forerunners to muddle through somehow. Future generations seem likely to do the same. Let's hope so.

Index